[Plutarch]
ESSAY ON THE LIFE AND POETRY OF HOMER

American Philological Association
American Classical Studies

Series Editor

David L. Blank

Number 40

[Plutarch]
ESSAY ON THE LIFE AND POETRY OF HOMER

edited by
J. J. Keaney and Robert Lamberton

[Plutarch]
ESSAY ON THE LIFE AND POETRY OF HOMER

edited by

J. J. Keaney
Robert Lamberton

Scholars Press
Atlanta, Georgia

[Plutarch]
ESSAY ON THE LIFE AND POETRY OF HOMER

edited by
J. J. Keaney and Robert Lamberton

© 1996
The American Philological Association

The cover illustration is from the engraved frontispiece of Joshua Barnes' extravagant edition of Homer (Cambridge, 1711). Thanks to Barnes, this *Essay* as well as numerous other texts that the Renaissance editors had favored, allegorical and otherwise, stood one last time as prefatory material to introduce the tirelessly curious reader to the *Iliad* and *Odyssey*.

Library of Congress Cataloging in Publication Data

De Homero. English & Greek.
   Essay on the life and poetry of Homer / (Plutarch) ; edited by J.J. Keaney, Robert Lamberton.
      p. cm. — (American classical studies ; no. 40)
   Includes bibliographical references and indexes.
   Text in Greek with English translation; critical apparatus in English.
   ISBN 0-7885-0259-X (alk. paper). — ISBN 0-7885-0260-3 (pbk. : alk. paper)
   1. Homer. 2. Authors, Greek—Biography. 3. Epic poetry, Greek—History and criticism. I. Plutarch. II. Keaney, John J. III. Lamberton, Robert. IV. Title. V. Series.
PA4035.A4P6 1996
883'.01—dc20
                                        96-13850
                                        CIP

Printed in the United States of America
on acid-free paper

CONTENTS

INTRODUCTION
    1. The History of the Essay   1
    2. Content and Aims   10
    3. The PresentEdition   29
    4. Acknowledgements   30

PRINCIPAL EDITIONS   33

FIRST TRANSLATIONS   37

ABBREVIATIONS AND BIBLIOGRAPHY   39

[PLUTARCH], ESSAY ON THE LIFE AND POETRY OF HOMER

    Analytic Table of Contents   45

    Text and Translation   54

    Apparatus   313

INDEX   315

GREEK INDEX   321

INTRODUCTION

1. The History of the Essay

"Several prefaces to Homer have survived from antiquity, but only a single systematic and comprehensive *Introduction* to the *Iliad* and *Odyssey*, such that a Greek who was anxious to be taught and curious to learn might really have used it with benefit as he undertook for the first time to read this poetry."[1] The Prussian Homerist Arthur Ludwich described the text before us in these terms in 1917, and although his praise echoes that of scholars of the 17th and 18th centuries,[2] and has been echoed in turn by more recent scholars,[3] the essay on the life and poetry of Homer attributed to Plutarch has remained relatively inaccessible, not only to those concerned with ancient literary criticism and the early history of Homer-reception, but to the scholarly community as well. There has been no easily accessible translation into a modern language, but more serious still, the Greek text itself long remained inadequately published.[4]

The *Essay on the Life and Poetry of Homer*[5] survived fortuitously as a parasite on the text of Homer and on the Planudean

---

[1] Ludwich (1917-18), 537.
[2] Cf. R.Schmidt (1850), 3, who cited Thomas Gale (ca. 1635-1702) qualifying the author of the longer life as *elegantem, ingeniosum, floridum, optimumque Homeri interpretem et encomiasten, item antiquum et minime neglegendum*, and Johann August Ernesti (1707-81) asserting that this is a treatise whose study *etiamnunc plurimum ad utiliter legendum Homerum prodesse posse*.
[3] Ziegler (1951), col. 878, described the piece as "die planmässigste, umfassendste und gehaltvollste der uns aus dem Altertum überkommen Einführungen in die Homerlektüre." See his remarks, cols. 873-74 on the need for a new edition.
[4] Cf. Ziegler (1951), cols. 873-74 and F. H. Sandbach in Plutarch, *Moralia* (Loeb), vol. 15, 403-4 (= Sandbach,1969). The earliest printed editions were prefaced to editions of Homer and are discussed below. The nineteenth-century editions are those of Wyttenbach (1800), Dübner (1882), and Bernardakis (1896), the two earlier ones accompanied by Latin translations. In 1990, the long-awaited new Teubner edition of Jan Fredrik Kindstrand filled a major gap in the scholarly literature. We were able to take advantage of Kindstrand's text and apparatus only in the final correction of the present volume, and we limit ourselves here to acknowledging significant differences between our text and his and points where we have followed his lead and corrected our text by his.
[5] The text has no definitive title and several descriptive labels with slight variations occur (see "Editions"), the most complete of which (Περὶ τοῦ βίου καὶ τῆς ποιήσεως τοῦ Ὁμήρου) we have expanded into *Essay on the Life and Poetry of Homer* (or, for brevity, the *Essay*). This text is the longer one of the manuscript tradition (B of Wyttenbach and others). The brief biography (A), prefaced to the *Essay* in mss. and eds. is here printed in its traditional place (though there is no

corpus of Plutarch's *Moral Essays*. The *editio princeps* of Homer (Florence, 1488), included it as introductory material, along with the *Life of Homer* attributed to Herodotus and Dio Chrysostom's essay *On Homer*. The first comprehensive edition of the *Moral Essays*, the Aldine (1509) omitted it, as did the Basel edition of 1542. Xylander published a Latin translation of the essay, along with the rest of the *Moral Essays*, in 1570 (repr. 1572), but omitted it from his 1574 edition of the Greek text, as did Stephanus in 1572. The first complete, annotated, critical edition of the *Moral Essays*, Wyttenbach's (1795-1830), included it among the pseudepigrapha. Since that time, there have been several attempts to establish its authorship, but even those scholars who have been convinced of its ultimate dependance on a genuine work or works of Plutarch have conceded that the version that has reached us has undergone substantial excerpting and editing since it left Plutarch's hand. The history of this controversy is fascinating in itself and deserves our attention here.

The first certain occurrence of the essay among the *Moralia* of Plutarch belongs to the late thirteenth century, when it was included, along with several other works now considered spurious, in the collection of the works of Plutarch assembled by the Byzantine scholar Maximus Planudes.[6] His conception of the Plutarchan *corpus* was overly generous by modern standards, but we owe to that generosity the preservation of several essays of tremendous value and influence, including the essay that still stands at the head of all modern editions of the *Moral Essays*, "The Education of Children."

The history of our text before the time of Planudes is lost, or nearly so. The *Essay* belongs to a large body of ancient Homer interpretation that has defied analysis and is largely impossible to date. Our text has affinities with the *Homeric Allegories* of "Heraclitus" and with an interpreter of Homer quoted by Stobaeus. Interpretations found in the *Essay* crop up in the scholia as well, but the complexity of the tradition is such that it is impossible to say that our author copied, or was copied by, any other. Numerous passages echo others in the authentic works of Plutarch, but here again, a common source often provides as credible an explanation as a direct borrowing of one text by the other. We can say, however, that a text of this sort could well have been written in the time of Plutarch, though later

---

reason to believe that it is by the same hand as the longer Essay), and referred to as the "Shorter Life". The titles given to the work in the mss. are "On the Life of Homer" (Εἰς τὸν βίον τοῦ Ὁμήρου) and "On Homer" (Περὶ Ὁμήρου, cf. Kindstrand, xi-xii).

[6] Russell (1972), 18-19, 147.

accretions may well have lengthened it. There is even a third-century papyrus (Pap. Lond. 734) containing meagre fragments of a work so similar to this one that it has been argued on that basis to be a copy of the lost *Homeric Studies* of Plutarch.[7]

Between that papyrus fragment of the third century and the earliest manuscripts, which are to be dated to the latter part of the thirteenth,[8] there is little trace of a work resembling the *Essay*. Of particular importance for the dissemination of the work was a manuscript (Ambrosianus Graecus 859) produced in the circle of Planudes.[9] The manuscript was written ca. 1296 and engendered many copies and copies of copies. We have no evidence where Planudes found this essay (though most of the other pseudepigrapha he included with the authentic works of Plutarch can be found attributed to Plutarch in the earlier manuscript tradition).[10] Nor, more important, do we know on what evidence he believed this work to be by Plutarch. What has occurred since his time is clearer, however, and a summary of the history of the scholarly controversy over the authorship of *The Life and Poetry of Homer* will serve as the best introduction to the problems raised by this authorless text.[11]

Superficially, the essay bears little resemblance to any other work attributed to Plutarch, and one might well ask how it came to form part of the *corpus*. It was unknown to the compiler of the so-called "Lamprias Catalogue" of the works of Plutarch, which may date to the fourth century.[12] That catalogue does, however, mention *Four Books of Homeric Studies* (Ὁμηρικῶν μελετῶν βιβλία δ'), fragments of which have

---

[7] Della Corte (1938). See on ch. 149 of the *Essay*, below.
[8] For an excellent survey of the manuscript tradition of Plutarch's *Moralia* (*Moral Essays*), see J. Irigoin in *Plutarque: Oeuvres Morales 1.1*, ccxxvii-cccii (= Irigoin, 1987).
[9] For Planudes' activity on Plutarch, see Wilson (1983), 235-36. Most of this manuscript was written by pupils, but Planudes wrote some pages himself: one of these, containing a portion of our text, is photographically reproduced in Turyn (1972), vol. 2, plate 66.
[10] The essay *On Music* and *The Life and Poetry of Homer* are the only pseudepigrapha included in the Planudean corpus of Plutarch whose pre-Planudean origins remain obscure. On this, see B. Einarson and Phillip de Lacy's introduction to "On Music" in vol. 14 of the Loeb *Moralia*, 344. Parisinus graecus 2679 and Berolinus graecus 183 present the first 136 chapters of the present work, without indication of title or author, as preface to Eustathius' commentaries on Homer. The former manuscript and the tradition it represents seem to be pre-Planudean. See Kindstrand, xii-xlviii on the manuscript tradition.
[11] Person (1957), 14-16, offers a concise summary of the positions taken by a variety of modern scholars.
[12] Sandbach (1967), 1-10, and with translation and notes in Sandbach (1969), 3-29.

been collected.[13] The attempts of modern scholars to trace *The Life and Poetry of Homer* to a genuine Plutarchan source have centered around the problem of this lost work. In fact, however, the little evidence we have for the nature and contents of the *Studies* suggests that the two are unconnected.[14]

For nearly two centuries after the *editio princeps* of 1488, the attribution of the essay to Plutarch seems to have gone largely unchallenged. The essay was often reprinted in editions of Homer, along with other prefatory material.[15] Chalcondyles had printed the Herodotean *Life of Homer* and Dio Chrysostom 53 *On Homer*, along with the *Essay*, and this pattern was imitated by Aldus Manutius (1504) and Antonius Francinus (1519). There were rival interpretive texts, though, including the partially preserved *Homeric Questions* of the Neoplatonist Porphyry and his remarkable essay "On the Cave of the Nymphs in the *Odyssey*." Both of these were prefaced to the 1541 Basel edition of Homer by Iacobus Micyllus and Ioachimus Camerarius, an edition that scorned the traditional triad of introductory texts. In editions of Plutarch, however, it was sometimes included and sometimes omitted, a clear indication that scholarly doubts had already been aroused, long before anything explicit appeared in print to call the attribution in question. Thus, when Thomas Gale, in 1671, proposed that the "Shorter Life" *only* (!) was to be attributed to Plutarch, and the longer one to Dionysius of Halicarnassus, he did little more than give concrete form to speculations that doubtless go back long before his time.

For the 15th and 16th centuries, however, "Plutarch" was one of the primary purveyors of information about Homer, as well as providing the bulk of the materials for the largely conventional and formulaic encomia of Homer that are characteristic of the period. Among the earliest of these paeans of praise is that of Poliziano (d. 1494), which, as Guillaume Budé soon pointed out, was in large part borrowed from "Plutarch."[16] The strategy of praising Homer by listing

---

[13] Sandbach (1967), 76-78, as well as Sandbach (1969), 238-41. If Sandbach's fragments in fact all belong to the "Studies," then that work would seem to be unrelated to the *Essay on the Life and Poetry of Homer*.
[14] Buffière (1956), 75-77.
[15] The list of major printed editions below, 33-35, gives an indication of the popularity of the text.
[16] Hepp (1961-62), 431, n. 1. Hepp does not locate the passage in Poliziano to which Budé referred, but the poem in Poliziano's *Silvae* entitled "Ambra" (with the explanatory subtitle, *in poetae Homeri ennaratione pronuntiata*) is the apparent target. Most of the poem consists of an allegorical/mythological extravaganza with little relevance to our text, but in the encomium proper (467 ff.), the catalogue

the kinds of knowledge he both possessed and imparted, along with the ideas of the philosophers that were to be traced to him, was widespread in the Renaissance, and the *Essay* was frequently the source, acknowledged or not, of these enumerations.[17] Although the *Essay* is not primarily a work of allegorization, its extraordinary claims for the scope of the wisdom and influence of Homer caused it to be associated with such anthologies of allegorical readings as the *Homeric Allegories* of Heraclitus, so that its fortunes rose and fell with those of that text, along with those of Eustathius and Cornutus. Thus the tradition of rhetorical eulogy could affirm the value and insight of these authors down through the seventeenth century and into the eighteenth.

The French manifestation of this development emerges clearly from Noémi Hepp's study of *Homère en France au xviie siècle*, along with the shorter study on the 16th century, already cited. French admirers of Homer echoed "Plutarch's" praise of the poet repeatedly,[18] but there is also a counter-current, represented by Tanneguy le Fèvre, whose discussion of Homer in *Les Poètes grecs* (1664) ignored the *Essay* and declared the (still more popular) Herodotean *Life* inauthentic.[19] Hepp sees the victory of this enlightened reaction against the interpretive tradition in the project brought before the Académie des Inscriptions in 1707 or 1708 by the Homerist Jean Boivin de Villeneuve, who proposed to undertake a new edition of Homer, in which the *Essay* along with all the other accretions that had stood between the reader and the text of the *Iliad* and *Odyssey* since the earliest printed editions were to be relegated to the obscurity of a third and final volume.[20]

If by the dawn of the 18th century the philologists of the Enlightenment had outgrown the texts that had traditionally

---

of the wisdom of Homer (476-589) contains a good deal of material that also occurs in the *Essay*. See also Grafton (1992), 154-55, 159-60.

[17] Hepp (1961-62), 419-21, citing Denis Lambin, Franciscus Portus, and Guillaume Paquelin.

[18] Hepp (1968): Urbain Chevreau (315-16), Louis Thomassin (327-33), Rapin (423-25).

[19] Hepp (1968), 310.

[20] Hepp (1968), 569-70. In fact, the "reaction" is not so clear-cut. Editions following Chalcondyles' *editio princeps* continued to print the *Essay* and the other prefatory material first, but the often-reprinted Aldine of 1504 had already relegated this material to the status of *postscripta*, and some subsequent editions based on the Aldine (e.g. the "Second Aldine" of 1517 and the 1563 Worms re-edition of the reworking of the Aldine text by Wolfgang Cephaleus) either omitted the secondary material entirely, or left the pages out of some copies while including them in others. See "Principal Editions," esp. 1517.

introduced readers to the *Iliad* and *Odyssey*, one great monument to the durability of this interpretive material was still to appear. When Joshua Barnes published his edition of Homer in Cambridge in 1711, he saw fit to preface the poems with the most complete assemblage of the inherited fantastic biographies, encomia, and allegorical interpretations ever assembled in a single edition.[21] It is difficult to imagine that this strategy was unrelated to the remarkable subterfuge by which he financed the edition, whose publication "was only made possible by persuading his wife, who had inherited a small fortune from her first husband, that the author of the Homeric poems was Solomon."[22] Thanks to the pious and credulous Mrs. Barnes, the enlightened 18th century saw a late flowering of the tradition of reading Homer over the shoulders of the biographers and the allegorists. Now, however, on the authority of Thomas Gale, Plutarch got credit only for the "Shorter Life" (A), with credit for the *Essay* proper going to Dionysius of Halicarnassus.[23]

Subsequent editions of Homer have tended to ignore the biographical and interpretive material entirely, or, in the spirit of Boivin's project, to relegate it to a final volume. This was the solution of Johann August Ernesti, whose Leipzig edition of 1759-64, based on the texts of the poems published by Samuel Clarke and his son in 1729-32 (and in turn on Barnes's text), added a fifth volume that included the minor Homerica as well as *Plutarchi Vita Homeri* [= A] *et De Homeri Poesi Incerti Auctoris* [= B]. The piece had not yet been relegated to the status of a historical oddity in Ernesti's day, though his reassertion of its claim to serve as a practical introduction for the young reader was undoubtedly belated, and can hardly have carried much conviction as his edition went on to be reprinted in the nineteenth century. He included it, he wrote, not simply because it was prefaced "to all the older editions, but also—and much more—because reading it can be very useful for the profitable reading of Homer—indeed it was once of great use to me, when I was young."[24]

---

[21] See "Principal Editions," 1711.
[22] Sandys (1920), vol. 2, 357.
[23] *Homeri Ilias et Odyssea*, ed. Joshua Barnes (1711), xxix.
[24] *Locum in hac Appendice feci etiam libello incerti Auctoris de Vita Homeri, sive potius de Poësi Homerica, non modo quod, antiquo instituto Demetrii, adjunctus est editionibus Homeri antiquioribus omnibus, sed etiam, et multo magis, quod ejus lectio plurimum ad utiliter legendum Homerum prodesse potest, mihi quidem olim juveni lectus multum profuit.* J. A. Ernesti, *Homeri Operum Appendix* [*Homeri Opera Omnia*, v] (1764), xiii [(1814), vii; (1824), viii-ix]. The 1814 and 1824 reprints added Wolf's *Prolegomena* to the collection of ancillary texts, alongside the *Essay*.

When Daniel Wyttenbach first printed the Essay in a comprehensive edition of the *Moralia* of Plutarch (1802), he labeled it inauthentic. This opinion was confirmed by Gustav Edward Benseler,[25] supported with cogent argumentation by Richard Volkmann,[26] and is still generally accepted, though not unquestioned.[27] Thus the *Essay* comes down to us with the traditional attribution to Plutarch largely discredited, and the attempts to associate the work with other known authors—principally Dionysius of Halicarnassus and Porphyry[28]—lacking substantive proof or vocal supporters.

If the form and style—and in particular the neglect of hiatus—are un-Plutarchan, nevertheless much of the content seems to echo passages in preserved authentic works of Plutarch. It is highly probable that the author was acquainted with Plutarch's writings and borrowed from them.[29] But there are striking contradictions of passages and opinions found in Plutarch, as well.[30] Plutarch, in any case, seems to provide a *terminus post quem* for this authorless text, and we must next ask whether other evidence might make it possible to move that *terminus* any later. The strongest argument that has been brought forward is based on the rhetorical definitions in the section of the *Essay* that deal with diction and rhetoric. These (*fide* Volkmann) point to the "later period" and specific agreement in the use of the term "political discourse" (πολιτικὸς λόγος) suggests the school of Hermogenes of Tarsus.[31] The latter, at the age of about 15, performed for Marcus Aurelius,[32] and thus his *floruit* is likely to fall close to the end of the second century. This provides an (albeit shaky) *terminus post quem*, leaving open the possibility that the *Essay* might belong to the last years of the second century.

---

[25] Benseler (1851), 537.
[26] Volkmann, (1869), 120-26; cf. Ziegler (1951), cols. 876-77, and the summary in Person (1957), 14.
[27] Buffière (1956), 72-77, surveys the problem. See esp. 74, n. 22, on the early history of the controversy.
[28] E. Clavier in Plutarque, Oeuvres, vol. 23, xiii-xiv (See "Earliest Translations; French"); Buffière (1956), 74; Volkmann (1869), 121-26.
[29] The passages were assembled by Bernardakis in his edition (vol. 7, xiv-xli). Cf. Buffière (1956), 75.
[30] These are assembled by Volkmann (1869), 121.
[31] Volkmann (1869), 120-21. At a number of points in his treatment of rhetorical matters, our author comes close to Hermogenes. See e.g. ch. 74, note.
[32] Radermacher (1913), col. 865. The only available biographical details come from the brief sketch in Philostratus' *Lives of the Sophists*, 2.7. The standard edition of Hermogenes remains Rabe's Teubner (*Rhetores Graeci*, vi, 1913). There is a useful translation of "On Types of Style" (Περὶ ἰδεῶν) by Cecil W. Wooten (1987).

8   *The Life and Poetry of Homer*

At this point, we reach the thorniest area in the recent discussion of the dating of the essay. Félix Buffière, whose work forms the foundation of the modern study of these ancillary texts, tried to locate the *Essay* early in the second century, not long after the time of Plutarch himself. Specifically, Buffière wished to establish that the essay pre-dated the work of the Neopythagorean Numenius—himself a shadowy figure who eludes precise dating.[33] The best modern estimates, however, place Numenius in the time of Marcus Aurelius or a little later, and so exactly in the time of Hermogenes, whose influence Volkmann found in the rhetorical portions of the *Essay*. Numenius was clearly a thinker of some originality, and much of the mysticizing allegory found in the essay "On the Cave of the Nymphs in the *Odyssey*" by the 3rd-century Neoplatonist Porphyry is explicitly attributed to him and to his "companion" Cronius.[34]

Buffière felt that a chronological sequence could be derived from these data. His argument is based on the comprehensive and inclusive nature of the *Essay*, its impulse to relate the whole of Greek thought to Homeric roots, and on the demonstrable existence of a Pythagoreanizing mystical strain of allegorical interpretation at least from the latter part of the second century, largely ignored by our author. Ps.-Plutarch, Buffière argued, would not have ignored Numenian mystical allegory, and so must have predated it. The argument is attractive, but Volkmann's, pointing to a slightly later date, is methodologically more convincing.

If, by this reasoning, we make the essay contemporary with Numenius or even post-Numenian, we must accept either that the author's decision to down-play mystical allegory was deliberate, or that he belonged to a circle that was ignorant of it[35]—and in either

---

[33] See Buffière (1956), 76-77, and Lamberton (1986), 54.
[34] Schrader (1902) assembled massive evidence for a common source for the *Essay*, Hermogenes, Dionysius of Halicarnassus, Porphyry, and some of the non-Porphyrian *scholia*, a source which he identified with the essays "On the Art of Rhetoric According to Homer" (Περὶ τῆς καθ' Ὅμηρον ῥητορικῆς) and "On the Figures in Homer" (Περὶ τῶν παρ' Ὁμήρῳ σχημάτων) of Telephus of Pergamon. The latter, by Schrader's reckoning (561-62) will have been approximately fifty years older than Hermogenes and perhaps twenty or thirty years older than Numenius. Nevertheless, if Schrader has made it possible to trace the rhetorical element of the essay to a rhetor a scant generation older than Numenius, while Volkmann's arguments point to a younger man, the fact remains that, dating the essay as early as possible, we would still have a work published in the lifetime of Numenius by an approximate contemporary of the Pythagorean.
[35] We do not, after all, have any testimonia to Numenius' accomplishments in this area before Porphyry, a century later. It is probable, moreover, that Numenius' discussion of Homer was merely incidental to a larger discussion of problematic

case he can provide no further help in dating the *Essay* or supplying a *terminus ante quem*. The probability seems to be that the work was not composed before the last quarter of the second century and, because of its unusual format and its rather plain style, which has not been convincingly compared with that of any other author, we are at a loss to set any unshakeable *terminus ante quem* earlier than Planudes himself, even though its content clearly indicates that the work belongs in the context of Greco-Roman polytheism and not in the Byzantine era.[36]

The *Essay*, then, is later than Plutarch, probably by two or three generations, and possibly by more, though there is nothing to show that it must be dated later than the year 200. By choice (or, less probably, out of ignorance) it does not include in developed form any of the mystical allegory we see emerge in the tradition that runs from Numenius to Porphyry and ultimately Proclus. It does, however, provide a global summary of earlier developments in the interpretation of Homer, on which the later tradition is built. Furthermore, the *Essay* gives us the perspective on the relationship of the Homeric poems to preclassical, classical, and Hellenistic Greek philosophy of an author who is remarkably impartial and who, while he sees a connection between Pythagoras and Homer, neither (like Numenius) attributes to the poet a doctrine of astral immortality, nor (like Proclus) finds in him illustrations of the elaborate demonology of the later Neoplatonists.

Given all of this, along with the explicitly pedagogical tone that is particularly striking in the opening sections, it seems clear that what we have before us is the work of a *grammaticus*, and in all probability a *grammaticus* of the end of the second century, or perhaps sometime in the third. He provides an introduction to Homer for the beginner, an introduction that has no particular philosophical axe to grind and no ulterior motive beyond that of simultaneously praising and making more accessible the language and thought of the poet. This, we may take it, is Homer as Homer was taught in the schools of the Roman Empire. Like the authors of modern pedagogical introductions, "Plutarch" describes Homer's language, his thought, his world-view,

---

passages in Plato, and that the idea of Numenius as an interpreter of Homer *per se* emerges from Porphyry's use of Numenius rather than the latter's real concerns. We should keep in mind the distinct possibility that Numenius and Cronius represent a tradition of mystical allegorical reading of archaic Greek poetry that, before the time of Plotinus and Porphyry, may have attracted little attention among those whose central concern was the understanding of Homer.

[36] The *communis opinio* previous to Buffière favored a date in the third or fourth century, but the *Essay* contains nothing that need be so late. See, for example, Scarpat (1952), 5-6.

and the content of the poems. The opportunity to view these matters through the optics of a pedagogue of Imperial date is offered by no other surviving text, and this underappreciated treatise deserves a privileged place in any assessment of the intellectual history of the period between Plutarch and Constantine.

2. Content and Aims

The *Essay on the Life and Poetry of Homer* is a rambling, encyclopedic work that does little to make the reader's task easier. The analytic table of contents that we have added (45-53) is intended to make clear the major sections and subsections and the overall organization of the work. The remainder of this *Introduction* is a synthetic survey of those aspects of the *Essay* that are most likely to be of interest to the modern reader: the claims the author makes on behalf of Homer the philosopher, the interpretive techniques that characterize the *Essay*, and the place of those claims and techniques in the history of Homer-interpretation in the Roman Empire.

Although the text before us mediated between readers and the *Iliad* and *Odyssey* for many generations, the author of the *Essay on the Life and Poetry of Homer* is unconcerned with interpretation *per se*. His project is to celebrate Homer not by twisting the meaning of the poems to correspond to one single philosophy but rather by demonstrating that Homer is the source of all philosophy—and not simply of philosophy, but of rhetoric and of many other human skills as well. His stance is seldom defensive, in the manner of the the Heraclitus of the *Homeric Allegories*. Moreover, in contrast to the latter, who attacks Plato repeatedly for the Socratic rejection of Homer,[37] and to later Platonists such as Proclus, determined to reconcile Plato with Homer,[38] "Plutarch" writes as if the conflict between the poet and the philosopher were a matter of complete indifference to him.

From this fact we may infer that the author did not set himself in the Platonic tradition: it would have been impossible for a Platonist to discuss Homer at length without coming to terms with the *Republic*. Hermann Schrader[39] realized that "Plutarch," Heraclitus, and the *Homeric Questions* of Porphyry all made use of a common source and he

---

[37] Heraclitus, *Homeric Allegories*, 4.76 ff.
[38] Lamberton (1986), 182-83. Closer to the time of our essay, Numenius also interpreted Homer with a view to reconciliation with Plato.
[39] Schrader (1880-82), 401-2.

argued that the source in question would have been the work of a Stoic. He seems even to have claimed that the author of the *Essay* was himself a Stoic,[40] but there is little reason to agree. It is certainly true that our author sometimes approves of Stoic doctrines,[41] yet he likewise describes several Stoic ideas as rooted in misunderstanding of Homer.[42] He finds in Homer the source not only of all reasonable traditions of thought, but also of numerous corrupt traditions that represent Homer's teachings in debased form. Epicurus, for example, was misled by Odysseus' praise of feasting in Od. 9, 5-11, because he did not realize that this dramatic utterance was subtly contrived by the speaker to please the sybaritic Phaeacians and did not represent Homer's own teaching.[43] Aristippus of Cyrene was similarly deceived (ch. 150) and it is clear that, without explicit condemnation, the author looks askance at these "hedonistic" philosophies. The fact that the Stoics are sometimes situated next to these deluded thinkers is good reason for doubting that the author would have described himself as a Stoic.

For example, the Stoic ideal of "indifference" (ἀπάθεια) is seen to be rooted in Homer (ch. 134), but is immediately contrasted with the more moderate Peripatatic ideal of μετριοπάθεια or "moderation in emotion" (ch. 135) which is found to have similar Homeric precedents. Later, however, in speaking of funeral customs, the author asserts that "τὸ ἀπαθές is impossible for humans" (ch. 189) and produces several passages to demonstrate that Homer approved of a moderate show of grief in such situations. Likewise, the Stoic doctrine that "virtue (ἀρετή) is sufficient for good fortune (εὐδαιμονία)" is seen to be Homeric in its origins (ch. 136) but here again the Peripatetic formulation is immediately brought in for comparison and the author makes it clear that Homer shares the latter opinion, considering εὐδαιμονία to be dependent not simply on ἀρετή, but also on various "benefits" or "good

---

[40] *Fide* Buffière (1956), 74, n. 22, who rejected the suggestion.
[41] Chs. 119, 143, 144.
[42] E.g., see ch. 119 in the light of ch. 120; 134 with 135 and 189; 136 with 137 and 141; and perhaps 127 with 128. The rather abrupt and surprising account of Stoic dependence on Homer for the heart as the seat of the authoritative and rational part of the soul (130) likewise seems to suggest that the Stoics have misunderstood.
[43] Ch. 150. This explanation fits nicely with the author's genuine sensitivity to the rhetorical subtleties of Homeric speeches and his emphasis on dramatic situations and rhetorical manipulation. Proclus (In Rep. 1, 131-32) defends the same passage, but does so by insisting on the difference between "pleasure" as such (ἡδονή) and the εὐφροσύνη ("good cheer") that Odysseus praised.

things" (ἀγαθά) that by no means issue automatically from ἀρετή (chs. 137-41).[44]

The author is, then, neither a Platonist nor a Stoic and, though he understates his position, he shares the disapproval of the Epicureans and related "hedonists" that is a commonplace of the (non-Epicurean) literature of the Roman Empire. He often presents Aristotelian or Peripatetic doctrines and opinions as acceptable, yet he speaks with respect of the teachings of "Pythagoras and Plato," an attitude that might seem contradictory. From our modern perspective, however, we are inclined to make too much of the conflict between Plato and Aristotle and to forget that Aristotle was an ally and not an enemy for much of the later Platonic tradition.[45] Our author's focus is on the practical, and he is generally unimaginative. He believes in the immortality of the soul (chs. 122 ff.), but does not explicitly choose between Stoic materialism (ch. 127) and the nonmaterial soul of Plato and Aristotle (ch. 128).[46] He looks to the philosophers neither for superhuman insights nor for fine distinctions, but primarily for practical moral precepts and for aids to the understanding of the world of his immediate experience. Pythagoras, Plato, and Aristotle are, for him, all participants in an essentially coherent tradition free of such contradictions as might inconvenience him. The positions he appears to prefer are, generally speaking, the more moderate ones, as the two examples of his reaction against elevated and difficult Stoic ideals have shown. His is an unpretentious but voracious intellect, unencumbered by any commitment to a particular philosophical school, engaged in a work that is essentially a popularization—a doxographer who focuses his doxography on the glorification of Homer.[47]

It will not be surprising from this description that "Plutarch" never feels the need to elaborate a theory of the nature of the linguistic

---

[44] See Dillon (1977), 44-45, as well as Schrader (1902), esp. 571-72, for a full discussion of the author's ideas concerning rhetoric and the dependence of those ideas on the Stoa. This dependence does not, of course, make our author into a Stoic.

[45] If the 2nd century was a crucial period in the self-definition of the philosophical schools as they were reborn under the Empire, the work of reconciliation (sometimes in the form of appropriation) was well under way by the 3rd. Porphyry's best-known work during the Middle Ages was his *Introduction* to Aristotle's *Categories* and in the *Life of Plotinus* (14) he observes that, to the greater glory of Plotinus' *oeuvre*, "Aristotle's treatment of metaphysics is concentrated into it."

[46] Cf. ch. 122, where he observes, as if it made no difference, "spirit (πνεῦμα) is the soul itself, or the vehicle (ὄχημα) of the soul."

[47] Hermann Diels appropriately devoted a chapter to the essay in his *Doxographi Graeci* (= Diels 1879), 88-99.

or literary sign, though he does offer a few hints on the nature of poetry, discussed below. True, Homer "hints at" various matters that are not made explicit and must be read between the lines,[48] but the relationship between text and subject is on the whole straightforward. He sets out to establish certain historical links, certain influences. It is the very scope of the undertaking—to trace *all* human accomplishments to Homer—that introduces an element of the outrageous, or perhaps better, of the sophistic exercise. Indeed, it is difficult to say just where the author's orderly program breaks down and eulogistic hyperbole takes over.

In general, the author repeats again and again the claim that the credit for a given discovery lies with Homer, though the idea in question is generally associated with some later thinker. Sometimes, we are permitted to believe that the idea in question was simply anticipated by Homer, but often it is explicitly stated that the later thinker got the idea from Homer and was not simply preceded by him, but actually copied him. Since the first part of the essay, where the method is established, deals not with philosophical positions, but with the tropes and figures of rhetoric, a broad analogy is established between the literary or rhetorical and the philosophical traditions. The analogy is not entirely convincing, but it is important to bear in mind that the author operates on the assumption that each of the writers and thinkers he mentions, from Thales and Pythagoras to Aristotle and Epicurus, knew the *Iliad* and *Odyssey* intimately and, moreover, that this assumption may be very close to the truth. Viewed in this light, the extraordinary "influences" claimed lose some of their absurdity, though the central thesis inevitably remains unsatisfying.

Homer, for "Plutarch," is an absolute source—there is no question of looking beyond him for his sources. The author does not consider Homer the earliest poet, but only one of the earliest (ch. 1), though that does not seem to alter his primal status. The attitude is not original, of course, and antecedents can be found at least as far back as Herodotus (2.54), for whom Homer and Hesiod had a primary creative role that rendered them in some sense personally responsible for the theology of the Greeks. Homer is conceived not as as a transmiter of traditions, but as a creative source for the information he conveys. In the *Essay*, though, the concept is elaborated and carried to a bizarre level of rhetorical exaggeration.

---

[48] See below, 15-18, on the vocabulary used to describe these evasive turns of language.

If we set aside the "Shorter Life" (long recognized as a separate work and probably a Byzantine composition),[49] the *Essay* opens with a celebration of the educational value of Homer, and specifically of the benefits to be had from him "in diction, understanding, and experience of the world" (ch. 1), followed by a selection of opinions on his life and date. The author believes the *Iliad* and *Odyssey* to be the only authentic works of Homer,[50] and distinguishes between them as celebrations, respectively, of strength of body and nobility of soul (ch. 4). Those, then, are the ideals of the two poems, but there is much in them that is far from ideal. At this point our author comes as close as he ever does to adopting a defensive stance, giving at least an indication that he is aware that Homer's educational value had been called in question. His response is to assert that both virtues and vices are a necessary part of the spectacle (ch. 4):[51]

> As a poet, he must depict not only good modes of action but bad ones as well, for without these, the unexpected and extraordinary deeds do not emerge, the hearing of which makes the listener able to choose the better course.

He views the experience of literature, or at least of Homer, as a participational act, one in which the reader is brought into unusual and morally ambiguous situations, and is expected to make value judgments. This implies that the creation of the meaning of a work of literature is an act of collaboration in which the reader has an active role—a conception that anticipates 20th-century developments in literary theory, from Sartre to post-war reception theory. The task of the author is to mix good and evil in order to cause his readers to use and so develop their own moral sense by coming to terms with extraordinary (παράδοξοι) situations. The same idea is repeated in the closing paragraph (ch. 218). Our author posits for the poet a goal of poetic

---

[49] See among others Volkmann (1869), 120. This "Shorter Life," if complete, looks like an introduction to the *Iliad* only, consisting as it does of general information about Homer's life and times, followed by a summary of the story of Troy that ends with the events with which the *Iliad* closes, and finally some observations about Homer's technique of starting that poem in the ninth year.
[50] Given the popularity of the *Batrachomyomachia* during the Renaissance and the conflicting ancient testimony on the extent of the Homeric *oeuvre*, "Plutarch's" support of what was to become the modern orthodoxy (likewise supported by Eustathius) was of considerable importance, and his authority is invoked in this context in the 17th century. See Hepp (1968), 92.
[51] Cf. Plutarch, *Demetrius*, 1, on negative exempla.

effectiveness that justifies the means of an "extraordinary and mythical treatment" of his material and of saying "some things that are highly improbable" (ch. 6). It is his task to capture the imagination, and these techniques are the most direct path to that end.

On one level, then, the mythic, fabulous element is simply window-dressing (albeit necessary window-dressing) for an experience that is fundamentally one of ethical training and exercise. On another level, though, the fabulous may be emblematic, metaphorical (ch. 5):

> Furthermore, he has made the gods converse with men
> not simply for the sake of exciting and astounding us,
> but in order to show, in this as well, that the gods care
> for mankind and are not indifferent.

Thus the treatment of the gods as anthropomorphic and playing parts in the lives and battles of men[52] is allegorical and constitutes an extended metaphor for divine providence. This apparently traditional explanation is expanded later in the essay (chs. 112 ff.) and eventually came to serve as the basis for the far more complex model of the Homeric fiction's representation of the divine to be found in the later Platonists.

Our author's first concern (chs. 7-73) is to examine Homer's diction, using the elaborate analytic vocabulary that has its roots in the rhetorical schools of the second century. He looks first at the variety of dialect forms and anachronisms (chs. 8-14),[53] then at the tropes and figures of rhetoric that can be traced to Homer (chs. 15-71).

In this opening section, our author defines allegory (ἀλληγορία) as a rhetorical figure closely related to irony (εἰρονεία) and to sarcasm (σαρκασμός), a figure that "says one thing through another" (ch. 70). The illustration given is Eumaeus' speech to Melanthius (Od. 22.195-96), when the latter is hanging in chains:

> Now, you'll keep your watch all night, Melanthius,
> in the sort of soft bed you deserve. . . .
>
> νῦν μὲν δὴ μάλα πάγχυ, Μελάνθιε, νύκτα φυλάξεις,
> εὐνῇ ἔνι μαλακῇ καταλέγμενος, ὥς σε ἔοικεν. . . .

---

[52] The verb ὁμιλέω, translated "converse" above, covers military as well as other sorts of interaction, and the author probably has in mind Books 20 and 21 of the *Iliad*. Proclus, at any rate, uses the same concept in a defense of those passages.
[53] Chs. 8-12 are edited with extensive commentary by Scarpat (1952).

which by modern definition is certainly sarcasm rather than allegory, and would not fall within the scope of "allegory" (outside of rhetoric) as understood by, for example, Plutarch.[54]

The fact that our author here employs ἀλληγορία as a technical term from the vocabulary of rhetoric does not prevent his using the same vocabulary in a broader and quite distinct sense later. In his rather confusing account of the relationship of the elements of the Homeric cosmos, he asserts that mist (ἀήρ) lies above earth, followed by *aither*, heaven, and finally, "Olympus," which is conceived as a kind of super-refined mist (ch. 96):

> In the lines in which the poet says that Hera, Zeus' sister, cohabits with him, he seems to be expressing these things allegorically, for Hera ["Ηρα] means "mist" [ἀήρ], the damp substance....

The verb ἀλληγορέω, then, can mean "express allegorically" in the sense "use the names of the gods to designate the elements of the universe." The author of the essay makes very sparing use of this complex of words but it is to this rather narrow category within the field of allegorical expression—the physical allegory traditionally associated with the Stoics, and perhaps going back to Theagenes of Rhegium in the 6th century—that he refers in the other instances as well. He is discussing the battle in Book 20 when he observes (ch. 102):

> The poet seems, in the division of the gods into those who help the Trojans and those who help the Greeks, to hint at the manner in which things constituted of opposite natures oppose one another, revealing their various natures allegorically.

Plutarch, in an often quoted passage (De aud. po. 19e-f) indicated that the word ἀλληγορία had in his day replaced ὑπόνοια ("hint" or "hidden meaning"), but that the meaning of the two terms was essentially the same, and our author, writing after Plutarch, provides support for this observation. He uses ὑπόνοια only once and the context easily explains the use of the old-fashioned word.[55] He is

---

[54] Cf. Plutarch, De aud. po. 19E-F.
[55] One should beware, however, of using the choice of vocabulary as a criterion of dating. Plutarch is undoubtedly reflecting a genuine shift in contemporary usage, but ὑπόνοια continued in use. In Hermias, for example (5th c.), who avoids

Introduction

asserting that the roots of theoretical discourse (physics, ethics, and dialectic) can be found in Homer (ch. 92):

> And if the knowledge is couched in enigmatic and mythic language, this should not be unexpected, for the cause is the nature of poetry and the custom of the ancients. They did this so that lovers of learning, delighted by a certain elegance, might more easily seek and more easily find the truth, while the ignorant would not scorn what they could not understand. That which is couched in hidden meanings [τὸ δι' ὑπονοίας σημαινόμενον] may be attractive where that which is spoken explicitly is useless.

Just as Numenius[56] believed that the dialogues of Plato were cryptic, a genre conceived around the avoidance of dogmatic assertions in order to avoid their political consequences, so early wisdom, in our author's assessment, in order to avoid the scorn of the ignorant, took on the form of poetry, which is thus by its very nature "enigmatic and mythic language" masking a hidden truth. This conception is clearly not original with our author; it can be traced to Plato (both the *Protagoras* and the pseudo-Platonic *Second Alcibiades* [147B]), and became, by way of these texts, a commonplace of later Platonists' discussions of archaic poetry.[57] The structures of meaning involved here never appeared simple to those who gave them careful attention. A simplistic attitude was appropriate only to the "ignorant," and in fact their inability to penetrate beyond the mask of the fiction is the very reason for the existence of that mask.

The characteristic verb by which the author of the *Essay* refers to the process by which poetic language points to meanings that lie beyond the superficial is αἰνίττομαι ("hint at"), related to the Homeric and Hesiodic noun αἶνος ("story," "fable," or "riddle") and thus having a sense that might be translated "refer to, obliquely, as in a riddle." The verb does not occur in Homer and the instances of the noun in the

---

the term ἀλληγορία, it seems to have reconquered its semantic turf (In Phaedrum 213, 19-22) and can also refer to an undesirable, or even obscene *sous-entendu* (In Phaedrum 202, 31-32). Cf. In Phaedrum 229, 20-21. Hermias' usage can be explained by way of Plato's own -- he may even be consciuosly avoiding anachronistic use of ἀλληγορία in talking about Plato.

[56] Frs. 23 and 24.
[57] E.g. Proclus, In Rep. 1, 186

Iliad tell us little,[58] but at *Odyssey* 14.508, where it refers to Odysseus' false tale told to Eumaeus to "hint" that he needs a coat, the noun αἶνος seems already to refer to a story told with an aim in view that goes beyond the superficially obvious sense—a story told for an ulterior motive. The word αἴνιγμα ("enigma," "riddle") belongs to the same complex, and our author explicitly associates αἰνίγματα with "mythical expression" (in ch. 92, cited above), in a phrase recalling the expression "extraordinary and mythical treatment" of ch. 6. The verb αἰνίττομαι can take various subjects: the poet "hints at" the Empedoclean doctrine of love and strife in Hera's speech to Zeus in the episode of the deception of Zeus (ch. 100), he "hints at" the strife of opposites in the battle of the gods in *Iliad* 20 (ch. 102), and he simply "hints" that he himself is acquainted with a theoretical sort of medicine (ch. 201). Similarly, in the song of Ares and Aphrodite, "the myth hints at" (ὁ μῦθος αἰνίττεται) the love and strife doctrine (ch. 101) and the transformations of Odysseus' crew "hint at" bestial reincarnations for bestial men (ch. 126). It is, then, an exceptionally flexible word, adaptable to many situations where an utterance implies something beyond its immediate and obvious sense.

This brief sketch of the *Essay*'s vocabulary, insofar as it relates to ambiguities and hidden meanings, has exhausted virtually all the uses of these words. The vast bulk of the exposition is concerned not with hidden meanings but with precedents to be found in Homer for the principles of later thinkers and writers. Hidden meanings enter the picture primarily in the discussion of "theoretical discourse," since, as we have seen, our author believes that it is the standard practice of early poetry to "hint at" truths of this order, rather than express them directly.

When he has completed his demonstration that Homer is the source of the various tropes and figures of diction (chs. 6-73), he goes on to divide human discourse (λόγος) into "historical" (ἱστορικός), "theoretical" or "contemplative" (θεωρητικός), and "political" (πολιτικός) and to ask whether in fact Homer can be shown to contain the "beginnings" or "first principles" (ἀρχαί) of all these modes (ch. 74). His method of demonstration here is sadly but characteristically unsatisfying. He attempts to reduce each mode of discourse to its most basic components and then to relate each of them by hook or by crook to Homer. Historical discourse he defines as that "containing the narration of past events" (ch. 6) and analyzes this into eight essential

---

[58] *Iliad* 23, 652 and 795.

elements belonging to every narrative (chs. 74-78).[59] When he has discovered all of these in Homer, he goes on to classify the various sorts of similes that contribute to Homer's narrative art (chs. 84-90), bringing the section on "historical discourse" to a rather abrupt close.

The "theoretical discourse" is analyzed into physics, ethics, and dialectic (ch. 92), though the treatment is not as rigorous as in the previous section, and the distinctions among the three categories are blurred. The initial discussion of physics includes a section on the gods and one on souls, followed by a gradual transition to ethics (chs. 133-44). There is, however, nothing that could be called a discussion of dialectic. Chapters 145 through 151 trace miscellaneous—largely "Pythagorean"—doctrines to Homer and, after a discussion of the borrowings of various later writers from the sayings (γνῶμαι) of Homer (chs. 151-60), the discussion of "political discourse" begins abruptly at ch. 161. The disparity between the announced content and what one actually finds in the essay might suggest that some meddling with the original document has occurred, but given the nature of the material it is difficult to build a strong case.

The thrust of the section on physics, narrowly defined, is to demonstrate that Homer provided the basis for Thales, Xenophanes, and Empedocles in their discussions of the first principles of the universe, and of the elements. Homer knew the order of the elements of the spherical universe (ch. 94), according to our author, and made them five: earth, mist, *aither*, heaven, and Olympus (chs. 94-95). Water seems to be subsumed in the single moist category "mist" (ἀήρ), at this point, but with no indication that the categories have been shifted, our author goes right on to develop a model (based on *Iliad* 15.187-88) in which the five elements are water (allotted to Poseidon), fire (Zeus) and mist (Hades), along with the shared elements, earth and Olympus, belonging to no individual god (chs. 97-98). Conflicting interpretations of Olympus as a mountain and as a fifth essence are simply juxtaposed with no attempt at reconciliation. In spite of the unresolved contradictions, our author's treatment of this material appears to be influenced by Aristotle's discussion of the first principles of the Presocratics in *Metaphysics* A. "Plutarch" goes on from the material principles to consider the dynamics of the structure of the universe,

---

[59] Volkmann (1869), 124, with n., noticed the similarity between our author's list of the eight "elements" (ἀφορμαί) of all narration and the nine *elementa circa quae versari videtur omnis narratio* of Quintilian (3, 6, 24 ff.), but in spite of the fact that six of our author's ἀφορμαί correspond nicely to six of Quintilian's *elementa*, the latter is writing of speeches at law, not narratives of past events, and even his discussion of the common categories has little to do with our author's.

quoting Empedocles on love and strife. He finds the same doctrine cryptically expressed both in the episode of the deception of Zeus and in the song of Ares and Aphrodite (chs. 100-01). The doctrine of the creative force of the interaction of opposites is likewise said to be expressed in the song of Ares and Aphrodite (ch. 99) and in the battle of the gods of *Iliad* 20 (ch. 102). Homer also showed the universe to be one and finite (ch. 103), he knew of the rotation of the sun (ch. 104), and he had certain other information about the sun, consistent with that of Aristotle (ch. 105). He knew all about the heavens and could have rivaled Aratus as an astronomical poet, had he chosen to do so. Likewise, he knew the nature and causes of such natural phenomena as earthquakes, eclipses, wind, and rain (chs. 106-11).

The section on physics now shifts from cosmology to doctrines concerning gods and souls,[60] to which we will turn in a moment. The information on the physical universe that could be claimed for Homer deserves another look. This material was exceptionally popular with the scholiasts, and the majority of "Plutarch's" points are made by the scholiasts as well, sometimes quoting substantial blocks of material verbatim in the form in which it appears in our author.[61] The attribution to Homer of certain ideas about the nature of the universe, ideas not archaic but quite acceptable to contemporary thinkers, was doubtless a commonplace. Our author is unique only in his systematic treatment of the matter, and in that his popular introduction attracted the attention of the copyists and of Planudes and so survived, whereas most of the works tapped by the scholiasts were lost. But "Plutarch" is doing two things at once here: he is demonstrating that the history of philosophy devolves from Homer—for this he is ultimately dependent

---

[60] It is as if "metaphysics" needed to be added to the categories of "theoretical discourse" to serve as a rubric for ch.s 112-21, though even that expedient would not comfortably accommodate chs. 122-31, on souls.

[61] In the section on physics (chs. 93-111), there are 44 citations of Homer along with three other references to easily identifiable passages (the song of Ares and Aphrodite, the war of the gods, and the description of the constellation called the "Cart" at *Iliad* 18, 487-90). Scholiasts, commenting on 20 of these passages, record observations identical or at least related to those of our author. In addition, ch. 106, without its final sentence, appears with only minor changes as a scholion on *Odyssey* 5, 272 (Schol. in Od. [Dindorf] vol. 1, 269), and most of ch. 109, including four citations, is similarly reproduced as a scholion on *Odyssey* 5, 295 (Schol. in Od. [Dindorf] vol. 1, 274). Many of "Plutarch's" points are doubtless made by the scholiasts commenting on passages other than those to which "Plutarch" attaches them, as well. As an example of this last situation, a scholiast on *Iliad* 11, 735 (Schol. in Il. [Erbse] vol. 3, 270) makes "Plutarch's" point that the sphericity of the earth was known to Homer. "Plutarch" discusses that passage in another context (ch. 105), but does not connect it with his claim that Homer's universe was spherical (ch. 94).

on Aristotle's summaries of Presocratic physics, though the material may reach him only by way of the doxographers—and secondly, he is demonstrating that an acceptable account of the world as we know and experience it can be found in the Homeric poems. The casual reference to Aratus (ch. 106) is suggestive. The implication is that Homer's experience and knowledge were limitless, but that the *Iliad* and *Odyssey*, because of their subjects and concerns, tap only a small part of that knowledge. It is clear that for our author the mind of Homer was a Gargantuan *abysme de science*. He seems, in fact, to have taken to heart the Sirens' claim to universal knowledge (*Odyssey* 12.189) and to have thoroughly identified Homer's Sirens with his Muse. The important point for him, though, is the vastness of that knowledge, and not any claim to special privilege. For "Plutarch," the *Iliad* and *Odyssey* constitute a vast encyclopedia with a complex, sometimes obscure structure of meaning. They have not, however, taken on the role of scripture, or of received revelation.

When our author goes on to discuss Homer as a source of knowledge concerning gods and souls, his assertions—given the extraordinarily exaggerated scope of his basic claims for the poet—are relatively modest. "All right-thinking men believe the gods exist, and Homer first among them" (ch. 112). Our author's initial formulation of Homer's distinction between gods and men sticks closely to Homeric vocabulary and concepts, adding only the un-Homeric abstraction φύσις (ch. 112):[62]

> Since the gods are immortal, it is the nature of their lives to be easy and endless and they have no need of food that the bodies of mortal creatures require.

Thus, since all living bodies are nourished by food and since the gods are not nourished in this way in the Homeric poems, therefore Homer conceived the gods to be non-material, "bodiless" (ἀσώματοι). The bodies that Homer created for the gods are the result of the needs of the poem—means justified first of all by the end of poetic effectiveness, and further, by the need of "reminding those who are less given to contemplation that the gods do, in fact, exist" (ch. 112). Homer's fashioning of the images of the gods emerges here as his great creative

---

[62] In the *Iliad* and *Odyssey*, φύσις appears only once, at *Odyssey* 10, 303, with reference to the "qualities" of the *moly* shown to Odysseus by Hermes. It is far from having the fully developed abstract sense that it developed in the philosophical vocabulary of the 4th c.

contribution. "Plutarch," however, cannot pass by the matter so quickly as Herodotus (2.53) had. He feels the need to establish Homer's motivation for this creativity and to relate the iconography of the gods to the esthetic needs of the poem. More important still, he wants to demonstrate that the concepts lying beyond the fiction and subtly communicated by it are acceptable ones.

The appeal is characteristically to current consensus: the "best philosophers" considered the highest god to be incorporeal and perceived by mind (νοῦς), rather than sense (αἴσθησις). A number of passages are mustered from Homer to illustrate that Zeus is at least in some sense isolated from the other gods and separate from them. Aside from being noetic, the primary qualities of this god are that he is all-knowing (πάντα ἐπιστάμενος) and pervades the universe (διέπων τὸ πᾶν) (ch. 114). Thus both providence (πρόνοια) and fate (εἱμαρμένη) are included in his vast wisdom. Several chapters (chs. 115-118) are devoted to the idea, already mentioned, that much of the force of the Homeric fiction is to illustrate the providence of the gods, a major component of which is "their desire for men to live justly" (ch. 118).

The source of the Stoic emphasis on fate as the deciding factor in human life is found in Homer (ch. 119). Characteristically, however, our author—without explicitly rejecting the Stoic position—asserts that true agreement with Homer will be found elsewhere, in the doctrines of Plato, Aristotle, and Theophrastus, all of whom are said to assert that the human will is free within a larger framework of necessity, a framework that may cause the free human impulse to produce unwanted results (ch. 120). In this discussion, "Plutarch" shows himself to be embroiled in one of the central problems of middle Platonism.[63] As did many Platonists, this author rejects the Stoic position in favor of one that is more moderate (i.e., in the context, less deterministic) and that he believes to have its roots in Plato and Aristotle.

This, according to "Plutarch" is Homer's teaching concerning the gods. The general conception bears the imprint, especially in its historical perspective, of the Aristotelian tradition. It is not, in any case, to be traced to the Stoa, and betrays concerns central to the Platonism of the early centuries of our era. The more important point is that it is a picture constructed entirely from the ideas, either explicitly

---

[63] Cf. Dillon (1977), 44-45 on this and on the debate over the sufficiency of virtue for happiness. Porphyry (Stobaeus Ecl. 1, 7, 42) likewise finds the Platonic position -- that life consists of an element of free will and an element of necessity -- to be anticipated by Homer.

cited or vaguely indicated, of later philosophers. The concern, again, is with Homer's prestige as a source for the philosophical tradition, and beyond that, with establishing that Homer offers an adequate account of reality, in line with the best received opinions.

Up to the beginning of the discussion of souls, "Plutarch" introduces no doctrines specifically designated as Pythagorean, but this subject is ushered in with the assertion that "of all the doctrines [concerning the soul], that of Pythagoras and Plato is the noblest, that the soul is immortal" (ch. 122). There are, as we shall see, certain doctrines that are, for our author, specifically Pythagorean, and others that are Platonic though borrowed from, or at least shared with, Pythagoras.[64] The immortality of the soul belongs in the latter category. The soul flits from the dying man and goes to Hades. This is identified, with the help of an etymology no doubt older than the *Cratylus*, as the "invisible" or "unseen" (ἀειδής) place.[65] "Plutarch" begs the question whether this is located above the earth or below, an issue of crucial importance for later commentators on the cosmology of Homer.[66] For our author, it is a matter of indifference, and he is able simply to offer both possibilities without feeling the need to reconcile them. The same sort of indifference to metaphysical subtleties emerges in more surprising from later in the chapter, where a Stoic model of the relationship of soul and body is discussed: "[Homer] knew all this well, that the blood is the food and sustanance of the spirit (πνεῦμα), and the spirit is either the soul itself, or the vehicle of the soul" (ch. 122). If we want to know *which*, we shall have to inquire elsewhere. Our author is content to present both possibilities, rather sympathetically confessing his inability to resolve the problem.

The individual human being, for Homer, is in any case the soul (ψυχή), and not the body, or the ghost (ch. 132). The etymological fantasy on the living body (δέμας) as the bondage (δεσμός) of the soul, and the dead body (σῶμα) as its tomb (σῆμα), is elaborated out of the *Cratylus* (400C)—perhaps the most persistent and productive of all the myriad interpretations by etymology.[67] The "philosophers" to whom these opinions are attributed are unspecified, but this entire section oscillates between the "Platonic" and the "Pythagorean." At this

---

[64] The idea of the philosophical dependence of Plato on Pythagoras is at least as old as Aristotle (Met. A 987a).
[65] "Plutarch" glosses ἀειδής with ἀόρατον to make the matter entirely clear. The same etymology occurs several times in Plato, and is specifically rejected by Socrates at *Cratylus* 404B.
[66] E.g. Proclus, In Rep. 2, 128-31.
[67] See De Vogel (1981).

point, however, Plato is left aside and metensomatosis is introduced as a properly Pythagorean doctrine that "was not beyond the understanding of Homer" (ch. 125). The talking horses of Achilles and the old dog that recognized Odysseus indicate that the souls of men and other animals are related, and the destruction of Odysseus' crew as punishment for killing the sacred cattle is viewed as a general indication that all animals are honored by the gods (ch. 125). Little more than a primitive animism is implied. The subsequent passage, however, on Circe as the symbol of the cycle of metensomatosis (ch. 126), to which "the intellectual man" (ὁ...ἔμφρων ἀνήρ), Odysseus, is immune, already suggests something more sophisticated and the patterns of the myths of Plato begin to be visible behind this hero who is liberated from reincarnation by the possession of reason (λόγος). The fact that λόγος is here identified with the Hermes of the myth likewise points back to the *Cratylus*. It points at the same time, however, to later developments of the same identification that lead, for example, to the identification, by the Naasenian Gnostics of the 1st and 2nd centuries, of the Hermes of the *nekyia* with the creative and redeeming λόγος, that is, with Christ.[68] Porphyry, in a fragment preserved in Stobaeus (Ecl. 1, 41, 60) develops the allegory of Circe, making it clear that this "Pythagorean" tradition became part of the Neoplatonists' reading of the passage.[69]

When Odysseus' descent to Hades is viewed as "separating soul from body" (ch. 126), we have fully entered that bizarre realm of Platonized Pythagoreanism where the influence of the legends of Pythagoras' own temporary death and resurrection becomes indistinguishable from that of the similar story of Er in the *Republic*. The important point here, though, from the present perspective, is that a comprehensive view of Odysseus the hero as an "intellectual man" freed by reason from the round of reincarnation, a hero whose heroism consists precisely in the denial of existence on the material plane and the attainment of a higher state, exists here in isolation from doctrines of astral immortality and elaborate demonologies. Whatever the later Neopythagorean and Neoplatonic contributions to the understanding of the poems, the core was already available for elaboration: a redefined Odysseus, far removed from the Homeric hero and transformed by a complex and unrecoverable process into a hero of the denial of the flesh.

---

[68] See Carcopino (1956), 180-82.
[69] For the text, translation, and discussion, see Lamberton (1986), 115-19.

After this discussion of ideas specifically identified as Pythagorean, "Plutarch" returns to the Stoic doctrine of the soul as an exhalation and demonstrates its Homeric roots (ch. 127). Again, however, without specifically rejecting the Stoic position, he juxtaposes the belief of "Plato and Aristotle" that the soul is nonmaterial, and likewise finds Homeric precedent for this, referring to the body as the "vehicle" of the soul (ch. 128, cf. ch. 122). He seems reluctant to resolve the apparent conflict of views, but it is significant—and perhaps suggestive of a surprisingly exact historical perspective—that just as the doctrine of immortality was attributed to "Pythagoras and Plato" and that of metensomatosis to Pythagoras alone, now a non-material soul is attributed *not* to Pythagoras, but only to Plato and Aristotle. Our author may have had a surprisingly clear idea of what was properly Pythagorean and what was properly Platonic, or at the very least, he will have taken to heart Aristotle's observation (Met. A, 989b-990a) that the Pythagoreans were exclusively concerned with the material, sensible universe.

"Plutarch" is more at home, in any case, with analysis and definition than with metaphysical speculation. Thus he proceeds (chs. 129-31) to elaborate upon the Homeric model of the soul, arguing that the poet divides it into a "rational" and an "irrational" part and then distinguishes within the latter the "appetitive" and the "passionate." Homer's supposed awareness of these categories is demonstrated by means of citations. The division is foreign to Aristotle,[70] and to the early Stoa, and must be traced to Plato. Although it is a doctrine de-emphasized by later Platonism, with its more complex psychology, it nevertheless emerges as a useful model in Porphyry.[71]

Before going on to the discussion of ethics, our author examines an essentially Stoic description of the soul (chs. 130-31), discussing in materialistic terms the origins of the emotions and the location within the body of the sources of anger and the appetites. Allowing the Platonic tripartite analysis to stand as a framework for his discussion, he moves glibly past it to demonstrate that Homer likewise provided the Stoics with the basic elements of their account of anger as merely a disturbance of the soul, itself conceived as unified and rational.

We may pass briefly over the section on ethics (the ἠθικὸν μέρος φιλοσοφίας, chs.132-44), having already mentioned that a Peripatetic (and moderate) account of the relationship between virtue and

---

[70] See the end of De Anima 1.
[71] Ap. Stobaeus, Ecl. 1, 41, 60. For a comprehensive treatment of the tripartite soul in the commentators on Homer, see Buffière (1956), 257-78.

happiness is explicitly preferred to the Stoic ideal. Our author is characteristically unable to accept the idea that moral excellence in the absence of wealth, health, beauty, etc., is sufficient for εὐδαιμονία. Here, in contrast to his treatment of most other topics, he sticks closely to a clearly defined position, which he shows by a series of citations to be that of Homer. The Stoic ideal, though, had its source in Homer as well, and specifically in the portrait of Odysseus, the "wisest and most reasonable of men" (ch. 136). We find that our author is capable of juxtaposing what appeared to be a Platonizing vision of Odysseus' heroism with a Stoicizing one. The suggestion is very strong that this versatile hero could become the expression of a variety of philosophical ideals and that, to a reader without prejudice and concerned only with the fullest appreciation of the text, the increased light thrown on the poem by each interpretation contributed to a cumulative enhancement of the text, in which the mutual contradictions of the interpretations became relatively unimportant.

After preferring the Peripatetic ethics to the Stoic, "Plutarch" returns briefly to the illustration, from Homer, of several Stoic positions (chs. 143-44) and concludes the section with the observation that Homer was the first to philosophize about ethics and physics.

He does not, however, go directly to the "political" aspect of Homer (the πολιτικὸς λόγος) as he had promised in ch. 74, but rather inserts eight chapters (chs. 145-52) on miscellaneous doctrines and sayings, the majority of them Pythagorean, and all, of course, rooted in Homer. He tells us first that Pythagorean arithmology and teachings on music are to be found "everywhere" in Homer (ch. 145). Homer has a tendency to use odd numbers for things with positive associations and even numbers for the opposite. Even the fact that Achilles sacrifices *four* horses and *twelve* Trojans on Patroclus' pyre is seen as a subtle indication that Homer does not approve of this excessive mourning (ch. 145, cf. ch. 190) and other examples are provided to show that a sacrifice should properly have an odd number of victims. The chapter ends with a panegyric on the number 9, which Homer is said to have favored.

Pythagoras is little more than a pretext for the discussion of music in Homer (chs. 147-48). The Pythagoreans held music in high esteem and so did Homer before them. The rest of the exposition is a rather banal catalogue of the uses of music in Homer and a demonstration that the poet distinguished between high and low pitch. Only one undeveloped hint of a more ambitious interpretation of Homeric music comes through here, when "Plutarch" observes, "Homer praises music when he is describing the Sirens, and says, 'But when he

has enjoyed it he goes away wiser'" (ch. 147). The praise of music in these lines sung by the Sirens is far from obvious. Indeed, from the context, we must read the lines as a sarcastic lie, and an allegory in the narrow, rhetorical definition only. In fact, the listener does not go away at all, as Circe has explicitly and vividly indicated a scant 150 lines earlier (*Odyssey* 12.45-46). Here, however, our author characteristically isolates the Sirens' song from its dramatic context to allow the passage to be read as praise of music. The Sirens thus take their place with Demodocus and Phemius in the complex Homeric self-portrait and self-advertisement of the artist.

After the passage on the philosophers misled by Homer (ch. 150), a series of short chapters demonstrates borrowings of the sayings of Homer by the sages, by Pythagoras, by the dramatists, and finally, by Theocritus and Aratus.

The section on the πολιτικὸς λόγος (chs. 161-98) is dominated by an analysis of Homer's rhetoric, focusing not on his diction (as in chs. 7-73), but rather on the rhetorical force of his speeches and his knowledge of the techniques of the rhetor (chs. 161-74). The central assertion is that Homer was himself an "artificer of discourse" (τεχνίτης λόγων). The following chapters are concerned with various topics loosely related to the πολιτικὸς λόγος: Homer's knowledge of the law, of the state, and its component parts and varieties (chs. 184-98).

After a brief discourse on the varied ages of the Homeric heroes and a longer one on Homer's knowledge of medicine (chs. 199-211) as well as seercraft, the *Essay* closes with the assertion that tragedy, comedy, and epigram are all literary forms founded by Homer, and with praise for the visual qualities of Homer's art (chs. 213-27). Homer was a sculptor of words, who "displayed to the imagination" things human and divine. The creator of Hephaestus and the shield is assimilated to his creation and the global and comprehensive artifact of Hephaestus becomes, implicitly, the Homeric *corpus* (ch. 216). It is indicative of the peculiar modernity of our author's literary sensitivity that the passage he selects for special analysis (the description of the scar of Odysseus, *Odyssey* 19.467 ff.) is precisely the one Eric Auerbach chose as emblematic of Homeric style,[72] and his discussion of the passage—different as it of course is from that of Auerbach—confirms the reader's impression that behind the dry persona of the *grammaticus*, "Plutarch" was in fact a perceptive analyst of Homeric style.

---

[72] Auerbach (1946), ch. 1.

The closing panegyric (ch. 218) returns to the mildly defensive note of the opening, again asserting that the depiction of evil alongside good is essential to art and to the esthetic experience. The last praise of Homer is perhaps the most curious: his limitless excellence is linked, in all seriousness, to the fact that those who have come after him have found in his poetry things he did not even put there! This is not an attack on the researchers in question. On the contrary, it serves to enhance the prestige of the Homeric encyclopedia that it can be put to uses that go beyond even the intentions of its author. This is the one point at which our author might appear to be talking about scripture, not archaic poetry, when he mentions with apparent approval certain people who "use the poetry for divination" (ch. 218), as if it were oracular, and others who rearrange its parts to make it express entirely new ideas—both practices that our author otherwise ignores. But notice the carefully maintained balance: "Plutarch" does not recommend these uses of the *Iliad* and *Odyssey*—he merely documents them. Simply because they are there, they redound to the greater glory of Homer.

The use of the poems for divination is puzzling. Leaving aside the incantatory use of the poems—claimed for early Pythagoreanism and apparently alive in Proclus' time—which is really something quite different, there seems to be no other early reference to the use of the text of Homer for magical purposes, let alone divination. The Roman emperors consulted the *sortes Vergilianae* as early as Hadrian[73] and it would appear to be an activity of this sort that is referred to here. The allegorical interpretation of Virgil and the elevation of the *Aeneid* into a sort of scripture, though a far more rapid development than in the case of Homer, is generally thought to be dependent on the previous transformation of Homer. However, the present instance may be one in which Roman practice influenced the use of the Greek epics, rather than the reverse. There is no reason to believe that divination by means of epic poetry predates Hadrian.[74] The notion of the ancients consulting Homeric *sortes* enjoyed a certain notoriety during the Renaissance, but "Plutarch" in the passage before us may well be responsible for that.[75]

---

[73] Historia augusta, Hadrian, 2, 8.

[74] The standard sources are quite vague on the dating of divination based on Homer -- cf. Halliday (1913), 217 -- but Bouché-Leclerq (1879-82), vol. 1, 195, suggests that it was "une méthode savante, qui n'a pu naître qu'après la prophétie orale et pour suppléer au défaut de l'inspiration défaillante." He may have had in mind a date as late as Plutarch, who wrote of the decline of the oracles. It seems impossible to document any "rhapsodomancy" before the time of Hadrian. Later references include a 4th-century magical papyrus using Homer (Pap. gr. mag. no. 7. Vol. 2, 1-45).

[75] Hepp (1961-62), 429-31.

Introduction   29

The shuffled pastiches or *centones* are likewise attested for the mid-2nd century, in a Christian Gnostic context.[76] Both of these elements of the use of Homer combine to reinforce those cited earlier in pointing to a date not far from 200 for the *Essay*.[77]

The cumulative evidence is encouraging, then, for a date for the *Essay* that would place it within a generation or two of the activities of Numenius. The piece seems, at any rate, to belong to that intellectual world and to provide a useful—if rhetorically overblown—account of the claims to wisdom that could be made for Homer by the commentators of the period that saw the first datable attempts to link the *Iliad* and *Odyssey* to the world-model of later Platonism and to transform their poet into a sage of limitless wisdom, with a direct and suprasensory perception of reality. The claims made by "Plutarch" for the scope of the wisdom of Homer are no doubt as old as the teachings of Socrates' contemporaries,[78] or older, but there is no reason to believe that they were ever, before or after, formulated so elaborately as in the *Essay*. One can only speculate as to the author's motives in selecting the material he did. One possibility is that he was well aware of the sort of meanings that Numenius and Cronius were distilling (or had distilled) from Homer, as they laid the foundation for the appropriation of the *Iliad* and *Odyssey* for the tradition of "Pythagoras and Plato," and that he deliberately stated the poet's traditional claim to encyclopedic wisdom in more traditional, and at the same time more generous terms. Whatever his reasons, "Plutarch" emerges as the vehicle of crucially important documentation of a stage of Homer interpretation intermediate between the (largely physical and ethical) allegories collected by Heraclitus and the Platonizing interpretations that come into their own in the preserved literature only with Porphyry, late in the third century.

3. The Present Edition

The goal of this bilingual edition is to make this important essay accessible to a larger public. As noted above, the need was long

---

[76] See Carcopino (1956), 190-91. Valentinus (fl. ca. 150), produced a *cento* discussed by Carcopino. Our earliest source for the description of such *centones* is Tertullian (d. ca. 225).
[77] They may, as Volkmann (1869, 121) argued, be reasons to date the essay to a later period than Plutarch's own, but only by a generation or two, not by centuries.
[78] They are parodied repeatedly in Plato's *Ion*.

felt for an improvement on the text as printed by the 19th-century editors down to Bernardakis. We undertook this task and had nearly completed it when the excellent Teubner edition of Jan Kindstrand appeared in 1990. Our own text is based on much the same principles as his, in particular with regard to the 13th-century Parisinus graecus 2697, which, for the first 136 chapters has been our principal guide. We worked as well with microfilms of Ambrosianus graecus 859 (C126 inf.), Riccardianus 30, and Vindobonensis Palatinus suppl. gr. 23 (88). Our text is on the whole more conservative than Kindstrand's, in that we have been reluctant to normalize the author's often crabbed style or to emend in situations where there are evident errors of fact (e.g. ch. 3 with note). The author's use of the definite article, for instance, is quite idiosyncratic, but we have left it as the manuscripts have it, except in a few instances. We have been more willing than Kindstrand to mark and leave a *locus desperatus* (†. . .†) when no emendation known to us was compelling. Our brief apparatus (183-84) accounts for all emendations and supplements we have printed. The reader in need of a richer apparatus will find an outstanding one in Kindstrand's edition, which has been invaluable in checking and correcting our own. Another important contribution to the study of our text, Michael Hillgruber's introduction and commentary on chapters 1-74 (Hillgruber [1994]) appeared when our book was in the final stages of revision, and we were therefore unable to make use of it.

The *Essay*'s pedagogic intent is everywhere evident, and the author is more likely to belabor the obvious than to write obscurely, with the result that he does not require constant comment or elucidation. Our notes are therefore limited to a sampling of comparanda and indications of sources, along with such explanation of obscure or unfamiliar matters as we thought might be helpful to the reader. In general, the text is the work of John Keaney and the introductory material and notes that of Robert Lamberton, though we both contributed to some extent to all aspects of the project. The translation we refined and corrected together, but since I have undertaken the final correction, the principal responsibility for its inevitable shortcomings rests with me. It will be noticed that the translations of the many citations from Homer sacrifice elegance to reflect as clearly as possible the point "Plutarch" is making, so that in a few cases the same Homeric passage has even been translated differently in different sections.

4. Acknowledgements

Our work would have been impossible without the microfilms provided by the Bibliothèque nationale in Paris, the Ambrosian Library in Milan, and the Österreichische Nationalbibliothek, Vienna. Two anonymous readers who undertook for the American Philological Association the considerable task of evaluating this study have our sincere gratitude for a wealth of constructive suggestions and corrections. Matthew Santirocco and David Blank, his successor as editor of the APA Monographs Series, have likewise contributed valuable advice and helped the project to fruition. The latter has been exceptionally generous in his meticulous advice and suggestions; it was he who pointed out to us the relevance of Lesbonax to our text. The final proofreading of the Greek text was carried out with the generous help of Washington University graduate students Barbara Manzara and Scott Bucholtz. Susan Rotroff contributed a great deal of time and insight to the correction of the remaining portion. Among the many librarians and keepers of books to whom we are indebted, the Director of the Gennadius Library in Athens, David Jordan, deserves our special thanks for help in elucidating thorny problems relating to the early printed editions of the text. Anne Kintner, Archivist of Grinnell College graciously allowed the engraved frontispiece of the Grinnell copy of Joshua Barnes' 1711 edition of Homer to be photographed for our cover. Our thanks as well to Gerald Lalonde for help on that part of the project.

> Robert Lamberton
> Washington University in St. Louis
> March, 1996

PRINCIPAL EDITIONS[1]

1488. [*Homeri Opera*] ed. Demetrios Chalcondyles. Florence: Bernardo and Nero Nerli, 1488. [9a-39b:] Πλουτάρχου εἰς τὸν βίον τοῦ Ὁμήρου. [The *editio princeps* of Homer and of *The Life and Poetry of Homer*, prefaced to the *Iliad* and *Odyssey*, along with the Herodotean *Life of Homer* and Dio Chrysostom, Or. 53: *On Homer*. Repr. Strasbourg, 1550, 1551.]

1504. *Homeri Opera* Venice: Aldus Manutius, 1504. [vol. 2, 516-604 (*fide* the hand-numbering in the Princeton copy):] Πλουτάρχου εἰς τὸν βίον τοῦ Ὁμήρου. [The same ancillary texts printed in the *editio princeps*, now divided into sections by large marginal capitals. The Aldine edition was reprinted at least five times between 1517 and 1542, though not always with the ancillary texts.]

1517. *Homeri Opera* Venice: Aldus Manutius, 1517. [In this second Aldine edition, an improved text of the *Lives* was printed on a sequence of 56 pages that were bound into the first volume of some copies, the second volume of others, and from some omitted entirely.]

1519. [*Homeri Opera*] ed. Antonius Francinus Varchiensis, Florence: in aedibus haeredum Philippi Juntae, 1519. [Vol. 1, 286a-335b:] Πλουτάρχου εἰς τὸν βίον τοῦ Ὁμήρου.

1525. [*Homeri Opera*] ed. Johannes Lonicerus, Strasbourg: apud Vuolf. Cephalaeum. [A reprint of the Aldine text, with variants]. [Vol. 2,] bb iiii [- gg viii:] Πλουτάρχου εἰς τὸν βίον τοῦ Ὁμήρου. [Reprinted 1534.]

1561. *Homeri Opera graeco-latina* ed. Sebastianus Castalio. Basel: Nicolaus Brylingerus, 1561. [2 vol. in 1. New pagination begins with the *Odyssey*. 2nd sequence, 266-317:] Πλουτάρχου εἰς τὸν βίον τοῦ Ὁμήρου. [A facing Latin translation added: *Plutarchi de Homeri vita*.]

---

[1] A more complete list, including partial editions, may be found in Kindstrand, lxiii-lxiv.

1566. *Plutarchi duo commentarii, apprime adolescentibus bonarum litterarum studiosis utiles: Quomodo adulescens poetas audire debeat; de Homeri poesi...latine redditi.* Tr. Wilhelm Xylander. Basel: J. Oporinum, 1566. [The title page goes on:] *Addidimus graeca, ab eodem recensita, emendata.* [This would seem to be the only edition of Xylander's Greek text. His Latin translation is, *fide* Person, the one reprinted all the way down to Dübner, and Xylander reprinted it in his Latin version of the *Moralia* (e.g. 1570, 1572), but the Greek was omitted from Xylander's Greek *Moralia* of 1574.]

1566. *Poetae Graeci heroici carminis...*, ed. Henri Estienne. Geneva: excudebat Henricus Stephanus, illustrius viri Haldrichi Fuggeri typographus, 1566. vii-xli: Πλουτάρχου περὶ τοῦ βίου καὶ τῆς ποιήσεως τοῦ Ὁμήρου. [No distinction is made between A and B, but the headers change from ΠΛΟΥΤ. ΠΕΡΙ ΤΟΥ ΒΙΟΥ ΟΜΗΡ. (ix) to ΠΛΟΥΤΑΡΧΟΥ......ΠΕΡΙ ΤΗΣ ΟΜΗΡΟΥ ΠΟΙΗΣΕΩΣ (x-xi - xxxviii-xxxix).]

1711. *Homeri Ilias et Odyssea* ed. Joshua Barnes. Cambridge: Crownfield [at the editor's expense], 1710-11. Vol. 1, xvi-xix = Πλουτάρχου περὶ τοῦ Βίου καὶ τῆς Ποιήσεως τοῦ Ὁμήρου [=A], xxix-lxxxii = Πλουτάρχου, ἢ μᾶλλον, Διονυσίου τοῦ Ἁλικαρνασσέως, περὶ τῆς Ὁμήρου Ποιήσεως [=B]. [The three traditional Lives, as well as one attributed to Proclus, two anonymous Lives, and *The Contest of Homer and Hesiod*, the first book of the *Homeric Questions* of Porphyry, as well as his essay on the Cave of the Nymphs in the *Odyssey* are included as prefatory material. The separation of the two parts of *The Life and Poetry of Homer* is credited to "Stephanus and other scholars," and the attribution of B to Dionysius of Halicarnassus to Thomas Gale (xxix)].

1759-64. *Homeri Opera Omnia* ed. J. A. Ernesti, following the edition of Samuel Clarke. 5 vols. Leipzig: Saalbach (*impensis G. Theophili Georgii*), 1759-64, reprinted Glasgow: Duncan, 1814; Leipzig: Weidmann, 1824. [Ernesti added to his re-edition of the Homer of Samuel Clarke (orig. 1729-32) a fifth volume entitled *Homeri Operum Appendix*, in which he included *Plutarchi Vita Homeri et De Homeri Poesi incerti auctoris* (1764: 141-260; 1814: 309-406; 1824: 159-259).]

Principal Editions

1800. *Plutarchi Chaeronensis Moralia* ed. Daniel Wyttenbach, vol. 5, part 2. Oxford: Clarendon, 1800. 1057-1247: *De Vita et Poesi Homeri*. [Wyttenbach was the first to print the essay with the *Moral Essays* of Plutarch, of which his edition constitutes the *editio princeps*, though many of the essays and groups of essays had been previously published. A brief note (p. 1057) labels both essays as pseudepigrapha.] [Reprinted Leipzig, 1834.]

1855. *Plutarchi opera* ed. F. Dübner, vol. 5 (*Fragmenta et pseudoplutarchea*), 100-164: *De Vita et poesi Homeri*. Paris: Didot, 1855.

1896. *Plutarchi Chaeronensis Moralia* ed. Gregory N. Bernardakis, vol 7 (*Fragmenta vera et spuria*): 329-462. Leipzig: Teubner, 1896.

1990. [Plutarchus] *De Homero* ed. Jan Fredrik Kindstrand. Leipzig: Teubner, 1990.

EARLIEST TRANSLATIONS[1]

Latin:

[Various complete Latin translations beginning in 1537 (*Homeri vita in Latinum tralata per Io. Rhellicanum, Tigurinum...Basileae per Belthasarem Lasium et Thomam Platterum*, 1537). That of Xylander (Holzmann), in 1566 (see "Principal Editions") became standard and was often reprinted.]

Italian:

Gratii, G. M., in M. A. Grandino, *Opuscoli morali di Plutarco Cheronese*, 1. Venice: Prati, 1598.

German:

Schulthess, Johann Georg. *Bibliothek der griechischen Philosophen*, 3. Zurich: Orell, Füssli u. Co., 1779.[2]

French:

Clavier, E., in *Oeuvres de Plutarque* translated by Jacques Amyot with notes and observations by MM. Brotier and Vauvilliers. New edition, corrected and augmented by E. Clavier. 25 vols. Paris: Cussac, 1801-05. [The essay in question is in vol. 23 (1804), 3-160.]

English:

Bevan, W. Lloyd, in *Plutarch's Complete Works*, vol. 3, 531-615: "The Life and Poetry of Homer." New York: Crowell, 1909. [A publisher's note (vol. 1, vii-viii) identifies Bevan as the translator and indicates that this "entirely new essay" has been added to the reprint of one of the seventeenth-century

---

[1] This list includes only the earliest translations into the European languages. In the cases of German and English, these appear to be the only existing ones to date. A further translation into French and one more into Italian were added in the 19th century. Cf. Kindstrand, lxiv-lxv.

[2] Omits the "Shorter Life" (*fide* Kindstrand, lxv).

translations of Plutarch, an essay "never before turned into English."]

ABBREVIATIONS

DK = Diels, H., *Die Fragmente der Vorsokratiker*, 10th ed., edited by Walther Kranz. 3 vols. Berlin: Weidmann, 1960-61.
Dox Gr = Diels, H. *Doxographi Graeci* [see "Bibliography"]
Kindstrand = [Plutarchus] *De Homero*, ed. Jan Fredrik Kindstrand [see "Principal Editions"]
LSJ = *A Greek-English Lexicon*, compiled by Henry George Liddell and Robert Scott, revised and augmented throughout by Sir Henry Stuart Jones, 9th edition, with supplement. Oxford: Oxford Univ. Press, 1968.
PW = *Paulys Realencyclopädie der Classischen Altertumswissenschaft*, neue Bearbeitung begonnen von Georg Wissowa. . . . Stuttgart: J. B. Metzler (succeeded after 1942 by Alfred Druckenmüller, Waldsee and Stuttgart, later Munich), 1894-1980.
SVF = von Arnim, Johann, ed., *Stoicorum Veterum Fragmenta*. 4 vols. Stuttgart: Teubner, 1903-24.

BIBLIOGRAPHY

Allen, Thomas W. *Homer. The Origins and the Transmission*. Oxford: Oxford Univ. Press, 1924.
———. [See also Monro, David B. and Thomas W. Allen, eds.]
Amyot, Jacques, trans., *Oeuvres de Plutarque* with notes and observations by MM. Brotier and Vauvilliers. New edition, corrected and augmented by E. Clavier. 25 vols. Paris: Cussac, 1801-05. [Clavier's translation of the *Essay* is in vol. 23, 3-160.]
Auerbach, Erich. *Mimesis*. Berne: A. Francke, 1946.
Benseler, Gustav Edward. *De hiatu in scriptoribus graecis*. Freiburg: J. G. Engelhardt, 1851.
Bernhardy, G. *Grundriss der griechischen Literatur*. Halle: Eduard Anton, 1877.
Blank, David L., ed., Lesbonax ΠΕΡΙ ΣΧΗΜΑΤΩΝ, 129-216 in K. Alpers et al., eds, *Sammlung griechischer und lateinischer Grammatiker*, vol. 7. Berlin: De Gruyter, 1988.
Bouché-Leclerq, A. *Histoire de la divination dans l'antiquité*. 4 vols. Paris: Leroux, 1879-82.
Buffière, Félix. *Les Mythes d'Homère et la pensée grecque*. Paris: Les Belles Lettres, 1956.

———, ed., Héraclite, *Allégories d'˙Homère*. Paris: Les Belles Lettres, 1962.

Burkert, Walter. *Lore and Science in Ancient Pythagoreanism*, tr. E. L. Minar, Jr. Cambridge: Harvard Univ. Press, 1972.

Carcopino, Jérôme. *De Pythagore aux apôtres: Etudes sur la conversion du monde romain*. Paris: Flammarion, 1956.

Castiglioni, Luigi. [Review of Ludwig Deicke, *Die Überlieferung der pseudoplutarchischen Schrift de vita et poesi Homeri*], *Gnomon* 16 (1940), 41-42.

Ciapporé, M. "Note sur un passage difficile du De vita et poesi Homeri:" 89-93 in *Mélanges offerts à Léopold Sédar Senghor. Langues, littérature, histoire ancienne*. Dakar: Les Nouvelles Editions Africaines, 1977.

Clavier, E. *see* Amyot, Jacques.

Deicke, Ludwig. *Die Überlieferung der pseudoplutarchischen Schrift de vita et poesi Homeri*. Göttingen: Vandenhoeck und Ruprecht, 1937. (= NGG, Philol.-Histor. Klasse, Fachgruppe I, Altertumswissenschaft, N.F., II, 2.)

Della Corte, Francesco. "Le ΟΜΗΡΙΚΑΙ ΜΕΛΕΤΑΙ di Plutarco e la ricomposizione del Pap. Lond. 734," *Rivista di filologia e d'instruzione classica* 66 (1938), 40-49.

De Vogel, C. J. "The Soma-Sema Formula: its Function in Plato and Plotinus Compared to Christian Writers," 79-95 in *Neoplatonism and Early Christian Thought: Essays in Honor of A. H. Armstrong*, M. J. Blumenthal and R. A. Markus, eds.. London: Variorum, 1981.

Diels, H. *Doxographi graeci*. (1st ed. 1879) 4th ed. Berlin: De Gruyter, 1965.

Dillon, John. *The Middle Platonists*. London: Duckworth, 1977.

———, ed., *Iamblichi Chalcidensis in Platonis Dialogos Commentariorum Fragmenta*. Philosophia antiqua, 23. Leiden: Brill, 1973.

Dodds, E. R., ed., Proclus, *Elements of Theology*. 2nd ed. Oxford: Oxford Univ. Press, 1963.

Fortenbaugh, William W., Pamela M. Huby, Robert N. Staples, and Dimitri Gutas, ed. and tr., *Theophrastus of Eresus: Sources for his Life, Writings, Thought and Influence*. 2 vols. Leiden: Brill, 1992.

Funke, Hermann. *Homer und seine Leser in der Antike*. Forschung an der Universität Mannheim: Vortrag Winter 76/77. Mannheim: Mannheim Kulturamt, 1977.

Gigon, Olof, ed., *Librorum deperditorum fragmenta* = *Aristotelis Opera ex rec. I Bekker. . . ed altera. . .*, vol. 3. Berlin: De Gruyter, 1987.

Gildersleeve, Basil Lanneau. *De Porphyrii studiis Homericis capitum trias*. Diss.: Göttingen, 1853.

Grafton, Anthony. "Renaissance Readers of Homer's Ancient Readers:" 149-72 in *Homer's Ancient Readers. The Hermeneutics of Greek Epic's Earliest Exegetes*, Robert Lamberton and John J. Keaney, eds. Princeton: Princeton Univ. Press, 1992.

Halliday, William Reginald. *Greek Divination: A Study of its Methods and Principles*. London: Macmillan, 1913.

Hepp, Noémi. "Homère en France au xvie siècle," *Atti della Accademia delle Scienze di Torino, ii. Classe di scienzi morali, storiche, e fililogiche*, 96 (1961-62), 389-508.

——— . *Homère en France au xviie siècle*. Bibliothèque française et romane, Centre de philologie et de littératures romanes, Strasbourg, Série C: Études littéraires, no. 18. Paris: Klincksieck, 1968.

Hillgruber, Michael. *Die pseudoplutarchische Schrift De Homero: Teil 1, Einleitung und Kommentar zu den Kapiteln 1-73*. Beiträge zur Altertumskunde, Band 57. Stuttgart: Teubner, 1994,

Hillyard, Brian. "The Medieval Tradition of Plutarch, De Audiendo," *Revue d'Histoire des Textes* 7 (1977), 1-56.

Irigoin, Jean. "Histoire du texte des 'Oeuvres Morales' de Plutarque:" ccxxvii-cccii in Plutarque, *Oeuvres Morales I, 1.*, Robert Flacelière, et al., eds., Paris: Les Belles Lettres (Budé), 1987.

Kindstrand, Jan Fredrik. *see* "Principal Editions" (1990).

Lamberton, Robert D. *Homer the Theologian, Neoplatonist Allegorical Reading and the Growth of the Epic Tradition*. The Transformation of the Classical Tradition, No. 9. Berkeley: Univ. of California Press, 1986.

Lausberg, H. *Handbuch der literarischen Rhetorik*. 3rd ed. Stuttgart: Steiner, 1990.

Lefkowitz, Mary R. *The Lives of the Greek Poets*. London: Duckworth, 1981.

Lévêque, Pierre. *Aurea Catena Homeri: Une Étude sur l'allégorie grecque*. Annales littéraires de l'Université de Besançon, vol. 27. Paris: Les Belles Lettres, 1959.

Ludwich, Arthur. "Plutarch über Homer," *Rheinisches Museum* 72 (1917-18), 537-93.

Marrou, Henri-Irénée. *Histoire de l'éducation dans l'antiquté*. 6th ed. Paris: Seuil, 1965.

Monro, David B. and Thomas W. Allen, eds., *Homeri Opera*. 5 vols. Oxford: Oxford Univ. Press, 1902-12.
Mosshammer, Alden A. *The Chronicle of Eusebius and Greek Chronographic Tradition*. Lewisburg: Bucknell Univ. Press, 1979.
Person, Klaus P. *Pseudo-Plutarchs Vita Homeri. Prolegomena zu einer kritischen Ausgabe*. Diss.: Göttingen, 1957.
Pfeiffer, Rudolf. *A History of Classical Scholarship From its Beginnings to the End of the Hellenistic Age*. Oxford: Oxford Univ. Press, 1968.
Radermacher, L. "Hermogenes (22)." PW 8 (1913): cols. 865-77.
Ramos Jurado, R. A. "La metáfora, su origen y tipos a la luz de un alegorista de Homero, el Pseudo-Plutarco," *Estudios clásicos* 26 [No. 87] (1984), 427-33.
———, "Notas críticas a De vita et poesi Homeri," *Habis* 15 (1984), 9-14.
Russell, D. A. *Plutarch*. London: Duckworth, 1972.
Rutherford, W. G. *A Study in the History of Annotation. Being Scholia Aristophanica III* (1905) Reprint: New York: Garland, 1987.
Sandbach, F. H., ed., *Plutarchi Moralia vii*. Leipzig: Teubner, 1967. [The "Lamprias Catalogue" and the 217 fragments, including those of the Ὁμηρικαὶ Μελεταί, are reprinted with translations and limited commentary in F. H. Sandbach, ed., *Plutarch's Moralia xv*, Cambridge, Mass., and London: Harvard and Heinemann (Loeb), 1969.]
Sandys, John Edwyn. *A History of Classical Scholarship*. 3 vols. (Cambridge, 1908; 3rd ed., 1920) Reprint: New York, Hafner, 1958.
Scarpat, Giuseppe. *I dialetti greci in Omero secondo un grammatico antico*. Studi grammaticali e linguistici, 2. Arona: Paideia, 1952.
Schmidt, Rudolf. *De Plutarchea quae vulgo fertur Homeri vita Porphyrio vindicanda*. (Programme d'Invitation à l'examen public du Collège royal français [Berlin], 27 Sept., 1850) Diss.: Berlin, 1850.
Schrader, Hermann. "Telephos der Pergamener ΠΕΡΙ ΤΗΣ ΚΑΘ' ΟΜΗΡΟΝ ΡΗΤΟΡΙΚΗΣ," *Hermes* 37 (1902): 530-81.
———, ed., *Porphyrii Quaestionum Homericarum ad Iliadem Pertenentium Reliquias*. 2 vols. Leipzig: Teubner, 1880-82.
———, ed., *Porphyrii Quaestionum Homericarum ad Odysseam Pertinentium Reliquias*. Leipzig: Teubner, 1890.

Sengebusch, Maximilian. "Homerica dissertatio prior:" 1-214 in *Homeri Ilias*, W. Dindorf, ed., pars I. Leipzig: Teubner, 1888.
Skiadas, Aristoxenos D. *Homer im griechischen Epigramm*. Studien und Untersuchungen, 2nd series. Athens: Ἀνθρωπιστική Ἑταιρεία, 1965.
Treu, Maximilian. "Zur Geschichte der Überlieferung von Plutarchs Moralia." I: Waldenburg in Schlesien, 1877; II: Städtisches Gymnasium zu Ohlau (wiss. Teil), Ohlau, 1881; III: Programm des Königl. Friedrichs-Gymnasiums zu Breslau, Breslau, 1884.
Turyn, Alexander. *Dated Greek Manuscripts of the Thirteenth and Fourteenth Centuries in the Libraries of Italy*. 2 vols. Urbana: Univ. of Chicago Press, 1972.
Volkmann, Richard. *Leben und Schriften des Plutarch von Chaeronea*. 1869. Reprint: Leipzig, Zentralantiquariat der D.D.R., 1970.
Wackernagel, Jacob. *Sprachliche Untersuchungen zu Homer*. Göttingen: Vandenhoeck und Ruprecht, 1916.
Wegehaupt, H. "Die Entstehung des Corpus Planudeum von Plutarchs Moralia," *Sitzungsberichte der königlich preussischen Akademie der Wissenschaften (phil.-hist. Klasse)* 1909, no. 41, 1030-46.
Weissenberger, Burkard. *Die Sprache Plutarchs von Chaeronea und die pseudoplatonischen Schriften*. Inaugural Dissertation, Würzburg, 1895.
Wilson, Nigel G. *Scholars of Byzantium*. London, Duckworth, 1983.
Wolff, Gustav. *Porphyrii de philosophia ex oraculis haurienda librorum reliquiae*. 1856. Reprint: Hildesheim: Georg Olms, 1962.
Wollenberg, Julius. *De Porphyrii studiis philologis capita quinque*. Diss.: Berlin, 1854.
Wooten, Cecil W., tr. *Hermogenes' On Types of Style*. Chapel Hill: Univ. of North Carolina Press, 1987.
Ziegler, Konrat. "Plutarchos von Chaironeia" [= Plutarchos 2], PW 41 [20B], cols. 636-962, 1951.

CONTENTS

A: The Shorter Life

1. Homer silent on the subject of his own origins
2. Ephorus of Cyme's account
3. Aristotle's account
4. The oracle and the death of Homer
5. The date of Homer: opinions
6. The Judgment of Paris (Il. 24.29-30) spurious
7. Summary of the story of Troy
8. Homer's technique of starting in the ninth year

B: The Essay on the Life and Poetry of Homer

Part One: Introduction (1-6)
1. Homer the greatest of poets and the first read
2. Homer's family and home: opinions
3. Homer's date: opinions
4. The works of Homer
5. Homer needed to present evil along with good
6. Homer's mythic treatment of his material

Part Two: Diction (7-73)
7. The heroic hexameter
8. Homer uses various dialects
9. Doric

10. Aeolic
11. Ionic
12. Attic
13. Syntactical peculiarities traced to dialect
14. Archaisms
15. Homer's tropes and figures. 1: The Tropes
    16. Neologism
    17. Neologism, cont.: epithets
    18. Catachresis
    19. Metaphor
    20. Metaphor, cont.: varieties
    21. Metalepsis
    22. Synecdoche
    23. Metonymy
    24. Antonomasia
    25. Antiphrasis
    26. Emphasis
27. Homer's tropes and figures. 2: The Figures
    28. Pleonasm
        29. Periphrasis
        30. Enallage; hyperbaton
        31. Parembole
        32. Palillogy; anadiplosis
        33. Epanaphora
        34. Epanodos (regressio)
    35. Homoeoteleuton
    36. Multiple figures in a single verse
    37. Parison

Contents

38. Paronomasia
39. Ellipsis
    40. Asyndeton
41. Asyntakton or alloiosis: types
    42. Shifts of gender
        43. Apparent shifts of gender
        44. Gender from sense
        45. Other shifts of gender
    46. Shifts of number
        47. Plural to singular
    48. Shifts of case
        49. Effective use in openings
        50. Genitive to nominative
    51. Archaic shifts of number
        52. e.g.: dual to singular
    53. Shifts of degree; shifts of verb forms
        54. Shifts of tense
        55. Shifts of voice
        56. Shifts of number
        57. Shifts of person; apostrophe
    58. Participles substituted for verbs
    59. Shifts of articles
    60. Prepositions: one used for another
        61. Wrong case after preposition
        62. Omission of prepositions
    63. Shifts of adverbs
    64. Shifts of conjunctions
65. Figures related to sense: proanaphoresis, epiphonesis

66. Prosopopoeia
67. Diantyposis
68. Irony
 69. Sarcasm
 70. Allegory
71. Hyperbole
72. Types of style: vigorous, delicate, intermediate
73. The flowery style

Part Three: Discourse (74-199)

74. Discourse: historical, theoretical, political
[Historical discourse in Homer (75-90):]
 75. Character
 76. Place
 77. Time
 78. Cause
 79. Instrument
 80. Deeds
 81. Impact
 82. Mode
 83. Conciseness of some of Homer's narratives
 84. Description by means of comparison
  85. Comparisons with small animals
  86. Animal comparisons, cont.
  87. Animal comparisons, cont.
  88. Animal comparisons: sea creatures
  89. Comparisons: human activities
  90. Comparisons: the elements

Contents 49

91. The remaining modes of discourse

[Theoretical discourse (92-160):]

    92. Divisions: physics, ethics, dialectic

    93. Physics: ideas of Thales and Xenophanes, four elements, traceable to Homer

      94. Order of the elements

      95. Order of the elements, cont.

      96. Zeus and Hera as *aither* and *aer*

      97. The anvils tied to Hera's feet

      98. Five-part division of the universe

      99. Love and strife

      100. Love and strife in Homer

      101. Love and strife: Song of Ares and Aphrodite

      102. Doctrine of opposites in the theomachy

      103. The universe one and finite

      104. The sun: rotation

      105. The sun: appearance

      106. The constellations

      107. Causes of earthquakes and eclipses

      108. Eclipses, cont.

      109. The winds

      110. The poles

      111. Evaporation and rain

      112. The gods: that they exist

          113. Homer's anthropomorphism

          114. One highest, noetic god

          115. Providence and fate contained in god's knowledge

116. Dignity of god, love of mankind
117. Gods always helping man
118. Divine providence, human piety
119. Homeric source of Stoic doctrine
120. Homer on fate comparable with Plato, Aristotle, Theophrastus
121. Providence overcomes chance
122. Souls: immortality
123. Soul identified as the individual
124. The body as the prison of the soul
125. Pythagorean metensomatosis
126. Circe, symbol of metensomatosis
127. Stoics follow Homer: exhalations
128. Non-material soul of Plato and Aristotle anticipated in Homer
129. Divisions of the soul
130. The heart, seat of the passionate soul
131. Sources of the emotions
132. [Ethics:] Aristotle on refined emotions
133. Virtues and vices
134. Stoic *apatheia* based on Homer
135. Peripatetic *metriopatheia*
136. Good things and happiness
137. Peripatetics' classes of good things
138. Good things in Homer: beauty, reasonableness, nobility
139. (cont.:) honor, offspring, society
140. (cont.:) wealth, strength, intelligence

Contents

141. (cont.:) secondary and tertiary
good things and happiness
142. Virtue useless unless active
143. Stoics: good men friends of the gods
144. Stoics: virtue can be taught

[Miscellaneous doctrines founded on Homer:]

145. Pythagorean arithmology
146. Arithmetic calculation
147. Pythagorean emphasis on music
148. Pitch
149. Pythagorean belief in silence
150. Philosophers misled by Homer
151. Sayings of the sages traced to Homer
152. The maxims of Homer
153. Copied by Pythagoras, Euripides
154. Pythagoras
155. Archilochus
156. Euripides
157. Aeschylus
158. Sophocles
159. Theocritus
160. Aratus

[Political discourse in Homer (161-199):]

161. The craft of rhetoric founded by Homer
162. Economy
163. Introductions
164. Speeches adapted to their audience
165. Nestor's speech in *Iliad* 1 analyzed

166. Agamemnon's rhetorical deviousness
167. Nestor's contribution
168. Diomedes' speech in *Iliad* 9
169. The embassy to Achilles
170. Rhetoric as a craft in Homer
171. Rhetorical craft in Homer: illustrations
172. Individual character of Homer's rhetors
173. Antithesis
174. Recapitulation

175. Law
176. The state: civic, military, and rustic lives
177. Senates
178. The king must be first
179. All must be subservient to their betters
180. Law declared by the elders
181. Deliberate crimes punished, involuntary ones pardoned
182. The three good states and opposites
183. (cont.)
184. Obligations: revere gods, honor family
185. (cont:) familial obligations
186. (cont.:) obligations to country, truthfulness
187. (cont.:) wives should not meddle
188. (cont.:) special demands of those going to war
189. Funeral customs: *apatheia* impossible
190. Homeric and modern customs
191. Multiple burials
192. Military tactics: varieties

Contents

193. Squadron leaders
194. The arrangement of the camp
195. The trench and the wall
196. Noble death in war
197. Rewards for heroes; threats to cowards
198. Wounds: varieties
199. The ages of man: heroes of all ages

[Part Four: Varia and Conclusion]

200. Medicine known to Homer
201. The categories of medicine
202. Theoretical medicine: signs
203. Theoretical medicine: causes
204. Practical medicine: chronic vs. acute
205. Dietetics
206. Uses of wine
207. Uses of exercise
208. Uses of a temperate climate
209. Cures for various complaints
210. Practical medicine: surgery
211. Practical medicine: pharmaceutics
212. Seercraft: Stoic categories known to Homer
213. Tragedy rooted in Homer
214. Comedy rooted in Homer
215. Epigram rooted in Homer
216. Homer's art visual: Homer a teacher of painting
217. The visual quality of Homer's art
218. Closing panegyric

[ΠΛΟΥΤΑΡΧΟΥ]

Περὶ Ὁμήρου [Α]

54A: The Shorter Life

1. περισσὸν μὲν ἴσως δόξειέ τισι πολυπραγμονεῖν περὶ Ὁμήρου, ποίων τε ἦν γονέων καὶ πόθεν· ἐπεὶ μηδὲ αὐτὸς ἠξίωσεν εἰπεῖν τὰ περὶ ἑαυτοῦ ἀλλ' οὕτως ἐγκρατῶς ἔσχεν ὡς μηδὲ τὴν ἀρχὴν τοῦ ὀνόματος ἐπιμνησθῆναι. ἐπεὶ δὲ ὡς πρὸς εἰσαγωγὴν τῶν ἀρχομένων παιδεύεσθαι χρήσιμος ἡ πολυπειρία, πειρασόμεθα εἰπεῖν ὅσα ἱστόρηται τοῖς παλαιοῖς περὶ αὐτοῦ.

2. Ἔφορος μὲν οὖν ὁ Κυμαῖος, ἐν συντάγματι τῷ ἐπιγραφομένῳ Ἐπιχωρίῳ (FGrHist 70 F1) Κυμαῖον αὐτὸν ἀποδεικνύναι πειρώμενος, φησὶν ὅτι Ἀπελλῆς καὶ Μαίων καὶ Δῖος ἀδελφοὶ Κυμαῖοι τὸ γένος· ὧν Δῖος μὲν διὰ χρέα μετῴκησεν εἰς Ἄσκρην, κώμην τῆς Βοιωτίας κἀκεῖ γήμας Πυκιμήδην ἐγέννησεν Ἡσίοδον. Ἀπελλῆς δὲ τελευτήσας ἐν τῇ πατρίδι Κύμῃ κατέλιπε θυγατέρα Κριθηίδα τοὔνομα προστησάμενος αὐτῇ τὸν ἀδελφὸν Μαίονα, ὃς διακορεύσας τὴν προειρημένην καὶ τὴν ἀπὸ τῶν πολιτῶν ἐπὶ τῷ γεγονότι δείσας κατάγνωσιν, ἔδωκεν αὐτὴν πρὸς γάμον Φημίῳ Σμυρναίῳ, διδασκάλῳ γραμμάτων. φοιτῶσα δὲ αὐτὴ ἐπὶ τοὺς πλυνούς, οἳ ἦσαν παρὰ τῷ Μέλητι, ἀπεκύησε τὸν Ὅμηρον ἐπὶ τῷ ποταμῷ καὶ διὰ τοῦτο Μελησιγένης ἐκλήθη. μετωνομάσθη δὲ Ὅμηρος, ἐπειδὴ τὰς ὄψεις ἐπηρώθη· οὕτω δὲ ἐκάλουν οἵ τε Κυμαῖοι καὶ οἱ Ἴωνες τοὺς τὰς ὄψεις πεπηρωμένους παρὰ τὸ δεῖσθαι τῶν

[PLUTARCH]

On Homer [A]

54A: The Shorter Life[1]

1. It might seem superfluous to some to be concerned with Homer's family and home, since he himself was so reticent in this regard that in the first place he never even mentioned his own name. Nevertheless, since a wide range of information is useful, in the guise of introduction, for those beginning their education, we shall try to set forth all the stories the ancients told about him.

2. Ephorus of Cyme[2] in his work entitled *Local History* [FGrHist 70 F1], trying to establish that the poet was a Cymean, says that there were three brothers, Apelles, Maion, and Dios, who were Cymeans by descent. Need forced Dios to emigrate to Ascra, a town in Boeotia, where he married Pykimede and had Hesiod for a son. Apelles died at home in Cyme, leaving a daughter named Critheis, whom he entrusted to his brother Maion. This Maion took her virginity, and afraid that his neighbors would realize what had happened, he married her off to a teacher named Phemius of Smyrna. She went down to the washing-places along the river Meles and gave birth to Homer alongside the river, whence he was called Melesigenes ["Born-of-Meles"]. Later, when he lost his sight, his name was changed to Homer [or "hostage"] because he was blind, for the Cymeans like the Ionians used to use this

---

[1] There are in fact two separate essays included under this title (No. 54 in the Planudean collection) in the manuscript tradition and the printed editions, though it was realized at an early date that the ninth paragraph (here, 54B, 1) represented a new beginning, and that the author of 54B compresses into two brief paragraphs (54B, 2-3) the largely mythic "biographical" material elaborated in 54A. The Shorter Life is closely comparable to the other biographies of Homer (cf. Allen [1924], ch. 1: "Lives of Homer" passim, and esp. 27-28, 31; also the OCT *Homeri Opera*, vol. 5, 239-45, where Allen published 54A, 1-5, and 54B, 1-3, juxtaposed with other biographical material). Below, references not specifically to the "shorter life" or to 54A are to the *Essay* proper, 54B.

[2] A pupil of Isocrates, d. ca. 330 BCE. His *Universal History* was an important source for Diodorus. The present passage represents the unique surviving fragment of his *Local History* (Ἐπιχώριος). The attempt to make Homer and Hesiod first cousins goes back at least to the early fifth century (Pherecydes of Athens fr. 167 Jacoby), and clearly represents an expansion from clues in the text of the poems (Phemius as Homer's stepfather, "Dios" from *Works and Days* 299).

55

ὁμηρευόντων, ὅ ἐστι τῶν ἡγουμένων. καὶ ταῦτα μὲν Ἔφορος.

3. Ἀριστοτέλης δὲ ἐν τῷ τρίτῳ Περὶ ποιητικῆς (F 20,1 Gigon) ἐν Ἴῳ φησὶ τῇ νήσῳ, καθ' ὃν καιρὸν Νηλεὺς ὁ Κόδρου τῆς Ἰωνικῆς ἀποικίας ἡγεῖτο, κόρην τινὰ τῶν ἐπιχωρίων γενομένην ὑπό τινος δαίμονος τῶν συγχορευτῶν ταῖς Μούσαις ἐγκύμονα, αἰδεσθεῖσαν τὸ συμβὰν διὰ τὸν ὄγκον τῆς γαστρός, ἐλθεῖν εἴς τι χωρίον τὸ καλούμενον Αἴγιναν, εἰς ὃ καταδραμόντας λῃστὰς ἀνδραποδίσαι τὴν προειρημένην καὶ ἀγαγόντας εἰς Σμύρναν οὖσαν ὑπὸ Λυδοῖς τότε, τῷ βασιλεῖ τῶν Λυδῶν ὄντι φίλῳ τοὔνομα Μαίονι χαρίσασθαι· τὸν δὲ ἀγαπήσαντα τὴν κόρην διὰ τὸ κάλλος γῆμαι. ἣν διατρίβουσαν παρὰ τῷ Μέλητι καὶ συσχεθεῖσαν ὑπὸ τῆς ὠδῖνος ἔτυχεν ἀποκυῆσαι τὸν Ὅμηρον ἐπὶ τῷ ποταμῷ. ὃν ἀναλαβὼν ὁ Μαίων ὡς ἴδιον ἔτρεφε, τῆς Κριθηίδος μετὰ τὴν κύησιν εὐθέως τελευτησάσης. χρόνου δὲ οὐ πολλοῦ διελθόντος καὶ αὐτὸς ἐτελεύτησε. τῶν δὲ Λυδῶν καταπονουμένων ὑπὸ τῶν Αἰολέων καὶ κρινάντων καταλιπεῖν τὴν Σμύρναν, κηρυξάντων δὲ τῶν ἡγεμόνων τὸν βουλόμενον ἀκολουθεῖν ἐξιέναι τῆς πόλεως, ἔτι νήπιος ὢν Ὅμηρος ἔφη καὶ αὐτὸς βούλεσθαι ὁμηρεῖν· ὅθεν ἀντὶ Μελησιγένους Ὅμηρος προσηγορεύθη.

4. γενόμενος δὲ ἐν ἡλικίᾳ καὶ δόξαν ἐπὶ ποιητικῇ κεκτημένος ἤδη ἐπηρώτα τὸν θεόν, τίνων τε ἦν γονέων καὶ πόθεν. ὁ δὲ ἀνεῖλεν οὕτως·
ἔστιν Ἴος νῆσος μητρὸς πατρίς, ἥ σε θανόντα
δέξεται· ἀλλὰ νέων ἀνδρῶν αἴνιγμα φύλαξαι (Anth. Pal. 14.65).
φέρεται δὲ καὶ ἕτερος χρησμὸς τοιοῦτος·

word for the blind, because they need to be led around like hostages. This is what Ephorus says.

3. Aristotle in the third book of the *Poetics* [F 20,1 Gigon][1] tells the story of a local girl on the island of Ios, at about the time when Neleus[2] the son of Codrus led out the colonists to Ionia, who became pregnant by one of the divinities that dance with the Muses and then, when her belly began to swell, was ashamed of what had happened and went off to a place called Aegina. Pirates captured her there and took her to Smyrna, which was under the Lydians at that time, and gave her to the king of Lydia, whose name was Maion and who was a friend of theirs. He fell in love with her because of her beauty and married her. The pains of childbirth came upon her while she was near the Meles river and she happened to give birth to Homer on its bank. Maion took the child and raised it as his own, though Critheis died shortly after giving birth. Soon, however, he died as well. At that time, the Lydians were under pressure from the Aeolians in war and decided they must give up Smyrna. The leaders announced that whoever wished to follow them should leave the city, and Homer, who was still a baby, said that he wished to go along [ὁμηρεῖν], and so came to be called Homer instead of Melesigenes.

4. When he grew up and had already acquired fame for his poetry, he asked the god who his parents were and where he was from, and the god answered:[3]

> The island of Ios is your mother's land, and shall receive you dead. But look out for the riddles of young men
> [*Palatine Anthology* 14.65].

Another oracle is preserved, as follows:

---

[1] To be referred to the third book of the dialogue *On the Poets* and not to a lost book of the *Poetics* (as Rose, who assigned ch. 3 and most of ch. 4 to the citation, and is followed by Gigon, realized).
[2] Neleus or Neileus, the mythic leader of the Ionian colonization, generally dated to the eleventh century.
[3] On these short poems and on Homer in Greek epigrams generally, see Skiadas (1965).

ὄλβιε καὶ δύσδαιμον· ἔφυς γὰρ ἐπ' ἀμφοτέροισι·
πατρίδα δίζηαι· μητρὶς δέ τοι, οὐ πατρίς ἐστι·
μητρόπολις ἐν νήσῳ ἀπὸ Κρήτης εὐρείης,
Μίνωος γαίης οὔτε σχεδὸν οὔτ' ἀποτηλοῦ.
ἐν τῇ σοι μοῖρ' ἐστὶ τελευτῆσαι βιότοιο,
εὖτ' ἂν ἀπὸ γλώσσης παίδων μὴ γνῷς ἐπακούσας
δυσξύνετον σκολιοῖσι λόγοις εἰρημένον ὕμνον.
δοιὰς γὰρ ζωῆς μοίρας λάχες, ἣν μὲν ἀμαυρὰν
ἠελίων δισσῶν, ἣν δ' ἀθανάτοις ἰσόμοιρον
ζῶντί τε καὶ φθιμένῳ· φθίμενος δ' ἔτι πολλὸν ἀγήρως
(Anth. Pal. 14.66).

μετ' οὐ πολὺν δὲ χρόνον πλέων ἐς Θήβας ἐπὶ τὰ Κρόνια (ἀγὼν δὲ οὗτος ἄγεται παρ' αὐτοῖς μουσικός) ἦλθεν εἰς Ἴον· ἔνθα ἐπὶ πέτρας καθεζόμενος ἐθεάσατο ἁλιεῖς προσπλέοντας ὧν ἐπύθετο εἴ τι ἔχοιεν. οἱ δὲ ἐπὶ τῷ θηρᾶσαι μὲν μηδὲν φθειρίσασθαι δὲ διὰ τὴν ἀπορίαν τῆς θήρας οὕτως ἀπεκρίναντο·

ὅσσ' ἕλομεν λιπόμεσθ', ὅσσ' οὐχ ἕλομεν φερόμεσθα
(Anth. Pal. 9.448),

αἰνισσόμενοι ὡς ἄρα, οὓς μὲν ἔλαβον τῶν φθειρῶν, ἀποκτείναντες κατέλιπον, οὓς δ' οὐκ ἔλαβον, ἐν τῇ ἐσθῆτι φέροιεν. ὅπερ οὐ δυνηθεὶς συμβαλεῖν Ὅμηρος διὰ τὴν ἀθυμίαν ἐτελεύτησε. θάψαντες δὲ αὐτὸν οἱ Ἰῆται μεγαλοπρεπῶς τοιόνδε ἐπέγραψαν αὐτοῦ τῷ τάφῳ·

ἐνθάδε τὴν ἱερὴν κεφαλὴν κατὰ γαῖα καλύπτει,
ἀνδρῶν ἡρώων κοσμήτορα θεῖον Ὅμηρον (Anth. Pal. 7.3).

> Oh happy and yet wretched man! (For you are bound to both
>   sorts of fortune.)
> You ask for your home: you have a motherland, not a
>   fatherland,
> a metropolis on an island neither near nor far
> from wide Crete, the land of Minos.
> It is your fate to end your days there
> when you hear from the tongues of children
> a song couched in crooked words—hard
> to understand—too much for you.
> A double fate hangs over you: the one, the darkening
> of your two suns; the other, a fate equal to that of the gods,
> which you will enjoy both alive and dead,
> for after death it is long and ageless
>   [*Palatine Anthology* 14.66].

Not long thereafter, sailing to Thebes on the feast of Kronos (when they hold a poetry contest in that city), he stopped on Ios.[1] He was sitting on a rock there and saw some fishermen approaching, and asked them if they had caught anything. They gave the following answer—not talking about fishing at all, but about the lice they'd been picking off themselves, precisely because there were no fish to catch—

> The ones we took we left behind, but the ones we missed we
>   have with us   [*Palatine Anthology* 9.448],

meaning that the lice they'd caught they'd killed and left, but the ones they'd missed were still in their clothes. Homer could not understand and the depression this caused killed him. The people of Ios gave him a sumptuous burial and this for an epitaph:

> This earth lies upon the holy head
> of divine Homer, marshal of heroes
>   [*Palatine Anthology* 7.3].

---

[1] There is a striking agreement—perhaps stemming from this (Aristotelian?) passage—among the ancient biographies of Homer, in proclaiming the place of his death to have been Ios.

εἰσὶ μέντοι οἳ καὶ Κολοφώνιον αὐτὸν ἀποδεικνύναι πειρῶνται, μεγίστῳ τεκμηρίῳ χρώμενοι πρὸς ἀπόδειξιν τῷ ἐπὶ τοῦ ἀνδριάντος ἐπιγεγραμμένῳ ἐλεγείῳ· ἔχει δὲ οὕτως·

    υἱὲ Μέλητος, Ὅμηρε, σὺ γὰρ κλέος Ἑλλάδι πάσῃ
      καὶ Κολοφῶνι πάτρῃ θῆκας ἐς ἀίδιον
    καὶ τάσδ᾽ ἀντιθέῳ ψυχῇ γεννήσαο κούρας
      δισσὰς ἡμιθέων γραψάμενος σελίδας.
    ὑμνεῖ δ᾽ ἡ μὲν νόστον Ὀδυσσῆος πολύπλαγκτον,
      ἡ δὲ τὸν Ἰλιακὸν Δαρδανιδῶν πόλεμον (Anth. Pal. 16.292).

ἄξιον δὲ μηδὲ τὸ ὑπὸ Ἀντιπάτρου τοῦ ἐπιγραμματοποιοῦ γραφὲν ἐπίγραμμα παραλιπεῖν, ἔχον οὐκ ἀσέμνως· ἔχει δὲ οὕτως·

    οἱ μέν σευ Κολοφῶνα τιθηνήτειραν, Ὅμηρε,
      οἱ δὲ καλὰν Σμύρναν, οἱ δ᾽ ἐνέπουσι Χίον·
    οἱ δ᾽ Ἴον, οἱ δ᾽ ἐβόασαν εὔκλαρον Σαλαμῖνα·
    οἱ δέ νυ τὰν Λαπιθᾶν ματέρα Θεσσαλίαν·
    ἄλλοι δ᾽ ἄλλο μέλαθρον ἀνίαχον· εἰ δέ με Φοίβου
      χρὴ λέξαι πινυτὰν ἀμφαδὰ μαντοσύναν,
    πάτρα τοι τελέθει μέγας Οὐρανός, ἐκ δὲ γυναικὸς
      οὐ θνατᾶς, ματρὸς δ᾽ ἔπλεο Καλλιόπας (Anth. Pal. 16.296).

5. γενέσθαι δὲ αὐτὸν τοῖς χρόνοις οἱ μέν φασι κατὰ τὸν Τρωικὸν πόλεμον οὗ καὶ αὐτόπτην γενέσθαι, οἱ δὲ μετὰ ἑκατὸν ἔτη τοῦ πολέμου, ἄλλοι δὲ μετὰ πεντήκοντα καὶ ἑκατόν. ἔγραψε δὲ ποιήματα δύο, Ἰλιάδα καὶ Ὀδύσσειαν· ὡς δέ τινες, οὐκ ἀληθῶς λέγοντες, γυμνασίας καὶ παιδιᾶς ἕνεκα Βατραχομυομαχίαν προσθεὶς καὶ Μαργίτην.

6. τοῦ δὲ Τρωικοῦ πολέμου καθ᾽ Ὅμηρόν τινές φασιν ἀρχὴν εἶναι τὴν τῶν θεῶν κρίσιν Ἥρας καὶ Ἀθηνᾶς καὶ Ἀφροδίτης, περὶ κάλλους ἐπ᾽ Ἀλεξάνδρου γενομένην· λέγειν γὰρ τὸν ποιητήν·

There are also people who try to prove that he was from Colophon, using as their proof three elegiac couplets inscribed on his statue:

> Homer, son of Meles, you secured eternal fame
>> for all Greece, and for your city of Colophon;
> your godlike soul gave birth to these two daughters
>> when you wrote the twin tomes of the demigods:
> the one sings the far-wandering homecoming of
>> Odysseus, the other, the Ilian war of the sons of
>>> Dardanus
>>>> [*Palatine Anthology* 16.292].

Finally, the poem written by Antipater of Sidon[1] the writer of epigrams should not be omitted—it shows a special kind of reverence:

> Some say, Homer, that Colophon was your nurse,
>> some beautiful Smyrna, some Chios;
> some shout for Ios, some for famous Salamis,
>> some for Thessaly, mother of the Lapiths.
> There is no agreement—but if I may speak
>> forth clearly in the wisdom of Apollo's oracle,
> Your homeland is great Heaven itself and your
>> mother no mortal, but Calliope
>>> [*Palatine Anthology* 16.296].

5.   Some say[2] he lived at the time of the Trojan War and saw it himself—some say he lived a hundred or a hundred and fifty years after it. He wrote two poems, the *Iliad* and the *Odyssey*, but some say—inaccurately—that he added the *Battle of Frogs and Mice* and the *Margites* for practice and amusement.

6.   Some claim that according to Homer the beginning of the Trojan War was Paris' judging of the beauty of the goddesses Hera, Athena, and Aphrodite, since the poet says,[3]

---

[1] Epigrammatist of the final quarter of the second century BCE.

[2] For a survey of the various dates for Homer proposed in antiquity, see Allen (1924), table (facing 32).

[3] In the many citations of Homer, we have followed the mss. of the *Essay* in both text and translation, and not the received text of Homer. The differences on the whole are slight, but our author frequently leaves out words and phrases that occur in the received text.

ὃς νείκεσσε θεάς, ὅτε οἱ μέσσαυλον ἵκοντο,
τὴν δ' ᾔνησ' ἥ οἱ πόρε μαχλοσύνην ἀλεγεινήν (Ω 29-30).
ἀλλ' οὐ πρέπον ὑπολαμβάνειν θεοὺς ὑπὸ ἀνθρώπων κεκρίσθαι οὔτε ὑπὸ Ὁμήρου δι' ἄλλων παρίσταται τοῦτο· ὅθεν εὐλόγως ἠθέτηνται οἱ προκείμενοι στίχοι.

7. ἄμεινον οὖν λέγειν ὅτι Ἀλέξανδρος ὁ Πριάμου παῖς, ἐπιθυμήσας Ἑλληνικοῦ βίου μαθεῖν ἀγωγήν, ἔπλευσεν εἰς Σπάρτην καὶ ἐπιξενωθεὶς Ἑλένῃ, Μενελάου κατὰ τὸν οἶκον οὐκ ὄντος, ἀνέπεισεν αὐτὴν ἀκολουθεῖν. ἐλθὼν δὲ εἰς τὴν Κρανάην καλουμένην νῆσον ἐμίγη πρῶτον τῇ γυναικὶ κἀκεῖθεν πλεύσας διὰ Σιδῶνος καὶ Φοινίκης ἧκεν ἐς Ἴλιον. ἐπιγνόντες δὲ οἱ περὶ Ἀγαμέμνονα καὶ Μενέλαον τὸ πεπραγμένον στρατιὰν ἤθροισαν ἐν Αὐλίδι πόλει τῆς Βοιωτίας. ἔνθα καὶ θυόντων αὐτῶν, δράκων ἐπὶ τὸ πλησίον ἀνελθὼν δένδρον στρουθοῦ νεοσσοὺς ὀκτὼ διέφθειρεν οἷς ἡ μήτηρ ἐνάτη συγκατείλεκτο. ἐμήνυε δὲ τὸ σημεῖον ὅτι ἐννέα ἔτη πολεμήσαντες τῷ δεκάτῳ αἱροῦσι τὴν Ἴλιον. ἡνίκα δὲ πλεύσαντες ἐπέβησαν τῆς Τροίας μετὰ πρώτην συμβολήν, καθ' ἣν ἀνῃρέθη Πρωτεσίλαος, Μενέλαόν τε καὶ Ὀδυσσέα πρέσβεις ἀπέστειλαν τὴν Ἑλένην ἀπαιτοῦντες. τῶν δὲ Τρώων ἀντειπόντων πάλιν συμβολὰς ἐποιοῦντο πολέμου καὶ ἐπικρατήσαντες τοὺς μὲν Τρῶας ἐντὸς τειχῶν κατέκλεισαν, αὐτοὶ δὲ εἰς δύο μερισθέντες τοὺς μὲν εἴασαν παρεδρεύειν τῇ πόλει, οἱ δὲ στρατηγοῦντος Ἀχιλλέως τὰς περικειμένας πόλεις ἐπόρθουν, συμμαχίας ἀφαιρούμενοι τοὺς Τρῶας. ἐξ ὧν μίαν ἑλόντες Χρῦσαν γέρας ἔδοσαν Ἀγαμέμνονι Χρυσηίδα, Χρύσου ἱερέως Ἀπόλλωνος θυγατέρα. ὁ δὲ ἐλθὼν ἐπὶ τὸν ναύσταθμον ἵνα λυτρώσηται τὴν παῖδα καὶ ὑβρισθεὶς ὑπὸ Ἀγαμέμνονος ηὔξατο τῷ Ἀπόλλωνι κολάσαι τοὺς Ἕλληνας. ἐπακούσας δὲ τῆς εὐχῆς ὁ θεὸς λοιμὸν ἔπεμψεν αὐτοῖς. καὶ τότε Ἀχιλλέως παραινέσαντος ἀποδοῦναι τὴν Χρυσηίδα Ἀγαμέμνων ὀργισθεὶς ἠπείλησεν ἀφαιρήσεσθαι τὸ Ἀχιλλέως γέρας Βρισηίδα· τὸν δὲ τὴν

> He judged the goddesses who came to his courtyard
> and chose the one who offered him terrible lust
> [Il. 24.29-30],

but the idea of gods being judged by men is unacceptable and Homer does not elsewhere mention this, so that the above verses are correctly taken to be spurious.[1]

7. It is better to say that Paris the son of Priam wanted to learn about the Greek way of life and sailed to Sparta. Since Menelaus was not at home he was entertained by Helen, and persuaded her to leave with him. He went off to the island of Kranae and there for the first time slept with the woman, then sailed to Sidon and Phoenicia and finally Troy. When Agamemnon, Menelaus, and the others learned what had happened they gathered an army at Aulis in Boeotia. There, when they were offering a sacrifice, a snake climbed into a nearby tree and killed eight sparrows in the nest, then the mother to make a total of nine. This sign revealed that after fighting for nine years they would take Troy in the tenth. When they landed at Troy, after the first battle in which Protesilaus was killed, they sent Menelaus and Odysseus as ambassadors to demand Helen. The Trojans refused and there was more fighting. The Greeks were victorious and closed the Trojans up within their walls, then divided themselves into two armies, one of which they left to lay siege to the city while the other, commanded by Achilles, ravaged the surrounding cities and deprived the Trojans of allies. One of these cities was Chryse and when they took that they gave Cressida, the daughter of a priest of Apollo named Chryses, to Agamemnon. Chryses went to the ships to ransom his daughter and was insulted by Agamemnon. He then prayed to Apollo to punish the Greeks. The god heard the prayers and sent a plague on them. Then, when Achilles proposed that Cressida be returned, Agamemnon became enraged and threatened to take Achilles' prize, Briseis. He then asked his mother Thetis to persuade Zeus to bring defeat on the Greeks.

---

[1] Schol. in Il. 24.23 and 24.25-30 indicate that various scholars athetized 24.23-30, or some part thereof. The spuriousness of the lone Iliadic reference to the Judgment of Paris was clearly a commonplace of Alexandrian criticism.

μητέρα Θέτιν αἰτήσασθαι παρὰ τοῦ Διὸς ἧτταν Ἑλλήνων. οὗ γενομένου Πάτροκλος προτραπεὶς ὑπὸ Νέστορος ἱκέτευσεν Ἀχιλλέα δοῦναι κἂν ἐπ' ὀλίγον τὴν πανοπλίαν αὐτῷ ἵνα τοὺς Τρῶας τῶν νεῶν ἀπώσηται. ἐξελθὼν δὲ Πάτροκλος καὶ γενναίως ἀριστεύσας μετ' οὐ πολὺ ἀνηρέθη. χαλεπήνας δὲ ὁ Ἀχιλλεὺς ἐπαύσατο μὲν τῆς πρὸς Ἀγαμέμνονα ἔχθρας, λαβὼν δὲ ἡφαιστότευκτον πανοπλίαν ἄλλους τε πολλοὺς ἀνεῖλεν καὶ τελευταῖον τὸν Ἕκτορα.

8. ἡ μὲν οὖν τάξις τῶν πραγμάτων ἐστὶν αὕτη· ὁ δὲ ποιητὴς ἀπὸ τοῦ ἐνάτου ἔτους ἤρξατο ἐπεὶ τὰ πρὸ τῆς Ἀχιλλέως μήνιδος ἀτονώτερα ἦν καὶ πράξεις οὐκ ἔχοντα λαμπρὰς οὐδὲ ἐπαλλήλους. συμμαχοῦντος γὰρ Ἕλλησιν Ἀχιλλέως

οὐδέποτε Τρῶες πρὸ πυλάων Δαρδανιάων

οἴχνεσκον· κείνου γὰρ ἐδείδισαν ὄβριμον ἔγχος (Ε 789-90).

ἀποστάντος δὲ τούτου θαρσήσαντες προῆλθον· καὶ τῆς μάχης ἐπίσης γενομένης πολυπρόσωποί τε καὶ συνεχεῖς τῶν ἡρώων ἀριστεῖαι κατέστησαν.

When this happened, Patroclus was persuaded by Nestor to ask Achilles to give him his armor—even if only for a short time—to drive the Trojans away from the ships. Patroclus went out, fought nobly, and was soon killed. Achilles in his sorrow laid aside his quarrel with Agamemnon, put on armor made by Hephaestus, and killed many of the Trojans and finally Hector.[1]

8. This is the order of events. The poet began from the ninth year because the action was less intense before Achilles' anger, and the heroic deeds were not spectacular or frequent. This was because, as long as Achilles was fighting on the Greek side,

> the Trojans never stepped outside their gates
> for they feared his strong spear   [Il. 5.789-90].

However, when he stopped fighting they were encouraged and came out, and when the fighting had become evenly balanced there were constant heroic encounters involving many individuals.[2]

---

[1] This summary of the Troy tale, supplying a sufficient "beginning" (ἀρχή) without recourse to the judgment of Paris and reducing the *Iliad* and necessary background information to a single paragraph, seems to give clear evidence that the "Shorter Life," though clearly a separate work, is indeed very close in purpose to the longer essay. Both are clearly introductions for the first-time reader. For the use of summary paraphrases in ancient education, see Plutarch De aud. po. 14E and Marrou (1965), 250.

[2] The "Shorter Life" (54A) would appear to be incomplete.

[ΠΛΟΥΤΑΡΧΟΥ]

Περὶ Ὁμήρου [Β]

54B: Essay on the Life and Poetry of Homer

1. Ὅμηρον τὸν ποιητὴν χρόνῳ μὲν τῶν πλείστων, δυνάμει δὲ πάντων πρῶτον γενόμενον εἰκότως ἀναγινώσκομεν πρῶτον, ὠφελούμενοι τὰ μέγιστα εἴς τε τὴν φωνὴν καὶ τὴν διάνοιαν καὶ τὴν τῶν πραγμάτων πολυπειρίαν. λέγωμεν δὲ περὶ τῆς τούτου ποιήσεως, πρότερον μνησθέντες διὰ βραχέων τοῦ γένους αὐτοῦ.

2. Ὅμηρον τοίνυν Πίνδαρος (fr.264 Snell-Maehler) μὲν ἔφη Χῖόν τε καὶ Σμυρναῖον γενέσθαι, Σιμωνίδης (fr. 147 Page; cf. Semonides fr. 29 Diehl) δὲ Χῖον, Ἀντίμαχος (fr. 130 Wyss) δὲ καὶ Νίκανδρος (271/2 fr. 36 Jacoby) Κολοφώνιον, Ἀριστοτέλης (F 20,1 Gigon) δὲ ὁ φιλόσοφος Ἰήτην, Ἔφορος (FGrHist 70 F1) δὲ ὁ ἱστορικὸς Κυμαῖον. οὐκ ὤκνησαν δέ τινες καὶ Σαλαμίνιον αὐτὸν εἰπεῖν ἀπὸ Κύπρου, τινὲς δὲ Ἀργεῖον, Ἀρίσταρχος δὲ καὶ Διονύσιος ὁ Θρᾷξ (fr. 47 Linke) Ἀθηναῖον. υἱὸς δὲ ὑπ' ἐνίων λέγεται Μαίονος καὶ Κριθηίδος, ὑπὸ δέ τινων Μέλητος τοῦ ποταμοῦ.

3. ὥσπερ δὲ τὰ τοῦ γένους αὐτοῦ διαπορεῖται, οὕτω καὶ τὰ περὶ τῶν χρόνων καθ' οὓς ἐγένετο. καὶ οἱ μὲν περὶ Ἀρίσταρχόν φασιν αὐτὸν γενέσθαι κατὰ τὴν τῶν Ἰώνων ἀποικίαν, ἥτις ὑστερεῖ τῆς τῶν Ἡρακλειδῶν καθόδου ἔτεσιν ἑξήκοντα, τὰ δὲ περὶ τοὺς Ἡρακλείδας λείπεται τῶν Τρωικῶν ἔτεσιν ὀγδοήκοντα. οἱ δὲ περὶ Κράτητα καὶ πρὸ τῆς Ἡρακλειδῶν καθόδου λέγουσιν αὐτὸν γενέσθαι, ὡς οὐδὲ ὅλα ἔτη ὀγδοήκοντα ἀπέχειν τῶν Τρωικῶν. ἀλλὰ παρὰ τοῖς πλείστοις πεπίστευται μετὰ ἔτη ἑκατὸν τῶν Τρωικῶν γεγονέναι οὐ πολὺ πρὸ

[PLUTARCH]

On Homer [B]

54B: The Essay on the Life and Poetry of Homer

1. It is appropriate that Homer, who in time was among the first of poets and in power was the very first, is the first we read. In doing so we reap a great harvest in terms of diction, understanding, and experience of the world. We shall discuss his poetry after a brief note on his family.

2. Pindar [fr. 264 Snell-Maehler] names both Chios and Smyrna as his home, and Simonides [fr. 147 Page; cf. Semonides fr. 29 Diehl] names Chios alone. Antimachus [fr. 130 Wyss] and Nicander [FGrHist 271/2 F36] say he was from Colophon, Aristotle the philosopher [F 20,1 Gigon],[1] Ios, and Ephorus the historian [FGrHist 70 F1], Cyme. Some have not hesitated to call him a Salaminian from Cyprus, others an Argive. Aristarchus and Dionysius Thrax [fr. 47 Linke] say he was an Athenian.[2] Some say he was the son of Maion and Critheis, but others make his father the river Meles.[3]

3. Just as there is disagreement about his origins, so also about the time in which he lived. The school of Aristarchus says that he was born about the time of the colonization of Ionia, which occurred 60 years after the return of the Heracleidae, and the latter event was 80 years after Troy. The school of Crates says he was born even before the return of the Heracleidae, and thus less than 80 years in all after the Trojan War. But the opinion to which most people subscribe is that he was

---

[1] See "Shorter Life" ch. 3, above.
[2] This same claim is made in "Life v" (Monro and Allen [1902-12],, vol. 5, 247.8). The question whether or not Aristarchus actually held such a belief has been much discussed. The earliest evidence seems to go back to the Augustan grammarian Aristonicus (schol. in Il. 13.197). See discussion in Pfeiffer (1968), 228, and below, ch. 12 with note 2.
[3] This summary of claims regarding Homer's city and the following passage on his date, doubling as they do 54A 2-4, make it clear that we have here the beginning of a new essay, presumably by another author.

τῆς θέσεως τῶν Ὀλυμπίων, ἀφ' ἧς ὁ κατὰ τὰς Ὀλυμπιάδας χρόνος ἀριθμεῖται.

4. εἰσὶ δὲ αὐτοῦ ποιήσεις δύο, Ἰλιὰς καὶ Ὀδύσσεια, διῃρημένη ἑκατέρα εἰς τὸν ἀριθμὸν τῶν στοιχείων, οὐχ ὑπὸ αὐτοῦ τοῦ ποιητοῦ ἀλλ' ὑπὸ τῶν γραμματικῶν τῶν περὶ Ἀρίσταρχον. ὧν ἡ μέν Ἰλιὰς ἔχει τὰς ἐν Ἰλίῳ πράξεις Ἑλλήνων τε καὶ βαρβάρων διὰ τὴν Ἑλένης ἁρπαγὴν καὶ μάλιστα τὴν Ἀχιλλέως ἐν τῷ πολέμῳ τούτῳ διαδειχθεῖσαν ἀλκήν, ἡ δὲ Ὀδύσσεια τὴν Ὀδυσσέως ἀνακομιδὴν εἰς τὴν πατρίδα ἀπὸ τοῦ Τρωικοῦ πολέμου καὶ ὅσα πλανώμενος ἐν τῷ νόστῳ ὑπέμεινε καὶ ὅπως τοὺς ἐπιβουλεύοντας τῷ οἴκῳ αὐτοῦ ἐτιμωρήσατο. ἐξ ὧν δῆλός ἐστι παριστὰς διὰ μὲν τῆς Ἰλιάδος ἀνδρείαν σώματος, διὰ δὲ τῆς Ὀδυσσείας ψυχῆς γενναιότητα.

5. εἰ δὲ μὴ μόνον ἀρετὰς ἀλλὰ καὶ κακίας ψυχῆς ἐν ταῖς ποιήσεσι παρίστησι, λύπας τε καὶ χαρὰς καὶ φόβους καὶ ἐπιθυμίας, οὐ χρὴ αἰτιᾶσθαι τὸν ποιητήν· ⟨ποιητὴν⟩ γὰρ ὄντα δεῖ μιμεῖσθαι οὐ μόνον τὰ χρηστὰ ἤθη ἀλλὰ καὶ τὰ φαῦλα—ἄνευ γὰρ τούτων παράδοξοι πράξεις οὐ συνίστανται—ὧν ἀκούοντα ἔνεστιν αἱρεῖσθαι τὰ βελτίω. πεποίηκε δὲ καὶ τοὺς θεοὺς τοῖς ἀνθρώποις ὁμιλοῦντας οὐ μόνον ψυχαγωγίας καὶ ἐκπλήξεως χάριν, ἀλλ' ἵνα καὶ ἐν τούτῳ παραστήσῃ ὅτι κήδονται καὶ οὐκ ἀμελοῦσι τῶν ἀνθρώπων οἱ θεοί.

6. καὶ τὸ μὲν ὅλον παρ' αὐτῷ διήγησις τῶν πραγμάτων παράδοξος καὶ μυθώδης κατεσκεύασται ὑπὲρ τοῦ πληροῦν ἀγωνίας καὶ θαύματος τοὺς ἐντυγχάνοντας καὶ ἐκπληκτικὴν τὴν ἀκρόασιν καθιστάναι. ὅθεν δοκεῖ τινα παρὰ τὸ εἰκὸς εἰρηκέναι. οὐ γὰρ ἀεὶ τὸ πιθανὸν ἕπεται ἐν ᾧ τὸ παράδοξον καὶ

born about 100 years after the Trojan War, not long before the establishment of the Olympic Games and the beginning of dating by Olympiads.[1]

4. There are two poems by Homer, the *Iliad* and the *Odyssey*, each divided into as many books as there are letters in the alphabet [24], not by the poet himself but by the scholars of the school of Aristarchus. The *Iliad* contains the deeds of the Greeks and foreigners at Troy, stemming from the rape of Helen, and particularly the glorious accomplishments of Achilles; the *Odyssey* contains Odysseus' return home after the Trojan War and all the things he endured in the wanderings of the journey and how he punished those who had plotted against his house. It is clear from this that in the *Iliad* he is presenting physical prowess, in the *Odyssey* the nobility of the soul.[2]

5. If he has presented in his poems not only the virtues but also the vices of the soul, the pains as well as the joys, the fears and the desires, the poet is not to be blamed. As a poet he must depict not only good character, but bad as well, for without this the unexpected and extraordinary deeds do not emerge, among which the listener can distinguish and select the best. Furthermore, he has made the gods converse with men not simply for the sake of exciting and astounding us, but in order to show, in this as well, that the gods care for mankind and are not indifferent.

6. In general, he cultivates an extraordinary and mythical treatment of events to fill his audience with anxiety and wonder and make the listener's experience deeply moving. This seems to be why he has said some things that are highly improbable, since credibility does not always follow when a narrative has been endowed with the

---

[1] This surprising chronology has been corrected and emended in various ways. The easiest solution is to emend "100 years" to "400 years" in the final sentence, thus accommodating the traditional date of the Trojan War, in the 12th century, with the first Olympiad, beginning in 776. Comparison with the chronographic tradition suggests that the mss. of "Plutarch" are faulty and misrepresent what the author must have found in his sources, but since the error is pervasive in the mss. (and this is what readers of "Plutarch" found before them), the error is retained here. On Homer in the chronographers, see Mosshammer (1979), 160.

[2] This reductive formulation of the content of the two poems anticipates the hermeneutics of Iamblichus, who is credited with the claim that each work (in practice, each dialogue of Plato) must be understood in terms of a single subject (σκοπός). See Dillon (1973), 92.

ἐπηρμένον πρόκειται. διὸ καὶ οὐ μόνον τὰ πράγματα μετεωρίζει καὶ ἐκτρέπει τῆς συνηθείας ἀλλὰ καὶ τοὺς λόγους. ὅτι δὲ ἀεὶ τὰ καινὰ καὶ ἔξω τοῦ προχείρου θαυμάζεται καὶ τὸν ἀκροατὴν ἐπάγεται παντί που δῆλον. πλὴν καὶ ἐν τοῖς μυθώδεσι τούτοις λόγοις, εἴ τις μὴ παρέργως ἀλλ' ἀκριβῶς ἕκαστα τῶν εἰρημένων ἐπιλέγοιτο, φανεῖται πάσης λογικῆς ἐπιστήμης καὶ τέχνης ἐντὸς γενόμενος καὶ πολλὰς ἀφορμὰς καὶ οἱονεὶ σπέρματα λόγων καὶ πράξεων παντοδαπῶν τοῖς μετ' αὐτὸν παρεσχημένος, καὶ οὐ τοῖς ποιηταῖς μόνον ἀλλὰ καὶ τοῖς πεζῶν λόγων συνθέταις ἱστορικῶν τε καὶ θεωρηματικῶν. ἴδωμεν γὰρ πρότερον τὴν τῆς λέξεως αὐτοῦ πολυφωνίαν, ἔπειτα καὶ τὴν ἐν τῇ πραγματείᾳ πολυμάθειαν. πᾶσα μὲν οὖν ποίησις, τάξει τινὶ τῶν λέξεων συντιθεμένων, ῥυθμῷ καὶ μέτρῳ παραλαμβάνεται· ἐπεὶ τὸ λεῖον καὶ εὐεπές, σεμνὸν ἅμα καὶ ἡδὺ γενόμενον, διὰ δὲ τοῦ τέρπειν εἰς τὸ προσέχειν ἐπάγεται. ὅθεν συμβαίνει κατὰ τὸ αὐτὸ μὴ μόνον τοῖς ἐκπλήττουσι καὶ θέλγουσι τέρπεσθαι, ἀλλὰ καὶ τοῖς πρὸς ἀρετὴν ὠφελοῦσι πείθεσθαι ῥᾳδίως.

7. τὰ δὲ Ὁμήρου ἔπη τὸ τελειότατον ἔχει μέτρον, τουτέστι τὸ ἑξάμετρον ὃ καὶ ἡρῷον καλεῖται· ἑξάμετρον μὲν ὅτι εἷς ἕκαστος στίχος ἔχει πόδας ἕξ—ὧν ὁ μέν ἐστιν ἐκ δύο συλλαβῶν μακρῶν, σπονδεῖος καλούμενος· ὁ δὲ ἐκ τριῶν μιᾶς μὲν μακρᾶς δύο δὲ βραχειῶν ὃς λέγεται δάκτυλος. καί εἰσιν ἀλλήλοις ἰσόχρονοι· αἱ γὰρ δύο βραχεῖαι μιᾶς μακρᾶς χρόνον ἐπέχουσιν· οὗτοι δὲ παραλλήλως συντιθέμενοι πληροῦσι τὸ ἑξάμετρον ἔπος. ἡρῷον δὲ λέγεται ὅτι διὰ τούτου τὰς τῶν ἡρώων πράξεις διηγεῖται.

8. λέξει δὲ ποικίλῃ κεχρημένος τοὺς ἀπὸ πάσης διαλέκτου τῶν Ἑλληνίδων χαρακτῆρας ἐγκατέμιξεν, ἐξ ὧν δῆλός ἐστιν πᾶσαν [μὲν] Ἑλλάδα ἐπελθὼν καὶ πᾶν ἔθνος.

extraordinary and the exalted. For this reason he not only elevates events and removes them from the normal sphere of experience, but does the same also with words. It is clear to everyone that that which is new and outside the realm of the everyday evokes wonder and captivates the imagination of the listener. Even in these mythical or fabulous passages, if one considers carefully and not superficially the specific things he has said, it becomes clear that he was adept at every kind of wisdom and skill and provides the starting points and so to speak the seeds of all kinds of discourse and action for those who come after him, not only for the poets but for writers of prose as well, both historical and speculative. Let us consider first the great variety of his diction and then his vast knowledge of things.

All poetry in which words are joined together according to some fixed order involves rhythm and meter, for that which is merely even and well put comes to command the attention through pleasure when it becomes awesome and beautiful. From this it comes about that a single work can not only please by those parts which astound and enchant, but also can have a persuasive or educative effect through those parts that are useful in the pursuit of virtue.

7. The poems of Homer are in the most perfect of meters, the hexameter, or "heroic meter." It is called "hexameter" because each verse has six feet, of two kinds: those with two long syllables, called "spondees," and those with three syllables, one long and the others short, called "dactyls." These are equal in duration because two shorts occupy the same amount of time as a single long. These two types of feet, taken together, constitute the hexameter line. It is called "heroic" because it is through this meter that Homer narrates the deeds of heroes.

8. Homer used a variegated diction, mingling together elements of all the dialects of the Greeks, and it is clear from this that he visited the whole of Greece and every one of its peoples.[1]

---

[1] See Scarpat (1952), an edition of chs. 8-14 with extensive commentary. In general, few of our author's claims about the dialectical origins of various phenomena in the Homeric poetic language are acceptable to modern linguists, but his system of classification of certain forms as "Doric," "Ionic," etc., was traditional from antiquity and still has descriptive value.

9. καὶ Δωριέων μὲν τῇ συνήθει τῆς βραχυλογίας ἐλλείψει κέχρηται, τὸ δῶμα λέγων δῶ·

αἶψα δέ οἱ δῶ

ἀφνειὸν πέλεται (α 392-3)
καὶ τὸ ὅτι ὅ

ὅ μοι αἰετὸς ἔκτανε χῆνας (τ 543)

καὶ τὸ ὀπίσω ἄψ, μεταβάλλων τὸ μὲν ο εἰς τὸ α, τὸ δὲ π καὶ τὸ σ εἰς τὸ συγγενὲς αὐτοῖς, καὶ τὸ ἄλλοτε ἄλλο

ἤδη γάρ με καὶ ἄλλο τεὴ ἐπίνυσσεν ἐφετμή (Ξ 249)

καὶ τὰ τοιαῦτα. ὁμοίως δὲ καὶ τὰ μέσα συντεμὼν λέγει τοὺς ὁμότριχας καὶ ὁμοετεῖς ὄτριχας καὶ οἰέτεας (Β 765 ambo). καὶ τὸν ὁμοπάτριον ὄπατρον (Λ 257) καὶ τὸ τρέμειν τρεῖν (Ε 256) καὶ τὸ τιμῶ τίω (Δ 257, Ι 378). τῶν αὐτῶν δέ ἐστι καὶ τὸ ὑπερβιβάζειν τὰ στοιχεῖα, ὡς ἐν τῷ κάρτιστοι (Α 266, 267) ἀντὶ τοῦ κράτιστοι.

10. Αἰολέων δὲ χρῆται ἐν τοῖς συνθέτοις τῇ συγκοπῇ καδδραθέτην (ο 494) λέγων ἀντὶ τοῦ κατέδραθον καὶ ὑββάλλειν (Τ 80) ἀντὶ τοῦ ὑποβάλλειν. καὶ ἐπὶ τοῦ παρατατικοῦ χρόνου τὰ τρίτα πρόσωπα λήγοντα παρὰ τοῖς ἄλλοις εἰς τὸ ει διὰ τοῦ η παρὰ τοῖς Αἰολεῦσιν ἐκφέρεται, ὡς ἐν τῷ ἐφίλη, ἐνόη. οὕτω καὶ Ὅμηρος ἐποίησεν

δίδη μόσχοισι λύγοισιν (L 105)

ἀντὶ τοῦ ἔδει, ὅ ἐστιν ἐδέσμει, καὶ

[Plutarch] 54B The Essay on the Life and Poetry of Homer

9. He makes use of the characteristic Doric trait of shortening words, which they themselves used for the sake of brevity, when he says δῶ for δῶμα,

> quickly his house [δῶ] becomes rich
> [Od. 1.392-3]

and ὅ for ὅτι,

> that [ὅ] the eagle killed my geese
> [Od. 19.543]

and ἄψ for ὀπίσω, changing the omicron to alpha, and the pi and sigma into the letter that combines their sounds, and ἄλλο for ἄλλοτε,

> for previously, another time [ἄλλο] you admonished me
> [Il. 14.249],

and other such things. Likewise cutting out the central elements of words he says ὄτριχας for ὁμότριχας and οἰετέας for ὁμοετεῖς, ὄπατρον for ὁμοπάτριον, τρεῖν for τρέμειν, and τίω for τίμω. Likewise Doric is his transposition of letters, as in κάρτιστοι for κράτιστοι.[1]

10. He uses the syncopy of the Aeolians as well,[2] in his compound words, saying καδδραθέτην for κατέδραθον, ὑββάλλειν for ὑποβάλλειν, and the third person singular imperfect ending, which among other Greeks is -ει, is changed to -η in Aeolic as in ἐφίλη, ἐνόη, and thus Homer says

> he bound [δίδη] them with willow shoots
> [Il. 11.105]

for ἔδει (i.e. "he bound"), and

---

[1] Doric inscriptions do, in fact, prefer καρτ- to κρατ-, but this phenomenon of Homeric dialect does not constitute a Doricism (Scarpat [1952], 36).
[2] Scarpat (1952), 38-55, discusses each of these "Aeolicisms," some of which are recognized as distinctively Aeolic by ancient and modern authorities, and others not.

τοὺς μὲν ἄρ' οὔτ' ἀνέμων διάη μένος ὑγρὸν ἀέντων (ε 478 = τ 440).

καὶ τὸ ἐναλλάσσειν ἐνίοτε τὸ σ εἰς τὸ δ, ὡς ἐν τῷ λέγειν ὀδμή (Ξ 415 al.) καὶ ἴδμεν (Α 124 al.). καὶ τὸ πλεονάζειν ἔν τισιν, ὡς τὸ εὔκηλος (Α 154, γ 263) ἀντὶ τοῦ ἔκηλος καὶ αὐτὰρ (Α 51 al.) ἀντὶ τοῦ ἀτὰρ καὶ κεκλήγοντες (Μ 125 al.) ἀντὶ τοῦ κεκληγότες. καὶ τὸ προστιθέναι τῷ δευτέρῳ προσώπῳ τῶν ῥημάτων τὸ θα, ὡς τὸ φῆσθα (Φ 186) καὶ εἴπησθα (Υ 250 al.). τὸν δὲ διπλασιασμὸν τῶν συμφώνων οἱ μὲν Δωριεῦσιν οἱ δὲ Αἰολεῦσι προσνέμουσιν, οἷόν ἐστιν

ἔλλαβε πορφύρεος θάνατος (Ε 83 al.)

καὶ

ὁππότερος τάδε ἔργα (Γ 321).

11. Ἰώνων δὲ ἴδιον ἔχει τὸ ἀφαιρέσει χρῆσθαι ἐν τοῖς παρῳχηκόσι χρόνοις τῶν ῥημάτων, ὡς τὸ βῆ (Α 34 al.) καὶ τὸ δῶκεν (Β 104 al.). ἔθος γὰρ ἔχουσι καὶ ἐπὶ τῶν παρῳχημένων χρόνων ἀπὸ τῶν αὐτῶν στοιχείων ἄρχεσθαι ἀφ' ὧν ἐστι καὶ ὁ ἐνεστώς. καὶ τὸ ὑφαιρεῖν τὸ ε ἐν τῷ ἱρεὺς (Ε 10 al.) καὶ ἴρηξ (Ν 62 al.). καὶ τὸ προστιθέναι τοῖς τρίτοις προσώποις τῶν ὑποτακτικῶν τὸ σι, οἷόν ἐστι τὸ ἔλθῃσι (Τ 191 al.) καὶ τὸ λάβῃσι (Ι 324 al.) καὶ ταῖς δοτικαῖς θύρῃσι (Β 788 al.), ὕλῃσι· καὶ τὸ λέγειν οὔνομα (Γ 325 al.) καὶ νοῦσον (Α 10 al.) τὸ ὄνομα καὶ τὴν νόσον· καὶ κεινὸν (cf. Γ 376, Δ 181) καὶ μεῖλαν (cf. Ω 79) ἀντὶ τοῦ κενόν καὶ μέλαν. καὶ τὸ μεταβάλλειν τὸ α, ἐπειδὰν ἐκτείνηται εἰς τὸ η, ὡς τὸ Ἥρη (Α 55 al.), Ἀθηναίη (Α 200 al.). ἔστι δὲ ὅτε καὶ ἐκ τοῦ ἐναντίου τὸ η εἰς τὸ α, ὡς τὸ λελασμένος (Π 538 al.) ἀντὶ τοῦ λελησμένος. καὶ τὸ διαιρεῖν τὰ περισπώμενα ῥήματα, φρονέων (Α 73 al.) καὶ νοέων· καὶ τὰς γενικὰς τὰς εἰς ους ληγούσας ὡς τὸ Διομήδεος (Ε 415 al.)· καὶ τῶν θηλυκῶν τὰς γενικὰς τὰς εἰς ων ληγούσας ὡς τὸ πυλέων (Η 1, Μ 340), νυμφέων (μ 318)· καὶ τῶν οὐδετέρων τὰς πληθυντικὰς εὐθείας τὰς εἰς τὸ η ληγούσας, ὡς τὸ στήθεα (Γ 397 al.), βέλεα (Θ 159 al.)· καὶ τὰς γενικὰς αὐτῶν ὁμοίως. ἰδίως δὲ λέγουσι καὶ τὸ τετράφαται (cf. Β 25, 62) καὶ τὰ τοιαῦτα.

nor did the might of the damp-blowing winds penetrate [διάη]
[Od. 5.478 = 19.440].

He also draws from Aeolic the substitution of delta for sigma, as in ὀδμή and ἴδμεν, the lengthening of certain syllables, as εὔκηλος for ἕκηλος and αὐτάρ for ἀτάρ, and κεκλήγοντες for κεκληγότες, and the addition of -θα to second person singular verbs, as φῆσθα, and εἴπησθα. The doubling of consonants some consider a Doric trait, some Aeolic, as in

red death took [ἔλλαβε] him   [Il. 5.83],

whichever one [ὁππότερος] [has done] these deeds
[Il. 3.321].

11.   He employs of the peculiarly Ionian usage of dropping the augment of past tense verbs, as βῆ and δῶκεν.[1] The Ionians begin the past tense forms with the same letter as the present. Likewise Ionian are the omission of epsilon from ἱρεύς and ἴρηξ, the adding of -σι to the third singular subjunctive as in ἔλθησι and λάβησι, as well as to plural datives (θύρῃσι, ὕλῃσι)[2] and saying οὔνομα and νοῦσον for ὄνομα and νόσον, and κεινόν and μεῖλαν for κενόν and μέλαν, and changing alpha, when lengthened, to eta as in Ἥρη, Ἀθηναίη, and the opposite shift from eta to alpha as in λελασμένος for λελησμένος and the separation of the vowels of contract verbs such as φρονέων and νοέων, and in genitives ending in -ους, as Διομήδεος, and genitives in -ων of feminine nouns, as πυλέων, νυμφέων, and in the nominative plurals of neuter nouns properly ending in eta, as στήθεα, βέλεα and likewise their genitives. It is also peculiar to them to say τετράφαται,[3] and other such things.

---

[1] The substantial Ionic element in the Homeric "dialect" is generally recognized by ancient and modern authorities.
[2] Some of the illustrations used in the section on dialect do not in fact occur in the received text of Homer, but it is often unclear whether our author would claim them as Homeric: in some cases, he is merely telling us what the typical dialect forms look like. Words for which no locus is offered in the facing Greek text are missing from the poems as transmitted. Emendations of the present essay have sometimes been suggested in order to accommodate the illustrations to the received text of Homer.
[3] I.e., for τετραμμένοι ἦσαν

Περὶ Ὁμήρου [Β]

12. μάλιστα δὲ τῇ Ἀτθίδι διαλέκτῳ κέχρηται· καὶ γὰρ ἐπίμικτος ἦν. καὶ ἐπεὶ λέγεται παρὰ τοῖς Ἀττικοῖς λεὼς ὁ λαός, κατὰ ταύτην τὴν συνήθειαν ἔστι παρ' αὐτῷ ὁ Πηνέλεως (Β 494 al.) καὶ τὸ χρέως (Λ 686 al.). ἔστι δὲ αὐτοῖς σύνηθες καὶ τὸ συναλείφειν ἐνίοτε καὶ ἀντὶ δύο ποιεῖν μίαν συλλαβήν· τὸ ἔπος τοὖπος, καὶ τὸ ἱμάτιον θοἰμάτιον, οἷς ἐστιν ὅμοιον

Τρῶες δὲ προὔτυψαν ἀολλέες (Ν 136 al.)

καὶ

πεδία λωτεῦντα (Μ 283)

ἀντὶ τοῦ λωτεύοντα. καὶ τὸ ὑφαιρεῖν τὸ η τῶν τοιούτων εὐκτικῶν, δοκοίης δοκοῖς, τιμῴης τιμῷς ἔστιν Ἀττικόν· ᾧ ἀκολούθως εἴρηται

ἄλλοι δὲ διακρινθεῖτε τάχιστα (Γ 102).

ὁμοίως δὲ καὶ τοῦτο Ἀττικόν·

οἱ πλέονες κακίους, παῦροι δέ τε πατρὸς ἀρείους (β 277),

ὃ λέγομεν κακίονες καὶ ἀρείονες. καὶ τὰς αἰτιατικὰς τῶν τοιούτων μὴ διαιρεῖν, τοὺς βοῦς, τοὺς ἰχθῦς,

βοῦς περιτεμνομένους (ω 112)

καὶ

12. Most of all, however, he uses the Attic dialect,[1] though mixed with others. And since λαός is pronounced λεώς in Attic, likewise by the same usage he says Πηνέλεως and χρέως. It is also customary for them sometimes to use crasis or contraction to make one syllable of two (for τὸ ἔπος they say τοὖπος, and for τὸ ἱμάτιον, θοιμάτιον), which is the same as

> the Trojans pressed forward [προὔτυψαν] in waves
> [cf. Il. 13.136, etc.],

and

> lotus plains [λωτεῦντα]   [Il. 12.283]

for λωτεύοντα. Likewise Attic is the suppression of eta in optatives like δοκοίης (which becomes δοκοῖς) and τιμῴης (which becomes τιμῷς). Following this rule, he says,

> let the rest of you come to a decision [διακρινθεῖτε] quickly
> [cf. Il. 3.102].

This is Attic as well:

> Most are worse [κακίους], few better [ἀρείους] than their fathers
> [Od. 2.277],

where we would say κακίονες and ἀρείονες, as is the usage of contracting accusatives like τοὺς βοῦς, τοὺς ἰχθῦς:

> cutting out cattle [βοῦς]   [cf. Od. 24.112],

and

---

[1] Many of the Atticisms listed here are noted by ancient grammarians, whose remarks are frequently taken up by Eustathius, but our author's insistence on the prevalence of Attic in the Homeric dialect appears, at least in the preserved literature, to be idiosyncratic. For his claim that Aristarchus and Dionysius Thrax said Homer was an Athenian, see ch. 2, above, with note. For the most thorough modern exploration of Atticism in the text of Homer, see Wackernagel (1916), esp. chs. 1 and 2.

ἰχθῦς ὄρνιθάς τε (μ 331).

κἀκεῖνο δὲ εἴρηται Ἀττικῶς

  οὐδέ τί μιν σθένεϊ ῥηγνῦσι ῥέοντες (Ρ 751),

ὡς ζευγνῦσι , ὀμνῦσι. καὶ τὸ ἐξαιρεῖν τὰ βραχέα Ἀττικόν, λούεται λοῦται, οἴομαι οἶμαι. οὕτως οὖν καὶ τὸ λύτο (Φ 114 al.) ἀντὶ τοῦ ἐλύετο. τῶν αὐτῶν ἐστι καὶ τὸ ἑώρων καὶ ἑωνησάμην, ἐκ περισσοῦ προστιθέντων τὸ ε· ὅθεν ἐστὶ καὶ τὸ ἐῳνοχόει (Δ 3, υ 255). καὶ τὸ συναιρεῖν τὸ ι ἐπὶ τῶν τοιούτων, ἠόνες (Ρ 265 al.), Νηρῇδες (Σ 38 al.) οὕτω καὶ τὸ

  σφῷ δὲ μάλ' ἠθέλετον (Λ 782).

καὶ ἐπὶ τῆς εἰς ι καθαρὸν ληγούσης δοτικῆς παρατελευτῶντος τοῦ α, κέραι κέρᾳ (Λ 385), γέραι γέρᾳ, σέλαι σέλᾳ (Θ 563 al.). ἔτι δὲ καὶ τοῦτο Ἀττικόν, τὸ λέγειν ἔστων (Α 338, α 273) καὶ ἐπέσθων (Ι 170) ἀντὶ τοῦ ἔστωσαν καὶ ἐπέσθωσαν. ἔστι δὲ καὶ ἡ τῶν δυϊκῶν χρῆσις τῆς συνηθείας καὶ Ὅμηρος χρῆται συνεχῶς. καὶ τὸ τοῖς θηλυκοῖς ἀρσενικὰ ἄρθρα ἢ μετοχὰς ἢ ἐπίθετα συντάσσειν, ὡς τὼ χεῖρε (Δ 523 al.), τὼ γυναῖκε. καὶ παρὰ Πλάτωνι ἰδέα ἄγοντε καὶ φέροντε (cf. *Phaedr.* 237D7), καὶ ἡ σοφὸς γυνὴ (cf. Phaedr. 235B7) καὶ ἡ δίκαιος. οὕτως οὖν καὶ Ὅμηρος ἐπὶ Ἥρας καὶ Ἀθηνᾶς ἔφη

  οὐκ ἂν ἐφ' ὑμετέρων ὀχέων πληγέντε κεραυνῷ (Θ 455)

καὶ

  ἤτοι Ἀθηναίη ἀκέων ἦν (Δ 22, Θ 459)

καὶ

fish [ἰχθῦς] and birds   [Od. 12.331].

He also says in the Attic manner,

> nor do they break [ῥηγνῦσι] it with the strength of their flowing
> [Il 17.751]

to which we may compare ζευγνῦσι and ὀμνῦσι. Likewise Attic is the removal of short vowels as in λοῦται for λούεται, οἶμαι for οἴομαι. Moreover, λύτο for ἐλύετο is comparable. Theirs too are ἑώρων and ἑωνησάμην, with the superfluous addition of the prothetic epsilon, as also ἐῳνοχόει. Likewise the contraction or diphthongization[1] of iota in forms such as ἠόνες, Νηρῇδες, and

> you two [σφῷ] were very willing
> [Il. 11.782],

and in datives ending in simple iota preceded by alpha: κέρᾳ, γέρᾳ, σέλᾳ. Attic as well says ἔστων and ἐπέσθων for ἔστωσαν and ἐπέσθωσαν. The use of the dual is likewise characteristic of the dialect, and Homer uses it constantly. Then, there is the use of masculine articles, participles, and adjectives with feminines, as τὼ χεῖρε, τὼ γυναῖκε, and even in Plato we find ἄγοντε καὶ φέροντε applied to feminines [*Phaedrus* 237D7], and ἡ σοφὸς γυνή [cf. *Phaedrus* 235B7] and ἡ δίκαιος. Thus Homer says of Hera and Athena,

> not if you were struck [πληγέντε] by lighting in your chariot
> [Il. 8.455],

and

> but Athena was silent [ἀκέων]   [Il. 4.22 = 8.459],

and

---

[1] Homeric Greek sometimes treats these iotas, juxtaposed with long vowels, as separate syllables, but often—and this is our author's point—treats the combination as a single long syllable. The latter phenomenon is reflected in our text by the Byzantine orthographic convention of placing the iota beneath the long vowel.

κλυτὸς Ἱπποδάμεια (Β 742).

13. καὶ περὶ τὴν σύνταξιν δὲ πολλὰ ἰδιώματα ἐχουσῶν τῶν διαλέκτων ὅταν εἴπῃ ὁ ποιητὴς

ἀλλ' ἄγ' ὀίστευσον Μενελάου κυδαλίμοιο (Δ 100)
Ἀττικὴν δείκνυσι τὴν συνήθειαν. ὅταν δὲ εἴπῃ

δέξατό οἱ σκῆπτρον (Β 186)
καὶ

Θέμιστι δὲ καλλιπαρῄῳ
δέκτο δέπας (Ο 87-8),
ἐν τούτοις δωρίζει.

14. ὅπως μὲν οὖν τὰς πάντων Ἑλλήνων φωνὰς ἀθροίζων ποικίλον ἀπεργάζεται τὸν λόγον καὶ χρῆται ποτὲ μὲν ταῖς ξέναις, ὥσπερ εἰσὶν αἱ προειρημέναι, ποτὲ δὲ ταῖς ἀρχαίαις, ὡς ὅταν λέγῃ ἄορ (Κ 484 al.) καὶ σάκος (Γ 335 al.), ποτὲ δὲ ταῖς κοιναῖς καὶ συνήθεσιν, ὡς ὅταν λέγῃ ξίφος (Α 194 al.) καὶ ἀσπίδα (Β 382 al.), δῆλον. καὶ θαυμάσειέ τις ὅτι καὶ κοιναὶ λέξεις παρ' αὐτῷ σῴζουσι τὸ σεμνὸν τοῦ λόγου. τοιοῦτον γὰρ τὸ

ἵππους τε ξανθὰς ἑκατὸν καὶ πεντήκοντα (Λ 680).

15. ἐπεὶ δὲ ὁ ἐγκατάσκευος λόγος φιλεῖ τὴν τοῦ συνήθους ἐξαλλαγὴν ὑφ' ἧς ἐναργέστερος ἢ σεμνότερος ἢ πάντως τερπνότερος γίνεται, καὶ ἡ μὲν τῶν λέξεων ἐκτροπὴ καλεῖται τρόπος, ἡ δὲ τῆς συνθέσεως σχῆμα—καὶ ἔστι τὰ εἴδη

famed [κλυτός] Hippodameia[1] [Il. 2.742].

13. Likewise, in syntax the dialects have many characteristic usages, so that when the poet says,

> come, shoot an arrow at proud Menelaus[2]
> [Il. 4.100],

he displays Attic usage, but when he says

> he received the scepter from him[3]
> [Il. 2.186]

and

> she received the cup
> from Themis of the pretty cheeks [Il. 15.87-88],

he is doricizing.

14. It is clear, then, that in mustering all the dialects of the Greeks, he creates a richly varied discourse and sometimes uses dialect expressions, as those just discussed, and sometimes archaic ones, as when he says ἄορ [sword] and σάκος [shield], though in some places he uses the common and ordinary words for those same things, ξίφος and ἀσπίς. One might wonder at the way even everyday words sustain the elevation of the Homeric discourse. For instance:

> Pale horses a hundred fifty [Il. 11.680].

15. Studied diction loves to escape the ordinary and thus to become more vivid and imposing and in general more pleasing. Modifications of diction involving only a word or two are called "tropes," those

---

[1] See ch. 42, below, where this phenomenon is again discussed, and this example cited.
[2] The author seems to take the odd genitive object as characteristically Attic.
[3] In this example and the following one, it is the use of the dative with δέχομαι to indicate the source or giver of the thing received that our author identifies as characteristically Doric. Lesbonax, "On the Figures" (περὶ σχημάτων) 9, calls this usage the "Sicilian figure" (Σικελικὸν σχῆμα) and cites the same examples.

τούτων ἐν τῇ τεχνολογίᾳ ἀναγεγραμμένα—θεασώμεθα τί τούτων Ὁμήρῳ παραλέλειπται ἢ τί ἕτερον ὑπὸ τῶν μετ' αὐτὸν εὕρηται, ὃ ἐκεῖνος οὐκ εἶπε πρῶτος.

16. τῶν τοίνυν τρόπων ὀνοματοποιία καὶ πάνυ συνήθης ἐστὶν αὐτῷ. οἶδε γὰρ τὴν παλαιὰν ἀρχὴν τῶν ὀνομάτων, ὅτι οἱ πρῶτοι τὰ πράγματα ὀνομάσαντες πολλὰ ἀπὸ τοῦ συμβεβηκότος προσηγόρευσαν καὶ τὰς ἀνάρθρους φωνὰς τοῖς ἐγγραμμάτοις ἐξετύπωσαν ὡς τὸ φυσᾶν (Σ 470 al.) καὶ τὸ πρίζειν καὶ τὸ μυκᾶσθαι (Ε 749 al.) καὶ τὸ βροντᾶν (Θ 133 al.) καὶ τὰ τούτοις ὅμοια. ὅθεν καὶ αὐτὸς ἐποίησέ τινα ὀνόματα οὐκ ὄντα πρότερον, πρὸς τὰ σημαινόμενα τυπώσας, οἷον τὸν δοῦπον (Δ 455 al.) καὶ τὸν ἄραβον (Κ 375) καὶ τὸν βόμβον καὶ τὸ ῥόχθει (ε 402 al.) καὶ τὸ ἀνέβραχε (Τ 13, φ 48) καὶ τὸ σίζε (ι 394) καὶ τὰ τοιαῦτα ὧν οὐκ ἂν εὕροι τις εὐσημότερα. καὶ πάλιν ἄλλας κοινὰς λέξεις ἐπ' ἄλλων πραγμάτων κειμένας ἐπ' ἄλλα μετέθηκεν, οἷόν ἐστι καὶ τοῦτο·

φλέγμα κακὸν φορέουσα (Φ 337)

ὃ σημαίνει τὴν κατὰ τὸ φλέγειν ἐνέργειαν· καὶ τὸν πυρετὸν (Χ 31) ἀντὶ τοῦ πυρός. οἷς ὅμοιόν ἐστι καὶ τὸ

χαλκοτύπους ὠτειλάς (Τ 25).

βούλεται γὰρ εἰπεῖν τὰς ὑπὸ τοῦ χαλκοῦ τετυπωμένας. καὶ ὅλως πολλῇ τῇ καινότητι τῶν λέξεων κέχρηται, μετὰ πολλῆς ἐξουσίας τὰ μὲν ἐξαλλάσσων

involving changes of syntax, "figures."[1] Their forms are written up in treatises on rhetoric. Let us consider which of these are not found in Homer and which he did not use first but were invented by those who came after him.

16. Taking the tropes first, onomatopoeia[2] is entirely familiar to him, for he knows the ancient origin of words and that the first men who gave names to things named many of them from circumstances relating to them, and impressed into language their inarticulate sounds. Consider for example φυσᾶν ["blow"], πρίζειν ["saw"],[3] μυκᾶσθαι ["moo"], βροντᾶν ["thunder"], and the like. Thus he himself invented certain words which had not been used before, designating things by their sounds, such as δοῦπον ["thump"], ἄραβον ["shudder"], βόμβον ["boom"], ῥόχθει ["splash"], ἀνέβραχε ["bubbled up"], σίζε ["hiss"], and the like, and no one could find clearer ones.

On other occasions, he transferred common words to new meanings, as

> wrapped in foul flame [Il. 21.337],

indicating the action of fire. He also used "fever" for "fire." This is the same sort of thing:

> bronze-struck wounds [Il. 19.25],

for he wants to talk about wounds *caused* by bronze. In general, he makes extensive use of innovative vocabulary, and with great freedom changes some words from their conventional meanings and makes others

---

[1] The best key to the complexities of the rhetorical literature is H. Lausberg's *Handbuch der literarischen Rhetorik* (= Lausberg 1990). Particularly helpful entries are mentioned in our notes below. For an overview of the tropes in interpretive contexts, and a synthesis of the treatises based on Tryphon, see Rutherford (1905), part 2 (181-350). David Blank pointed out to us the relevance, as well, of the short treatise "On Figures" (περὶ σχημάτων) of Lesbonax, most of whose examples of figures are drawn from Homer, and whose concerns and definitions often resemble our author's. See Blank (1988) for text and comment.

[2] One of the "fourteen ordinary tropes" of Tryphon. See Rutherford (1905), 238-49. Though the examples represent "onomatopoeic" formations in the modern sense, the term is broader and refers to word-formation (neologism) in general. Tryphon defines seven subcategories.

[3] πρίζειν (the reading of the mss.) does not occur in the received text of Homer. Barnes' emendation τρίζειν ("squeak") (Il. 2.314, etc.) may well be correct.

παρὰ τὴν συνήθειαν, τὰ δὲ εὐσημότερα καθιστάς, ἕνεκα τοῦ κάλλος καὶ μέγεθος ἐμποιεῖν τοῖς λόγοις.

17. πολλὴ δέ ἐστιν αὐτῷ καὶ ἡ τῶν ἐπιθέτων εὐπορία, ἅπερ οἰκείως καὶ προσφυῶς τοῖς ὑποκειμένοις ἡρμοσμένα δύναμιν ἴσην ἔχει τοῖς κυρίοις ὀνόμασιν· ὥσπερ τῶν θεῶν ἑκάστῳ ἰδίαν τινὰ προσηγορίαν προστίθησι, τὸν Δία μητιέτην (Α 175 al.) καὶ ὑψιβρεμέτην (Α 354 al.) καὶ τὸν Ἥλιον ὑπερίονα (Θ 480 al.) καὶ τὸν Ἀπόλλωνα Φοῖβον (Α 43 al.) καλῶν. μετὰ δὲ τὴν ὀνοματοποιίαν ἴδωμεν καὶ τοὺς ἄλλους τρόπους.

18. κατάχρησις μὲν δή, ἥπερ ἀπὸ τοῦ κυρίως δηλουμένου μεταφέρει τὴν χρῆσιν ἐφ' ἕτερον οὐκ ἔχον ὄνομα κύριον, ἔστι παρὰ τῷ ποιητῇ, ὅταν λέγῃ σειρὴν χρυσείην (Θ 19)· σειρὰ γὰρ κυρίως ἐπὶ τοῦ σχοινίου τάσσεται. καὶ ὅταν εἴπῃ αἰγείην κυνέην (ω 231)· ἡ μὲν γὰρ περικεφαλαία κέκληται κυνέη παρ' αὐτῷ, ἐπεὶ ἐκ δέρματος κυνὸς γίνεσθαι αὐτὴν ἔθος ἦν, ἡ δὲ αἰγεία δηλονότι ἐστὶ δέρμα αἰγός.

19. μεταφορὰ δέ, ἥπερ ἐστὶν ⟨λέξις⟩ ἀπὸ τοῦ κυρίως δηλουμένου πράγματος ἐφ' ἕτερον μετενηνεγμένη κατὰ τὴν ἀμφοῖν ἀνάλογον ὁμοιότητα, καὶ πολλὴ καὶ ποικίλη ἐστὶ παρ' αὐτῷ· οἷόν ἐστιν

ἧκεν ἀπορρήξας κορυφὴν ὄρεος μεγάλοιο (ι 481)

καὶ

νῆσον, τὴν πέρι πόντος ἀπείριτος ἐστεφάνωται (κ 195).

more meaningful, all for the general purpose of infusing beauty and grandeur into his diction.

17. He makes very extensive use of epithets,[1] which are so appropriately and intimately fitted to what they modify as to have just the same force as proper names. Thus he provides each of the gods with his particular descriptive epithet, as when he calls Zeus "wise" and "high-thunderer," and the sun "Hyperion" ["passer-over"] and Apollo "Phoibos" ["brilliant"]. So much for the creation of words, now for the other tropes.

18. Catachresis[2] (the transfer of a word from its primary meaning to designate something that does not have a word to describe it) is found in the poet in expressions like σειρὴν χρυσείην ["golden chain"], since σειρά primarily means "rope." Likewise, when he says αἰγείην κυνέην ["goatskin cap"] he uses the same trope, since he uses κυνέη to mean simply "cap" when it really should mean "a cap made of dogskin," but "goatskin" here clearly refers to the skin of a goat.

19. Metaphor[3] (the transfer [of a word] from its primary meaning to designate something else according to the principle of analogy or similarity between the two) is very common in Homer, as in

> He came, breaking off the head of a mountain
> [Od. 9.481],

or

> An island wreathed by the infinite sea
> [Od. 10.195],

---

[1] Not a figure or trope, but widely discussed as contributing to an ornamented style. See e.g. Aristotle, *Rhetoric* 1405b21-27, and Lausberg (1990) par. 676.

[2] Another of the "fourteen ordinary tropes," Rutherford (1905), 209-11. The term is applied to a variety of modest transfers of words from their primary meanings to designate other things. This trope may be considered a low-grade, unpretentious, and in some instances unavoidable "level" ("der maximale Habitualisierungsgrad" Lausberg [1990] par. 577; cf. 562). of metaphor, metonymy, or synecdoche.

[3] Another of the "fourteen ordinary tropes," Rutherford (1905), 203-09. Cf. Lausberg (1990) par. 554-64. The trope of metaphor is widely treated as a compressed form of comparison, or a simile with ellipsis of "like" or "as." On metaphor in this text, see Ramos Jurado (1984).

ὃν γὰρ λόγον ἔχει ἡ κορυφὴ πρὸς ἄνθρωπον, τοῦτον καὶ ἡ ἀκρώρεια πρὸς τὸ ὄρος· καὶ ὃν στέφανος πρὸς τοῦτον ᾧ περίκειται, τὸν αὐτὸν καὶ θάλασσα πρὸς νῆσον. ἀλλὰ τὸ χρήσασθαι τοῖς ὁμοίοις ἀντὶ τῶν κυρίων ὀνόμασιν εὐειδέστερον καὶ ἐναργέστερον ποιεῖ τὸν λόγον.

20. εἰσὶ δὲ καὶ παρ' αὐτῷ μεταφοραὶ ποικίλαι· αἱ μὲν ἀπὸ ἐμψύχων ἐπὶ ἔμψυχα, οἷον

φθέγξατο δ' ἡνίοχος νηὸς κυανοπρῴροιο (fr. 16 Allen)

ἀντὶ τοῦ ναύτης, καὶ

βῆ δὲ μετ' Ἀτρείδην Ἀγαμέμνονα ποιμένα λαῶν (cf. Ξ 22)

ἀντὶ τοῦ βασιλέα. αἱ δὲ ἀπὸ ἐμψύχων ἐπὶ ἄψυχα, οἷον

ὑπαὶ πόδα νείατον Ἴδης (Β 824)

τὴν ὑπώρειαν καὶ

οὖθαρ ἀρούρης (Ι 141 = 283)

τὸ γόνιμον. ἀπὸ δὲ ἀψύχων ἐπὶ ἔμψυχα, οἷον

σιδήρειόν νύ τοι ἦτορ (Ω 205 = 521)

ἀντὶ τοῦ σκληρόν. ἀπὸ δε ἀψύχων ἐπὶ ἄψυχα, οἷον

σπέρμα πυρὸς σῴζων (ε 490)

ἀντὶ τοῦ γόνιμον ἀρχήν. ὥσπερ δὲ ὀνομάτων, ⟨οὕτω⟩ καὶ ῥημάτων εἰσὶ παρ' αὐτῷ μεταφοραί, οἷον

ἠιόνες βοόωσιν ἐρευγομένης ἁλὸς ἔξω (Ρ 265)

for the "head" has the same relationship to a man that a peak has to a mountain, and as the wreath is to the man whom it crowns, so is the sea to the island. The use of such expressions in place of the proper words makes the discourse more beautiful and more vivid.

20. He uses various kinds of metaphors, some from animate creatures to other animate creatures:

> The charioteer of the blue-prowed ship called out
> [fr. incert. 16 Allen]

for "sailor," and

> He went up to Atreus' son Agamemnon, shepherd of the people
> [cf. Il. 14.22],

for "king." There are also those moving from animate to inanimate, such as

> Under the lowest foot of Ida [Il. 2.824]

for "slope,"

> Udder of farmland [Il. 9.141],

to indicate its fertility—and from inanimate to animate:

> Your heart is iron [Il. 24 205],

for "hard"—and inanimate to inanimate:

> Saving the seed of fire [Od. 5 590],

for "generative principle." There are metaphors involving verbs as well as nouns in Homer:

> The headlands howl, protruding from the sea
> [Il. 17.265],

ἀντὶ τοῦ ἠχοῦσιν.

21. ἕτερος τρόπος ἐστὶν ἡ καλουμένη μετάληψις, κατὰ συνωνυμίαν σημαίνουσα πρᾶγμά τι διάφορον οἷον

ἔνθεν δ' αὖ νήσοισιν ἐπιπροέηκα θοῇσι (ο 299).

βούλεται γὰρ σημῆναι τὰς κυρίως λεγομένας ὀξείας νήσους, ἐπεὶ συνωνυμεῖ τὸ θοὸν τῷ ὀξεῖ· ὀξὺ δὲ οὐ μόνον τὸ κατὰ κίνησιν ταχύ ἐστιν ἀλλὰ καὶ τὸ κατὰ σχῆμα προηγούμενον εἰς λεπτότητα. τοιοῦτόν ἐστι καὶ τὸ

ἐγὼ δ' ἐθόωσα παραστάς (ι 327).

22. ἄλλος τρόπος ἡ συνεκδοχὴ λεγομένη, ἀπὸ τοῦ κυρίως σημαινομένου ἕτερόν τι τῶν ὑπὸ τὸ αὐτὸ γένος ὄντων παριστᾶσα. καὶ ἔστιν ὁμοίως καὶ ὁ τρόπος οὗτος ποικίλος. ἐκδεχόμεθα γὰρ ἤτοι ἀπὸ τοῦ ὅλου τὸ μέρος, οἷον

οἱ δ' ἰθὺς πρὸς τεῖχος εὔδμητον βόας αὔας (Μ 137)·

ἀπὸ γὰρ τῶν βοῶν τὰς βύρσας, ἐξ ὧν αἱ ἀσπίδες, δηλοῦν βούλεται. ἢ ἀπὸ μέρους τὸ ὅλον, οἷον

21. Another trope is called metalepsis,[1] in which by synonymy a word designates something different [from its usual sense]:

> Thence I sent my ships among the swift [ὀξύς] islands
> [Od. 15.299].

This refers to islands which are properly called "sharp" or "jagged," since "swiftness" and "sharpness" are related and ὀξύς means not only "swift," with regard to movement, but also, with regard to shape, "brought to a point." The following example is the same sort of thing:

> Standing next to him, I swiftened [i.e. "sharpened"] the end
> [Od. 9.327].

22. Another trope called synecdoche[2] involves the use of a word to indicate something other than what it primarily means, but something in the same class. This trope is of various sorts. For example, the use of the whole to designate the part:

> They rushed the well-built wall, lifting high their dried bulls
> [Il. 12.137],

for by "bulls" he means "hides of bulls," out of which shields are made. There is also the sort that goes from the part to the whole:

---

[1] Another of the "fourteen ordinary tropes," Rutherford (1905), 222-226. According to Tryphon (whose discussion is close to our author's and who uses the same primary illustration, metalepsis occurs when as word "by synonymy designates its homonym." That is, to paraphrase Rutherford (223), if X and Y are synonyms, i.e. different names for A, but X is also a name for B (by homonymy) then by metalepsis Y can also be used to designate B. So, since ὀξύς and θοός are synonyms meaning "swift", but ὀξύς is a homonym and also means "sharp" or "jagged", then by metalepsis Homer uses θοός to describe islands (which can be "jagged", but not literally "swift").

[2] Another of the "fourteen ordinary tropes," Rutherford (1905), 228-38. This polymorphous trope is regularly subdivided, but most definitions involve quantity: i.e., the use of the name of the part for the whole or the name of the whole for the part (Lausberg [1990] par. 572-77). Rutherford notes that "Plutarch" enumerates nine types (as does Quintilian), while other rhetorical writers list as many as thirteen.

τοιήνδ' αὖ κεφαλὴν ποθέω (cf. α 343)·

ἀπὸ γὰρ τῆς κεφαλῆς τὸν ἄνδρα σημαίνει. καὶ ὅταν λέγῃ λευκώλενον (Α 55 al.) τὴν καλὴν καὶ εὐκνήμιδας (Α 17 al.) τοὺς εὐόπλους. ἢ ἀπὸ ἑνὸς τὰ πολλά, ὡς ὅταν εἴπῃ ἐπὶ τοῦ Ὀδυσσέως

ἐπεὶ Τροίης ἱερὸν πτολίεθρον ἔπερσεν (α 2)·

οὐ γὰρ μόνος ἀλλὰ σὺν τοῖς ἄλλοις Ἕλλησι τὴν Τροίαν ἐπόρθησεν. ἀπὸ δὲ τῶν πολλῶν τὸ ἕν, οἷον

στήθεά θ' ἱμερόεντα (Γ 397),

τουτέστι τὸ στῆθος. ἀπὸ δὲ εἴδους ⟨τὸ⟩ γένος, ⟨οἷον⟩

μαρμάρῳ ὀκρυόεντι βαλών (Μ 380 = ι 499)·

εἶδος γάρ ἐστι λίθου ὁ μάρμαρος. ἀπὸ δὲ γένους τὸ εἶδος, οἷον

ὄρνιθας γνῶναι καὶ ἐναίσιμα μυθήσασθαι (β 159)·

οὐ γὰρ πάντας ἀλλὰ τοὺς μαντικοὺς ὄρνιθας εἰπεῖν βούλεται. ἀπὸ δὲ τῶν παρεπομένων τὴν πρᾶξιν, οἷον

Πάνδαρος, ᾧ καὶ τόξον Ἀπόλλων αὐτὸς ἔδωκεν (β 827)·

ἀπὸ γὰρ τοῦ τόξου τὴν περὶ τὸ τόξον ἐμπειρίαν δηλοῖ. καὶ

ἑζόμενοι λεύκαινον ὕδωρ (μ 172)

καὶ

οἱ δὲ πανημέριοι σεῖον ζυγόν (γ 486 = ο 184)·

ἀπὸ γὰρ τοῦ συμβαίνοντος ἐπὶ μὲν τοῦ προτέρου τὸ ἤλαυνον, ἐπὶ δὲ τοῦ δευτέρου τὸ ἔτρεχον δηλοῖ. ἀπὸ δὲ τοῦ προηγουμένου τὸ ἀκόλουθον·

[Plutarch] 54B *The Essay on the Life and Poetry of Homer* 91

> I long for that head   [cf. Od. 1.343],

for by "head" he means the man himself. Other examples are "white-armed" for "beautiful" and "well-greaved" for "well-equipped." Then there is the sort of synecdoche that goes from one to many, as when it is said of Odysseus

> After he sacked the holy city of Troy
> [Od. 1.2],

for he did not sack Troy alone, but along with the other Greeks. Likewise, it may go from the many to the one, as in "lovely breasts" [Il. 3.397] for "breast," or from the specific to the class, as in "hurling chilling marble" [Il. 12.380 = Od. 9.499], for marble is a kind of stone, and this is what is meant, and it may likewise go from the class to the specific instance, as in

> Know birds and speak ominous words
> [Od. 2.159],

for he means knowledge not of all birds, but specifically of those that are prophetic. Synecdoche may also go from the attendant thing to the action itself:

> Pandarus, to whom Apollo himself gave the bow
> [Il. 2.827],

for by the "bow" he means skill as an archer, and this is likewise seen in

> seated, they whitened the water
> [Od. 12.172],

and

> All day long they shook the yoke
> [Od. 3.486],

because (by way of the attendant thing) the first means "they rowed," and the second means "drove on." Also, this trope can indicate the consequence by mentioning that which precedes it:

λῦσε δὲ παρθενίην ζώνην (λ 245)·

ἀκολουθεῖ γὰρ τούτῳ τὸ διεκόρουσεν. ἀπὸ δὲ τοῦ ἀκολούθου τὸ προηγούμενον ὡς ὅταν ἐναρίζειν (Α 191 al.) λέγῃ τὸ φονεύειν ἀπὸ τοῦ σκυλεύειν.

23. ἔστι δὲ καὶ ἄλλος τρόπος ἡ μετωνυμία, λέξις ἐπ' ἄλλου μὲν κυρίως κειμένη, ἄλλο δὲ κατ' ἀναφορὰν σημαίνουσα, οἷόν ἐστι παρ' αὐτῷ τὸ

ἦμος ὅτ' αἰζηοὶ Δημήτερα κωλοτομεῦσι (fr. 15 Allen)·

τὸν γὰρ πύρινον καρπὸν δηλοῖ, ἀπὸ τῆς εὑρούσης Δήμητρος ὀνομάσας. καὶ ὅταν εἴπῃ

σπλάγχνα δ' ἄρ' ἀμπείραντες ὑπείρεχον Ἡφαίστοιο (Β 426)·

ἐν γὰρ τῷ τοῦ Ἡφαίστου ὀνόματι τὸ πῦρ λέγει. ὅμοιον δέ ἐστι τοῖς εἰρημένοις καὶ τοῦτο·

ὅς κεν ἐμῆς γε

χοίνικος ἅπτηται (τ 27-8).

λέγει γὰρ τὰ ἐμπεριεχόμενα τῇ χοίνικι.

24. ἔστι καὶ ἄλλος τρόπος ἡ ἀντωνομασία, λέξις δι' ἐπιθέτων ἢ συσσήμων ὄνομα ἴδιον σημαίνουσα, ὡς ἐν τούτῳ·

> He took off her virginal belt   [Od. 11.245],

for this action is actually *followed* by his raping her (and it is to this that the poet refers). It can also indicate something that goes before by mentioning the consequence, as in the use of ἐναρίζειν, which properly means "despoil," to mean "kill."

23.   There is another trope called metonymy,[1] which is the use of a word to designate something other than what it usually means, but related. The poet says,

> When boys who cut the clods harvest Demeter
> [fr. incert. 15 Allen]

and means the wheat itself but uses the name of its discoverer, Demeter. Likewise, when he says,

> The spitted guts were held over Hephaestus
> [Il. 2.426]

he uses the name "Hephaestus" for fire. This example is similar:

> whoever touches my basket
> [Od. 19.27-28],

where he is referring to that which is contained in the basket.

24.   There is another trope called antonomasia[2] in which an epithet or word of related meaning is used to refer to the name itself, as in this:

---

[1] See Rutherford (1905), 226-228. Tryphon, who lists it among his "fourteen ordinary tropes," again shares a primary illustration (Hephaestus = fire in Il. 2.426). Lausberg [1990] par. 565-71 indicates that a wide range of substitutions of words fall under this designation, often difficult to distinguish from synecdoche.

[2] See Rutherford (1905), 272-73; Lausberg (1990) par, 580-81. This trope is generally (as here) restricted to the substitution of a descriptive term or some periphrasis for a proper name.

Πηλείδης δ' ἐξαῦτις ἀταρτηροῖς ἐπέεσσιν

Ἀτρείδην προσέειπε (Α 223-4)·

δηλοῖ γὰρ διὰ τούτων τόν τε Ἀχιλλέα καὶ τὸν Ἀγαμέμνονα. καὶ πάλιν

θάρσει, Τριτογένεια, φίλον τέκος (Θ 39 = Χ 183)

καὶ ἐν ἄλλοις

Φοῖβος ἀκερσεκόμης (Υ 39)·

τὸ μὲν γὰρ τὴν Ἀθηνᾶν τὸ δὲ τὸν Ἀπόλλωνα δηλοῖ.

25. ἔστι καὶ ἡ ἀντίφρασις λέξις τὸ ἐναντίον ἢ τὸ παρακείμενον σημαίνουσα ὡς ἐν τούτῳ·

οὐδ' ἄρα τώ γε ἰδὼν γήθησεν Ἀχιλλεύς (Α 330)·

βούλεται γὰρ εἰπεῖν τὸ ἐναντίον, ὅτι ἰδὼν αὐτοὺς ἐλυπήθη.

26. ἔστι καὶ ἡ ἔμφασις, ἥπερ δι' ὑπονοίας ἐπίτασιν τοῦ λεγομένου παρίστησιν, οἷον

αὐτὰρ ὅτ' εἰς ἵππον κατεβαίνομεν, ὃν κάμ' Ἐπειός (λ 523)·

ἐν γὰρ τῷ κατεβαίνομεν τὸ μέγεθος τοῦ ἵππου ἐμφαίνει. ὅμοιον δὲ κἀκεῖνο

> The son of Peleus again spoke unkind words
> to the son of Atreus
> > [Il. 1.223-24],

where Achilles and Agamemnon are meant. And again,

> Take courage, Tritogeneia, dear child
> > [Il. 8.39]

and elsewhere,

> Phoibos with unshorn hair   [Il. 20.39],

for the first indicates Athena, the second, Apollo.

25.   There is also antiphrasis,[1] when an expression signifies the opposite of its obvious meaning, as in

> Achilles did not rejoice when he saw them
> > [Il. 1.330],

for he means the opposite, that he was greatly displeased when he saw them.

26.   There is also emphasis,[2] which by things implied adds tension to what is actually said, as in

> When we were climbing down into the horse that Epeios made
> > [Od. 11.523],

for the size of the horse appears in the choice of the verb "were climbing down into." This is the same:

---

[1] See Rutherford (1905), 270-71. Our author is close to Tryphon, who has the same illustration. The more familiar term for this particular sort of substitution of one phrase for another is litotes (Lausberg [1990] par. 586-88).

[2] See Rutherford (1905), 264-66. Tryphon again uses the same first illustration. The term is variously used and what it designates is sometimes difficult to distinguish from allegory (Lausberg [1990] par. 578, 905).

πᾶν δ' ὑπεθερμάνθη ξίφος αἵματι (Π 333 = Υ 476)·

καὶ γὰρ ἐν τούτῳ παρέχει μείζονα ἔννοιαν, ὡς βαπτισθέντος οὕτως τοῦ ξίφους ὥστε θερμανθῆναι. τοιοίδε μὲν οἱ τῶν λέξεων τρόποι ὑπὸ Ὁμήρου πρώτου πεποιημένοι.

27. ἴδωμεν δὲ καὶ τὰς τῆς συντάξεως ἐκτροπάς, τὰ καλούμενα σχήματα, εἰ καὶ ταῦτα πρῶτος Ὅμηρος ὑπέδειξε. τὸ δὲ σχῆμά ἐστι λόγος ἐξηλλαγμένος τοῦ ἐν ἔθει κατά τινα πλάσιν κόσμου ἢ χρείας χάριν. κάλλος μὲν γὰρ τοῖς λόγοις περιτίθησι διὰ τῆς ποικιλίας καὶ μεταβολῆς τοῦ λόγου καὶ σεμνοτέραν ἀπεργάζεται τὴν φράσιν, χρειώδης δέ ἐστιν εἰς τὸ ἐξᾶραι καὶ ἐπιτεῖναι τὰς ἐμφύτους ποιότητας καὶ δυνάμεις τῶν πραγμάτων.

28. τῶν δὲ σχημάτων τὰ μὲν κατὰ πλεονασμὸν ποιεῖ, ἐνίοτε μὲν διὰ τὸ μέτρον, ὡς τοῦτο·

χρυσοῦ δὲ στήσας Ὀδυσεὺς δέκα πάντα τάλαντα (Τ 247, cf. Ω 232)·

τὸ γὰρ πάντα μηδὲν συντελοῦν ἔγκειται. ἔστι δὲ ὅτε κόσμου χάριν, ὡς τὸ

ἦ μάλα δὴ τέθνηκε Μενοιτίου ἄλκιμος υἱός (Σ 12)·

τὸ γὰρ μάλα μηδὲν συντελοῦν ἔγκειται, πλεονάζει δὲ κατὰ συνήθειαν Ἀττικήν.

29. ἄλλοτε δὲ διὰ πλειόνων λέξεων τὸ σημαινόμενον ἀποδίδωσιν, ὃ καλεῖται περίφρασις, ὡς ὅταν λέγῃ υἷας Ἀχαιῶν (Α 240 al.) τοὺς Ἀχαιοὺς καὶ

> Every sword was hot with blood
> [Il. 16.333 and 20.476],

for here as well a further sense is added, in that the swords were so soaked with blood as to become hot.

These are the tropes first used by Homer.

27. Let us also examine the modifications of syntax, the so-called "figures," to see if Homer was the first to use these as well. The figure is a turn of phrase that departs from the usual rules, for the sake of ornament or utility. Figures add beauty to the discourse by introducing change and variety, and they make the style more majestic. Figures are useful to draw out and extend the inherent qualities and power of the material.

28. Among the figures is pleonasm,[1] the use of excess words, sometimes for the meter, as in this instance:

> Odysseus put up ten whole talents of gold
> [Il. 19.247, cf. 24.232],

for the word "whole" adds nothing to the sense. Sometimes this is done for the sake of ornament:

> Surely the strong son of Menoitios is dead
> [Il. 18.12],

for the "surely" [μάλα] is a typically Attic pleonasm.

29. Sometimes he establishes his meaning by the use of several words where one would do, and this is called periphrasis,[2] as when he

---

[1] More frequently called a "trope" (though terms "trope" and "figure" are not used consistently by the rhetorical writers), and one of Tryphon's "fourteen ordinary tropes." See Rutherford (1905), 255-57. The term is variously used of words or parts of compounds not relevant to thier immediate context or contributing substantially to the sense (Lausberg [1990] par. 462, 1).

[2] Quintilian (8.6.59) has much the same definition we find here (Lausberg [1990] par. 907).

βίην Ἡρακληείην (Β 638 al.) τὸν Ἡρακλέα.

30. καὶ τὰ τοιαῦτα δὲ κατὰ ἐναλλαγὴν σχηματίζει, τὴν εἰθισμένην τάξιν ἀναστρέφων, καὶ ἤτοι ἐν μέσῳ μηδὲν ἐντιθείς, ὡς εἶναι τὴν μετάθεσιν ἀγχίστροφον, ὅπερ ἰδίως ἀναστροφὴ καλεῖται, ὡς ἐν τῷ ὄρνιθες ὥς (Γ 2). ποτὲ δὲ καὶ μέσας λέξεις ἐντίθησι, ὃ καλεῖται ὑπερβατόν ὡς ἐν τούτῳ

αἱματόεις, ὥς τίς τε λέων κατὰ ταῦρον ἐδηδώς (Ρ 542)·

ἀντὶ τοῦ λέων ταῦρον κατεδηδώς. καὶ λέξιν μὲν οὕτως ὑπερβιβάζει· ἐνίοτε δὲ καὶ ὅλον λόγον, ὡς ἐν τούτῳ·

ὣς ἔφατ', Ἀργεῖοι δὲ μέγ' ἴαχον, ἀμφὶ δὲ νῆες
σμερδαλέον κονάβησαν ἀυσάντων ὑπ' Ἀχαιῶν,
μῦθον ἐπαινήσαντες Ὀδυσσῆος θείοιο (Β 333-5)·

τὸ δὲ ἑξῆς ἐστιν "Ἀργεῖοι δὲ μέγ' ἴαχον μῦθον ἐπαινήσαντες Ὀδυσσῆος θείοιο."

31. τοῦ δὲ αὐτοῦ εἴδους ἔχεται καὶ ἡ καλουμένη παρεμβολή, ὅταν ἔξωθέν τινα μηδὲν προσήκοντα τοῖς προκειμένοις ἐμβάλληται, ἃ κἂν ἐξέλῃ τις οὐδὲν τῆς συντάξεως ἀφαιρεῖ, οἷόν ἐστι

calls the Greeks "the sons of the Achaeans" and Heracles "the strength of Heracles."

30. He also forms expressions of the following sort by enallage,[1] inverting the usual word-order, sometimes inserting nothing between the words and so creating an abrupt transposition, which is properly called anastrophe,[2] as in

> birds resembling [Il. 3.2],

and sometimes inserting words in the middle, which is called hyperbaton,[3] or transposition, as in

> bloody, like a lion that has devoured a bull [κατὰ ταῦρον ἐδηδώς]
> [Il. 17.542],

for λέων ταῦρον κατεδηδώς. He transposes single words in this way, and sometimes whole expressions, as in

> So he spoke, and the Argives gave a shout—and all around, the ships resounded terribly with the shouting of the Greeks— approving what godlike Odysseus had said
> [Il. 2.333-35].

In the usual order it would be, "The Argives gave a shout, approving what godlike Odysseus had said."

31. Of the same sort is *parembole*,[4] where something from outside and utterly foreign to what has preceded is brought in, which could be removed without altering the syntax. For example,

---

[1] Lat. *mutatio* or *immutatio*. See Rutherford (1905), 311 with notes, on the figure ἀλλοίωσις. The term is used in the rhetorical literature to designate a wide range of "changes" of syntax.
[2] One of the "fourteen ordinary tropes" (Rutherford [1905] 251-52). See Lausberg [1990] par. 713. Tryphon offers (among others) the same illustration.
[3] Rutherford (1905) 252-55. Like our author, Tryphon, in his list of the "fourteen ordinary tropes," places hyperbaton after anastrophe, and he offers exactly the same illustrations. See Lausberg (1990) par. 716-17.
[4] This figure, which we might translate "insertion" or "parenthesis" (Lat. *interpositio*), is relatively infrequently mentioned in the rhetorical literature. See Lausberg (1990), par. 860, who distinguishes this as a "thought-hyperbaton" from true hyperbaton (above), since here it is ideas rather than parts of sentences that are transposed.

> ναὶ μὰ τόδε σκῆπτρον, τὸ μὲν οὔ ποτε φύλλα καὶ ὄζους
> φύσει, ἐπεὶ δὴ πρῶτα τομὴν ἐν ὄρεσσι λέλοιπεν,
> οὐδ' ἀναθηλήσει· περὶ γάρ ῥά ἑ χαλκὸς ἔλεψε (Α 234-6)

καὶ τὰ ἑξῆς, ὅσα περὶ τοῦ σκήπτρου λέγει· εἶτα ἐπιφέρει τὸ ἀκόλουθον τῇ ἀρχῇ

> ἦ ποτ' Ἀχιλλῆος ποθὴ ἵξεται υἷας Ἀχαιῶν
> σύμπαντας (Α 240-1).

32. ἔστι παρ' αὐτῷ καὶ ἡ παλιλλογία, ἐπανάληψις οὖσα μέρους τινὸς λόγου ἢ πλειόνων λέξεων ἐπαναλαμβανομένων, ὃ καὶ ἀναδίπλωσις καλεῖται· οἷόν ἐστι

> τοῦ δ' ἐγὼ ἀντίος εἶμι, καὶ εἰ πυρὶ χεῖρας ἔοικεν·
> εἰ πυρὶ χεῖρας ἔοικε, μένος δ' αἴθωνι σιδήρῳ (Υ 371-2).

ποτὲ δὲ παρεντιθεμένων ἄλλων τινῶν καὶ τῶν αὐτῶν πάλιν ἀντιλαμβανομένων, ὡς ἐν τῷ

> ἀλλ' ὁ μὲν Αἰθίοπας μετεκίαθε τηλόθ' ἐόντας,
> Αἰθίοπας, τοὶ διχθὰ δεδαίαται, ἔσχατοι ἀνδρῶν (α 22-3).

ἔστι δὲ τὸ σχῆμα κίνησιν ἐμφαῖνον τοῦ λέγοντος καὶ ἅμα κινοῦν τὸν ἀκροατήν.

> I swear by this scepter, which will never bear leaves or branches
> since it left its trunk behind in the mountains,
> nor will it flourish again for the iron has stripped away its bark   [Il. 1.234-36],

and so forth—all he says about the scepter. Then he completes the opening idea:

> That indeed one day a craving for Achilles shall come upon the sons of the Achaeans   [Il. 1.240].

32.   He also uses palillogy,[1] which is the repetition of a part of a statement, either immediately repeating a number of words (when it is called anadiplosis), as in

> I shall go to him even if his hands are like fire,
> if his hands are like fire and his strength like shining iron
>   [Il. 20.371-72],

or adding other words before the repetition, as in

> But he's gone to the Ethiopians, far away,
> the Ethiopians, divided into two nations, the furthest of men
>   [Od. 1.22-23].

This figure both reveals the emotion of the speaker and deeply affects the listener.

---

[1] Lat. *reduplicatio*. See Lausberg (1990), par. 619. Tryphon calls this sort of repetition ἐπανάληψις, likewise using Od. 1.22-23 as an illustration (Rutherford [1905] 268-70).

33. τοῦ αὐτοῦ γένους ἐστὶ καὶ ἡ ἐπαναφορά, ὅταν ἐν ἀρχῇ πλειόνων κώλων ταὐτὸν μόριον ἐπαναλαμβάνηται· τούτου δὲ παράδειγμα παρὰ τῷ ποιητῇ

    Νιρεὺς αὖ δὴ Σύμηθεν ἄγε τρεῖς νῆας ἐίσας,
    Νιρεὺς Ἀγλαΐης υἱὸς Χαρόποιό τ᾽ ἄνακτος,
    Νιρεύς, ὃς κάλλιστος ἀνὴρ ὑπὸ Ἴλιον ἦλθεν (Β 671-3).

καὶ ἔστιν ὁμοίως τὸ σχῆμα οἰκειότατον κινήσεως καὶ εὐεπείας.

34. ἔστι παρ᾽ αὐτῷ καὶ ἡ ἐπάνοδος, ἥπερ ἐστὶν ὅταν δύο ὀνόματα καὶ πράγματα προτιθείς τις, μήπω τοῦ νοῦ πέρας ἔχοντος, ἐπανίῃ ἐφ᾽ ἑκάτερον τῶν ὀνομάτων, ἀποδιδοὺς τὸ τῆς διανοίας ἐλλιπές, ὡς ἐν ἐκείνῳ

    Ἄρης τε βροτολοιγὸς Ἔρις τ᾽ ἄμοτον μεμαυῖα (Ε 518)·
    ἡ μὲν ἔχουσα Κυδοιμὸν ἀναιδέα δηιοτῆτος·
    Ἄρης δ᾽ ἐν παλάμῃσι πελώριον ἔγχος ἐνώμα (Ε 593-4).

ἔργον δὲ τοῦ σχήματος ποικιλία καὶ σαφήνεια.

35. ὑπάρχει δὲ καὶ ⟨τὸ⟩ ὁμοιοτέλευτον σχῆμα παρ᾽ αὐτῷ ἐν ᾧ τὰ κῶλα εἰς ὁμοίας τῷ ἤχῳ λέξεις τελευτᾷ, τὰς αὐτὰς συλλαβὰς ἐν τοῖς πέρασιν ἔχοντα, οἷόν ἐστι

    χρὴ ξεῖνον παρεόντα φιλεῖν, ἐθέλοντα δὲ πέμπειν (ο 74)·

καὶ πάλιν

    Οὔλυμπόνδ᾽, ὅθι φασὶ θεῶν ἕδος ἀσφαλὲς αἰεί

33. Of the same class is epanaphora,[1] when the same expression is repeated at the beginnings of several clauses. An example from the poet is

> Nireus, also, from Syme, brought three smooth ships,
> Nireus, son of Aglaia and lord of Charopos,
> Nireus, the most beautiful man who came beneath Ilion
> [Il. 2.671-73].

This figure as well is suited to exciting the emotions and to elegance of diction.

34. He also has the figure epanodos,[2] which occurs when someone has already mentioned two names and two things, and without completing the thought he comes back to each of the names and then completes the sentence, as

> Murderous Ares and incessantly raging Strife—
> she who presides over the battle din, whose maw is never sated with fighting—
> and Ares shook an enormous spear in his hands
> [cf. Il. 5.592-94].

The function of this figure is the addition of variety and clarity.

35. There is also homoeoteleuton [i.e., rhyme][3] in Homer, a figure in which the phrases [i.e., cola] end in words with the same sound and identical final syllables, as

> One must hold a present guest dear [φιλεῖν] but when he wishes,
> send him on his way [πέμπειν]
> [Od. 15.74],

and this,

> to Olympus, where they say the sure seat of the gods always

---

[1] Lat. *repetitio*. Tryphon treats this as well, again with the same example, under the heading ἐπανάληψις (see Rutherford [1905], 268-70; see also Lausberg (1990), pars. 616-29.
[2] Lat. *regressio*. Another of the varieties of repetition: Lausberg (1990), par. 798.
[3] See Lausberg (1990), par. 725-28.

ἔμμεναι· οὔτ' ἀνέμοισι τινάσσεται οὔτε ποτ' ὄμβρῳ

δεύεται οὔτε χιὼν ἐπιπίλναται, ἀλλὰ μάλ' αἴθρη

πέπταται ἀνέφελος, λευκὴ δ' ἐπιδέδρομεν αἴγλη (ζ 42-5).

ὅταν δὲ εἰς ὀνόματα ὁμοίως κλινόμενα λήγωσιν αἱ περίοδοι ἢ τὰ κῶλα, καὶ ταῦτα εἰς πτώσεις ὁμοίας, ὁμοιόπτωτον τοῦτο ἰδίως ὀνομάζεται· οἷόν ἐστιν

ἠΰτε ἔθνεα εἶσι μελισσάων ἀδινάων,

πέτρης ἐκ γλαφυρῆς αἰεὶ νέον ἐρχομενάων (Β 87-8).

τὰ δὲ εἰρημένα καὶ τὰ τοιαῦτα μάλιστα προστίθησι τῷ λόγῳ χάριν καὶ ἡδονήν.

36. δεῖγμα δὲ τῆς περὶ τὴν σύνθεσιν φιλοτεχνίας, ὅτι πολλάκις καὶ δυσὶ σχήμασιν ἐν τοῖς αὐτοῖς ἔπεσι κέχρηται, τῇ τε ἐπαναφορᾷ καὶ τῷ ὁμοιοτελεύτῳ, ὡς ἐν ἐκείνῳ

εὖ μέν τις δόρυ θηξάσθω, εὖ δ' ἀσπίδα θέσθω,

εὖ δέ τις ἵπποισιν δεῖπνον δότω ὠκυπόδεσσιν

εὖ δέ τις ἅρματος ἀμφὶς ἰδὼν πολέμοιο μεδέσθω (Β 382-4).

37. τούτων ἔχεται κἀκεῖνο τὸ σχῆμα τὸ καλούμενον πάρισον, ὃ γίνεται ἐκ δυοῖν ἢ καὶ πλειόνων κώλων, ἴσας ἀλλήλαις τὰς λέξεις ἐχόντων. καὶ τοῦτο δὲ πρῶτος Ὅμηρος ἐποίησεν, εἰπών

αἴδεσθεν μὲν ἀνήνασθαι, δεῖσαν δ' ὑποδέχθαι (Η 93).

> endures [ἔμμεναι]; neither do winds shake it [τινάσσεται] nor ever a shower
> wet it [δεύεται] nor snow come near [ἐπιπίλναται] but cloudless sky
> is spread over it [πέπταται] and white radiance is shed on it
> [Od. 6.42-45].

When periods or cola end with nouns similarly declined and in the same case, this figure is given the specific name *homoioptoton*,[1] as

> As the tribes of bees go forth swarming [ἀδινάων]
> out of the smooth rock endlessly coming [ἐρχομενάων]
> [Il. 2 87-88].

These and things of this sort primarily add grace and pleasure to the discourse.

36. It is an indication of the craftsmanship of Homer in composition that he often uses two figures in the same verses, as in this example epanaphora[2] combined with homoeoteleuton:[3]

> Well let a man sharpen [θηξάσθω] his spear, well set [θέσθω] his shield,
> well let him feed his swift horses,
> well let him look over his chariot, mindful of fighting
> [Il. 2.382-84].

37. The figure called parison[4] belongs with these. It consists of two or even more cola with exactly equal words. Homer was the first to use this, saying,

> They were ashamed to reject, afraid to accept
> [Il. 7.93],

---

[1] See Lausberg (1990), pars. 729-31. The figure is variously distinguished from the preceding.
[2] Ch. 33, above.
[3] Ch. 35, above.
[4] Not consistently distinguished from *isocolon* in the rhetorical writers. See Lausberg (1990), esp. par. 736. The criterion is more frequently that the number and pattern of syllables in the two phrases be identical, but this is not required by our author's definition.

καὶ πάλιν

    μηνιθμὸν μὲν ἀπορρῖψαι, φιλότητα δ' ἑλέσθαι (Π 282).

καὶ τοῦτο δὲ ὅτι πολὺν ἔχει τῆς φράσεως κόσμον, εὔδηλον.

38. τῆς δὲ ὁμοίας χάριτος ἔχεται καὶ ἡ παρονομασία, ὅταν παρὰ τὸ προκείμενον ἕτερον ὄνομα ἐμφερὲς τεθῇ εὐθὺς κατὰ σύμμετρον διάστημα, οἷόν ἐστιν

    οὐδὲ γὰρ οὐδὲ Δρύαντος υἱός, κρατερὸς Λυκόεργος,

    δὴν ἦν (Ζ 130-1)·

καὶ ἐν ἄλλῳ·

    τῶν ἦ τοι Πρόθοος θοὸς ἡγεμόνευε (Β 758).

39. καὶ τὰ μὲν προειρημένα ἤτοι κατὰ πλεονασμὸν ἢ κατά τινα ποιὰν πλάσιν σχηματίζεται. ἄλλα δὲ κατὰ ἔνδειαν λέξεως, ὧν ἐστὶν ἡ καλουμένη ἔλλειψις, ὅταν καὶ ἄνευ τοῦ ῥηθῆναί τινα λέξιν ἐκ τῶν προειρημένων ἡ διάνοια φαίνηται, οἷόν ἐστι

    δώδεκα δὴ σὺν νηυσὶ πόλεις ἀλάπαξ' ἀνθρώπων,

    πεζὸς δ' ἑνδεκά φημι (Ι 328-9)·

λείπει γὰρ τὸ ἀλαπάξαι, νοεῖται δὲ ἐκ τῶν προειρημένων. κἀκεῖνο δὲ λέγεται κατὰ ἔλλειψιν

    εἷς οἰωνὸς ἄριστος ἀμύνεσθαι περὶ πάτρης (Μ 243)·

ἐνδεῖ γὰρ τὸ ἐστί. καὶ

and again

> To cast aside anger and to take up friendship
> [Il 16.282]

and it is quite clear that this figure is a great ornament to discourse.

38. Paronomasia[1] is equally graceful, when a word is immediately followed by a word that answers to it, as in

> Neither did the son of Dryas, strong Lycurgus
> exist for long [δὴν ἦν]
> [Il. 6.130-31]

and elsewhere,

> and swift Prothoos [Προθόος θοός] led them
> [Il. 2.758].

39. The figures discussed to this point are characterized either by pleonasm or by some manner of rearranging the words, but others are characterized by the *absence* of words or expressions. One of these is called ellipsis,[2] when, even though an expression is not actually voiced, that which leads up to it makes the meaning clear. For instance,

> I claim to have taken by ship twelve cities of men,
> on foot, eleven   [Il 9.328-29].

The second "to have taken" is left out, but is understood from what goes before. The following, too, is expressed by ellipsis,

> One best omen: to guard the state
> [Il. 12.243],

since the verb "to be" is left out, and

---

[1] Lat. *annominatio*. A "(pseudo-)etymological play" with the sound of words and word-endings (Lausberg [1990], par. 637).
[2] Another of the "fourteen ordinary tropes," the mirror-image of pleonasm (ch. 28, above). See Rutherford (1905), 257-58.

ὦ πόποι, ἦ μοι ἄχος μεγαλήτορος Αἰνείαο (Υ 293)·
λείπει γὰρ τὸ πάρεστιν ἢ συμβέβηκεν ἤ τι τοιοῦτον. καὶ ἄλλα πολλὰ εἴδη τῆς ἐλλείψεώς ἐστι παρ' αὐτῷ· ἔργον δὲ τοῦ σχήματος τάχος.

40. τοιοῦτόν ἐστι καὶ τὸ ἀσύνδετον, ὁπόταν ἐξαιρῶνται οἱ σύνδεσμοι οἱ συνδέοντες τὴν φράσιν, ὅπερ οὐ μόνον τάχους ἀλλὰ καὶ ἐμφάσεως παθητικῆς χάριν γίνεται, οἷόν ἐστι καὶ τοῦτο·
ᾔομεν ὡς ἐκέλευες ἀνὰ δρυμά, φαίδιμ' Ὀδυσσεῦ,
εὕρομεν ἐν βήσσῃσι τετυγμένα δώματα καλά (κ 251-2)·
ἐν τούτοις γὰρ ὁ καί σύνδεσμος ἐξῄρηται, τὸν τάχιστον τρόπον τῆς ἀπαγγελίας ζητοῦντος τοῦ λέγοντος.

41. ἔστιν ἐν τοῖς σχήμασι καὶ τὸ καλούμενον ἀσύντακτον, ὃ καὶ ἀλλοίωσις καλεῖται, ἐπειδὰν ἡ συνήθης τάξις ἀλλοία γένηται, καὶ ἔστι ποικίλη ἕνεκα τοῦ κόσμον ἢ χάριν ἐμποιεῖν τοῖς λόγοις, τῆς μὲν συνήθους τάξεως οὐ δοκούσης ἀκολουθεῖν, †ἐπί τι ἴδιον ἀναφορᾶς ἐχούσης ἀκολουθίαν†.

42. συμβαίνει δὲ πολλαχῶς περὶ τὰ γένη τῶν ὀνομάτων ἐναλλασσομένων, οἷόν ἐστι τὸ κλυτὸς Ἱπποδάμεια (Β 742) ἀντὶ τοῦ κλυτὴ καὶ

> Alas, what pain for great-hearted Aeneas!
> [Il. 20.293]

since "comes upon me" or "I feel" or something of the sort is left out. There are many other forms of ellipsis in Homer, and the function of the figure is rapidity.

40.   Of this sort is the figure asyndeton,[1] where the bonds that hold the expression together are removed, and this occurs not only for the sake of speed, but also for the emotional effect, as in

> We went as you said, through the oak scrub, glorious Odysseus,
> we found a fine house built in the thicket
> [Od. 10.251-52].

In these verses the conjunction "and" is left out, since the speaker is trying to report the information as quickly as possible.

41.   Among the figures is also the so-called *asyntakton* or *alloiosis*,[2] where the normal syntax is changed and varied for the sake of adding grace and ornament to the discourse. The usual syntax appears not to follow, but rather there is a change with regard to some peculiar characteristic.[3]

42.   A frequent form of this figure is the changing of the genders of nouns, as κλυτὸς Ἱπποδάμεια [Il. 2.742][4] for κλυτή and θῆλυς ἐέρση [Od.

---

[1] A type of ellipsis and the opposite of polysyndeton, asyndeton consists of the omission of co-ordinating conjunctions. See Lausberg (1990), pars. 709-11; Rutherford (1905), 324.

[2] Lat. *mutatio*. Both terminology and definition are idiosyncratic here (cf. Lausberg [1990], par. 509). The first term (ἀσύντακτον) seems not to be used elsewhere of a figure or trope, but does occur with the sense "irregular," "in violation of the rules." "Plutarch" lumps together here a large group of "irregularities" or "shifts" of gender, number, case, tense, etc. See Rutherford (1905), 310-12, esp. 311 (on ἀλλοίωσις).

[3] The Greek is probably corrupt in the last part of this sentence, and the translation represents an attempt to accommodate the odd received text to the definition at hand, as well as the examples given in the following chapters.

[4] The same example is used in ch. 12 above, where these shifts of gender are likewise identified as characteristically Attic. Lesbonax (2) also cites the same example, identifying this shift of gender as the "Euboean figure."

θῆλυς ἐέρση (ε 467) ἀντὶ τοῦ θήλεια. σύνηθες γὰρ ἦν τοῖς παλαιοῖς, καὶ μάλιστα τοῖς Ἀττικοῖς, χρῆσθαι τοῖς ἀρσενικοῖς καὶ ἀντὶ τῶν θηλυκῶν ὡς κρείττοσι καὶ δυνατωτέροις· οὐκ ἀμέτρως μέντοι οὐδὲ ἀλόγως, ἀλλ' ὅταν δέῃ χρῆσθαι ὀνόματι ἐπιθέτῳ ἐκτὸς ὄντι τοῦ σώματος περὶ οὗ ἐστιν ὁ λόγος. περὶ μὲν γὰρ τὸ σῶμά ἐστιν· ὁ μέγας, ἡ μεγάλη, ὁ καλός, ἡ καλή, καὶ τὰ τοιαῦτα· ἐκτὸς δέ, οἷον ἔνδοξος, εὐτυχής. καὶ γὰρ καθολικῶς πάντα τὰ σύνθετα κοινά ἐστιν ἑκατέρου τοῦ γένους. καὶ ὅταν κοινῶς ἀρσενικῷ καὶ θηλυκῷ ὀνόματι ἐπιφέρηται ῥῆμα ἢ μετοχή, τὸ ἀρσενικὸν ἐπικρατεῖ, ὡς ἐν τούτῳ·

παρθενικαί τε καὶ ἠίθεοι ἀταλὰ φρονέοντες (Σ 567).

43. τινὰ δὲ καὶ παρὰ τὴν τῶν διαλέκτων ἰδιότητα ἢ τὴν τότε συνήθειαν λέγεται διαφόρως· οἷόν ἐστιν

ἔχει δέ τε κίονας αὐτός,
μακράς, αἳ γαῖάν τε καὶ οὐρανὸν ἀμφὶς ἔχουσιν (α 53-4).

44. πολλάκις δὲ καὶ μετὰ λόγου ἐναλλάσσει τὰ γένη, ὡς ἐν τούτῳ·
δῶρόν τοι καὶ ἐγώ, τέκνον φίλε, τοῦτο δίδωμι (ο 125)·
τὸ μὲν γὰρ τέκνον οὐδέτερον ὄνομα, ἐπήνεγκε δὲ ἀρσενικὸν τὸ φίλε, πρὸς τὸ πρόσωπον ἀποτείνας τὸν λόγον. ὅμοιόν ἐστι καὶ τὸ ἀπὸ τῆς Διώνης πρὸς τὴν Ἀφροδίτην εἰρημένον

τέτλαθι, τέκνον ἐμόν, καὶ ἀνάσχεο κηδομένη περ (Ε 382).
τῆς δὲ αὐτῆς ἀναλογίας κἀκεῖνο ἔχεται

ἦλθε δ' ἐπὶ ψυχὴ Θηβαίου Τειρεσίαο

5.467], for θήλεια. It was customary among the ancients, and particularly the people of Attica, to use masculines for feminines, as stronger and more dynamic—not excessively or unreasonably, but when an adjective was used to designate qualities not inherent in the person or thing in question. These qualities are inherent in bodies: that they are "big" or "beautiful"—but that they are "glorious" or "blessed" do not constitute inherent qualities. Moreover, in general all compound adjectives have the same form for masculine and feminine. And when the same verb or participle applies to both masculine and feminine nouns, the masculine prevails, as in

> girls and youths of tender thought [φρονέοντες]
> [Il. 18.567].

43. Occasional expressions violate all the norms, however, both of dialect and of ancient custom:

> and he holds the lofty columns[1]
> that keep earth and heaven apart
> [Od. 1.53-54].

44. Often he modifies gender according to sense, as

> I as well give you this gift, dear child [φίλε τέκνον][2]
> [Od. 15.125],

for τέκνον ["child"] is neuter but he has attached to it the masculine form φίλε, since the reference is to a person. Likewise, when Dione says to Aphrodite,

> Bear up, my child [τέκνον], and endure, though grieved
> [κηδομένη]   [Il. 5.382]

this works on the same principle, as does

> The soul [ψυχή] of Theban Tiresias came,

---

[1] The author singles out these lines because of the treatment of κίων ("column") as a feminine rather than a masculine noun, but the usage is common even in fifth-century Attic Greek (LSJ s.v.).
[2] Another of the illustrations of the "Euboean figure" in Lesbonax (2).

χρύσεον σκῆπτρον ἔχων (λ 90-1).

τὸ γὰρ ἔχων οὐ πρὸς τὴν ψυχὴν ἀλλὰ πρὸς τὸ γένος τοῦ σώματος, τουτέστι πρὸς τὸν Τειρεσίαν, ἥρμοσε. πολλάκις γὰρ οὐ πρὸς τὸν λόγον ἀλλὰ πρὸς τὸ σημαινόμενον ποιεῖται τὴν ἀπόδοσιν ὡς ἐν τούτῳ·

πᾶσιν ὀρίνθη θυμός, ἐκίνηθεν δὲ φάλαγγες,

ἐλπόμενοι παρὰ ναῦφιν ἀμύμονα Πηλείωνα (Π 280-1)·

τὸ γὰρ ἐλπόμενοι οὐχ αἱ φάλαγγες ἀλλ' οἱ ἄνδρες ἐξ ὧν αἱ φάλαγγες συνεστᾶσι.

45. καὶ κατ' ἄλλον δὲ τρόπον τὰ γένη ἐξαλλάσσει, ὡς ὅταν εἴπῃ

νεφέλη δέ μιν ἀμφιβέβηκε

κυανέη· τὸ μὲν οὔποτ' ἐρωεῖ (μ 74-5)·

ἐπεὶ γὰρ συνωνύμως λέγεται νεφέλη καὶ νέφος, προειπὼν τὴν νεφέλην, ἐπήνεγκε τὸ οὐδέτερον νέφος. ὅμοια δέ ἐστι τούτῳ κἀκεῖνα τὰ ἔπη

τῶν δ', ὥς τ' ὀρνίθων πετεηνῶν ἔθνεα πολλά,

χηνῶν ἢ γεράνων ἢ κύκνων δουλιχοδείρων,

ἔνθα καὶ ἔνθα πέτονται ἀγαλλόμεναι πτερύγεσσι

κλαγγηδὸν προκαθιζόντων(Β 459-60, 462-3)·

προθεὶς γὰρ γενικῶς τὰ τῶν ὀρνίθων γένη, ἅπερ οὐδετέρως λέγεται, ἐπήνεγκε τὸ θηλυκὸν

ἔνθα καὶ ἔνθα πέτονται ἀγαλλόμεναι πτερύγεσσι (Β 462)

εἶτα

κλαγγηδὸν προκαθιζόντων (Β 463),

holding [ἔχων] a golden scepter [Od. 11.90-91],

for ἔχων does not agree with ψυχή but is masculine to agree with "Tiresias."[1] Often the gender respects the sense and not the actual words:

> All their souls were excited and the battle-columns [φάλαγγες] were shaken
> anticipating [ἐλπόμενοι] the handsome son of Peleus, by the ships   [Il. 16.280-81]—

ἐλπόμενοι agrees not with φάλαγγες but rather with the men, of whom the columns are composed.

45. Homer also switches gender in another way, when he says,

> a dark cloud [νεφέλη] surrounds it;
> it never withdraws   [Od. 12.74-75],

since for "cloud" both the feminine νεφέλη and the neuter νέφος are in use, and though he has just said νεφέλη, he acts (in the next phrase) as if he had used the neuter νέφος. These verses are the same:

> These, as the many races [ἔθνη] of winged birds,
> geese, cranes, or long-necked swans,
> fly here and there, rejoicing in their wings,
> as they settle down noisily [Il. 2.459-60, 462-63],

for, having first said broadly "the races of birds" [a neuter], he then introduced a feminine

> fly here and there, rejoicing [ἀγαλλόμεναι][2], in their wings,

then [returns to the neuter in],

> as they settle down [προκαθιζόντων] noisily
>   [Il. 2.463],

---

[1] On this same passage, compare ch. 123 below.
[2] Modern editors print a neuter (ἀγαλλόμενα) here.

ἀποδιδοὺς τὸ οἰκεῖον τῷ γενικῷ ὀνόματι τῶν ἐθνῶν.

46. Ἅμα δὲ τοῖς γένεσι καὶ τοὺς ἀριθμοὺς ἐναλλάσσει πολλάκις ὁ ποιητὴς λέγων

ἡ πληθὺς ἐπὶ νῆας Ἀχαιῶν ἀπονέοντο (Ο 305)·
προθεὶς γὰρ τὸ ἑνικὸν ἐπήγαγε τὸ πληθυντικόν, δηλονότι πρὸς τὸ σημαινόμενον ἀναφέρων, ἐπειδήπερ ἡ πληθὺς τῇ μὲν προσηγορίᾳ ἐστὶν ἑνικόν, πολλοὺς δὲ ἐν αὐτῷ περιείληφεν.

47. ἐκ τοῦ ἐναντίου δέ ἐστι τὸ ὅμοιον, ἐπειδὰν προτεθέντος τοῦ πληθυντικοῦ τὸ ἑνικὸν ἐπενεχθῇ ὡς ἐν τούτῳ·

οἱ δ᾽ ἄλκιμον ἦτορ ἔχοντες,
πρόσσω πᾶς πέτεται (Π 264-5).
τὸ γὰρ πᾶς τῷ λόγῳ ἑνικόν ἐστι, τέτακται δὲ ἐπὶ πλήθους, ἴσον δυνάμενον τῷ πάντες. τῆς δὲ αὐτῆς ἰδέας τοῦ σχήματός ἐστι κἀκεῖνο·

οἱ δὲ Πύλον, Νηλῆος εὐκτίμενον πτολίεθρον
ἷξον· τοὶ δὲ ἐπὶ θινὶ θαλάσσης ἱερὰ ῥέζον (γ 4-5)·
νοοῦνται γὰρ οἱ Πύλιοι.

48. περὶ δὲ τὰς πτώσεις γίνεται ἀλλοίωσις παρ᾽ αὐτῷ, εὐθείας μὲν καὶ κλητικῆς ἐναλλασσομένης ἐν τοῖς τοιούτοις·

αὐτὰρ ὁ αὖτε Θυέστ᾽ Ἀγαμέμνονι λεῖπε φορῆναι (Β 107)
καὶ

making the agreement go back to the general word "races" [ἔθνη].

46. As well as gender, the poet often changes number, as when he says

> the crowd made their way back to the ships of the Achaeans
> [Il. 15.305],

for starting from the singular he brings in the plural, clearly preferring the sense to the usual rule, since πληθύς ["crowd"] is singular in number but represents many individuals.

47. There is also the opposite case, where he starts with the plural and shifts to the singular, as in

> those with stout hearts,
> every one [πᾶς] flies forward
> [Il. 15.264-65],

where the word πᾶς, is singular but refers to many individuals and has the same force as the plural πάντες. This belongs to the same category:

> they arrived at Pylos, the well-built city of Neleus,
> and they [sc. the inhabitants] were sacrificing on the shore
> [Od. 3.4-5].

for the Pelians are understood as the subject of the verb.

48. He also has *alloiosis* of case, switching nominative and vocative as in this example,

> and Thyestes[1] left it to Agamemnon to bear
> [Il. 2.107],

and

---

[1] The author takes the elided Θύεστ[α] to represent a vocative, an explanation of such odd Homeric masculine nominatives in alpha that was offered by Hellenistic scholarship (e.g. schol in Il. 2.107 [Aristonicus]) and remains current.

νεφεληγερέτα Ζεῦς (Α 511 al.)

καὶ

δός, φίλος· οὐ γάρ μοι δοκέεις ὁ κάκιστος Ἀχαιῶν (ρ 415)
γενικῆς δὲ καὶ δοτικῆς ἐν τῷ τοιούτῳ·

Τρωσὶν μὲν προμάχιζεν Ἀλέξανδρος θεοειδής (Γ 16)
ἀντὶ τοῦ Τρώων. καὶ ἐκ τοῦ ἐναντίου

ἡ δ' αὐτοῦ τετάνυστο περὶ σπέους γλαφυροῖο (ε 68)
ἀντὶ τοῦ περὶ σπέει γλαφυρῷ. καὶ τούτων δέ ἐστιν ἡ αἰτία αὕτη, ὅτι συγγένειάν τινα ἐδόκουν ἔχειν πρὸς ἀλλήλας ἥ τε εὐθεῖα καὶ ἡ αἰτιατικὴ καὶ ἡ κλητική. διὸ καὶ ἐν τοῖς οὐδετέροις εἰσὶν αἱ αὐταί, καὶ ἐν πολλοῖς τῶν ἀρσενικῶν καὶ θηλυκῶν ἥ τε εὐθεῖα καὶ ἡ κλητική ἐστιν ἡ αὐτή. ὁμοίως δὲ καὶ ἡ γενικὴ πρὸς τὴν δοτικὴν ἔχει τινὰ συγγένειαν. ταῦτα δὲ καὶ ἐν τοῖς δυϊκοῖς ἀριθμοῖς ἐπὶ πάντων τῶν ὀνομάτων εὑρίσκεται. ὅθεν εἰκότως παρὰ τὴν συνήθειαν τὰς πτώσεις ἐναλλάσσει. ἐνίοτε δὲ καὶ λόγον ἐστὶν εὑρεῖν τῆς ἐξαλλαγῆς, ὡς ἐν τῷ

ἐπιστάμενοι πεδίοιο (Ε 222 = Θ 106)

καὶ

διέπρησσον πεδίοιο (Β 785 al.)

ἴσον τῷ ἐπέρων διὰ τοῦ πεδίου.

49. εὖ δὲ ἔχει παρ' αὐτῷ ἡ τῶν πτώσεων μεταβολὴ ἐν ἀρχῇ τῶν δύο ποιήσεων, ἐν ἑκατέρᾳ γὰρ προθεὶς τὴν αἰτιατικὴν ἐπήνεγκε τὴν εὐθεῖαν, εἰπών

μῆνιν ἄειδε, θεά, ...

ἣ μυρί' Ἀχαιοῖς ἄλγε' ἔθηκε (Α 1-2)

> Cloud-gatherer Zeus [νεφεληγερέτα Ζεύς]
> [Il. 1.511 etc.],

and

> Give, my friend [φίλος], since you don't look like the basest of the Greeks [Od. 17.5]

and genitive and dative, as in

> Godlike Paris fought in the front of the Trojans [Τρωσίν]

for Τρώων, and in reverse,

> The [vine] was spread there around the smooth cave [σπείους]
> [Od. 5.68],

for σπέει. The reason is this: the nominative, accusative, and vocative are considered to be related to one another. Thus in neuter nouns they are the same, and in many masculine and feminine nouns as well the nominative and the vocative are the same. Likewise the genitive is related to the dative. This is found in the duals of all nouns. For this reason, Homer switches the cases—quite appropriately—according to these relationships. In some instances the reason for the change is apparent, as in "coming on the plain" [πεδίοιο] and "they crossed the plain" [πεδίοιο], which is like "they crossed through the plain" [διὰ τοῦ πεδίου].

49. He makes good use of the shifting of cases at the beginning of each of the poems, starting in each instance with the accusative and going to the nominative:[1]

> Goddess, sing the wrath [μῆνιν]...
> ... which [ἥ] set myriad woes on the Greeks
> [Il. 1.1-2],

---

[1] Lesbonax (19A) calls this the "Periegetic figure," though he uses different illustrations (one of which appears every bit as regular and unremarkable as the familiar ones cited here).

καὶ

> ἄνδρα μοι ἔννεπε, Μοῦσα, πολύτροπον, ὃς μάλα πολλὰ
> πλάγχθη   (α 1-2).

50. ἔστι δὲ ὅτε τῇ γενικῇ τὴν εὐθεῖαν ἐπιφέρει, ὡς ἐν τούτῳ·

> τῶν οἳ νῦν βροτοί εἰσι (Α 272).

51. πολλὰ δὲ καὶ ἑτέρως σχηματίζει, ὡς ἔχει καὶ τὸ

> φημὶ γὰρ οὖν κατανεῦσαι ὑπερμενέα Κρονίωνα
> ἤματι τῷ, ὅτε νηυσὶν ἐπ' ὠκυπόροισιν ἔβαινον
> Ἀργεῖοι Τρώεσσι φόνον καὶ κῆρα φέροντες,
> ἀστράπτων δ' ἐπιδέξι', ἐναίσιμα σήματα φαίνων (Β 350-3).

τούτῳ δὲ ὅμοιόν ἐστι κἀκεῖνο·

> ὁ δ' ἀγλαΐηφι πεποιθώς,
> ῥίμφα ἑ γοῦνα φέρει (Ζ 510-11).

καὶ ταῦτα δὲ ἐξήνεγκε κατά τινα ἀρχαϊκὴν συνήθειαν καὶ οὐδὲ ταῦτα ἀλόγως. εἰ γάρ τις τὰς μετοχὰς ἀναλύσειεν εἰς ῥήματα, εὕροι ἂν τὸ ἀκόλουθον· τὸ γὰρ ἀστράπτων ἴσον ἐστὶ τῷ ὅτε ἤστραπτε, καὶ τὸ πεποιθὼς τῷ ἐπεὶ πέποιθε. τούτοις ἐστὶ κἀκεῖνα παραπλήσια·

> οἱ δὲ δύο σκόπελοι, ὁ μὲν οὐρανὸν εὐρὺν ἱκάνει (μ 73)

and

> Muse, sing the versatile man [ἄνδρα], who [ὅς] wandered much [Od. 1.1-2].

50. There are situations where he shifts from the genitive to the nominative, as here:

> of those [τῶν] who [οἵ] are now alive
> [Il. 1.272].

51. Many other passages use other sorts of figures, as[1]

> For I say the powerful son of Kronos nodded assent
> that day, when the Greeks went onto their swift ships
> bringing death and doom to the Trojans,
> flashing his lightning on the right, showing favorable signs
> [Il. 2.350-53].

This is like

> he trusting in his glory
> his swift knees carry him
> [Il. 6.510-11].

He made these shifts in the archaic manner, and not unreasonably—for if one resolved these participles into verbs, the sequence would be found. "Flashing his lightning" [ἀστράπτων] is the equivalent of "when he flashed his lightning" [ὅτε ἤστραπτε], and "trusting" [πεποιθώς], of "since he trusted" [ἐπεὶ πέποιθε]. Parallel to these are:

> and the two crags, one reaches wide heaven
> [Od. 12.73],

---

[1] In the first passage, Zeus is first mentioned in the accusative, but is later modified by nominative participles. In the second example, there is an abrupt shift in the opposite direction, from nominative to accusative. This last is Lesbonax's "Argolic figure," (nominative participle agreeing with accusative followed by infinitive), which he illlustrates with the same two passages of Homer cited here (23A, 23B).

καὶ
>τὼ δὲ διακρινθέντε ὁ μὲν μετὰ λαὸν Ἀχαιῶν
>ἤι', ὁ δ' ἐς Τρώων ὅμαδον κίε (Η 306-7).

καὶ τὰ τοιαῦτα. οὐκ ἄλογον γὰρ τὸν μέλλοντα περὶ δυεῖν τινων λέγειν τὸ κοινὸν αὐτῶν προτάξαι τὴν εὐθεῖαν πτῶσιν ἐν ἑκατέρῳ φυλάξαντα· ὅτι δὲ τὸ κοινὸν τοῦ λόγου χάριν πολλὴν ἐπιφαίνει, πρόδηλον.

52. ἔστι δὲ ὅπου τὴν κοινὴν πτῶσιν προθεὶς τὸν περὶ ἑνὸς ἐπιφέρει λόγον, ὡς ἐν τούτῳ·
>ἄμφω δ' ἑζομένω γεραρώτερος ἦεν Ὀδυσσεύς (Γ 211).

53. καὶ τὰ εἴδη δὲ τῶν ὀνομάτων ἐξαλλάσσει πολλάκις· ποτὲ μὲν ἐξ ὑπερβολῆς τιθεὶς τὸ συγκριτικὸν ἀντὶ τοῦ ἁπλοῦ, ὡς τὸ
>σαώτερος ὥς κε νέηαι (Α 32).

ποτὲ δὲ καὶ τὸ ὑπερθετικὸν ὁμοίως ἀντὶ τοῦ ἁπλοῦ, ὡς τὸ
>δικαιότατος Κενταύρων (Λ 832).

τοιαύτη μὲν ἡ ἐξαλλαγὴ ἐν τοῖς ὀνόμασιν. ἐν δὲ τοῖς ῥήμασι γίνεται ἐξαλλαγὴ τῶν μὲν ἐγκλίσεων, ὡς ὅταν τὸ ἀπαρέμφατον ἀντὶ τοῦ προστακτικοῦ παραληφθῇ, οἷον
>θαρσῶν νῦν, Διόμηδες, ἐπὶ Τρώεσσι μάχεσθαι (Ε 124)

and

> the two separating, the one went among the Greek host,
> and the other went into the throng of the Trojans
> [Il. 7.306-07],

and the like. It is not unreasonable in speaking of something that is going to happen to two people that he should put the [dual] common element first and use the nominative in both instances, and it is evident that the common expression is very graceful.

52.   Sometimes he begins with the [dual] common expression and then talks only about one person, as in

> the two sitting, Odysseus was more imposing
> [Il. 3.211].

53.   He often changes the forms of nouns and adjectives as well, sometimes by hyperbole[1] using comparative for positive, as

> so you'll go more safely
> [Il. 1.32],

sometimes as well the superlative for the positive, as

> most just of Centaurs   [Il. 11.832].

These are the sorts of shifts he makes in nouns and adjectives. There are also shifts in verbs, including shifts of mood, as when the infinitive is used for an imperative:[2]

> Now, taking heart, Diomedes, fight [μάχεσθαι] the Trojans
> [Il. 5.124],

---

[1] The modest examples of hyperbole, or exaggeration, noted here are not the sort usually discussed by the rhetorical writers, who tend to warn against exaggeration. See ch. 71, below.
[2] An "Ionian and Dorian figure" according to Lesbonax (15A, 17B), who finds other illustrations in Homer.

ἀντὶ τοῦ μάχου· ἢ τὸ ὁριστικὸν ἀντὶ τοῦ εὐκτικοῦ, οἷον

    πληθὺν δ' οὐκ ἂν ἐγὼ μυθήσομαι οὐδ' ὀνομήνω (Β 488)

ἀντὶ τοῦ μυθησαίμην καὶ ὀνομήναιμι. καὶ ἐκ τοῦ ἐναντίου ⟨τὸ⟩ εὐκτικὸν ἀντὶ τοῦ ὁριστικοῦ, οἷον

    καὶ νύ κεν ἔνθ' ἀπόλοιτο Ἄρης (Ε 388)

ἀντὶ τοῦ ἀπώλετο.

54. τῶν δὲ χρόνων, ὅταν ὁ ἐνεστὼς ἀντὶ τοῦ μέλλοντος τεθῇ, ὡς ἐν τούτῳ·

    τὴν δ' ἐγὼ οὐ λύσω, πρίν μιν καὶ γῆρας ἔπεισιν (Α 29)

ἀντὶ τοῦ ἐπελεύσεται. ἢ ἀντὶ τοῦ παρῳχηκότος

    ἔνθ' ἦ τοι πλυνοὶ ἦσαν ἐπηετανοί, πολὺ δ' ὕδωρ

    καλὸν ὑπεκπρορέει (ζ 86-7)

ἀντὶ τοῦ ἔρρεε. καὶ ὁ μέλλων ἀντὶ τοῦ ἐνεστῶτος

    οἱ μὲν δυσομένου Ὑπερίονος, οἱ δ' ἀνίοντος (α 24)·

ἢ ἀντὶ τοῦ παρῳχηκότος

    δείδω μὴ δὴ πάντα θεὰ νημερτέα εἴπῃ (ε 300)

ἀντὶ τοῦ εἶπε.

55. καὶ διαθέσεις δὲ ἐναλλάσσονται παρ' αὐτῷ πολλάκις καὶ τίθεται ἀντὶ ἐνεργητικῶν παθητικὰ ἢ μέσα, οἷον

for μάχου; or when the indicative is used for the optative:

> I will not tell [μυθήσομαι] the multitude, nor name [ὀνομήνω] them [Il. 2.488]

instead of "could not tell" [μυθησαίμην] and "could not name" [ὀνομήναιμι] and the opposite, optative for indicative:

> and now Ares might perish [ἀπόλοιτο] there
> [Il. 5.388],

for "would have perished" [ἀπώλετο].

54.   There are shifts of tense as well, including present for future, as in the following:

> I won't release her, not until old age comes on her [ἔπεισιν]
> [Il. 1.29],

for "will come on her." There is also present for past:

> there, there were year-round washing places, and abundant good water flows out through them
> [Od. 6.86-87],

instead of "flowed;" as well as future for present:

> some, where the sun is going to set, some where it rises
> [Od. 1.24],

or for past:

> I fear the goddess says [εἴπῃ] everything unfailingly
> [Od. 5.300]

for "said" [εἶπε].[1]

55.   He often has shifts of voice, using middle or passive for active:

---

[1] This is in fact the reading adopted by all modern editors.

ἕλκετο δ' ἐκ κολεοῖο μέγα ξίφος (Α 194)
ἀντὶ τοῦ εἷλκε· καὶ
καθορώμενος αἶαν (Ν 4)
ἀντὶ τοῦ ὁρῶν. καὶ τοὐναντίον τὸ ἐνεργητικὸν ἀντὶ τοῦ παθητικοῦ
δωρήσσω τρίποδα χρυσούατον (fr. 17 Allen)
ἀντὶ τοῦ δωρήσομαι.

56. ἔστι δὲ ἰδεῖν ὅπως καὶ τοὺς ἀριθμοὺς ἐναλλάσσων τὸν πληθυντικὸν ἀντὶ τοῦ ἑνικοῦ τίθησιν, ὡς πολλάκις ἐν τῇ συνηθείᾳ, εἴ τις περὶ αὑτοῦ λέγων ὡς ἐπὶ πολλοὺς ἀναφέρει τὸν λόγον, ὡς ἐν τούτῳ·
τῶν ἀμόθεν γε, θεὰ θύγατερ Διός, εἰπὲ καὶ ἡμῖν (α 10)
ἀντὶ τοῦ ἐμοί.

57. γίνεται δὲ παρ' αὐτῷ καὶ κατὰ πρόσωπα μεταβολή· καθ' ἕνα μὲν τρόπον οὕτως
ἄλλοι μὲν γὰρ πάντες, ὅσοι θεοί εἰσ' ἐν Ὀλύμπῳ,
σοί τ' ἐπιπείθονται, καὶ δεδμήμεσθα ἕκαστος (Ε 877-8).
πολλῶν γὰρ ὄντων τῶν θεῶν, ἐν οἷς ἐστι τὸ λέγον πρόσωπον, ἑκάτερον καλῶς ἐξενήνοχε, τό τε πείθονται καὶ τὸ δεδμήμεσθα. καθ' ἕτερον δὲ τρόπον, ὅταν τὸ νῦν ἐάσας ἀφ' ἑτέρου ἐφ' ἕτερον πρόσωπον μεταβῇ· ὅπερ ἰδίως ἀποστροφὴ καλεῖται, τῷ δὲ παθητικῷ κινεῖ καὶ ἄγει τὸν ἀκροώμενον, οἷόν ἐστι καὶ τοῦτο·

> He drew himself [ἕλκετο] the great sword from its sheath
> [Il. 1.194],

for εἷλκε ["drew"] and

> gazing over [καθορώμενος] the land
> [Il. 13.4],

for ὁρῶν; and the opposite, active for passive:

> I shall grant [δωρήσω] a golden-eared tripod
> [fr. incert. 17, Allen]

for δωρήσομαι.

56. There are instances where he shifts number, using the plural for the singular, as is common usage, where someone who is talking about himself speaks as if more than one person were concerned:

> These things from some point, goddess daughter of Zeus, tell us
> [Od. 1.10]

for "me."

57. There are shifts of person as well. One type is this:

> All the other gods, as many as are on Olympus,
> obey you, and we submit to you, each of us
> [Il. 5.877-78].

Since there are many gods and the speaker is among them, both the third person plural form "[they] obey you" and the second person plural "we submit to you" are appropriate.

Another type (specifically called apostrophe[1]) is seen where he abandons the person in which he has been speaking and moves from one to another. This is very emotional and moves the listener:

---

[1] See Rutherford (1905) 313-14 and Lausberg (1990) par. 762-65. The term is not confined to the narrower modern usage (for second-person addresses, usually to absent individuals) but applies to all shifts of person, including the characteristically Homeric shifts from third-person narrative to dramatic first-person speeches and scenes.

Περὶ Ὁμήρου [Β]

> Ἕκτωρ δὲ Τρώεσσιν ἐκέκλετο, μακρὸν ἀΰσας
> νηυσὶν ἐπισσεύεσθαι, ἐᾶν δ' ἔναρα βροτόεντα·
> ὃν δ' ἂν ἐγὼν ἀπάνευθε νεῶν ἑτέρωσε νοήσω (Ο 346-8)·

ἀπὸ γὰρ τοῦ διηγηματικοῦ μετέβαλεν εἰς τὸ μιμητικόν. καὶ ἐν αὐτῷ δὲ τῷ διηγηματικῷ πολλάκις χρῆται τῇ ἀποστροφῇ

> ἀμφὶ σέ, Πηλέος υἱέ, μάχης ἀκόρητοι Ἀχαιοί (Υ 2).

ἀλλὰ καὶ ἐν τῷ μιμητικῷ πολλάκις χρῆται τῇ ἀποστροφῇ καὶ μεταβολῇ τῶν προσώπων, ὡς ἐν τούτῳ

> ἦ δὴ παισὶν ἐοικότες ἀγοράασθε
> νηπιάχοις, οἷς οὔ τι μέλει πολεμήϊα ἔργα,
> Ἀτρεΐδη, σὺ δ' ἔθ', ὡς πρίν, ἔχων ἀστεμφέα βουλήν,
> ἄρχευ' Ἀργείοισιν ἀνὰ κρατερὰς ὑσμίνας (Β 337-8, 344-5).

καὶ ἕτερον δὲ εἶδος ἀποστροφῆς ἐστι τοιοῦτον·

> Τυδεΐδην δ' οὐκ ἂν γνοίης ποτέροισι μετείη (Ε 85)·

ἔστι γὰρ ἀντὶ τοῦ οὐκ ἄν τις γνοίη. καὶ πάλιν

> ὀδμὴ δ' ἡδεῖα ἀπὸ κρητῆρος ὀδώδει
> θεσπεσίη, τότ' ἂν οὔ τοι ἀποσχέσθαι φίλον ἦεν (ι 210-11).

58. καὶ μετοχαῖς δὲ χρῆται ἀντὶ ῥημάτων, ὡς ἐν τῷ

> ἥ τ' ἐνὶ κήπῳ
> καρπῷ βριθομένη (Θ 306-7)

ἀντὶ τοῦ βρίθεται. καὶ

> Hector called on the Trojans with a great shout
> to leave the spoils and rush upon the ships:
> "And whomever I find away from the ships. . . ."
> [Il. 15.346-48].

Here he shifts from the narrative style to the dramatic-mimetic. He often uses apostrophe in the middle of a narrative passage:

> Around you, son of Peleus, the Greeks insatiate of battle
> [Il. 20.2],

but in dramatic-mimetic passages he also often uses apostrophe as well as shifts of person, as in

> You speak like feeble children,
> with no knowledge of war. . . .
> Agamemnon, keep your resolve firm and
> lead the Greeks in the harsh strife
> [Il. 2.337-38 and 344-45].

This is another form of apostrophe:

> You would not have known which side Diomedes was on
> [Il. 5.85],

for "one would not have known," and again,

> A sweet, magical smell came from the mixing bowl—
> Then, you know, it was no pleasure to hold back
> [Od. 9.210-11].

58. Likewise he uses participles in place of verbs, as in

> and she, in the garden,
> weighted down [βριθομένη] with fruit
> [Il. 8.306-07],

for "is weighted down," and

> ἔνθ᾽ οἵ γ᾽ εἰσέλασαν πρὶν εἰδότες (ν 113)

ἀντὶ τοῦ πρὶν εἰδέναι.

59. καὶ τὰ ἄρθρα δὲ ἐναλλάσσει πολλάκις, ἀντὶ τῶν προτακτικῶν τοῖς ὑποτακτικοῖς χρώμενος, οἷον

> τοὺς ἔτεκε Ζεφύρῳ ἀνέμῳ ἅρπυια Ποδάργη (Π 150)

καὶ τοὐναντίον

> καὶ θώρηχ᾽. ὃ γάρ ἦν οἱ, ἀπώλεσε πιστὸς ἑταῖρος (Σ 460).

60. οὕτω καὶ τὰς προθέσεις εἴωθε μεταλλάσσειν·

> χθιζὸς ἔβη μετὰ δαῖτα (Α 424)

ἀντὶ τοῦ ἐπὶ δαῖτα· καὶ

> νοῦσον ἀνὰ στρατὸν ὦρσε κακήν (Α 10).

61. ὁμοίως δὲ καὶ προθέσει πτῶσιν ὀνόματος οὐκ οἰκείαν ἐπιφέρει, ὡς ἐν τούτῳ·

> μή πως καὶ διὰ νύκτα μενοινήσωσι μάχεσθαι (Κ 101)

ἀντὶ τοῦ διὰ νυκτός.

they put in here before they knew[1]
>[Od. 13.113],

for πρὶν εἰδέναι.

59. He also shifts articles, using the postpositive [i.e. the relative pronoun] instead of the prepositive [i.e. the definite article],[2]

> a breastplate; what he had, his dear companion lost
> [Il. 18.460],

and the opposite:

> those [τούς] the Harpy Podarge bore to the West Wind
> [Il. 16.150].

60. In the same way he was accustomed to switch prepositions:

> Yesterday, he went after dinner [μετὰ δαῖτα]
> [Il. 1.424]

for "for dinner" [ἐπὶ δαῖτα], and

> he aroused an evil sickness up [ἀνά] the camp
> [Il. 1.10].

61. Likewise, he will use the wrong case after a preposition, as in

> lest they be planning to fight by night [διὰ νύκτα]
> [Il. 10.101],

for διὰ νυκτός.

---

[1] The author clearly misunderstood this verse (as Clavier noted). The translation above reflects what the author must have thought it meant, but in fact πρὶν εἰδότες here means not "before they knew" but "knowing it in advance."

[2] That is, Homer sometimes uses, in place of relative pronouns, forms that to our author look like articles, and vice versa. The examples are reversed in the mss., but we have put them back in their logical order in the translation.

62. ἐνίοτε δὲ ἀφαιρεῖ τὰς προθέσεις, οἷον

τῆς ὅ γε κεῖτ' ἀχέων (Β 694)

ἀντὶ τοῦ περὶ ἧς καὶ

ποτιδέγμενος εἴ τι μιν εἴποι (ψ 91)

ἀντὶ τοῦ προσείποι. καὶ ἄλλας προθέσεις ὁμοίως τὰς μὲν ὑπαλλάσσει τὰς δὲ ἀφαιρεῖ.

63. καὶ ἐπιρρήματά τινα ἐναλλάσσει, τοῖς εἰς τόπον καὶ τοῖς ἐν τόπῳ καὶ τοῖς ἐκ τόπου ἀδιαφόρως χρώμενος, οἷον

οἱ δ' ἑτέρωσε καθῖζον (Υ 151)

ἀντὶ τοῦ ἑτέρωθι καὶ

Αἴας δ' ἐγγύθεν ἦλθεν (Η 219 al.)

ἀντὶ τοῦ ἐγγύς.

64. ἔστι δὲ παρ' αὐτῷ καὶ τῶν συνδέσμων ἐναλλαγή, οἷον

εὐνῇ δ' οὔ ποτ' ἔμικτο· χόλον δ' ἀλέεινε γυναικός (α 433)

ἀντὶ τοῦ χόλον γὰρ ἀλέεινε γυναικός. ταῦτα μὲν δὴ κατὰ λέξιν ἐστὶ σχήματα, οἷς καὶ ἄλλοι πάντες οὐ μόνον ποιηταὶ ἀλλὰ καὶ πεζῶν λόγων συνθέται κέχρηνται.

65. ἔστι δὲ καὶ ἡ διάνοια παρ' αὐτῷ πολλοῖς εἴδεσιν ἐσχηματισμένη, ὧν ἐστι καὶ ἡ προαναφώνησις, ἥτις γίνεται ὅταν τις διηγούμενος μεταξὺ τὸ ἐν

62. Sometimes he leaves out prepositions, as in

> he lay grieving her [Il. 2.694],

for "over her," and

> looking to see if she would say [εἴποι] anything to him [Od. 23.91],

for "address" [προσείποι]. There are other prepositions as well, some of which he changes and some of which he omits.

63. He also shifts adverbs, making no distinction between those indicating place-to-which, place-in-which, and place-from-which,

> they sat to the other side [ἑτέρωσε] [Il. 20.151],

for "on the other side" [ἑτέρωθι], and

> Ajax came near [ἐγγύθεν] [Il. 7.219 etc.],

for ἐγγύς.

64. He shifts conjunctions as well, as in

> But he never yet slept with her; and [δέ] he avoided his wife's anger [Od. 1.433],

instead of *"for* [γάρ] he was avoiding." These are stylistic figures which many others have used, not only poets but writers of prose as well.

65. There are also many figures in Homer's works that relate to meaning, such as *proanaphonesis*,[1] which occurs when in the middle of

---

[1] This "figure" (which we might call "prediction") is seldom mentioned, but has a clear usefulness in describing the very characteristic habit of the Homeric narrator of leaping suddenly forward in time to demonstrate his knowledge of the future. See Rutherford (1905), 279-80. The brief treatment of its opposite ("speaking from hindsight") is less susceptible to generalization.

ἑτέροις τάξιν ἔχον τοῦ ῥηθῆναι προλέγῃ, ὡς ἐν τούτῳ·

ἦ τοι ὀιστοῦ τε πρῶτος γεύσεσθαι ἔμελλεν (φ 98)

καὶ ἡ ἐπιφώνησις, οἷόν ἐστι

ῥεχθὲν δέ τε νήπιος ἔγνω (Ρ 32).

66. ἔστι παρ' αὐτῷ πολὺ καὶ ποικίλον τὸ τῆς προσωποποιίας. πολλὰ μὲν γὰρ καὶ διάφορα πρόσωπα εἰσάγει διαλεγόμενα, οἷς καὶ ἤθη παντοῖα περιτίθησιν. ἐνίοτε δὲ καὶ τὰ μὴ ὄντα πρόσωπα ἀναπλάσσει, ὡς ὅταν εἴπῃ

ἦ κε μέγ' οἰμώξειε γέρων ἱππηλάτα Πηλεύς (Η 125).

67. ἔστι δὲ καὶ ἡ διατύπωσις, ἐξεργασία πραγμάτων ἢ γενομένων ἢ ὄντων ἢ πραχθησομένων εἰς τὸ παραστῆσαι ἐναργέστερον τὸ λεγόμενον, ὡς ἐν τούτῳ·

ἄνδρας μὲν κτείνουσι, πόλιν δέ τε πῦρ ἀμαθύνει,
τέκνα δέ τ' ἄλλοι ἄγουσι βαθυζώνους τε γυναῖκας (Ι 593-4),

ἢ πρὸς τὸ οἶκτον κινῆσαι

δύσμορον, ὅν ῥα πατὴρ Κρονίδης ἐπὶ γήραος οὐδῷ
νούσῳ ἐν ἀργαλέῃ φθίσει κακὰ πολλ' ἐπιδόντα·
υἱέας τ' ὀλλυμένους ἑλκυσθείσας τε θύγατρας,
καὶ θαλάμους κεραϊζομένους, καὶ νήπια τέκνα

a narrative one anticipates and brings up something which has its place elsewhere in the work, as in this:

> Indeed he was to be the first to taste the arrow
> [Od. 21.98],

and its opposite *epiphonesis*, as

> Even a fool knows after the fact
> [Il. 17.32].

66. The figure prosopopoeia[1] ("character-making") is abundant and varied in Homer, for he brings in many different characters to whom he gives all sorts of qualities. Sometimes he even evokes those who are not characters in the work, as when he says,

> Ah, old horse-taming Peleus would weep terribly
> [Il. 7.125].

67. There is also *diatyposis*[2] ("vivid description"), which is the depiction of past, present, or future events to add vividness to the discourse, as in this:

> They kill the men and fire levels the city;
> Others lead away their children and deep-waisted women
> [Il. 9.593-94],

or in order to evoke pity:

> Unfortunate man, for father Zeus will destroy him in old age
> with hideous sickness, when he has seen many terrible things:
> his sons killed, his daughters raped,
> their bedrooms plundered, and the little children

---

[1] Lat. *fictio personae*. Lausberg (1990), pars. 826-29; Rutherford (1905), 138 with n. 1, 328-29. This is one of the most broadly exploited ornaments in oratory, where the speaker's mimetic adoption of a persona other than his own turns the speech into a one-actor drama. That the *Iliad* and *Odyssey* should be thought of in these terms underlines the oddness of this presentation of Homer-as-rhetor.

[2] Lat. *evidentia* or *illuminatio*. See Longinus 20.1, and Lausberg (1990), pars. 810-19; Rutherford (1905), 328.

βαλλόμενα προτὶ γαίῃ ἐν αἰνῇ δηϊοτῆτι (Χ 60-4).

68. ἔστι καὶ ἡ εἰρωνεία παρ' αὐτῷ, λόγος διὰ τοῦ ἐναντίου δηλῶν τὸ ἐναντίον μετά τινος ἠθικῆς ὑποκρίσεως, οἷόν ἐστι τὸ τοῦ Ἀχιλλέως

ὁ δ' Ἀχαιῶν ἄλλον ἑλέσθω

ὅς τις οἷ τ' ἐπέοικε καὶ ὃς βασιλεύτερός ἐστιν (Ι 391-2).
ἐμφαίνει γὰρ ὅτι οὐκ ἂν ἕτερον εὕροι βασιλικώτερον. καὶ τὸ

ἀλλ', Ὀδυσεῦ, σὺν σοί τε καὶ ἄλλοισιν βασιλεῦσι

φραζέσθω νήεσσιν ἀλεξέμεναι δήϊον πῦρ (Ι 346-7).
καὶ οὗτος μὲν ὁ τρόπος ἐστίν, ὅταν περὶ αὐτοῦ λέγῃ τις εὐτελῶς, ἵνα τὴν ἐναντίαν δόξαν παράσχῃ· ἕτερος δὲ ὅταν τις ἄλλον ἐπαινεῖν προσποιῆται τῇ ἀληθείᾳ ψέγων· καὶ τοῦτό ἐστι ⟨τὸ⟩ παρ' Ὁμήρου λεγόμενον ὑπὸ Τηλεμάχου·

Ἀντίνο', ἦ μευ καλὰ πατὴρ ὣς κήδεαι υἱός (ρ 397)·

τῷ γὰρ ἐχθρῷ λέγει, ὡς πατὴρ υἱοῦ πεφρόντικας. καὶ πάλιν, ὅταν χλευάζων τις ἐπαίρῃ τὸν πέλας, ὡς οἱ μνηστῆρες,

ἦ μάλα Τηλέμαχος φόνον ἡμῖν μερμηρίζει,

ἤ τινας ἐκ Πύλου ἄξει ἀμύντορας ἠμαθόεντος,

ἤ νυ καὶ ἐκ Σπάρτηθεν, ἐπεί νύ περ ἵεται οὕτως (β 325-7).

hurled to the ground in bitter war
[Il. 22.60-64].

68. He also uses irony[1]—that is, statements which, because they are delivered with a certain hypocrisy, mean exactly the opposite of what they say, as when Achilles says,

Let him pick another of the Greeks
who is more like him, and more kingly
[Il. 9.391-92],

where he is really saying that he would not find anyone more kingly. Likewise,

But, Odysseus, let him consult with you and the other kings
to save the ships from raging fire
[Il. 9.346-47].

This is the figure used when someone underrates himself to create just the opposite impression, and it is another [related] one when one pretends to praise someone else but is in fact censuring him. This is present when Homer has Telemachus say,

Antinous, indeed you love me as a father loves a son
[Od. 17.397],

since he is speaking to an enemy, and saying "you have treated me like a son." It is the same when one praises one's neighbor mockingly, as the suitors do in these lines:

Surely Telemachus is plotting our death:
he ill bring allies either from sandy Pylos
or from Sparta, since this is what he's set on
[Od 2.325-27].

---

[1] Lausberg (1990) par. 902; Rutherford (1905), 271-72, cf. 214, n. 34. Along with sarcasm (ch. 69, below), often a subcategory of allegory (ch. 70, below).

69. ἔστι δέ τι εἶδος εἰρωνείας καὶ ὁ σαρκασμός, ἐπειδάν τις διὰ τῶν ἐναντίων ὀνειδίζῃ τινὶ μετὰ προσποιήτου μειδιάματος, ὡς Ἀχιλλεύς,

    τοῖσι μὲν ἔμπεδα κεῖται, ἐμεῦ δ' ἀπὸ μούνου Ἀχαιῶν

    εἵλετ', ἔχει δ' ἄλοχον θυμαρέα, τῇ παριαύων

    τερπέσθω (Ι 335-7).

70. τούτοις παραπλησίως ἔχει καὶ ἡ ἀλληγορία, ἥπερ ἕτερον δι' ἑτέρου παρίστησιν, οἷόν ἐστι τοῦτο·

    νῦν μὲν δὴ μάλα πάγχυ, Μελάνθιε, νύκτα φυλάξεις,

    εὐνῇ ἔνι μαλακῇ καταλέγμενος, ὡς ἐπέοικε (χ 195-6).

τὸν γὰρ ἐν δεσμοῖς ὄντα καὶ ἀνηρτημένον ἐν κοίτῃ ἁπαλῇ ὑπνώσειν λέγει.

71. κέχρηται πολλάκις καὶ τῇ ὑπερβολῇ, ἥτις ὑπεραίρουσα τὴν ἀλήθειαν πολλὴν ἐπίτασιν ἐμφαίνει, οἷον

    λευκότεροι χιόνος, θείειν δ' ἀνέμοισιν ὁμοῖοι (Κ 437).

τοιούτοις μὲν δὴ τρόποις καὶ σχήμασι χρησάμενος Ὅμηρος καὶ τοῖς μετ' αὐτὸν ὑποδείξας τῆς ἐπὶ τούτοις εὐδοξίας πρὸ πάντων δικαίως τυγχάνει.

72. ἐπεὶ δὲ καὶ χαρακτῆρές εἰσι τῶν λόγων τὰ καλούμενα πλάσματα, ὧν τὸ μὲν ἁδρόν, τὸ δὲ ἰσχνόν, τὸ δὲ μέσον λέγεται, ἴδωμεν εἰ πάντα ἐστὶ παρ'

69. Sarcasm[1] is also a form of irony, when someone attacks someone else by saying the opposite of what he means, with a false smile on his face, as Achilles:

> Their gifts are safe, but mine alone
> is confiscated and *he* has a lovely woman—may he
> have pleasure lying with her!
> [Il. 9.335-37].

70. Very close to these is allegory,[2] which says one thing through another, as in

> Now you'll keep your watch all night, Melanthius,
> in the sort of soft bed you deserve
> [Od. 22.195-96],

for he is hanging in chains and the speaker says he will sleep in a soft bed.

71. He often uses hyperbole[3] as well, which goes beyond the truth and exaggerates, to give force to the discourse, as

> Whiter than snow and as fast as the winds
> [Il. 10.437].

Since he used such tropes and figures and passed them on to those who followed, Homer rightly receives the credit for them before all others.

72. Inasmuch as there are various kinds of styles (the so-called *plasmata*),[4] specifically, the grand, the plain, and the intermediate,

---

[1] Often a subcategory of irony (Lausberg [1990], pars. 583, 1244).
[2] Lausberg (1990), pars. 895-901; Rutherford (1905), 211-13. Allegory is for "Plutarch" first and foremost a trope of rhetoric.
[3] Lausberg (1990), pars. 909-10; Rutherford (1905), 262-64. See ch. 53, above.
[4] Cf. Demetrius *On Style*, where the classification is more elaborate, with four "simple types of style" (ἁπλοῖ χαρακτῆρες) only one of which (ἰσχνός, "plain") occurs in this list. Our author's "grand" (ἁδρόν) style is roughly equivalent to Demetrius' "elevated" (μεγαλοπρεπές) style, likewise exemplified by Thucydides (Demetrius 36, 39-40).

Ὁμήρῳ, τῶν μὲν μετ᾽ αὐτὸν ποιητῶν ἢ λογογράφων ἐπιτηδευσάντων ἕν τι τούτων ἑκάστου, ὧν καὶ ἔστι παραδείγματα, Θουκυδίδου μὲν τὸ ἁδρὸν, Λυσίου δὲ τὸ ἰσχνόν, Δημοσθένους δὲ τὸ μέσον. τὸ μὲν οὖν ἁδρὸν πλάσμα ἐκεῖνό ἐστι τὸ καὶ τῇ τῶν λέξεων καὶ τῇ τῶν νοημάτων κατασκευῇ μεγάλας ἔχον ἐμφάσεις, οἷόν ἐστιν

    ὣς εἰπὼν σύναγεν νεφέλας, ἐτάραξε δὲ πόντον,

    χερσὶ τρίαιναν ἑλών· πάσας δ᾽ ὀρόθυνεν ἀέλλας

    παντοίων ἀνέμων· σὺν δὲ νεφέεσσι κάλυψε

    γαῖαν ὁμοῦ καὶ πόντον· ὀρώρει δ᾽ οὐρανόθεν νύξ (ε 291-4).

ἰσχνὸν δὲ τὸ καὶ τῇ ὕλῃ τῶν πραγμάτων μικρὸν καὶ τῇ λέξει κατεξεσμένον, οἷόν ἐστι τοῦτο·

    ὣς εἰπὼν οὗ παιδὸς ὀρέξατο φαίδιμος Ἕκτωρ.

    ἂψ δ᾽ ὁ πάις πρὸς κόλπον ἐϋζώνοιο τιθήνης

    ἐκλίνθη ἰάχων, πατρὸς φίλου ὄψιν ἀτυχθείς,

    ταρβήσας χαλκόν τε ἰδὲ λόφον ἱππιοχαίτην (Ζ 466-9).

μέσον δὲ τὸ ἑκατέρου τούτων μεταξύ, τοῦ μὲν ἰσχνότερον, τοῦ δὲ ἁδρότερον, οἷον

    αὐτὰρ ὁ γυμνώθη ῥακέων πολύμητις Ὀδυσσεύς,

    ἆλτο δ᾽ ἐπὶ μέγαν οὐδόν, ἔχων βιὸν ἠδὲ φαρέτρην

    ἰῶν ἐμπλείην, ταχέας δ᾽ ἐκχεύατ᾽ ὀϊστοὺς

    αὐτοῦ πρόσθε ποδῶν, μετὰ δὲ μνηστῆρσιν ἔειπεν (χ 1-4).

73. ὅτι δὲ καὶ τὸ ἀνθηρὸν εἶδος τῶν λόγων ἐστὶ πολὺ παρὰ τῷ ποιητῇ, κάλλος ἔχον καὶ χάριν εἰς τὸ τέρπειν καὶ ἥδειν ὥσπερ ἄνθος, τί ἄν τις καὶ λέγοι; μεστὴ γάρ ἐστιν ἡ ποίησις τῆς τοιαύτης κατασκευῆς. ἡ μὲν δὴ τῆς φράσεως ἰδέα τοιαύτην ἔχει ποικιλίαν παρὰ τῷ Ὁμήρῳ, οἵαν διήλθομεν, ὀλίγα παραδείγματα θέμενοι, ἐξ ὧν ἔστι καὶ τὰ ἄλλα κατανοεῖν.

let us see if all of these are to be found in Homer. Later poets and writers each cultivated only one such mode, so that Thucydides is exemplary for the grand style, Lysias for the plain, and Demosthenes, the intermediate. The grand style is that which creates strong impressions through the fashioning of language and ideas:

> So he spoke, and drew together the clouds and shook the sea,
> trident in hand, and stirred up every blast
> of every wind, hiding land and sea in cloud.
> He brought down night upon the earth
>
> [Od. 5.291-94].

The plain style is that in which the substance of the events is slight and the language very polished, as in:

> So spoke brilliant Hector and reached out for his son,
> but the child cried and shrank back to his nurse's breast,
> afraid to look at his father—
> scared of the bronze and the horse-mane crest
>
> [Il. 6.466-69].

The intermediate style is that which falls between these, plainer than the one but grander than the other:

> Stripped of his rags, crafty Odysseus
> leapt to the great threshold with his bow and quiver
> full of arrows, showering them before him.
> Then he spoke to the suitors... [Od. 22.1-4].

73. Why would one think it necessary to add that the flowery style—with beauty and grace to warm the heart, like a flower—is frequently encountered in the works of the poet? His poetry is filled with this sort of thing. The form of the diction of Homer's poetry shows tremendous variety, as we have demonstrated with a few examples. These will be sufficient to suggest the rest.

74. ἐπεὶ δὲ παντὸς τοῦ ἀσκουμένου παρ' ἀνθρώποις λόγου, ὁ μέν τίς ἐστιν ἱστορικὸς ⟨ὁ δὲ θεωρητικὸς⟩ ὁ δὲ πολιτικός, φέρε θεασώμεθα εἰ καὶ τούτων εἰσὶν αἱ ἀρχαὶ παρ' αὐτῷ. ὁ μὲν δὴ ἱστορικός ἐστιν ὁ τῶν γεγονότων πραγμάτων ἔχων διήγησιν. πάσης δὲ διηγήσεως ἀφορμαὶ γίνονται πρόσωπον, [αἰτία,] τόπος, χρόνος, ⟨αἰτία,⟩ ὄργανον, πρᾶξις, πάθος, τρόπος, καὶ οὐδὲν ἔξω τούτων ἐν ἱστορίᾳ περιέχει οὐδεμία διήγησις. οὕτως ἔστι παρὰ τῷ ποιητῇ πολλὰ πράγματα ὡς γεγονότα ἢ ὄντα διηγουμένῳ, ἐνίοτε δὲ καὶ ἐν ἑκάστῳ τούτων διηγήσεις εὑρεῖν ἔστι.

75. προσώπου μέν, ὡς τὸ τοιόνδε·

ἦν δέ τις ἐν Τρώεσσι Δάρης ἀφνειός, ἀμύμων,

ἱρεὺς Ἡφαίστοιο, δύω δέ οἱ υἱέες ἤστην,

Φηγεὺς Ἰδαῖός τε, μάχης εὖ εἰδότε πάσης (Ε 9-11)

καὶ ἐν οἷς εἴδη τινῶν διαγράφει, ὡς ἐπὶ τοῦ Θερσίτου·

φολκὸς ἔην, χωλὸς δ' ἕτερον πόδα· τὼ δέ οἱ ὤμω

κυρτώ, ἐπὶ στῆθος συνοχωκότε· αὐτὰρ ὕπερθεν

φοξὸς ἔην κεφαλήν, ψεδνὴ δ' ἐπενήνοθε λάχνη (Β 217-9).

καὶ ἄλλα πολλά, ἐν οἷς ἢ γένος ἢ εἶδος ἢ τρόπον ἢ πρᾶξιν ἢ τύχην προσώπου διέξεισι πολλάκις, ὡς ἐν τούτοις·

Δάρδανον αὖ πρῶτον τέκετο νεφεληγερέτα Ζεύς (Υ 215).

74. Since the field of human discourse is divided into the historical, the theoretical, and the political, let us consider whether all of these may be found to have their origins in Homer. The historical is that which contains the narration of past events. The subjects of all narratives are character, place, time, cause, instrument, deed, impact, and manner, and no narrative contains within it any element beyond these.[1] The poet describes many things, both past and present, and numerous descriptions of every one of these elements are to be found.

75. He has descriptions of character, such as the following:

> There was a man named Dares among the Trojans, rich and famous,
> a priest of Hephaestus. He had two sons,
> Phegeus and Idaios, experienced in every sort of fighting
> [Il. 5.9-11].

Among these, he gives physical descriptions of some, as in the case of Thersites:

> He was lame, crippled in one foot, his shoulders
> humped and twisted over his chest. His head came
> to a point and his hair was thin
> [Il. 2.217-19].

There is a multitude of other places where he describes the type or physical characteristics or manners, deeds, or fortunes of a character, as in this:

> First, cloud-gathering Zeus begat Dardanus
> [Il. 20.215],

---

[1] This sort of classification of the elements of discourse (usually called "circumstances" [περιστάσεις]) is reminiscent of the "preliminary exercises" (προγυμνάσματα) that formed the first stage of rhetorical education, but it is admittedly difficult to understand just how the present classification contributes to the reader's understanding of Homer. Cf. Hermogenes "On Invention" (περὶ εὑρέσεως) 3.5 for a closely comparable list of the "circumstances." His six "circumstances" all occur here, but our author adds "instrument" and splits the "event" (πρᾶγμα) of Hermogenes into πρᾶξις, here translated "deed," and πάθος "impact," on which, see the following note.

καὶ τὰ ἑξῆς.

76. τόπου δὲ ἔστι παρ' αὐτῷ διήγησις, ὁποῖα περὶ τῆς νήσου τῆς γειτνιώσης τῇ τῶν Κυκλώπων λέγει, ἐν οἷς τὸ εἶδος τοῦ τόπου διαγράφει καὶ τὸ πηλίκον καὶ τὸ ποιὸν αὐτοῦ καὶ τὰ ἐν αὐτῷ καὶ τὰ παρ' αὐτῷ· καὶ περὶ τῶν παρακειμένων τῷ ἄντρῳ τῆς Καλυψοῦς

ὕλη δὲ σπέος ἀμφὶ πεφύκει τηλεθόωσα
κλήθρη τ' αἴγειρός τε καὶ εὐώδης κυπάρισσος (ε 63-4).
καὶ τὰ ἑξῆς. καὶ μυρία ἄλλα τοιαῦτα.

77. χρόνου δέ, οἷον
ἐννέα δὲ βεβάασι Διὸς μεγάλου ἐνιαυτοί (Β 134)
καὶ
χθιζά τε καὶ πρωίζ' ὅτ' ἐς Αὐλίδα νῆες Ἀχαιῶν
ἠγερέθοντο κακὰ Πριάμῳ καὶ Τρωσὶ φέρουσαι (Β 303-4).

78. αἰτίας δὲ ἐν οἷς ἐμφαίνει δι' ὃ γίνεταί τι ἢ γέγονεν, οἷά ἐστι τὰ ἐν ἀρχῇ τῆς Ἰλιάδος εἰρημένα

τίς τ' ἄρ σφωε θεῶν ἔριδι ξυνέηκε μάχεσθαι;
Λητοῦς καὶ Διὸς υἱός· ὁ γὰρ βασιλῆι χολωθεὶς
νοῦσον ἀνὰ στρατὸν ὦρσε κακήν· ὀλέκοντο δὲ λαοί·
οὕνεκα τὸν Χρύσην ἠτίμησ' ἀρητῆρα
Ἀτρεΐδης (Α 8-12)

καὶ τὰ ἑξῆς. ἐν γὰρ τούτοις λέγει τὰς αἰτίας τῆς μὲν Ἀχιλλέως καὶ Ἀγαμέμνονος διαφορᾶς τοῦ δὲ λοιμοῦ τὸν Ἀπόλλωνος χόλον, τοῦ δὲ χόλου τὴν ὕβριν τὴν εἰς

and so forth.

76.   He also has descriptions of place, as in what he says of the island next to that of the Cyclopes, where he describes the physical aspect of the place, its size and quality, and the things in it and nearby. He also says, concerning the things around the cave of Calypso,

> A rich, green wood lay about the cave,
> alder and poplar and sweet-smelling cypress
> [Od. 5.63-64],

and so forth—there are thousands of other examples.

77.   He has descriptions of time, such as;

> Nine of great Zeus' years have passed
> [Il. 2.134]

and

> Yesterday and the day before when the Greek ships
> were gathered at Aulis to bring evil upon Priam and the Trojans
> [Il. 2.303-04].

78.   There are passages such as that at the beginning of the *Iliad* in which he describes the causes why something happens or has happened:

> Which god set those two to angry fighting?
> The son of Zeus and Leto, for he was angered at the king
> and aroused an evil sickness in the camp, and the people were
>   dying,
> because the son of Atreus failed to honor Chryses,
> his priest   [Il. 1.8-12],

and the rest. Here he states the cause both of the dispute of Achilles and Agamemnon and of the plague, namely the wrath of Apollo—and

τὸν ἱερέα τοῦ δαίμονος.

79. ὀργάνου δὲ †τὴν διήγησιν ὁποίαν διέξεισι τῆς ἀσπίδος†, ἣν Ἥφαιστος Ἀχιλλεῖ κατεσκεύασε, καὶ ἄλλη σύντομος περὶ τοῦ Ἕκτορος δόρατος

>ἔνθ' Ἕκτωρ εἰσῆλθε Διῒ φίλος, ἐν δ' ἄρα χειρὶ
>ἔγχος ἔχ' ἑνδεκάπηχυ· πάροιθε δὲ λάμπετο δουρὸς
>αἰχμὴ χαλκείη, περὶ δὲ χρύσεος θέε πόρκης (Ζ 318-20).

80. πράξεως δὲ διηγήσεις εἶεν ἂν ἄλλαι τε καὶ αἱ τοιαίδε·

>οἱ δ' ὅτε δὴ ῥ' ἐς χῶρον ἕνα ξυνιόντες ἵκοντο,
>σύν ῥ' ἔβαλον ῥινούς, σὺν δ' ἔγχεα καὶ μένε' ἀνδρῶν
>χαλκεοθωρήκων· ἀτὰρ ἀσπίδες ὀμφαλόεσσαι
>ἔπληντ' ἀλλήλῃσι, πολὺς δ' ὀρυμαγδὸς ὀρώρει (Δ 446-9 = Θ 60-3).

81. πάθους δὲ διήγησίς ἐστιν ἐν ᾗ τὸ συμβαῖνον ἐξ αἰτίου ἢ ἐνεργείας σαφηνίζεται· ὁποῖά φησι περὶ τῶν ὑπὸ ὀργῆς ἢ φόβου ἢ λύπης κατεσχημένων ἢ τιτρωσκομένων ἢ ἀποκτιννυμένων ἢ ἄλλο τι τοιοῦτον πασχόντων. οἷον ἐξ αἰτίου μὲν

>ἀχνύμενος· μένεος δὲ μέγα φρένες ἀμφὶ μέλαιναι
>πίμπλαντ', ὄσσε δέ οἱ πυρὶ λαμπετόωντι ἐίκτην (Α 103-4 = δ 661-2),

ἐξ ἐνεργείας δὲ

>αἵματί οἱ δεύοντο κόμαι Χαρίτεσσιν ὁμοῖαι
>πλοχμοί θ', οἳ χρυσῷ τε καὶ ἀργύρῳ ἐσφήκωντο (Ρ 51-2).

the cause of this wrath, namely the offense against the priest of the god.

79. An example of how he describes instruments occurs in the description of the shield prepared by Hephaestus, another brief one in that of the spear of Hector:

> Hector dear-to-Zeus went forth with a fifteen-foot
> spear in his hand—the bronze point shone
> before him, and a golden ring ran around it
> [Il. 6.318-20].

80. There are, of course, many descriptions of deeds, including this sort:

> When these came together
> they crashed shields, crashed swords and rage of heroes
> armored in bronze. Bulging shields pressed
> on one another and a great din was stirred up
> [Il. 4.446-49 = 8.60-63].

81. Descriptions of impact [πάθος][1] occur when he displays what comes about as a result of some cause or action, as when he speaks of those who are gripped by anger or fear or pain, or of those who are wounded or killed or suffer something of the sort. First, from a cause:

> in a rage—his darkened mind was filled
> with anger and his eyes gleamed like fire
> [Il. 1.103-04 = Od. 4.661-62]—

and from an action:

> His hair like that of the Graces was wet with blood
> and his braids, bound with silver and gold
> [Il. 17.51-52].

---

[1] This category resists smooth translation. The term πάθος refers, properly, to anything that happens to, or affects, an individual. Thus emotion (in the first example) falls in the same category as a wound (in the second example).

82. ὁ δὲ τρόπος ἐστὶ ποιητικὸς πράξεως ἢ παθήματος ἢ σχέσεώς τινος, καθ' ἣν τὸ μὲν ὡδέ πῃ ἐνεργεῖ καὶ πάσχει, τὸ δὲ ὡδέ πως ἔχει, καὶ πάσῃ ἀκολουθεῖ τοιαύτη διηγήσει. παράδειγμα δὲ αὐτοῦ τὸ τοιόνδ' ἂν εἴη

 τὸν δ' Ὀδυσεὺς κατὰ λαιμὸν ἐπισχόμενος βάλεν ἰῷ·
 ἐκλίνθη δ' ἑτέρωσε, δέπας δέ οἱ ἔκπεσε χειρὸς
 βλημένου· αὐτίκα δ' αὐλὸς ἀνὰ ῥῖνας παχὺς ἦλθεν
 αἵματος ἀνδρομέοιο (χ 15, 17-9)

καὶ τὰ ἑξῆς.

83. ἔστι δὲ διήγησις παρ' αὐτῷ ὡς μέν ἐπὶ τὸ πλεῖστον πλατεῖαν φράσιν καὶ ἐξεργασίαν ἁρμόζουσαν τοῖς ὑποκειμένοις ἔχουσα. ἐνίοτε δὲ εὔτονος, ὡς ἡ τοιαύτη

 κεῖται Πάτροκλος, νέκυος δὲ δὴ ἀμφιμάχονται
 γυμνοῦ· ἀτὰρ τά γε τεύχε' ἔχει κορυθαίολος Ἕκτωρ (Σ 20-1).

τοῦτο δὲ τὸ εἶδος πολλάκις ἐστὶ χρήσιμον. τὸ γὰρ τάχος τῶν λόγων εὐτονώτερον καθίστησι καὶ τὸν λέγοντα καὶ τὸν ἀκροώμενον καὶ ῥᾳδίως τυγχάνει τοῦ προκειμένου.

84. διηγεῖται δὲ ποτὲ μὲν ψιλῶς, ποτὲ δὲ μετὰ εἰκόνος ἢ ὁμοιώσεως ἢ παραβολῆς, εἰκόνος μέν, ὡς ὅταν εἴπῃ

 ἡ δ' ἴεν ἐκ θαλάμοιο περίφρων Πηνελόπεια
 Ἀρτέμιδι ἰκέλη ἠὲ χρυσῇ Ἀφροδίτῃ (ρ 36-7 = τ 53-4),

ὁμοιώσεως δέ, οἷον

 αὐτὸς δὲ κτίλος ὣς ἐπιπωλεῖται στίχας ἀνδρῶν (Γ 196).

παραβολῆς δέ, ὅταν παραπλησίων πραγμάτων παράθεσιν ποιήσηται, ἔχουσαν ἀνταπόδοσιν τὴν ἀπὸ τοῦ προκειμένου διηγήματος. καὶ ἔστι παρ' αὐτῷ ποικίλα τὰ εἴδη τῶν παραβολῶν. συνεχῶς γὰρ καὶ πολυτρόπως παρατίθησι ταῖς τῶν

82. Manner is that which gives rise to an action or experience or condition, according to which a thing is acted upon and acts in a certain way, or is in a certain state. Homer pursues this sort of description everywhere. An example of this would be the following:

> Odysseus shot an arrow through his throat
> and he slumped to one side, his cup falling from his hand,
> as it hit him. Immediately a thick spurt of blood
> came from his nostril   [Od. 22.15, 17-19],

and so forth.

83. Descriptions in Homer generally employ more expansive diction and treatment, fitting the scope of the material, but sometimes there is terse description, as

> Patroclus lies dead and they fight around the naked
> corpse, while Hector of the crested helmet has the arms
>   [Il. 18.20-21].

This sort of style is often useful for its rapidity. It makes both speaker and listener more attentive and more easily gets to the point.

84. Sometimes he describes simply, sometimes with an image or comparison or illustration. For example, he uses an image when he says,

> Penelope came from the bedroom
> looking like Artemis or golden Aphrodite
>   [Od. 17.36-37 = 19.53-54],

a comparison, when he says,

> He went like a ram through the ranks of men
>   [Il. 3.196],

and an illustration, when he draws a comparison with some similar thing, substituting this for the description of the matter at hand. The modes of illustration in Homer are multiple and he continuously and in

ἀνθρώπων πράξεσι καὶ σχέσεσι ζῴων ἄλλων ἐνεργείας καὶ φύσεις.

85. καὶ ἔστι μὲν ὅτε ἀπὸ τῶν ἐλαχίστων ποιεῖται τὴν ὁμοίωσιν οὐ πρὸς τὸ μέγεθος τοῦ σώματος ἀλλὰ πρὸς τὴν φύσιν ἑκάστου ἀφορῶν· ὅθεν τὴν μὲν ἰταμότητα ἀπείκασε μυίᾳ

καί οἱ μυίης θάρσος ἐνὶ στήθεσσιν ἔθηκε (Ρ 570)
καὶ τὴν συνέχειαν τῷ αὐτῷ ζῴῳ
ἠύτε μυιάων ἁδινάων ἔθνεα πολλά (Β 469).
τὸν δὲ ἀθροισμὸν καὶ τὴν πολυπλήθειαν μετ' εὐταξίας μελίσσαις
ἠύτε ἔθνεα εἶσι μελισσάων ἁδινάων (Β 87).
οὕτω δὲ καὶ τὴν ὀργὴν καὶ τὴν δίωξιν ἔδειξεν εἰπὼν
σφήκεσσιν ἐοικότες ...
εἰνοδίοισι (Π 259-60)
καὶ ἔτι προσθεὶς
οὓς παῖδες ἐριδμαίνουσιν ἔθοντες (Π 260),
ἵνα μᾶλλον τὸ ἐκ φύσεως αὐτῶν θυμοειδὲς τῷ ἀπὸ τῶν παίδων ἐρεθισμῷ ἐπιτείνῃ. ἐπὶ δὲ συνεχοῦς φωνῆς φησιν
ἐσθλοί, τεττίγεσσιν ἐοικότες (Γ 151).
λαλίστατον γὰρ τὸ ζῷον καὶ ἄπαυστον ἐν τούτῳ.

86. τῶν δὲ ἀσυντάκτως φερομένων φωνὰς παμμιγεῖς οὕτως εἴκασεν·
ἠύτε περ κλαγγὴ γεράνων πέλει οὐρανόθι πρό (Γ 3).

various ways juxtaposes the actions and qualities of other creatures with the deeds and conditions of men.[1]

85.   He makes comparisons with very small animals which focus not on bodily size but on the specific nature of the creatures concerned. Hence the fly provides an image for boldness,

>   And she put in his breast the boldness of a fly
>   [Il. 17.570],

and for a great swarming,

>   As the many tribes of swirling flies
>   [Il. 2.469]

and bees provide an image for mustering, and for order in huge numbers,

>   As the tribes of bees go forth swarming
>   [Il. 2.87].

Thus he describes both rage and diligent pursuit when he says, "Like wayside wasps" and adds, "that little boys like to annoy" [Il. 16.259-60], in order to intensify their natural propensity to anger through the provocation by the boys. Referring to continuous talking, he speaks of "noble speakers, like cicadas" [Il. 3.151], for this is the most talkative of creatures and never stops.

86.   For the mingled shouting of men rushing along in a disorderly manner he used this image:

>   As the clamor of cranes descends from heaven
>   [Il. 3.3],

---

[1] As Clavier points out in a note, *ad loc.*, the author here distinguishes between two sorts of similes: those that mention first the element in the narrative to which a comparison is to be made and then the thing to which it is compared (the ὁμοίωσις, here translated "comparison"), and those where the outside element is first described and the point of comparison within the narrative identified only thereafter (the παραβολή, here translated "illustration").

τὰ δὲ εἰς τάξιν καθιστάμενα πλήθη τοῖς ⟨καθιπταμένοις⟩ ὀρνέοις ὁμοιοῖ
    κλαγγηδὸν προκαθιζόντων (Β 463),
τὴν δὲ ὀξύτητα τῆς τε ὄψεως καὶ τῆς πράξεως ποτὲ μὲν ἱέρακι παραβάλλει
    ὠκέι φασσοφόνῳ, ὅς τ' ὤκιστος πετεηνῶν (Ο 238),
ποτὲ δὲ ἀέτῳ
    ὅν τε καὶ ὑψόθ' ἐόντα πόδας ταχὺς οὐκ ἔλαθε πτώξ (Ρ 676).
παρίστησι γὰρ τὴν ὀξυδέρκειαν ἐν τῷ πόρρωθεν ἰδεῖν, τὸ δὲ τάχος ἐν τῷ ποδωκέστατον ζῷον ἑλεῖν. τὸν δὲ ἐκπλαγέντα πρὸς ὄψιν πολεμίου δράκοντος ὁράματι προσείκασεν, οὐκ ὀκνήσας οὐδὲ ἀπὸ τῶν ἑρπετῶν παραδείγματα λαβεῖν·
    ὡς δ' ὅτε τίς τε δράκοντα ἰδὼν παλίνορσος ἀπέστη (Γ 33),
ἀπὸ δὲ τῶν ἄλλων ζῴων δειλίας μὲν ἀπὸ τοῦ λαγωοῦ λαμβάνει καὶ ἀπὸ τῶν ἐλάφων ὁμοίως
    τίφθ' οὕτως ἔστητε τεθηπότες ἠύτε νεβροί (Δ 243);
κυνῶν δὲ ὁτὲ μὲν ἀλκήν
    ὡς δ' ὅτε καρχαρόδοντε δύω κύνε, εἰδότε θήρης (Κ 360),
ὁτὲ δὲ φιλοτεκνίαν
    ὡς δὲ κύων ἀμαλῇσι περὶ σκυλάκεσσι βεβῶσα (υ 14),

[Plutarch] 54B *The Essay on the Life and Poetry of Homer* 151

and he compares the orderly troops to winged flocks of birds,

> as they settle down noisily   [Il. 2.463],

and for sharpness of vision and swiftness of action he sometimes uses the illustration of a falcon,

> the swift one, the dovekiller, fastest of birds
> [Il. 15.238]

and sometimes that of an eagle,

> that the swift-footed hare does not escape, though he is high overhead   [Il. 17.676]

for he indicates the quality of keensightedness in the fact that the eagle spots his prey from far away, that of swiftness in his taking the swiftest of beasts. He compares a man stunned by the sight of an enemy to one seeing a snake, scorning not even the reptiles as sources of imagery:

> As when a man leaps back at the sight of a snake
> [Il. 3.33].

Among the other animals he uses rabbits and likewise deer for timidity:

> Why do you stand there trembling like fawns?
> [Il. 4.243],

dogs, sometimes for bravery:

> Like two dogs that love to bite, trained for the hunt
> [Il. 10.360],

and at times for love of offspring:

> like a bitch protecting her helpless puppies
> [Od. 20.14],

ὁτὲ δὲ προθυμίαν πρὸς τὸ φυλάσσειν

    ὡς δὲ κύνες περὶ μῆλα δυσωρήσωνται ἐν αὐλῇ (Κ 183).

87. ἁρπαγὴν δ' ἅμα θυμικῶς καὶ ἰταμῶς πρασσομένην λύκοις εἴκασεν·

    ὡς δὲ λύκοι ἄρνεσσιν ἐπέχραον ἢ ἐρίφοισι (Π 352).

τὸ δὲ ἄλκιμον καὶ ἄτρεπτον διά τε ἀγρίων συῶν καὶ παρδάλεων καὶ λεόντων ἔδειξε, μερίζων ἑκάστῳ τὸ πρὸς τὴν φύσιν οἰκεῖον· τῶν μὲν συῶν τὴν ὁρμήν, ἣν ἔχει πρὸς μάχην, ἀνυπόστατον ποιῶν

    Ἰδομενεὺς δ' ἄρ' ἐνὶ προμάχοις συῒ εἴκελος ἀλκὴν (Δ 253)·

τῶν δὲ παρδάλεων τὸ ἄπαυστον τῆς τόλμης

    ἀλλά τε καὶ περὶ δουρὶ πεπαρμένη οὐκ ἀπολήγει (Φ 577)·

λεόντων δὲ τὸ μέλλον μὲν εἰς τέλος δὲ γενναῖον

    οὐρῇ δὲ πλευράς τε καὶ ἰσχία ἀμφοτέρωθεν

    μαστίεται (Υ 170-1).

πάλιν δὲ παραβάλλει δρόμον ἀνδρὸς γενναίου ἵππῳ τροφῆς κεκορεσμένῳ

    ὡς δ' ὅτε τις στατὸς ἵππος ἀκοστήσας ἐπὶ φάτνῃ (Ζ 506 = Ο 263)

καὶ τοὐναντίον βραδεῖαν πορείαν, ἀήττητον ἐν τῷ καρτερεῖν, οὕτως ἔδειξεν·

    ὡς δ' ὅτ' ὄνος παρ' ἄρουραν ἰὼν ἐβιήσατο παῖδας (Λ 558).

σχῆμα δὲ βασίλειον καὶ ὑπερέχον ἐτύπωσε διὰ τούτων·

and sometimes for diligence at keeping watch:

> As dogs keep painful watch over flocks in the pen
> [Il. 10.183].

87. He uses the image of wolves for angry, rash rapaciousness:

> As wolves fall on lambs or little goats
> [Il. 16.352].

He describes boldness and unflinchingness by means of the images of wild boars and leopards and lions, giving each the specific quality natural to it and depicting the irresistible lust for battle of the boar,

> and Idomeneus, like a boar in strength, fought among the first
> [Il. 4.253],

the fierce stamina of the leopard,

> but he does not give up, even when run through by the spear
> [Il. 21.577],

the slowness to wrath and then the noble bravery of the lion,

> He swishes his tail around his sides and flanks
> on both sides [Il. 20.170-71].

Again, he illustrates the gait of a noble warrior through a horse sated with grain,

> as when a tied horse has filled himself at the manger
> [Il. 6.506 = 15.263],

and on the contrary, for one who is slow but insuperable in his endurance, he uses this description:

> as when an ass going through the cropland is attacked by boys
> [Il. 11.558],

and he characterizes a noble and outstanding figure thus:

ἠΰτε βοῦς ἀγέληφι μέγ' ἔξοχος ἔπλετο πάντων (Β 480).

88. οὐκ ἀπέλιπε δὲ οὐδὲ τὰς τῶν θαλασσίων ζῴων ὁμοιότητας, πολύποδος μὲν τὸ παράμονον καὶ δυσαπόσπαστον τῶν πετρῶν

ὡς δ' ὅτε πουλύποδος θαλάμης ἐξελκομένοιο (ε 432),

δελφῖνος δὲ τὸ ἡγεμονικὸν καὶ κρατιστεῦον τῶν ἄλλων

ὡς δ' ὑπὸ δελφῖνος μεγακήτεος ἰχθύες ἄλλοι (Φ 22).

89. πολλάκις δὲ τὰ ὑπὸ ἀνθρώπων πρασσόμενα ἄλλαις ὁμοίαις πράξεσι παραβάλλει, ὥσπερ ἐν τούτῳ

οἱ δ', ὥς τ' ἀμητῆρες ἐναντίοι ἀλλήλοισι (Λ 67),

τὴν ἔνστασιν καὶ καρτερίαν δεικνύων τῶν ἀνδρῶν. τῷ δὲ ἀγεννῶς δακρύοντι ὀνειδίζει μετ' ἐναργοῦς ὁμοιώσεως

τίπτε δεδάκρυσαι, Πατρόκλεις, ἠΰτε κούρη

νηπίη (Π 7-8);

90. ἐτόλμησε δὲ καὶ τοῖς στοιχείοις παραβαλεῖν πράξεις ἀνθρωπίνας, ὡς ἐν τούτῳ·

ὣς ἔφατ'. Ἀργεῖοι δὲ μέγ' ἴαχον, ὡς ὅτε κῦμα

ἀκτῇ ἐφ' ὑψηλῇ, ὅτε κινήσῃ Νότος ἐλθὼν

προβλῆτι σκοπέλῳ· τὸν δ' οὔ ποτε κύματα λείπει

παντοίων ἀνέμων, ὅτ' ἂν ἔνθ' ἢ ἔνθα γένωνται (Β 394-7).

[Plutarch] 54B The Essay on the Life and Poetry of Homer 155

> Like the bull in the herd, he was far the most remarkable of all
> [Il. 2.480].

88.   He did not fail to use sea creatures for comparisons. With respect to the octopus, he exploits his perseverance and the difficulty of getting him free of the rocks:

> drawn forth like an octopus from his bed
> [Od. 5.432],

and of the dolphin, his dominance and supremacy over the others:

> as all the other fishes pursued by the dolphin of the deep
> [Il. 21.22].

89.   Often he compares human actions to one another as in this:

> like reapers, one opposite the other
> [Il. 11.67]

showing the stamina and endurance of the heroes. With an enlightening comparison he rebukes a man who is weeping in a cowardly manner:

> Why are you weeping, Patroclus, like a little girl? [Il. 16.7-8].

90.   He was also bold to use the natural elements to illustrate human actions, as in

> So he spoke, and the Greeks gave a great shout, as when a wave
> crashes on a high cliff, when the south wind comes,
> a jutting headland—the waves never leave it in peace
> no matter which wind blows, from whatever side
> [Il. 2.394-97],

ἐν οἷς δῆλός ἐστι καὶ ὑπερβολῇ καὶ αὐξήσει κεχρημένος. οὐ γὰρ ἤρκεσε κύματος ἤχῳ τὴν κραυγὴν ἀπεικάσαι, ἀλλὰ τῶν προσφερομένων ἀκτῇ ἐφ' ὑψηλῇ, ὅπου μετεωριζόμενον τὸ κῦμα μείζονα ἦχον ἀποτελεῖ· καὶ οὐχ ἁπλῶς κῦμα, ἀλλὰ τὸ κινηθὲν ἀπὸ Νότου, τοῦ μάλιστα τὰ ὑγρὰ κινοῦντος· καὶ ἐπὶ σκοπέλῳ προβλῆτι, τῷ ἀνατεταμένῳ εἰς τὸ πέλαγος καὶ περικλυζομένῳ ὑπ' αὐτοῦ, ὃς καὶ ἀδιάλειπτον ἔχει τὸν κλύδωνα, ὁπόθεν ἂν προσπίπτωσιν οἱ πνέοντες ἄνεμοι. τοιαῦτα μέν ἐστι τὰ τῆς ἐν τῷ διηγεῖσθαι ἐξεργασίας παρ' αὐτῷ· ἅπερ ἔνεστι καὶ ἐπὶ τῶν πολλῶν κατανοεῖν ἐκ τῶν ὀλίγων παραδειγμάτων.

91. σκεψώμεθα δὲ καὶ τὰ λοιπὰ εἴδη τῶν λόγων, εἰ ἔστι παρὰ τῷ Ὁμήρῳ πρώτῳ καὶ τὰς ἐννοίας αὐτῶν λαβόντι καὶ ἐναργῶς κατασκευάσαντι. ὁμοίως ὀλίγα παραδείγματα παρατεθέντα καὶ τὰ ἄλλα νοεῖν παρασκευάσει.

92. ὁ δὲ θεωρητικὸς λόγος ἐστὶν ὁ περιέχων τὰ καλούμενα θεωρήματα, ἅπερ ἐστὶ γνῶσις τῆς ἀληθείας γινομένη μετὰ τέχνης, ἀφ' ὧν ἔστι τὴν φύσιν τῶν ὄντων, θείων τε καὶ ἀνθρωπίνων πραγμάτων, κατανοεῖν, καὶ τὰς περὶ τὸ ἦθος ἀρετὰς καὶ κακίας διαιρεῖν, καὶ εἴ τινι τέχνῃ λογικῇ μετέρχεσθαι τὴν ἀλήθειαν προσήκει, μανθάνειν. ταῦτα δὲ μετεχειρίσαντο οἱ ἐν φιλοσοφίᾳ διατρίψαντες, ἧς ἐστι μέρη τὸ φυσικὸν καὶ ἠθικὸν καὶ διαλεκτικόν. ἐν δὴ πᾶσι τούτοις τὰς ἀρχὰς καὶ τὰ σπέρματα ἐνδιδόντα Ὅμηρον εἰ καταμάθοιμεν, πῶς οὐκ ἂν εἴη πρὸ πάντων θαυμάζεσθαι ἄξιος; εἰ δὲ δι' αἰνιγμάτων καὶ μυθικῶν λόγων τινῶν ἐμφαίνεται τὰ νοήματα, οὐ χρὴ παράδοξον ἡγεῖσθαι· τούτου γὰρ αἴτιον ⟨ἡ⟩ ποιητικὴ καὶ ⟨τὸ⟩ τῶν ἀρχαίων ἦθος, ὅπως οἱ μὲν φιλομαθοῦντες μετά τινος εὐμουσίας ψυχαγωγούμενοι ῥᾶον ζητῶσί τε καὶ εὑρίσκωσι τὴν ἀλήθειαν, οἱ δὲ ἀμαθεῖς μὴ καταφρονῶσι τούτων ὧν οὐ δύνανται συνιέναι. καὶ γάρ ἐστί πως τὸ μὲν δι' ὑπονοίας σημαινόμενον ἀγωγόν, τὸ δὲ φανερῶς λεγόμενον εὐτελές.

[Plutarch] 54B *The Essay on the Life and Poetry of Homer*

where he has clearly used hyperbole[1] in combination with amplification. It was not enough to compare the shout to the noise of a wave but he went on to talk of waves crashing "on a high cliff," where the wave is lifted up and the noise becomes even louder—and not just any wave, but specifically a wave driven by the South Wind, which moves the most water, and upon a "jutting headland," that cuts into the sea and is surrounded by it so that the roar is constant, from whichever side the winds blow. This is the sort of care he takes with his descriptions, and these few examples will give an indication of the many others.

91. Let us also consider the remaining modes of discourse and whether it is clear that they were first thought up and developed by Homer. Here, likewise, a few examples set side by side will make it possible to get an idea of the rest.

92. Theoretical discourse[2] is that which concerns objects of speculation, which is to say, the knowledge of the truth acquired systematically. This is the road to understanding the nature of reality and of divine and human matters, to distinguishing on the ethical plane those things which are good and those which are bad, and to learning any rule of reasoning appropriate for reaching the truth. These things have been handled by those who have studied philosophy, which includes physics, ethics, and dialectic. Indeed, if we should find that Homer provides the beginnings and seeds of all of these, how then would he not deserve the greatest admiration? And if he reveals these ideas through enigmatic and mythic language, this should not be unexpected, for the reason is the nature of poetry and the custom of the ancients. They did this so that lovers of learning, delighted by a certain elegance, might more easily seek and find the truth, while the ignorant would not scorn what they could not understand. That which is signified through hidden meanings may be attractive where that which is said explicitly is of little value.[3]

---

[1] See ch. 71, above.
[2] On the doxographic portion of the essay, see Diels (1879 = Dox Gr), 88-99.
[3] This programmatic statement may be compared with Plato, *Protagoras* 316D and Proclus In Rep. 1.44.14. See Lamberton (1986), 41, 185.

93. ἀρξώμεθα τοίνυν ἀπὸ τῆς τοῦ παντὸς ἀρχῆς καὶ γενέσεως, ἣν Θαλῆς ὁ Μιλήσιος (cf. 11 A 12 D-K) εἰς τὴν τοῦ ὕδατος οὐσίαν ἀναφέρει καὶ θεασώμεθα εἰ πρῶτος Ὅμηρος τοῦθ᾽ ὑπέλαβεν, εἰπὼν

Ὠκεανός θ᾽ ὅς περ γένεσις πάντεσσι τέτυκται (Ξ 246).

μετ᾽ ἐκεῖνον δὲ Ξενοφάνης ὁ Κολοφώνιος (cf. 21 B 33 D-K), ὑφιστάμενος τὰς πρώτας ἀρχὰς εἶναι τὸ ὕδωρ καὶ τὴν γῆν, ἔοικε σπάσαι τὴν ἀφορμὴν ταύτην ἐκ τῶν Ὁμηρικῶν τούτων·

ἀλλ᾽ ὑμεῖς μὲν πάντες ὕδωρ καὶ γαῖα γένοισθε (Η 99).

σημαίνει γὰρ τὴν ἀνάλυσιν εἰς τὰ γεννητικὰ στοιχεῖα τοῦ παντός. ἡ δὲ μάλιστα ἀληθὴς δόξα τέσσαρα στοιχεῖα συνίστησι, πῦρ, ἀέρα, ὕδωρ, γῆν. ταῦτα δὲ καὶ Ὅμηρος εἰδὼς φαίνεται, μνημονεύων ἐν πολλοῖς αὐτῶν ἑκάστου.

94. καὶ τὴν τάξιν δὲ αὐτῶν ὅπως ἔχει κατέμαθεν. ὅτι μὲν γὰρ ἡ γῆ κατωτάτω πάντων ἐστί, θεασώμεθα· σφαιροειδοῦς γὰρ ὄντος τοῦ κόσμου, ὁ μὲν περιέχων τὰ πάντα οὐρανὸς τὸν ἄνω τόπον ἐπέχειν εἰκότως λέγοιτ᾽ ἄν, ἡ δὲ γῆ, ἐν μέσῳ οὖσα πανταχόθεν, κατωτέρω τοῦ περιέχοντός ἐστι. τοῦτο δὴ ὁ ποιητὴς ἐν τούτοις μάλιστα δηλοῖ, ἐν οἷς φησιν ὁ Ζεύς, ⟨εἰ⟩ ἀπὸ τοῦ Ὀλύμπου σειρὰν ἀνάψαιτο, τὴν γῆν καὶ τὴν θάλασσαν ἀνασπάσειν, ὡς πάντα μετέωρα γενέσθαι

ἀλλ᾽ ὅτε κεν καὶ ἐγὼ πρόφρων ἐθέλοιμι ἐρύσσαι
αὐτῇ κεν γαίῃ ἐρύσαιμ᾽ αὐτῇ τε θαλάσσῃ·
σειρὴν μέν κεν ἔπειτα περὶ ῥίον Οὐλύμποιο
δησαίμην, τὰ δέ κ᾽ αὖθι μετήορα πάντα γένοιτο (Θ 23-6).

93. Let us begin therefore from the first principle and beginning of all things,[1] which Thales the Milesian [fr. A12 DK] traces to water. And let us consider whether Homer first took this position, when he said,[2]

> and Okeanos who gave birth to all things
> [Il. 14.246].

After Thales, Xenophanes of Colophon [fr. B33 DK], claiming that the first principles are water and earth, seems to have gotten that idea from this verse of Homer:

> but may you all become water and earth
> [Il 7.99],

for he refers here to the dissolution of the universe into the elements that produced it. The truest doctrine establishes four elements, fire, mist, water, and earth, and Homer clearly knew this as well, since he mentions each of these in many places.

94. Moreover, he had learned their true order.[3] We shall see that the earth is the lowest of all, for since the cosmos is spherical, heaven, which surrounds it all, might appropriately be said to have the highest place, and the earth, being in the center and equidistant from it all around, is below that which surrounds it. The poet makes this very clear in the verses where Zeus says that if he should hang a chain from Olympus, he would draw up the earth and the sea, so that they would be suspended:

> But if I should take it into my head to pull,
> I'd haul up the earth and the sea themselves
> and tie the chain around the peak of Olympus
> and all those things would be suspended there
> [Il. 8.23-26].

---

[1] The section on physics (93-111) is especially rich in material that appears as well in the scholia. See above, "Introduction," 19-21, with **n.** 61.
[2] Diels (Dox Gr, 93-94) notes that Stobaeus (1.10.2 and 6) makes similar use of these two citations and echoes our text on the significance of the latter.
[3] See Heraclitus, *Homeric Allegories* 40 on the golden chain of Il. 15.18-20 (below, ch. 97), as well as Lévêque (1959).

95. ὑπὲρ δὲ γῆς ὄντος τοῦ ἀέρος, τὸν αἰθέρα ὑψηλότερον εἶναί φησιν οὕτως

εἰς ἐλάτην ἀναβὰς περιμήκετον, ἣ τότ' ἐν Ἴδῃ
ἀκροτάτῃ πεφυυῖα δι' ἠέρος αἰθέρ' ἵκανε (Ξ 287-8),
τοῦ δὲ αἰθέρος ἀνωτέρω τὸν οὐρανὸν

ὣς οἱ μὲν μάρναντο· σιδήρειος δ' ὀρυμαγδὸς
χάλκεον οὐρανὸν ἷκε δι' αἰθέρος ἀτρυγέτοιο (Ρ 424-5)
καὶ ἔτι ἐν τούτοις·

ἠερίη δ' ἀνέβη μέγαν οὐρανὸν Οὔλυμπόν τε (Α 497).
τὸ γὰρ καθαρώτερον τοῦ ἀέρος, ἀνωτάτω ὄν, καὶ τὸ μάλιστα ἀπέχον τῆς γῆς καὶ τῶν ἐξ αὐτῆς ἀναθυμιάσεων ὡς ὅλον λαμπρὸν φασιν Ὄλυμπον προσηγορεῦσθαι.

96. ἐν οἷς δέ φησιν ὁ ποιητὴς συνοικεῖν τῷ Διὶ τὴν Ἥραν οὖσαν ἀδελφὴν δοκεῖ ταῦτα ἀλληγορεῖσθαι, ὅτι Ἥρα μὲν νοεῖται ὁ ἀήρ, ἥπερ ἐστὶν ὑγρὰ οὐσία, διὸ καὶ λέγει

ἠέρα δ' Ἥρη
πίτνα πρόσθε βαθεῖαν (Φ 6-7).
Ζεὺς δὲ ὁ αἰθήρ, τουτέστιν ἡ πυρώδης καὶ ἔνθερμος οὐσία·

Ζεὺς δ' ἔλαχ' οὐρανὸν εὐρὺν ἐν αἰθέρι καὶ νεφέλῃσιν (Ο 192).

95.[1] Given that mist lies above earth, he says here that the *aither* is higher yet:

> Climbing a massive fir, which then grew on the peak
> of Ida and passed through the mist into the *aither*
> [Il. 14.287-88],

and here that heaven is above the *aither*:

> So they fought, and the iron din
> came to bronze heaven through the barren *aither*
> [Il. 17.424-25],

and again in this:

> Through the mist[2] she went up to great heaven and Olympus
> [Il. 1.497],

for they say the purest and highest mist and the furthest from the earth and its exhalations is called "Olympus," since it is "all radiant" [ὅλον λαμπρόν].

96. In the lines in which the poet says Hera, Zeus' sister, cohabits with him, he seems to be allegorizing as follows: that Hera ["Ηρη] represents "mist" [ἀήρ][3]—the damp substance—and so he says,

> Hera spread deep mist
> before them [Il. 21.6-7],

and Zeus represents the *aither*, the fiery, hot substance:[4]

> Zeus' portion was wide heaven in the *aither* and clouds
> [Il. 15.192].

---

[1] Stobaeus 1.22.2 echoes the whole of this chapter (Dox Gr, 95-96).
[2] The author takes ἠερίη to be derived from ἀήρ, and hence to mean "misty" or possibly (as here translated) "through the mist," but it is certainly a temporal adjective (cf. ἦρι) meaning "early in the morning."
[3] A commonplace. See e.g. Heraclitus, *Homeric Allegories* 40.3.
[4] Another commonplace. See Heraclitus, *Homeric Allegories* 36, 40.

ἀδελφοὶ μὲν οὖν ἔδοξαν διὰ τὴν συνάφειαν καὶ τὴν κατά τι ὁμοιότητα ὅτι ἄμφω κοῦφοι καὶ κινούμενοι· σύνοικοι δὲ καὶ ὁμόλεκτροι, ὅτι ἐξ αὐτῶν συνιόντων γεννᾶται τὰ πάντα· διὸ καὶ ἐν τῇ Ἴδῃ συνέρχονται καὶ ἡ γῆ αὐτοῖς φύει τὰς πόας καὶ τά ἄνθη.

97. τοῦ δὲ αὐτοῦ λόγου ἔχεται κἀκεῖνα, ἐν οἷς φησιν ὁ Ζεὺς κρέμασθαι τὴν Ἥραν καὶ ἐξάπτεσθαι τῶν ποδῶν αὐτῆς ἄκμονας δύο, τουτέστι τὴν γῆν καὶ τὴν θάλασσαν. μάλιστα δὲ ἐν ἐκείνοις ἐξεργάζεται τὸν περὶ στοιχείων λόγον. δι᾽ ὧν ὁ Ποσειδῶν λέγει αὐτῷ

τρεῖς γάρ τοι Κρόνου εἰμὲν ἀδελφεοί, οὓς τέκε Ῥέα
Ζεὺς καὶ ἐγώ, τρίτατος δ᾽ Ἀίδης ἐνέροισιν ἀνάσσων (Ο 187-8)

καί

τριχθὰ δὲ πάντα δέδασται, ἕκαστος δ᾽ ἔμμορε τιμῆς (Ο 189),

καὶ ὅτι ἐν τῇ τοῦ παντὸς νομῇ Ζεὺς μὲν ἔλαχε τὴν τοῦ πυρὸς οὐσίαν, Ποσειδῶν δὲ τὴν τοῦ ὕδατος, Ἅιδης δὲ τὴν τοῦ ἀέρος· τοῦτον γὰρ λέγει ζόφον ἠερόεντα (Μ 240 al.), ἐπειδὴ φῶς οἰκεῖον οὐκ ἔχει, ἀλλ᾽ ὑπὸ ἡλίου καὶ σελήνης καὶ τῶν ἄλλων ἄστρων καταλάμπεται.

98. τετάρτη δὲ κατελείφθη καὶ κοινὴ πάντων ἡ γῆ. ἡ μὲν γὰρ τῶν τριῶν στοιχείων οὐσία κινεῖται ἀεί, μόνη δὲ ἀκίνητος ἡ γῆ μένει, ᾗ καὶ τὸν Ὄλυμπον προσέθηκεν· εἰ μὲν γὰρ ὄρος ἐστίν, ὡς μέρος τῆς γῆς, εἰ δὲ τοῦ οὐρανοῦ τὸ λαμπρότατον καὶ καθαρώτατον, ὡς καὶ ταύτης οὔσης ἐν τοῖς στοιχείοις πέμπτης οὐσίας, ὅπερ ᾠήθησάν τινες τῶν ἐνδόξων φιλοσόφων. ὥστε κατὰ τὸ εἰκὸς κοινὰ ὑπέθετο εἶναι, τήν τε γῆν κατωτάτω διὰ βαρύτητα, καὶ τὸν Ὄλυμπον ἀνωτάτω ὄντα διὰ κουφότητα, ὅτι εἰς ταῦτα αἱ μεταξὺ φύσεις πῇ μὲν

They seemed on the one hand brother and sister on account of the connection and a certain similarity between these elements, in that they are both light and mobile, and on the other hand they seemed sharers of home and bed because all things come to be from their union. This is why, when they come together on Ida, the earth also produces grass and flowers for them.

97. The same idea is contained in the verses where Zeus says he hung Hera up and attached two anvils to her feet—that is, the earth and the sea. Homer develops the idea of the elements most fully in the passage where Poseidon says to Zeus,[1]

> There are three of us brothers born of Kronos and Rhea—
> Zeus and I, and third there is Hades who rules over those below
> [Il. 15.187-88],

and

> The universe was divided in three and each had his share of honor   [Il. 15.189],

and says that in the distribution of the universe Zeus received the element fire, Poseidon, water and Hades, the mist, for he calls his portion "misty gloom" [ζόφον ἠερόεντα] since it has no light of its own but is lit by the sun and moon and the other stars.

98. The fourth, earth, is left over, and is common to all three. It is the nature of the first three elements to move continually and only the earth—to which the poet adds Olympus—remains motionless. For if Olympus is a mountain, it is therefore part of the earth, but if it is the most radiant and pure portion of heaven, then it is a fifth essence among the elements, which indeed has been the opinion of certain famous philosophers.[2] Thus he took it to be appropriate for these to be shared: the earth, which is lowest because of its weight, and Olympus,

---

[1] In fact, Poseidon is speaking to Iris. Diels (Dox Gr, 89-90) pointed out the resemblance of the following treatment of the elements to Heraclitus, *Homeric Allegories* 41 on the same passage. See Buffière's remarks *ad loc.* in his edition of Heraclitus (Buffière [1962], 50, with n. 3).

[2] Compare [Aristotle] *On the Universe* 400a.

καταφέρονται, πῇ δὲ ἀναφέρονται.

99. τῆς δὲ τῶν στοιχείων φύσεως ἐξ ἐναντίων συνεστώσης, ξηρότητός τε καὶ ὑγρότητος καὶ θερμότητος καὶ ψυχρότητος, ὑπὸ δὲ τῆς πρὸς ἄλληλα ἀναλογίας καὶ κράσεως ἐναπεργαζομένης τὸ πᾶν καὶ μεταβολὰς μὲν μερικὰς ὑπομενούσης τοῦ δὲ παντὸς λύσιν μὴ ἐπιδεχομένης, Ἐμπεδοκλῆς (fr. 31 B 17.7-8 D-K) ἔφη τὰ ὅλα συνεστάναι οὕτως·

ἄλλοτε μὲν φιλότητι συνερχόμεν' εἰς ἓν ἅπαντα
ἄλλοτε δ' αὖθις ἕκαστα φορούμενα νείκεος ἄχθει,
τὴν μὲν συμφωνίαν καὶ ἕνωσιν τῶν στοιχείων φιλίαν προσαγορεύσας, νεῖκος δὲ τὴν ἐναντίωσιν.

100. πρὸ δὲ τούτου Ὅμηρος τὴν φιλίαν καὶ τὸ νεῖκος ἐκείνοις αἰνίσσεται, ἐν οἷς φησιν ἡ Ἥρα παρ' αὐτῷ·

εἶμι γὰρ ὀψομένη πολυφόρβου πείρατα γαίης,
Ὠκεανόν τε, θεῶν γένεσιν, καὶ μητέρα Τηθύν,
τοὺς εἶμ' ὀψομένη, καί σφ' ἄκριτα νείκεα λύσω (Ξ 200-1, 205).

101. τοιοῦτον δέ τι καὶ τὴν Ἀφροδίτην καὶ τὸν Ἄρην ὁ μῦθος αἰνίσσεται, τῆς μὲν ταὐτὸ δυναμένης ὃ παρὰ τῷ Ἐμπεδοκλεῖ ἡ φιλία, τοῦ δὲ ὃ παρ' ἐκείνῳ τὸ νεῖκος. ὅθεν ποτὲ μὲν σύνεισιν ἀλλήλοις, ποτὲ δὲ διαλύονται· ἐλέγχει δὲ αὐτοὺς Ἥλιος. καὶ δεσμεῖ μὲν αὐτοὺς Ἥφαιστος, λύει δὲ Ποσειδῶν. ἐν οἷς δῆλόν ἐστιν ὅτι ἡ ἔνθερμος καὶ ἡ ξηρὰ οὐσία καὶ ἡ ταύτῃ ἐναντία, ἡ ψυχρά τε καὶ ὑγρά, ποτὲ μὲν συνάγουσι τὰ πάντα, ποτὲ δὲ λύουσιν.

102. ἀκολουθεῖ δὲ τούτοις καὶ τὸ παρὰ τοῖς ἄλλοις ποιηταῖς εἰρημένον, ὅτι ἐκ τῆς Ἄρεως καὶ Ἀφροδίτης συνουσίας Ἁρμονία συνέστηκεν,

which is highest because of its lightness, since the intermediate elements are suspended above the one and below the other.

99.[1] Since the nature of the elements emerges from opposites (dryness and wetness, heat and cold), and this nature generates the universe by the correspondences and minglings of the elements and tolerates partial change but does not allow the dissolution of the universe, Empedocles said that the universe was constituted thus:

> They all at one time come together into one through love
> and at another are polarized by the hostility of strife
> [fr. B17.7-8 DK],

calling the harmony and unity of the elements "love" and their opposition "strife."

100. But before Empedocles, Homer hinted at "love and strife" in what he has Hera say:

> I am going to the limits of the fruitful earth,
> to see Okeanos, begetter of gods, and mother Tethys.
> I am going to see them and I shall end their continual strife
> [Il. 14.200-01, 205].

101. The myth hints at something similar in Ares and Aphrodite,[2] for she has the same force as what Empedocles calls "love" and Ares, what the philosopher calls "strife." This is why they sometimes come together and are sometimes separated—but the sun denounces them, Hephaestus chains them, and Poseidon frees them. In these verses it is clear that the hot, dry essence and its opposite, the cold wet one, sometimes draw the universe together and sometimes pull it apart.

102. What the other poets have said takes its lead from these verses—that Harmony comes from the mating of Ares and Aphrodite,[3]

---

[1] Chs. 99 and 100 are found nearly verbatim in Stobaeus 1.10.11b. (Dox Gr, 88-89).
[2] Cf. Heraclitus, *Homeric Allegories*, 69.
[3] For this claim in the context of a demonstration that Homer here "confirms the Empedoclean theory" of the role of love and strife, see Heraclitus, *Homeric Allegories*, 69.10.

ἐξ ἐναντίων, βαρέων τε καὶ ὀξέων, κιρναμένων ἀλλήλοις ἀναλόγως. ὅπως δὲ ἀντίκειται ἀλλήλοις τὰ τῆς ἐναντίας φύσεως τετυχηκότα, αἰνίττεσθαι ἔοικεν ὁ ποιητὴς καὶ ἐν τῇ παράταξει τῶν θεῶν, ἐν ᾗ πεποίηκε τοὺς μὲν τοῖς Ἕλλησι, τοὺς δὲ τοῖς Τρωσὶ βοηθοῦντας, ἀλληγορικῶς ἐμφαίνων τὰς δυνάμεις ἑκάστου· καὶ τὸν μὲν Φοῖβον τῷ Ποσειδῶνι ἀντιτάσσει, τὸ θερμὸν καὶ ξηρὸν τῷ ὑγρῷ καὶ ψυχρῷ· τὴν δὲ Ἀθηνᾶν τῷ Ἄρει, τὸ λογιστικὸν τῷ ἀλογίστῳ, τουτέστιν τὸ ἀγαθὸν τῷ κακῷ, τὴν δὲ Ἥραν τῇ Ἀρτέμιδι, τὸν ἀέρα τῇ σελήνῃ, ὅτι ὁ μὲν σταθερός, ἡ δὲ πολυκίνητος· τὸν δὲ Ἑρμῆν τῇ Λητοῖ, ὅτι ὁ μὲν λόγος ἀεὶ ζητεῖ καὶ μέμνηται, ἡ δὲ λήθη τούτῳ ἐστὶν ἐναντίον· τὸν δέ Ἥφαιστον τῷ ποταμῷ κατὰ τὸν αὐτὸν λόγον, καθ' ὃν τὸν ἥλιον τῇ θαλάσσῃ· θεατὴν δὲ τῆς μάχης τὸν πρῶτον θεὸν καὶ ἐπὶ τούτῳ γεγηθότα.

103. ἐκ δὲ τῶν προειρημένων ἅμα καὶ τοῦτο ὑποδεικνὺς Ὅμηρος φαίνεται, ὅτι εἷς ἐστιν ὁ κόσμος καὶ πεπερασμένος. εἰ γὰρ ἄπειρος ἦν, οὐκ ἂν εἰς ἀριθμὸν πέρας ἔχοντα διῃρεῖτο. καὶ ἐν τῷ ὀνόματι σημαίνει τὸ † σιωπᾶν †, ὡς καὶ ἐν ἄλλοις πολλοῖς χρῆται ἀντὶ τοῦ ἑνικοῦ τῷ πληθυντικῷ. σαφέστερον δὲ τὸ αὐτὸ δηλοῖ ἐν τῷ εἰπεῖν πείρατα γαίης (Ξ 200 al.), καὶ πάλιν
ἐν οἷς φησιν
οὐδ' εἴ κε τὰ νείατα πείραθ' ἵκηται
γαίης καὶ [πάλιν ἐν οἷς] πόντοιο (Θ 478-9)
καὶ ἐν τῷ
ἀκροτάτῃ κορυφῇ πολυδειράδος Οὐλύμποιο (Α 499 = Θ 3).

that is, harmony of opposites: the ponderous and the swift mixed proportionately together. The poet seems, in the division of the gods into those who help the Greeks and those who help the Trojans, to hint at the manner in which things possessing opposite natures oppose one another, and he reveals their various powers allegorically.[1] He sets Apollo against Poseidon, hot and dry against wet and cold; Athena against Ares, rational against irrational (that is, good against evil); Hera against Artemis, mist against the moon (also because the one is stationary, the other very mobile); Hermes against Leto, because reason is always inquiring and remembering, and forgetfulness [λήθη] is the opposite of this; Hephaestus against the river for the same reason as the sun against the sea. He also makes the first god a spectator of the battle, taking pleasure in it.

103. From what has been said, it is likewise clear that Homer is tacitly indicating that the universe is one and finite.[2] For if it were infinite, it would not be susceptible to analysis into a finite number of parts. The plural πάντα ["all"] is used to indicate the universe,[3] just as in many other situations he uses the plural for the singular. He shows this still more clearly when he says, "limits of the earth" [Il. 14.200, etc.] and again when he says,

> Not if he should come to the nether limits
> of earth and sea   [Il. 8.478-79]

and in

> On the highest peak of many-ridged Olympus
>   [Il. 1.499 = 8.3],

---

[1] See Heraclitus, *Homeric Allegories*, 52-58 and Proclus In Rep., 1.87-90 on the theomachy in the *Iliad* and the various allegorical interpretations current in the imperial period. Cf. Lamberton (1986), esp. 216-21.

[2] What is attributed to Homer here is in general the Aristotelian position, in contrast to that of the Epicureans, who postulated an infinite universe of matter (or atoms and void) with multiple κόσμοι scattered through it. The passage is echoed in Stobaeus, 1.21.4.

[3] The text is corrupt. Our translation follows the solution of Bernardakis ad loc., who supplied πάντα from Il. 15.189, observing that this verse (cited in ch. 97, above) seems to be explained here. Bernardakis also reviews the solutions of Wyttenbach and Dübner.

ὅπου γάρ ἐστιν ἀκρότης, ἐκεῖ καὶ πέρας.

104. ὅπως δὲ καὶ περὶ Ἡλίου γινώσκει, οὐκ ἄδηλον· ὅτι κυκλοφορικὴν ἔχων δύναμιν ποτὲ μὲν ὑπὲρ γαίης φαίνεται αὖθις δὲ ὑπὸ γῆν ἄπεισι, καὶ τοῦτο δῆλον ποιεῖ λέγων

ὦ φίλοι, οὐ γάρ τ' ἴδμεν ὅπη ζόφος οὐδ' ὅπη ἠώς
οὐδ' ὅπη ἡέλιος φαεσίμβροτος εἶσ' ὑπὸ γαῖαν,
οὐδ' ὅπη ἀνεῖται (κ 190-2).

καὶ ὅτι ἀεὶ ὑπὲρ ἡμᾶς ἰών, καὶ διὰ τοῦτο Ὑπερίων (Θ 480 al.) προσαγορευόμενος ὑπὸ αὐτοῦ τοῦ ποιητοῦ, τήν τε ἀνατολὴν ἐκ τοῦ περιέχοντος τὴν γῆν ὕδατος, τουτέστι τοῦ ὠκεανοῦ, ποιεῖται καὶ εἰς αὐτὸν καταδύεται, δηλοῖ σαφῶς, τὴν μὲν ἀνατολὴν κἀν τούτοις

ἠέλιος δ' ἀνόρουσε, λιπὼν περικαλλέα λίμνην,
οὐρανὸν ἐς πολύχαλκον, ἵν' ἀθανάτοισι φαείνη (γ 1-2),

τὴν δὲ δύσιν

ἐν δ' ἔπεσ' Ὠκεανῷ λαμπρὸν φάος ἠελίοιο,
ἕλκον νύκτα μέλαιναν ἐπὶ ζείδωρον ἄρουραν (Θ 485-6).

105. δείκνυσι δ' αὐτοῦ καὶ τὸ εἶδος

λαμπρὸς δ' ἦν ἠέλιος ὥς (τ 234)

καὶ τὸ μέγεθος

εὖτε γὰρ ἠέλιος φαέθων ὑπερέσχεθε γαῖαν (Λ 735)

καὶ ἔτι μᾶλλον ἐν τούτῳ

[Plutarch] 54B The Essay on the Life and Poetry of Homer

for where there is a peak there is a limit.

104. It is also clear that he knows about the sun[1]—that it has the power to rotate and is sometimes above the earth, and sometimes goes beneath—and he shows this when he says,

> Friends, we can find neither the dusk nor the dawn—
> neither the place where the sun that brings light to mortals
> goes beneath the earth,
> nor where it rises   [Od. 10.190-92]

and in that it is always passing over us, the poet calls the sun Hyperion. He also clearly indicates that it rises out of the waters that surround the earth (i.e. Ocean), and sets back into them. He describes the rising in these verses,

> The sun rose into brassy heaven,
> leaving his lovely lake, to shine for the immortals
>   [Od. 3.1-2],

and the setting in these,

> The shining light of the sun fell into Ocean,
> drawing down black night on the fruitful earth
>   [Il. 8.484-85].

105. He also indicates its outward appearance:

> He was radiant as the sun   [Od. 19.234],

and its size,

> for as the shining sun is larger than the earth[2]
>   [Il. 11.735],

which he describes more clearly here:

---

[1] Cf. Stobaeus, 1.25.7 (Dox Gr, 96).
[2] The line actually means, in context, "when the shining sun was above the earth," but the translation given above is intended to indicate our author's apparent understanding of the line.

ἦμος δ' ἡέλιος μέσον οὐρανὸν ἀμφιβεβήκει (Θ 68 = δ 400)
καὶ τὴν δύναμιν
Ἥλιος, ὃς πάντ' ἐφορᾷ καὶ πάντ' ἐπακούει (λ 109 = μ 323)
καὶ τὸ ἔμψυχον καὶ τὸ ἐπὶ τῇ κινήσει αὐτοπροαίρετον, ἐν οἷς ἀπειλεῖ
δύσομαι εἰς Ἀίδαο καὶ ἐν νεκύεσσι φαείνω (μ 383)
καὶ ἐπὶ τούτῳ ὁ Ζεὺς αὐτὸν παρακαλεῖ
Ἠέλι', ἤ τοι μὲν σὺ μετ' ἀθανάτοισι φάεινε
καὶ θνητοῖσι βροτοῖσιν ἐπὶ ζείδωρον ἄρουραν (μ 385-6).
ἐξ ὧν δηλοῖ ὅτι οὐ πῦρ ἐστιν ὁ ἥλιος ἀλλ' ἑτέρα τις κρείσσων οὐσία· ὅπερ καὶ Ἀριστοτέλης ὑπέλαβεν, εἴ γε τὸ μὲν πῦρ ἐστιν ἀνωφερὲς καὶ ἄψυχον καὶ ⟨εὐ⟩διάλειπτον καὶ φθαρτόν, ὁ δὲ ἥλιος κυκλοφορητικὸς καὶ ἔμψυχος καὶ ἀίδιος καὶ ἄφθαρτος.

106. καὶ τῶν ἄλλων δὲ τῶν κατὰ τὸν οὐρανὸν ἄστρων ὅτι οὐκ ἀπείρως Ὅμηρος εἶχε φανερόν ἐστιν ἐξ ὧν πεποίηκε
Πληιάδας θ' Ὑάδας τε τό τε σθένος Ὠρίωνος (Σ 486)

and when the sun had strode across half of heaven[1]
[Il. 8.68 = Od. 4.400],

and its powers,

the Sun, who sees all and hears all
[Od. 11.109 = 12.323].

He likewise indicates that it has a soul and is self-determining in motion, in the lines where the sun threatens:

I shall go down to Hades and shine among the dead
[Od. 12.383].

Zeus asks him not to do this,

Sun, go on shining among immortals
and mortal men on the fruitful earth
[Od. 12.385-86].

In these lines, Homer shows that the sun is not fire, but rather some other, more powerful substance, which is exactly Aristotle's position,[2] for while fire is borne upwards, is soulless, intermittent, and perishable, the sun for its part has a circular motion and a soul, and is eternal and imperishable.

106. That Homer was acquainted with the other stars of heaven is clear from this:

the Pleiades, the Hyades, and strong Orion
[Il. 18.486].

---

[1] The author seems to envision the sun crossing half of heaven with a single stride—or he may take ἀμφιβεβήκει more abstractly to mean "contain." In any case, the verb means simply "strode across" and not "contained in his stride." A scholiast *ad loc.* (bT schol. on Il 8.68) indicates that this verse proves that the sun is larger than heaven.
[2] e.g. *Meteorology* 355a. The implied contrast is with a mechanistic Stoic view of the issue.

καὶ τὴν Ἄρκτον [Σ 487-90] τὴν ἀεὶ στρεφομένην περὶ τὸν ἀειφανῆ πόλον τὸν βόρειον καὶ διὰ τὸ μετέωρον μὴ ἁπτομένην τοῦ ὁρίζοντος, ὅτι ἐν ἴσῳ χρόνῳ ὅ τε μικρότατος κύκλος, ἐν ᾧ ἐστιν Ἄρκτος, καὶ ὁ μέγιστος, ἐν ᾧ Ὠρίων, στρέφεται ἐν τῇ τοῦ κόσμου περιφορᾷ· καὶ τὸν βραδέως δυόμενον Βοώτην, ὅτι πολυχρόνιον ποιεῖται τὴν κατάδυσιν [ε 272], οὕτω πεπτωκὼς θέσει, ὥστε ὀρθὸν καταφέρεσθαι καὶ συγκαταδύεσθαι τέσσαρσι ζῳδίοις, τῶν πάντων εἰς ὅλην τὴν νύκτα μεριζομένων ἓξ ζῳδίων. εἰ δὲ μὴ πάντα τὰ περὶ τῶν ἄστρων θεωρούμενα διεξῆλθεν, ὡς Ἄρατος ἢ ἄλλος τις, οὐ χρὴ θαυμάζειν· οὐ γὰρ τοῦτο προέκειτο αὐτῷ.

107. οὐκ ἀγνοεῖ δὲ τὰς αἰτίας τῶν περὶ τὰ στοιχεῖα συμπτωμάτων, οἷον σεισμῶν καὶ ἐκλείψεων. ἐπεὶ γὰρ ἡ γῆ σύμπασα μετέχει ἐν ἑαυτῇ ἀέρος τε καὶ πυρὸς καὶ ὕδατος, ὑφ' ὧν καὶ περιέχεται, κατὰ τὸ εἰκὸς ἐν βάθει αὐτῆς συνίστανται ἀτμοὶ πνευματώδεις. τούτους φασὶν ἔξω μὲν φερομένους κινεῖν τὸν ἀέρα εἰρχθέντας δὲ ἀνοιδαίνειν, εἰς τὸ ἔξω βιαζομένους. ⟨τοῦ δὲ⟩ ἀνειλεῖσθαι τὸ πνεῦμα ἐντὸς τῆς γῆς τὴν θάλασσαν αἰτίαν εἶναι νομίζουσιν, ἐμφράσσουσαν ἐνίοτε τὰς εἰς τὸ ἔξω διόδους, ἔστι δὲ ὅτε ὑποχωροῦσαν αὐτὴν κατερείπειν τῆς γῆς τινα μέρη. καὶ τοῦτο οὖν Ὅμηρος εἰδὼς τὴν αἰτίαν τῶν σεισμῶν τῷ Ποσειδῶνι ἀνατίθησι γαιήοχόν (Ι 183 al.) τε αὐτὸν καὶ ἐνοσίχθονα (Η 445 al.) προσαγορεύων.

108. ἐπεὶ δέ, τῶν πνευμάτων ἐντὸς τῆς γῆς καθειργνυμένων, νηνεμίαι συμβαίνουσι καὶ ζόφοι καὶ ἀμαυρώσεις τοῦ ἡλίου, σκεψώμεθα εἰ καὶ τοῦτο συνεῖδε. πεποίηκε γὰρ τὸν Ποσειδῶνα σείοντα τὴν γῆν μετὰ τὴν Ἀχιλλέως ἔξοδον ἐπὶ τὴν μάχην. προειρήκει δὲ ἐπὶ τῆς προτεραίας, ὁποία ἦν ἡ τοῦ ἀέρος κατάστασις· ἐπὶ μὲν τοῦ Σαρπηδόνος

Ζεὺς δ' ἐπὶ νύκτ' ὀλοὴν τάνυσε κρατερῇ ὑσμίνῃ (Π 567)

He also knew the Bear [Il. 18.487-90], always revolving around the permanently visible north pole star and never passing below the horizon, because of its elevation. He knew that the smallest circle (that of the Bear) and the largest (that of Orion) turn in the revolution of the cosmos in exactly the same time. He knew that Boötes is slow to set, since he makes its setting take a long time [Od. 5.272], because its position is such that it is borne along upright to set with four zodiacal signs while the entire night is divided among six signs. If he did not go into the entire matter of astronomy as for instance Aratus does, this is no wonder, since that is not his subject.[1]

107. He is not ignorant of the causes of such events affecting the elements as earthquakes and eclipses.[2] Since the entire earth contains within itself mist and fire and water and is also surrounded by these, it would seem there are misty vapors in the depths of it also, and they say that these move outward and cause motion in the mist, and when they are shut in they swell upwards, forcing their way out. Furthermore, it is believed that the cause of the mist's being packed within the earth is the sea, which sometimes blocks the exit-paths, and there are times also when it withdraws and parts of the earth collapse. It was because Homer knew all these things that he attributed the cause of earthquakes to Poseidon, calling him "Earth-supporter" [Γαιήοχος] and "Earthshaker" ['Ενοσίχθων].

108. Since when the vapors are closed up within the earth there are periods of calm and darkness and eclipses of the sun, let us examine whether he knew this as well.[3] He depicted Poseidon shaking the earth after Achilles joined the battle and in the account of the previous day's fighting he had described how the mist [ἀήρ] came down—for he said with regard to the episode of Sarpedon's death,

> Zeus spread deadly night over the fighting
> [Il. 16.567],

---

[1] The tacit implication may be that, among the early hexameter poets, the precedents of the *Phaenomena* of Aratus were to be sought in the (lost) *Astronomy* attributed to Hesiod, rather than in Homer.
[2] See Aristotle, *Meteorology* 364-69.
[3] Aristotle, *Meteorology*, 367a, 20-30.

καὶ πάλιν ἐπὶ τοῦ Πατρόκλου

οὐ δέ κε φαίης

οὔτε ποτ' ἠέλιον σόον ἔμμεναι οὔτε σελήνην·

ἠέρι γὰρ κατέχοντο (Ρ 366-8).

καὶ μετ' ὀλίγον ὁ Αἴας εὔχεται

Ζεῦ πάτερ, ἀλλὰ σὺ ῥῦσαι ὑπ' ἠέρος υἷας Ἀχαιῶν,

ποίησον δ' αἴθρην, δὸς δ' ὀφθαλμοῖσιν ἰδέσθαι (Ρ 645-6).

μετὰ δὲ τὸν σεισμόν, τοῦ πνεύματος ἔξω καταστάντος, σφοδροὶ γίνονται ἄνεμοι, ὅθεν ἡ Ἥρα φησὶν

αὐτὰρ ἐγὼ Ζεφύροιο καὶ ἀργέσταο Νότοιο

εἴσομαι ἐξ ἁλόθεν χαλεπὴν ὄρσουσα θύελλαν (Φ 334-5).

εἶτα τῇ ὑστεραίᾳ τοὺς ἀνέμους ἡ Ἶρις ἐπὶ τὴν πυρὰν τοῦ Πατρόκλου παρακαλεῖ

οἱ δ' ὀρέοντο

πνοιῇ ὑπὸ λιγυρῇ νέφεα κλονέοντες ὄπισθεν (Ψ 212-3).

οὕτως δὲ καὶ τὴν ἔκλειψιν τοῦ ἡλίου φυσικῶς γινομένην ὅταν ἡ σελήνη ἐν τῇ πρὸς αὐτὸν συνόδῳ κατὰ κάθετον ἐπελθοῦσα ἐπισκοτήσῃ, εἰδὼς φαίνεται. προειπὼν γὰρ ὅτι ἐλεύσεται ὁ Ὀδυσσεὺς

τοῦ μὲν φθίνοντος μηνός, τοῦ δ' ἱσταμένοιο (ξ 162 = τ 307),

and again with regard to that of Patroclus,

> You would have said...
> that both the sun and moon were sick
> for they were wrapped in mist
> [Il. 17.366-68],

and a little later Ajax prays,

> Father Zeus, save the sons of the Achaeans from the mist!
> Give us bright sky so that we can see with our eyes
> [Il. 17.645-46].

After the earthquake, when the exhalation has come forth, there are violent winds, for Hera says:

> but I shall rouse the harsh gale of the West Wind
> or the brightening South Wind, from the sea
> [Il. 21.334-35],

and on the following day Iris calls the winds down upon the pyre of Patroclus:

> these were stirred up
> with a shrill blast, driving the clouds before them
> [Il. 23.212-13].

He clearly also knew that eclipses of the sun occur naturally when the moon, in her path near the sun, passes directly underneath and blocks it out.[1] For, having predicted that Odysseus will arrive home

> when one moon is wasted and another coming to be
> [Od. 14.162 = 19.307]—

---

[1] This observationally sound account of solar eclipses is at least as old as Empedocles (fr. B42 DK). The fact that our author juxtaposes it with the theory based on vapors is perhaps explained by the fact that Aristotle had done the same (above, chs. 107 and 108 with notes).

τουτέστιν ὅτε ἅμα παύεται καὶ ἄρχεται ὁ μήν, συνιούσης τῷ ἡλίῳ τῆς σελήνης, ἅμα τῷ ἐλθεῖν αὐτόν φησιν ὁ μάντις πρὸς τοὺς μνηστῆρας

 ἆ δειλοί, τί κακὸν τόδε πάσχετε; νυκτὶ μὲν ὑμέων

 εἰλύαται κεφαλαί τε πρόσωπά τε νέρθε τε γοῦνα·

 εἰδώλων δὲ πλέον πρόθυρον, πλείη δὲ καὶ αὐλή

 ἐρχομένων ἐρεβόσδε ὑπὸ ζόφον· ἥλιος δὲ

 οὐρανοῦ ἐξαπόλωλε, κακὴ δ' ἐπιδέδρομεν ἀχλύς (υ 351-2, 355-7).

109. καὶ ἀνέμων δὲ φύσιν ἀκριβῶς κατενόησεν· ὧν τὴν μὲν γένεσιν ἐκ τῶν ὑγρῶν εἶναι· τοῦ μὲν γὰρ ὕδατος ἡ μεταβολὴ εἰς ἀέρα γίνεται, ὁ δὲ ἄνεμός ἐστιν ἀὴρ ῥέων. τοῦτο δὲ ἔν τε ἄλλοις πολλοῖς ἐμφαίνει καὶ ἐν οἷς φησιν

   ἀνέμων ... μένος ὑγρὸν ἀέντων (ε 478 = τ 440),

τὴν δὲ τάξιν αὐτῶν ὡς ἔχει διέθηκε

 σὺν δ' Εὖρός τε Νότος τ' ἔπεσε Ζέφυρός τε δυσαής,

 καὶ Βορέης αἰθρηγενέτης μέγα κῦμα κυλίνδων (ε 295-6)·

τούτων γὰρ ὁ μὲν ἀπὸ ἀνατολῆς ὁρμᾶται ὁ δὲ ἀπὸ μεσημβρίας ὁ δὲ ἀπὸ δύσεως ὁ δὲ ἀπὸ ἄρκτου. καὶ ὁ μὲν Ἀπηλιώτης ὑγρὸς ὢν μεταβάλλει εἰς Νότον θερμὸν ὄντα, ὁ δὲ Νότος λεπτυνόμενος εἰς Ζέφυρον, ὁ δὲ Ζέφυρος, ἔτι μᾶλλον λεπτυνόμενος, εἰς Βορέαν ἀποκαθαίρεται· διὸ

 κραιπνὸν Βορέην, τὰ δὲ κύματα ἄξεν (ε 385).

καὶ τὴν ἀντίθεσιν δὲ αὐτῶν φυσικῶς ἐξηγήσατο

 ἄλλοτε μέν τε Νότος Βορέῃ προέηκε φέρεσθαι,

 ἄλλοτε δ' αὖτ' Εὖρος Ζεφύρῳ εἴξασκε διώκειν (ε 331-2).

that is, at the end and the beginning of the month, when the moon comes into conjunction with the sun—he has the seer further predict his coming to the suitors in the following terms:

> Wretches, what evil lies upon you! Your heads
> and faces are wreathed in night, and your limbs below!
> The hall is full of ghosts, the courtyard full as well,
> moving through the dark gloom. The sun is wiped
> from heaven and an evil mist has settled in
> [Od. 20.351-52, 355-57].

109.   He also perceived the precise nature of the winds, that they have their origin in humidity—for water changes into mist and wind is running mist.[1] He reveals this in many places, including

> the might of the damp-blowing winds
> [Od. 5.478 = 19.440].

He placed the winds in their proper order:

> Eurus and Notus fell in together and stormy Zephyrus
> and Boreas born of the *aither*, rolling up a great wave
> [Od. 5.295-96],

for the first of these comes from the East, the second from the South, the third from the West, and the last from the North. Wet Apeliotes turns into warm Notus, and Notus thins out into Zephyr, and thinning out still more is purified into Boreas. Hence,

> [She urged] swift Boreas upon him and broke the waves before
>   him   [Od. 5.385].

He has also explained their opposition as it actually occurs,

> At one moment Notus would toss him to Boreas,
> the next, Eurus gave him to Zephyrus to drive
> [Od. 5.331-32].

---

[1] See Xenophanes, fr. B30 DK, and Aristotle, *Meteorology*, 359 ff.

110. ἠπίστατο δὲ κἀκεῖνος ὅτι ὁ βόρειος πόλος ὑπὲρ γῆν ἐστι μετέωρος, ὡς καθ' ἡμᾶς τοὺς ἐν τῷ κλίματι τούτῳ κατοικοῦντας, ὁ δὲ νότιος ἐκ τοῦ ἐναντίου βαθύς· ὅθεν ἐπὶ μὲν τοῦ βορείου φησὶ

καὶ Βορέης αἰθρηγενέτης, μέγα κῦμα κυλίνδων (ε 296),
⟨ἐπὶ δὲ τοῦ νοτείου

ἔνθα νότος μέγα κῦμα ποτὶ σκαιὸν ῥίον ὠθεῖ (γ 295).
καὶ τῷ μὲν κυλίνδων⟩ τὴν ἄνωθεν ἐμπίπτουσαν φορὰν τοῦ ἀνέμου ἐμφαίνει, τῷ δὲ ὠθεῖ τὴν ἀπὸ τοῦ κοιλοτέρου πρὸς τὸ ἄναντες βίαν.

111. ὅτι δὲ καὶ ἡ τῶν ὑετῶν γένεσίς ἐστιν ἐκ τῆς τῶν ὑγρῶν ἀναθυμιάσεως, ἐπεδήλωσεν εἰπὼν

κατὰ δ' ὑψόθεν ἧκεν ἐέρσας
αἵματι μυδαλέας ἐξ αἰθέρος (Λ 53-4)
καὶ
αἱματοέσσας δὲ ψιάδας κατέχευεν ἔραζε (Π 459).
προειρήκει γὰρ
τῶν νῦν αἷμα κελαινὸν ἐΰρροον ἀμφὶ Σκάμανδρον
ἐσκέδασ' ὀξὺς Ἄρης, ψυχαὶ δ' Ἀϊδόσδε κατῆλθον (Η 329-30).
ὅθεν δῆλόν ἐστιν ὅτι τὰ ἀναφερόμενα ἀπὸ τῶν περὶ γῆν ὑδάτων ὑγρά, ἀναπεφυρμένα τῷ αἵματι, τοιαῦτα ἄνωθεν κατηνέχθη. τοῦ δὲ αὐτοῦ λόγου

110. He also knew that the north pole [of the heavens] is suspended above the earth, from the perspective of those who live where we do, and that the south pole is deep below on the other side. Thus he says about the North Wind,

> Boreas born of the *aither*, rolling up a great wave
> [Od. 5.296],

and about the South Wind,

> Then Notus pushed a great wave against the left-hand cliff
> [Od. 3.295],

and when he says "rolling" he is indicating that the motion of that wind is downwards, but by "pushed" he indicates a force moving upwards from the hollows of the swell.

111. He also showed that the source of rain is the evaporation of waters, in this passage:[1]

> Down fell drenching showers of blood
> from the *aither* [Il. 11.53-54],

and in

> He poured down drops of blood on the ground
> [Il. 16.459],

for he had previously said,

> Swift Ares has scattered their black blood
> along the running Scamander, and their souls have gone to
> Hades [Il. 7.329-30],

and so it is clear that the moisture borne upwards from the waters on the surface of the earth was mixed with blood, and came down from above in the same condition. The same idea is found in the line:

---

[1] The idea is a commonplace, going back at least to Anaximander (fr. A11 DK = Hippolytus, Ref. 1.6.7).

ἔχεται κἀκεῖνο

ἤματ' ὀπωρινῷ ὅτε λαβρότατον χέει ὕδωρ (Π 385).

τότε γὰρ ὁ ἥλιος ἐκ βάθους ἀνασπῶν διὰ ξηρότητα τῆς γῆς τὰ ὑγρὰ θολερὰ καὶ γεώδη ἀναφέρει, τὰ δὲ ὑπὸ βάρους λάβρα καταρρήγνυται. αἱ μὲν οὖν ὑγραὶ ἀναθυμιάσεις ὑετοὺς γεννῶσιν, αἱ δὲ ξηραὶ ἀνέμους. ὅταν δὲ νέφει ἐναποληφθῇ ἄνεμος, ἔπειτα βίᾳ ῥήξῃ τὸ νέφος, βροντὰς καὶ ἀστραπὰς ἀποτελεῖ, εἰ δὲ ἐκπίπτοι ἡ ἀστραπή, κεραυνὸν ἀφίησιν. ὅπερ εἰδὼς ὁ ποιητὴς λέγει τὰ τοιαῦτα·

ἀστράψας δὲ μάλα μεγάλ' ἔκτυπε (Ρ 595)

καὶ ἐν ἄλλοις

Ζεὺς δ' ἄμυδις βρόντησε καὶ ἔμβαλε νηὶ κεραυνόν (μ 415 = ξ 305).

112. θεοὺς δὲ εἶναι πάντες οἵ γε ὀρθῶς φρονοῦντες νομίζουσι, καὶ πρῶτος Ὅμηρος. ἀεὶ γὰρ μέμνηται τῶν θεῶν, λέγων μάκαρες θεοί (Α 406 al.), ῥεῖα ζώοντες (Ζ 138 al.). ἀθάνατοι γὰρ ὄντες ῥᾳδίαν καὶ ἄπαυστον ἔχουσι τὴν τοῦ ζῆν φύσιν καὶ οὐ δέονται τροφῆς, ἧς δεῖται τῶν θνητῶν ζῴων τὰ σώματα·

οὐ γὰρ σῖτον ἔδουσ', οὐ πίνουσ' αἴθοπα οἶνον·

τοὔνεκ' ἀναίμονές εἰσι καὶ ἀθάνατοι καλέονται (Ε 341-2).

113. ἐπεὶ δ' ἐδεῖτο ἡ ποίησις θεῶν ἐνεργούντων, ἵνα τὴν γνώμην αὐτῶν ⟨τῇ⟩ αἰσθήσει τῶν ἐντυγχανόντων παραστήσῃ, περιέθηκεν αὐτοῖς σώματα· οὐδὲν δὲ ἄλλο σώματος εἶδος ἢ τοῦ ἀνθρώπου δεκτικόν ἐστιν ἐπιστήμης καὶ λόγου· ⟨ᾧ⟩ προσεικάσας ἕκαστον τῶν θεῶν μετὰ τοῦ κοσμῆσαι μεγέθει τε καὶ

> An autumn day, when Zeus sends the rain crashing down
> [Il. 16.385],

for then the sun draws moisture from the depths, since the earth is dried out and the water comes up muddy and full of earth and bursts forth violently because of the weight. Moreover, the damp exhalations produce rain but the dry ones produce winds. When wind is intercepted by a cloud it smashes the cloud by its force and produces thunder and lightning and, if the lightning drops down, a thunderbolt. Knowing this, the poet says things of this sort:

> He shot forth lightnings and thundered loudly
> [Il. 17.595]

and elsewhere,

> At the same time, Zeus thundered and cast a thunderbolt at the ship [Od. 12.415 = 14.305].

112. All right-thinking people believe the gods exist,[1] and Homer first among them, for he constantly mentions the gods, calling them, "blessed gods living at ease," for since they are immortal it is the nature of their lives to be easy and endless and they have no need of food, which the bodies of mortal creatures require:

> For they eat no grain nor do they drink bright wine
> and so they are bloodless and are called immortals
> [Il. 5.341-42].

113. Since the poem needed active gods, he provided them with bodies, in order to communicate the idea of them to the perception of his audience. No kind of body except the human is capable of receiving knowledge and reason, and thus he gave each of the gods a human form, enhanced in size and beauty. At the same time, he initiated the

---

[1] The section on theology (112-21) presents Homer's anthropomorphic deities as a function of his fiction (113), while insisting on the truth of the notion of divine providence.

κάλλει ἅμα καὶ τοῦτο ὑπέδειξε τὸ εἰκόνας καὶ ἀγάλματα θεῶν εἰς ἀνθρώπων εἶδος ἠκριβωμένα ἱδρῦσθαι, ὑπὲρ τοῦ παρέχειν ὑπόμνησιν καὶ τοῖς ἔλασσον φρονοῦσιν, ὅτι εἰσὶ θεοί.

114. τούτων δὲ πάντων ἀρχηγὸν καὶ ἡγεμόνα τὸν πρῶτον θεὸν νομιζόντων τῶν ἀρίστων φιλοσόφων ἀσώματον ὄντα καὶ νοήσει μᾶλλον καταληπτόν, καὶ Ὅμηρος ταῦτα ὑπολαμβάνων φαίνεται, παρ' ᾧ λέγεται ὁ Ζεὺς
πατὴρ ἀνδρῶν τε θεῶν τε (Α 544 al.)
καὶ
ὦ πάτερ ἡμέτερε Κρονίδη, ὕπατε κρειόντων (Θ 31 al.).
καὶ αὐτὸς μὲν ὁ Ζεύς φησιν
ὅσσον ἐγὼ περί τ' εἰμὶ θεῶν περί τ' εἰμὶ ἀνθρώπων (Θ 27).
ἡ δὲ Ἀθηνᾶ πρὸς αὐτόν
εὖ νυ καὶ ἡμεῖς ἴδμεν ὅ τοι σθένος οὐκ ἐπιεικτόν (Θ 32).
εἰ δὲ δεῖ καὶ τοῦτο ζητῆσαι, εἰ νοητὸν ἠπίστατο τὸν θεόν, οὐκ ἄντικρυς μέν, ἅτε καὶ ἐν ποιήσει πολὺ τὸ μυθῶδες ἐχούσῃ, ὅμως δέ ἐστι καταμαθεῖν ἐν οἷς φησιν
εὗρεν δ' εὐρύοπα Κρονίδην ἄτερ ἥμενον ἄλλων (Α 498)
καὶ ἐν οἷς αὐτὸς λέγει
ἀλλ' ἤ τοι μὲν ἐγὼ μενέω πτυχὶ Οὐλύμποιο
ἥμενος, ἔνθ' ὁρόων φρένα τέρψομαι (Υ 22-3).

tradition of giving precise human form to images and statues of the gods, for the sake of reminding those who are less given to contemplation that the gods do, in fact, exist.[1]

114. The best philosophers have considered the first god, the ruler and leader of all, to be incorporeal and perceptible rather by thought [νόησις] [than by the senses] and Homer clearly takes this position as well, when he calls Zeus "father of gods and men," (Il. 1.544 etc.) and

> Son of Kronos, our father, highest of rulers
> [Il. 8.31, etc.].

Zeus himself says,

> as much as I am above gods and men
> [Il 8.27],

and Athena says to him,

> We see clearly that your strength is incomparable
> [Il. 8.32].

If we must also ask whether he knew that god is perceived by mind [i.e. that he is νοητός], we must say that Homer does not say as much explicitly, since he expresses himself in poetry that contains a large mythic element, but that he was aware of this fact may nevertheless be gathered from such phrases as:

> She found far-seeing Zeus sitting apart from the others
> [Il. 1.498],

and when he himself says,

> But myself I shall stay back, sitting on the ridges of Olympus,
> and delight my heart watching from there
> [Il. 20.22-23].

---

[1] That Homer's anthropomorphic gods are part of the screen of Homeric fiction was, at least from the Hellenistic period, tacitly acknowledged by all those who gave the poems any theological authority.

ἡ γὰρ μόνωσις αὕτη καὶ τὸ μὴ καταμιγνύειν τοῖς ἄλλοις θεοῖς ἑαυτὸν ἀλλὰ χαίρειν ἑαυτῷ συνόντα καὶ χρώμενον ἡσυχίαν ἄγοντι καὶ ἀεὶ διακοσμοῦντι τὰ πάντα τὴν τοῦ νοητοῦ θεοῦ φύσιν παρίστησιν. οἶδε δὲ ὅτι νοῦς ἐστιν ὁ θεὸς ὁ πάντα ἐπιστάμενος καὶ διέπων τὸ πᾶν· φησὶ γὰρ ὁ Ποσειδῶν

ἦ μὰν ἀμφοτέροισιν ὁμὸν γένος ἠδ' ἴα πάτρη,

ἀλλὰ Ζεὺς πρότερος γεγόνει καὶ πλείονα ᾔδει (Ν 354-5)

καὶ τοῦτο πολλάκις·

ἔνθ' αὖτ' ἄλλ' ἐνόησε (Ψ 140 al.).

τοῦτο σημαίνει ὅτι ἀεὶ διανοεῖται.

115. τῆς δὲ τοῦ θείου διανοίας ἔχεται καὶ ἡ πρόνοια καὶ ἡ εἱμαρμένη, περὶ ὧν εἴρηνται λόγοι πολλοὶ παρὰ τοῖς φιλοσόφοις· τούτων δὲ πάντων τὰς ἀφορμὰς Ὅμηρος παρέσχε. τὰ μὲν γὰρ τῆς προνοίας τῶν θεῶν τί ἂν καὶ λέγοι τις, ὅπου διὰ πάσης τῆς ποιήσεως οὐ μόνον πρὸς ἀλλήλους ὑπὲρ τῶν ἀνθρώπων διαλέγονται ἀλλὰ καὶ καταβάντες ἐπὶ τὴν γῆν τοῖς ἀνθρώποις ὁμιλοῦσιν; ὀλίγα δὲ παραδείγματος ἕνεκα θεασώμεθα, ἐν οἷς ἐστιν ὁ Ζεὺς λέγων πρὸς τὸν ἀδελφόν

ἔγνως, ἐννοσίγαιε, ἐμὴν ἐνὶ στήθεσι βουλήν,

ὧν ἕνεκα ξυνάγειρα· μέλουσί μοι ὀλλύμενοί περ (Υ 20-1)·

καὶ ἐν ἄλλοις

ὢ πόποι, ἦ φίλον ἄνδρα διωκόμενον περὶ τεῖχος

ὀφθαλμοῖσιν ὁρῶμαι, ἐμὸν δ' ὀλοφύρεται ἦτορ (Χ 168-9).

116. ἔτι δὲ τὸ βασιλικὸν ἀξίωμα καὶ τὸ φιλάνθρωπον ἦθος ἐμφαίνει εἰπών

πῶς ἂν ἔπειτ' Ὀδυσῆος ἐγὼ θείοιο λαθοίμην,

ὃς περὶ μὲν νόον ἐστὶ βροτῶν, πέρι δ' ἱρὰ θεοῖσιν

This isolation and refusal to mix with the other gods, as well as Zeus' pleasure at being alone and at ease, overseeing the universe—these reveal the nature of the intelligible god. Thus Homer knows that god is a mind [νοῦς], with universal knowledge, governing the universe. Poseidon says:

> Indeed our family is the same and we had one father
> but Zeus was born first and knew more
> [Il. 13.354-55],

and this frequent expression,

> He, on the contrary, had other things in mind,
> [Il. 23.140, etc.]

indicates that Zeus is constantly thinking.

115. Both providence and fate are part of the intention of god. Many ideas concerning these things have been expressed by the philosophers, and Homer provided the starting points for all of them. As far as the providence of the gods is concerned, what more could one say, when throughout the poetry the gods not only discuss men but even come down to earth to mingle with them? Let us consider a few examples. Zeus says to his brother,

> Earthshaker, you knew my intention in gathering
> you all together: I am concerned for them, even if they are
> mortal [Il. 20.20-21],

and elsewhere [when he sees Hector pursued by Achilles], he says,

> Alas, I see a man dear to me chased around the walls
> and my heart is sore [Il. 22.168-69].

116. He also reveals regal dignity and love of mankind when he says,

> How could I forget divine Odysseus,
> who excels among all men in wits [νοῦς] and has given

ἀθανάτοισι δέδωκε, τοὶ οὐρανὸν εὐρὺν ἔχουσιν (α 65-7);
ἐν οἷς ὁρᾶν ἔστιν ὅτι ἐπήνεσε τὸν ἄνδρα πρῶτον ἐπὶ τῷ νοῦν ἔχειν, δεύτερον δὲ ἐπὶ τῷ σέβειν τοὺς θεούς.

117. πῶς δὲ καὶ αὐτοῖς τοῖς ἀνθρώποις ὁμιλοῦντας καὶ συμπονοῦντας ποιεῖ τοὺς θεούς, ἐν πολλοῖς ἔστι καταμαθεῖν· ὥσπερ καὶ τὴν Ἀθηνᾶν ποτὲ μὲν τῷ Ἀχιλλεῖ ἀεὶ δὲ τῷ Ὀδυσσεῖ, καὶ τὸν Ἑρμῆν τῷ Πριάμῳ καὶ αὖ πάλιν τῷ Ὀδυσσεῖ, καθόλου δὲ ἀεὶ τοὺς θεοὺς τοῖς ἀνθρώποις παραστατεῖν οἴεται· φησὶ γὰρ

 καί τε θεοὶ ... ἐοικότες ἀλλοδαποῖσι,
 παντοῖοι τελέθοντες, ἐπιστρωφῶσι πόληας,
 ἀνθρώπων ὕβριν τε καὶ εὐνομίην ἐφορῶντες (ρ 485-7).

118. τῆς δὲ προνοίας τῶν θεῶν ἴδιόν ἐστι τὸ βούλεσθαι δικαίως τοὺς ἀνθρώπους βιοῦν· καὶ τοῦτό φησιν ὁ ποιητὴς ἐναργέστατα

 οὐ γὰρ σχέτλια ἔργα θεοὶ μάκαρες φιλέουσιν,
 ἀλλὰ δίκην τίουσι καὶ αἴσιμα ἔργ' ἀνθρώπων (ξ 83-4)

καὶ

 Ζεύς, ὅς τ' ἄνδρεσσι κοτεσσάμενος χαλεπήνῃ
 οἳ βίῃ ⟨εἰν⟩ ἀγορῇ σκολιὰς κρίνωσι θέμιστας (Π 386-7).

ὥσπερ γὰρ τοὺς θεοὺς προνοουμένους τῶν ἀνθρώπων εἰσάγει, οὕτω καὶ τοὺς ἀνθρώπους μεμνημένους αὐτῶν ἐν πάσῃ τύχῃ· καὶ ὁ μὲν εὐημερῶν στρατηγός φησιν

 ἔλπομαι, εὐχόμενος Διί τ' ἄλλοισίν τε θεοῖσιν,
 ἐξελάαν ἐνθένδε κύνας κηρεσσιφορήτους (Θ 526-7).

ὁ δὲ κινδυνεύων

[Plutarch] 54B The Essay on the Life and Poetry of Homer

> many sacrifices to the gods who hold wide heaven?
> [Od. 1.65-67].

Here, one can see that he approves of the man first for his mind [νοῦς] and secondly for his reverence for the gods.

117. In many passages one sees how he makes the gods mingle with men and work alongside them. Athena helps Achilles occasionally and Odysseus constantly, and Hermes aids Priam and then again Odysseus. In general, Homer believes that the gods are always standing beside men, for he says,

> and the gods in the guise of strangers, taking on
> all sorts of shapes, wander through the cities
> and see both the crimes and the lawfulness of men
> [Od. 17.485-87].

118. One inherent aspect of the providence of the gods is their desire for men to live justly, and the poet expresses this very clearly:

> The gods do not like wicked deeds,
> rather, they honor justice and the seemly acts of men
> [Od. 14.83-84],

and,

> Zeus becomes enraged and punishes men
> who enforce crooked judgment in council
> [Il. 16.386-87].

Just as he shows the gods to be providentially concerned with mankind, he also shows men thinking of the gods in every situation. The fortunate general says,

> I hope and pray to Zeus and the other gods
> that I may drive away these dogs whom their fate has brought here
> [Il. 8.526-27]

and the general in peril says,

Ζεῦ πάτερ, ἀλλὰ σὺ ῥῦσαι ὑπ' ἠέρος υἷας Ἀχαιῶν (Ρ 645)
καὶ πάλιν ὁ μὲν κτείνας
ἐπειδὴ τόνδ' ἄνδρα θεοὶ δαμάσασθαι ἔδωκαν (Χ 379),
ὁ δὲ θνήσκων
φράζεο νῦν, μή τοί τι θεῶν μήνιμα γένωμαι (Χ 358).

119. πόθεν οὖν ἄλλοθεν ἢ ἐκ τῶν εἰρημένων ἐστὶ τὸ δόγμα ἐκεῖνο τῶν Στωικῶν, τὸ δὴ ἕνα μὲν εἶναι τὸν κόσμον συμπολιτεύεσθαι δὲ ἐν αὐτῷ θεοὺς καὶ ἀνθρώπους δικαιοσύνης μετέχοντας φύσει; καὶ γὰρ ὅταν εἴπῃ
Ζεὺς δὲ Θέμιστ' ἐκέλευσε θεοὺς ἀγορήνδε καλέσσαι·
τίπτ' αὖτ', ἀργικέραυνε, θεοὺς ἀγορήνδ' ἐκάλεσσας;
ἦ τι περὶ Τρώων καὶ Ἀχαιῶν μερμηρίζεις (Υ 4, 16-7);
τί ἄλλο ὑποδείκνυσιν ἢ ὅτι νόμῳ πόλεως ὁ κόσμος διοκεῖται καὶ προβουλεύονται οἱ θεοί, ἐξάρχοντος τοῦ θεῶν τε καὶ ἀνθρώπων πατρός;

120. τὴν δὲ περὶ τῆς εἱμαρμένης δόξαν δείκνυσιν ἐν ἐκείνοις σαφῶς·
μοῖραν δ' οὔ τινά φημι πεφυγμένον ἔμμεναι ἀνδρῶν,
οὐ κακὸν οὐδὲ μὲν ἐσθλόν, ἐπὴν τὰ πρῶτα γένηται (Ζ 488-9).
καὶ ἐν οἷς ἄλλοις κρατύνει τὴν δύναμιν τῆς εἱμαρμένης. ἡγεῖται μέντοι καὶ αὐτός, ὥσπερ καὶ μετ' αὐτὸν οἱ δοκιμώτατοι τῶν φιλοσόφων, Πλάτων καὶ

> Father Zeus, save the sons of the Achaeans from the mist!
> [Il. 17.645];

the victorious soldier says,

> since the gods have let me overcome this man
> [Il. 22.379],

and the one who is dying,

> Consider, lest you face the wrath of the gods on my account
> [Il. 22.358].

119. Now from where, if not from what Homer has said, does the teaching of the Stoics come—that the universe is one, inhabited as a city by gods and men who participate, by their natures, in justice? When he says,

> Zeus ordered Themis to call the gods to council. . . .
> Why have you again called the gods to council, wielder of thunder?
> Are you concerned about the Trojans and Greeks?
> [Il. 20.4, 16-17]

what else is he showing than that the universe is managed by civic laws, that the gods are the ruling council, and the father of gods and men presides over them?

120. He reveals his teaching concerning fate clearly in these lines:

> I say that no man, whether good or bad,
> has ever escaped his fate, once he has entered this world
> [Il. 6.488-89],

and elsewhere, when he confirms the power of fate. He is nevertheless of the same opinion as the most respected of philosophers after him,

Ἀριστοτέλης καὶ Θεόφραστος, οὐ πάντα καθ' εἱμαρμένην παραγίνεσθαι, ἀλλά τι καὶ ἐπὶ τοῖς ἀνθρώποις εἶναι, ᾧ ὑπάρχει μὲν τὸ ἑκούσιον, τούτῳ δέ πως συνάπτειν τὸ κατηναγκασμένον, ὅταν τις πράξας ὃ βούλεται εἰς ὃ μὴ βούλεται ἐμπέσῃ. καὶ ταῦτα σαφῶς ἐν πολλοῖς δεδήλωκεν, ὥσπερ καὶ ἐν ταῖς ἀρχαῖς ἑκατέρας τῆς ποιήσεως, ἐν μὲν τῇ Ἰλιάδι λέγων τὴν ὀργὴν τοῦ Ἀχιλλέως αἰτίαν τῆς ἀπωλείας τῶν Ἑλλήνων γενέσθαι καὶ τότε τὴν Διὸς βούλησιν ἐκτελεσθῆναι, ἐν δὲ τῇ Ὀδυσσείᾳ τοὺς ἑταίρους τοῦ Ὀδυσσέως διὰ τὴν αὐτῶν ἀβουλίαν ὀλέθρῳ περιπεσεῖν· ἐξήμαρτον γὰρ ἁψάμενοι τῶν ἱερῶν τοῦ Ἡλίου βοῶν, ἐξὸν ἀποσχέσθαι αὐτῶν· καὶ γὰρ ἦν προειρημένον

τὰς εἰ μέν κ' ἀσινέας ἐάᾳς νόστου τε μέδηαι

καί κεν ἔτ' εἰς Ἰθάκην κακά περ πάσχοντες ἵκοισθε·

εἰ δέ κε σίνηαι, τότε τοι τεκμαίρομ' ὄλεθρον (λ 110-2 = μ 137-9).

οὕτως τὸ μὲν μὴ ἀδικῆσαι ἐπ' αὐτοῖς, τὸ δὲ ἀδικήσαντας ἀπολέσθαι ἐκ τῆς εἱμαρμένης ἀκόλουθον ἦν.

121. ἔνεστι δὲ καὶ τὸ ἄλλως συμβαῖνον ἐκ προνοίας διαφυγεῖν, ὅπερ ἐν τούτῳ παρίστησιν·

ἔνθα δὲ καὶ δύστηνος ὑπὲρ μόρον ὤλετ' Ὀδυσσεύς,

εἰ μὴ ἐπὶ φρεσὶ θῆκε θεὰ γλαυκῶπις Ἀθήνη·

ἀμφοτέρῃσι δὲ χερσὶν ἐπεσσύμενος λάβε πέτρης,

τῆς ἔχετο στενάχων, εἵως μέγα κῦμα παρῆλθεν (ε 436, 427-9).

ἐνταῦθα γὰρ ἐκ τοῦ ἐναντίου κινδυνεύων ὑπὸ τύχης ἀπολέσθαι, ἐκ προνοίας ἐσώθη.

[Plutarch] 54B The Essay on the Life and Poetry of Homer

Plato, Aristotle, and Theophrastus,[1] that everything does not come about through fate, but a certain amount falls under the control of men, who have freedom of will, though an element of necessity is somehow attached to this, whenever they do as they want but consequently fall into situations they do not want. He has shown this clearly in many passages, as in the beginnings of both poems, for in the *Iliad* he says that the anger of Achilles was the cause of the destruction of the Greeks, and then that the will of Zeus was accomplished, and in the *Odyssey* the companions of Odysseus met with disaster through their own folly, for they made the mistake of touching the cattle sacred to the sun, when they could have kept away from them. It had been predicted:

> If you leave them unharmed and think of your homecoming,
> you might yet come to Ithaca, though after much suffering,
> but if you harm them, then I predict ruin
> [Od. 11.110-12 = 12.137-39].

Thus the responsibility not to commit the crime was theirs, but their being destroyed if they did was a consequence of fate.

121.   It is also possible, through divine providence, to escape what would otherwise inevitably occur, as Homer shows in the following passage:

> Then wretched Odysseus would have been destroyed against fate,
> if gray-eyed Athena had not put a thought in his head.
> He quickly grabbed the rock with both hands
> and held tight, groaning, until the great wave passed
> [Od. 5.436, 427-29].

In this instance, conversely, when he was in danger of being destroyed by chance, he was saved by providence.

---

[1] See, e.g. Plato, *Laws* 904C; Aristotle, *Metaphysics* 6, 1026a-27b. The evidence for Theophrastus' position on the matter is predictably less satisfactory: Fortenbaugh et al. (1992) cite this passage as the earliest evidence, supplemented by Stobaeus (1.6.17c) and Alexander of Aphrodisias, *Supplement to the De Anima* 186.13-14 and 28-31 Bruns.

122. καθάπερ δὲ περὶ τῶν θείων πολλοὶ καὶ ποικίλοι λόγοι παρὰ τοῖς φιλοσόφοις τὰς πλείστας ἀφορμὰς ἐξ Ὁμήρου λαβοῦσιν, οὕτω καὶ περὶ τῶν ἀνθρωπείων πραγμάτων, ὧν πρῶτον περὶ τῆς ψυχῆς πειρασώμεθα. τὸ μὲν δὴ τῶν δογμάτων Πυθαγόρου καὶ Πλάτωνος γενναιότατόν ἐστι, τὸ εἶναι τὴν ψυχὴν ἀθάνατον, ᾗ καὶ πτερὰ τῷ λόγῳ προστίθησιν ὁ Πλάτων (*Phaedr.* 251B7 al.). τίς οὖν τοῦτο πρῶτον ἀνεφώνησεν ἢ Ὅμηρος εἰπὼν ἄλλα τε καὶ ταῦτα

ψυχὴ δ' ἐκ ῥεθέων πταμένη Ἄιδόσδε βεβήκει (Π 856 = Χ 362);

εἰς τὸν ἀειδῆ καὶ ἀόρατον εἴτε ἀέρα θείη τις εἴτε ὑπόγειον τόπον. καὶ ἐν μὲν τῇ Ἰλιάδι ποιῶν τὴν τοῦ Πατρόκλου ψυχὴν ἐφισταμένην κοιμωμένῳ τῷ Ἀχιλλεῖ

ἦλθε δ' ἐπὶ ψυχὴ Πατροκλῆος δειλοῖο (Ψ 65)

καὶ λόγους αὐτῷ περιτίθησιν, ἐν οἷς καὶ τοῦτο λέγει

τῆλέ με εἴργουσι ψυχαί, εἴδωλα καμόντων (Ψ 72).

ἐν δὲ τῇ Ὀδυσσείᾳ δι' ὅλης τῆς Νεκυίας τί ἄλλο ἢ τὰς ψυχὰς δείκνυσι μετὰ θάνατον διαμενούσας καὶ φθεγγομένας ἅμα τῷ πιεῖν τοῦ αἵματος; καὶ γὰρ τοῦτο ᾔδει, ὅτι τὸ αἷμα νομὴ καὶ τροφή ἐστι τοῦ πνεύματος, τὸ δὲ πνεῦμά ἐστιν αὐτὴ ἡ ψυχὴ ἢ ὄχημα τῆς ψυχῆς.

123. ἐναργέστατα δὲ κἀκεῖνο ἀπέφηνεν, ὅτι τὸν ἄνθρωπον οὐδὲν ἄλλο ἢ τὴν ψυχὴν νομίζει, ἐν οἷς λέγει

ἦλθε δ' ἐπὶ ψυχὴ Θηβαίου Τειρεσίαο,
χρύσεον σκῆπτρον ἔχων (λ 90-1).

122. Just as among the many and varied opinions of philosophers concerning divine things most have their source in Homer, the same is true with regard to human matters.[1] Let us consider first that which concerns the soul. Of all the doctrines, that of Pythagoras and Plato is the noblest, that the soul is immortal—whence Plato also gives it wings [*Phaedrus* 251B, etc.]. Who first expressed this except Homer, when he said among other things,

> The soul fluttered from his limbs and went to Hades
> [Il. 16.856 = 22.362]?

That is, to the unseen or invisible [ἀειδῆ καὶ ἀόρατον] place, whether one makes this mist [ἀήρ], or an underground place. He also expressed this in the *Iliad* when he made the soul of Patroclus stand beside the sleeping Achilles:

> The soul of miserable Patroclus came to him
> [Il. 23.65].

Homer gives him speech, to say among other things,

> The souls, images of the dead, keep me away
> [Il. 23.72].

Likewise, in the entire journey to the dead in the *Odyssey*, what does he show but souls surviving after death and, when they drink blood, speaking? He knew as well that blood is the food and nourishment of the spirit, and the spirit is the soul, or the vehicle of the soul.

123. He furthermore reveals very clearly that he considers man to be nothing other than soul, when he says,

> The soul of Theban Tiresias came,
> holding a golden scepter   [Od. 11.90-91],

---

[1] Chs. 122-31, on Homeric psychology (or doctrines concerning the soul), match closely the preceding section on the gods, attributing to Homer belief in an immortal, immaterial soul.

ἐπίτηδες γὰρ ἀπὸ τοῦ τῆς ψυχῆς ὀνόματος εἰς τὸ ἀρσενικὸν μετέβαλεν, ἵνα δείξῃ ὅτι ἡ ψυχὴ ἦν ὁ Τειρεσίας. καὶ ἐν τοῖς ἑξῆς πάλιν

τὸν δὲ μετ' εἰσενόησε βίην Ἡρακληείην,
εἴδωλον· αὐτὸς δὲ μετ' ἀθανάτοισι (λ 601-2).

καὶ γὰρ ἐν τούτοις πάλιν ἐδήλωσεν, ὅτι τὸ μὲν εἴδωλον, ὅπερ ἦν ἀποπτάμενον τοῦ σώματος, οὐκέτι ⟨τι⟩ τῆς ἐκείνου ὕλης ἐφελκόμενον ἐφαντάζετο, τὸ δὲ καθαρώτατον τῆς ψυχῆς ἀπελθὸν αὐτὸς ἦν ὁ Ἡρακλῆς.

124. ὅθεν κἀκεῖνο δοκεῖ τοῖς φιλοσόφοις τὸ εἶναι τὸ σῶμα τρόπον τινὰ τῆς ψυχῆς δεσμωτήριον. καὶ τοῦτο δὲ Ὅμηρος πρῶτος ἐδήλωσε· τὸ μὲν γὰρ τῶν ζώντων ἀεὶ δέμας προσαγορεύει, ὡς ἐν τούτοις·

οὐ δέμας οὐδὲ φυήν (Α 115 al.)

καὶ

δέμας δ' ἤικτο γυναικὶ (δ 796 al.)

καὶ

ἦ τοι ἐμὴν ἀρετήν, εἶδός τε δέμας τε (σ 251).

τὸ δὲ ἀποβεβληκὸς τὴν ψυχὴν οὐδὲν ἄλλο ἢ σῶμα καλεῖ, ὡς ἐν τούτοις·

for he deliberately shifted from the gender of "soul" [ψυχή] to the masculine [in the participle ἔχων, "bearing"], in order to show that the "soul" was Tiresias himself.[1] He indicates this again in the subsequent lines:

> Then he noticed the strength of Heracles,
> an image, for he himself was with the immortals
> [Od. 11.601-02],

for in these he shows moreover that he imagined that the "image" that had fled the body was no longer dragging along anything of the substance of the body,[2] and that the purest part of the soul, which had departed, was Heracles himself.

124. From this, philosophers also held the opinion that the body is in some sense a prison for the soul, and it was Homer who first revealed this, for he always calls the "body" of a living man a δέμας,[3] as in

> Neither in body nor in character
> [Il. 1.115, etc.],

and

> With a body like a woman's [Od. 4.796, etc.],

and

> Indeed, my virtue, my form and body...
> [Od. 18.251].

That body from which the soul has departed, however, he calls nothing other than σῶμα, as in

---

[1] In ch. 44, above, this same passage is discussed as an example of the gender of a modifier following the sense rather than the gender of the noun modified.

[2] This passage has been emended (e.g. by Bernardakis) to yield a different sense, based on the concept of the εἴδωλον, the "image" or "ghost" as in fact dragging along some matter with it and therefore resembling the dead person. The received text seems rather to place the emphasis on the verb εἰσενόησε (Hom.: εἰσενόησα) and to insist that the perception was noetic, as opposed to visual.

[3] Cf. Stobaeus, 1.41.10 (Dox Gr 96).

σῶμα δὲ οἴκαδ' ἐμὸν δόμεναι πάλιν (Η 79 = Χ 342)

καὶ

σώματ' ἀκηδέα κεῖται ἐνὶ μεγάροις Ὀδυσῆος (ω 187)

καὶ

σῶμα γὰρ ἐν Κίρκης μεγάρῳ κατελείπομεν ἡμεῖς (λ 53).
τὸ γὰρ αὐτό, ζῶντος μὲν τοῦ ἀνθρώπου, δεσμὸς ἦν τῆς ψυχῆς, τελευτήσαντος δέ, ὡσπερεὶ σῆμα καταλείπεται.

125. τούτῳ δὲ ἕπεται καὶ ἕτερον δόγμα τοῦ Πυθαγόρου, τὸ μεταβαίνειν τὰς ψυχὰς τῶν τελευτησάντων εἰς ἕτερα σωμάτων εἴδη. ἀλλ' οὐδὲ τοῦτο τῆς Ὁμήρου διανοίας ἐκτός ἐστιν· ὁ γὰρ ποιήσας καὶ τὸν Ἕκτορα τοῖς ἵπποις διαλεγόμενον καὶ τὸν Ἀντίλοχον καὶ αὐτὸν τὸν Ἀχιλλέα καὶ μὴ ὅτι διαλεγόμενον ἀλλὰ καὶ ἀντακούοντα, καὶ τὸν κύνα πρὸ τῶν ἀνθρώπων καὶ τῶν οἰκείων ἐπιγινώσκοντα τὸν Ὀδυσσέα, τί ἄλλο ἢ τὴν κοινωνίαν τοῦ λόγου καὶ συγγένειαν τῆς ψυχῆς τῶν ἀνθρώπων καὶ τῶν ἄλλων ζῴων παρίστησι; καὶ οἱ τὰς βοῦς Ἡλίου καταφαγόντες καὶ ἐκ τούτων ὀλέθρῳ περιπεσόντες ἐλέγχουσιν, ὅτι οὐ μόνον βόες ἀλλὰ καὶ πάντα τὰ ἄλλα ζῷα, ὡς τῆς αὐτῆς φύσεως ζωτικῆς μετέχοντα, τιμᾶται ὑπὸ τῶν θεῶν.

126. καὶ τὸ μεταβάλλειν δὲ τοὺς ἑταίρους τοῦ Ὀδυσσέως εἰς σύας καὶ τὰ τοιαῦτα ζῷα τοῦτο αἰνίττεται, ὅτι τῶν ἀφρόνων ἀνθρώπων αἱ ψυχαὶ μεταλλάττουσιν εἰς εἴδη σωμάτων θηριωδῶν, ἐμπεσοῦσαι εἰς τὴν τοῦ παντὸς ἐγκύκλιον περιφοράν, ἣν Κίρκην προσαγορεύει καὶ κατὰ τὸ εἰκὸς Ἡλίου παῖδα

> to return my body home   [Il. 7.79 = 22.342],

and

> Unburied bodies lie in Odysseus' halls
> [Od. 24.187],

and

> We left his body behind in Circe's hall
> [Od. 11.53].

That same thing which is a prison or bond for the soul, when the man is still alive, is left behind as a monument or memorial.[1]

125.   Another doctrine of Pythagoras follows from this one, namely that the souls of the dead enter bodies of other sorts. But neither was this foreign to the understanding of Homer, for when he depicted Hector talking to his horses, as well as Antilochus and Achilles himself, and not only speaking but getting answers—and when he depicted his dog recognizing Odysseus before people did, even those of his own household—what else was he showing than that the souls of men and animals share the capacity for rational discourse and are related? Those who ate the cattle of the sun and were destroyed for it demonstrate that not only cattle but all other creatures as well, inasmuch as they participate in the same animate nature, are honored by the gods.

126.   Likewise, the transformation of the companions of Odysseus into pigs and such animals hints at the fact that the souls of unthinking men are transferred into bestial sorts of bodies as they fall into the circular rotation of the universe, which he calls Circe[2] and

---

[1] Plato, *Cratylus*, 400B-C. The point is that the word for the living body (δέμας) echoes, or perhaps imitates, the word for "bondage" (δεσμός) while that used by Homer for the dead body (σῶμα) echoes the word for "grave monument" (σῆμα). The notion has a long history, on which see De Vogel (1981).

[2] "Plutarch" associates Κίρκη with (ἐν)κύκλιον, "cyclical, rotating."

ὑποτίθεται, οἰκοῦσαν ἐν τῇ Αἰαίῃ νήσῳ· ταύτην δὲ ἀπὸ τοῦ αἰάζειν καὶ ὀδύρεσθαι τοὺς ἀνθρώπους ἐπὶ τοῖς θανάτοις κέκληκεν. ὁ δὲ ἔμφρων ἀνήρ, αὐτὸς ὁ Ὀδυσσεύς, οὐκ ἔπαθε τὴν τοιαύτην μεταβολήν, παρὰ τοῦ Ἑρμοῦ, τουτέστι τοῦ λόγου, τὸ ἀπαθὲς λαβών· αὐτὸς δὲ οὗτος, καὶ εἰς Ἅιδου κάτεισιν, ὥσπερ εἶναι λέγων χωρίζειν τὴν ψυχὴν ἀπὸ τοῦ σώματος καὶ θεατὴς ψυχῶν τῶν τε ἀγαθῶν καὶ φαύλων γινόμενος.

127. αὐτὴν δὲ τὴν ψυχὴν οἱ Στωικοὶ ὁρίζονται πνεῦμα συμφυὲς καὶ ἀναθυμίασιν αἰσθητικήν, ἀναπτομένην ἀπὸ τῶν ἐν σώματι ὑγρῶν, Ὁμήρῳ ἀκολουθήσαντες λέγοντι

εἰς ὅ κ' ἀυτμὴ

ἐνὶ στήθεσσι μένῃ (Ι 609-10 = Κ 89-90)

καὶ πάλιν

ψυχὴ δὲ κατὰ χθονὸς ἠΰτε καπνός (Ψ 100),

ἐν οἷς τὸ μὲν ζωτικὸν πνεῦμα ἅτε ἔνικμον ἀυτμῇ δηλοῖ, τὸ δὲ κατασβεννύμενον ἤδη καπνῷ ἀπεικάζει. καὶ αὐτῷ δὲ τῷ τοῦ πνεύματος ὀνόματι κέχρηται ἐπ' αὐτῆς

ὣς εἰπὼν ἔμπνευσε μένος μέγα ποιμένι λαῶν (Ο 262 = Υ 110)

καὶ

θυμὸν ἀποπνείων (Δ 524 = Ν 654)

appropriately makes a child of the sun, living in the island of Aiaia.[1] He has given the island this name from people's wailing[2] and lamenting over the dead. The wise man, however, Odysseus himself, did not undergo this kind of transformation, for he received impassivity from Hermes, which is to say, from reason.[3] Odysseus himself also goes down to Hades—as if he were saying that it is possible to separate the soul from the body—and views both good and evil souls.

127. The Stoics define the soul as the breath of life [πνεῦμα] that is inherent in us, an exhalation capable of sense-perception, rising from the moisture within the body, and in this they follow Homer, where he says,

> as long as breath remains in the chest [Il. 9.609-10 = 10.89-90]

and again,

> and the soul [slipped] beneath the ground like smoke [Il. 23.100],

where he presents the living spirit [πνεῦμα], because it is moist, as "breath," while that which is already extinguished he compares to smoke.

He even uses "spirit" [πνεῦμα] and related words to refer to the soul:

> So speaking, he inspired great strength in the shepherd of the people [Il. 15.262 = 20.110],

and

> his soul expiring [Il. 4.524 = 13.654],

---

[1] Cf. Plutarch fr. 200 (Sandbach) = Stobaeus 1.49.60. The passage is attributed by the mss. of Stobaeus to Porphyry, but Bernardakis, followed by Sandbach, claimed it for Plutarch.
[2] I.e. Αἰαίη is understood to be derived from αἰάζειν.
[3] On Hermes as λόγος, see above ("Introduction"), 24.

καὶ

> ἡ δ' ἐπεὶ οὖν ἄμπνυτο καὶ ἐς φρένα θυμὸς ἀγέρθη (Χ 475).

τουτέστι τὸ πνεῦμα διεσπαρμένον συνελέξατο· καὶ

> αὖθις δ' ἀμπνύνθη· περὶ δὲ πνοιὴ Βορέαο
> ζώγρει ἐπιπνείουσα κακῶς κεκαφηότα θυμόν (Ε 697-8).

τοῦ γὰρ λιποθυμοῦντος τὸ πνεῦμα ῥιπίσασα ἡ ἔξωθεν πνοὴ συμφυὴς οὖσα ζῶντα αὐτὸν κατέστησε. συναίρεται δὲ τῷ λόγῳ ὅτι καὶ ἐπὶ τοῦ ἐκτὸς πνεύματος τῷ τῆς ψυχῆς ὀνόματι κέχρηται εἰπὼν

> ἦκα μάλα ψύξασα (Υ 440).

βούλεται γὰρ εἰπεῖν ἀντιπνεύσασα.

128. Πλάτων δὲ καὶ Ἀριστοτέλης τὴν ψυχὴν ἀσώματον εἶναι ἐνόμισαν, ἀεὶ μέντοι περὶ σῶμα εἶναι καὶ τούτου ὥσπερ ὀχήματος δεῖσθαι· διὸ καὶ ἀπαλλασσομένην τοῦ σώματος τὸ πνευματικὸν ἐφέλκεσθαι πολλάκις καθάπερ ἐκμαγεῖον ἣν ἔσχε τῷ σώματι μορφὴν διαφυλάσσουσαν. οὕτως οὖν καὶ Ὅμηρος οὐδαμοῦ τῆς ποιήσεως εὑρεθήσεται σῶμα τὴν ψυχὴν καλῶν, ἀλλὰ τὸ ἐστερημένον ψυχῆς ἀεὶ τούτῳ τῷ ὀνόματι προσαγορεύει, ὡς καί τινων ἐν τοῖς πρόσθεν ἐμνημονεύσαμεν.

129. τῆς δὲ ψυχῆς ἐχούσης, ὡς καὶ τοῖς φιλοσόφοις δοκεῖ, τὸ μὲν λογικὸν ἐνιδρυμένον τῇ κεφαλῇ, τὸ δὲ ἄλογον, καὶ τούτου τὸ μὲν θυμικὸν ἐνοικοῦν τῇ καρδίᾳ, τὸ δὲ ἐπιθυμητικὸν ἐν τοῖς περὶ τὴν γαστέρα· ἆρ' οὖν οὐ πρότερος Ὅμηρος εἶδε τὴν τούτου διαφοράν, ὃς ἐποίησεν ἐπὶ μὲν τοῦ Ἀχιλλέως τὸν λογισμὸν τῷ θυμῷ μαχόμενον καὶ ἐν τῇ αὐτῇ ῥοπῇ διανοούμενον ἢ

and

> When she recovered her spirit and gathered her wits
> [Il. 22.475],

that is, gathered up her scattered spirits. Likewise,

> Again he got his breath and around him the breath of Boreas revived him, breathing spirit into him even as he was dying
> [Il. 5.697-98].

In the last example, the external wind, being of the same substance as the spirit of the dying man, fans it and brings him back to life. This doctrine is likewise supported by the fact that he uses "soul" [ψυχή and related words] for the breath, even outside the body, saying,

> with a gentle puff of breath [ψύξασα]
> [Il. 20.440],

when he means "breathing out" [ἀντιπνεύσασα].

128. Plato and Aristotle considered the soul to be nonmaterial and always to be attached to the body and to require this as a vehicle, and for this reason even when it has been freed from the body it often draws the spiritual matter [τὸ πνευματικόν] with it, retaining, like a wax tablet, the shape it had by virtue of the body.[1] Thus, nowhere in his poems will you find Homer calling the soul a "body" [σῶμα], but that which is deprived of soul he consistently designates by this name, as we have noted in some of the previous examples.

129. The soul, as the philosophers believe, contains a rational part, seated in the head, and an irrational part, and this latter part is further subdivided into the passionate, dwelling in the heart, and the appetitive, in the region of the stomach.[2] Now, was not Homer the first to see this difference, depicting in Achilles the rational part doing battle with the passionate, and showing him in a single moment

---

[1] This procedure as explained here provides a precedent for the Neoplatonists' idea of an astral body. See Dodds (1963), 317.
[2] This tripartite division is conventionally represented as Platonic dogma, based on *Republic* 4, 436A ff.

ἀμύνασθαι τὸν λελυπηκότα ἢ παῦσαι τὸν χόλον;

 ἕως ὃ ταῦθ' ὥρμαινε κατὰ φρένα καὶ κατὰ θυμόν (Α 193 al.),

τουτέστι τὴν φρόνησιν καὶ τὴν ἀντικειμένην αὐτῷ θυμικὴν ὀργήν, ἧς τὴν φρόνησιν ἐπικρατοῦσαν πεποίηκε· τοῦτο γὰρ αὐτῷ ἡ ἐπιφάνεια τῆς Ἀθηνᾶς βούλεται. καὶ ἐν ἄλλοις δὲ ποιεῖ τὸν λογισμὸν τῷ θυμῷ παραινοῦντα καὶ ὥσπερ ἄρχοντα τῷ ὑποτεταγμέμῳ κελεύοντα

 τέτλαθι δή, κραδίη· καὶ κύντερον ἄλλο ποτ' ἔτλης (υ 18).

καὶ πολλάκις μὲν τῷ λογισμῷ πείθεται τὸ θυμούμενον, ὡς ἐν τούτοις·

 ὣς ἔφατ', ἐν στήθεσσι καθαπτόμενος φίλον ἦτορ·

 τῷ δ' αὖτ' ἐν πείσῃ κραδίη μένε τετληκυῖα (υ 22-3).

ὁμοίως δὲ καὶ τὸ λυπούμενον

 ἀλλὰ τὰ μὲν προτετύχθαι ἐάσομεν ἀχνύμενοί περ,

 θυμὸν ἐνὶ στήθεσσι φίλον δαμάσαντες ἀνάγκῃ (Σ 112-3 = Τ 65-6).

ἐνίοτε δὲ περιγινόμενον τὸν θυμὸν τοῦ λογισμοῦ παρίστησιν· ὅπερ οὐκ ἐπαινῶν ἀλλὰ ψέγων φανερός ἐστιν, ὡς ὁ Νέστωρ τῷ Ἀγαμέμνονι τὴν εἰς τὸν Ἀχιλλέα ὕβριν ὀνειδίζων φησὶν

 οὔ τι καθ' ἡμέτερόν γε νόον· μάλα γάρ τοι ἔγωγε

 πολλ' ἀπεμυθεόμην· σὺ δὲ σῷ μεγαλήτορι θυμῷ

 εἴξας ἄνδρα φέριστον, ὃν ἀθάνατοί περ ἔτισαν,

 ἠτίμησας (Ι 108-11).

ὅμοια δὲ τούτοις καὶ ὁ Ἀχιλλεὺς πρὸς τὸν Αἴαντα λέγει

intending either to attack the one who caused his grief or to restrain his rage?

> While he pondered these things in his mind [κατὰ φρένα] and
> in his soul [κατὰ θυμόν]
> [Il. 1.193, etc.]—

that is, rational thought [φρόνησις] and its opposite, passionate anger [θυμικὴ ὀργή], which he depicts as overcome by rational thought, for this is the meaning of the apparition of Athena. In other passages as well he depicts the rational element advising the passionate soul and giving it orders, as a ruler to a subordinate:

> Be strong, my heart, you've borne worse than this
> [Od. 20.18],

and often rage obeys the rational part, as in these verses:

> Thus he spoke, addressing his heart in his chest
> and his heart obeyed and remained calm
> [Od. 20.22-23],

as does grief,

> Let these things lie in the past, painful though it is,
> taming the heart in our breasts to necessity
> [Il. 18.112-13 = 19.65-66].

Sometimes he depicts the passionate soul overcoming the rational, though clearly with disapproval rather than approval. Thus Nestor speaks to Agamemnon, criticizing his anger toward Achilles:

> Nor is this according to my mind. I tried everything
> to dissuade you, but you yielded to your passionate
> heart and dishonored the best of men, to whom
> the gods themselves give honor
> [Il. 9.108-11].

Achilles says similar things to Ajax:

πάντα τί μοι κατὰ μοῖραν ἐείσω μυθήσασθαι·

ἀλλά μοι οἰδάνεται κραδίη χόλῳ, ὁππότ' ἐκείνου

μνήσομαι, ὅς μ' ἀσύφηλον ἐν Ἀργείοισιν ἔρεξεν (Ι 645-7).

οὕτω δὲ καὶ ὑπὸ φόβου ἔστιν ὅτε ὁ λογισμὸς ἐξίσταται, ὅπου Ἕκτωρ μὲν διανοεῖται ὑποστῆναι τὴν πρὸς τὸν Ἀχιλλέα μάχην

βέλτερον αὖτ' ἔριδι ξυνελαυνέμεν ὅττι τάχιστα·

εἴδομεν ὁπποτέρῳ κεν Ὀλύμπιος εὖχος ὀρέξῃ (Χ 129-30).

εἶτ' ἀναχωρεῖ πλησίον γενομένου τοῦ Ἀχιλλέως

Ἕκτορα δ', ὡς ἐνόησεν, ἕλε τρόμος· οὐδ' ἄρ' ἔτ' ἔτλη

αὖθι μένειν· ὀπίσω δὲ πύλας λίπε, βῆ δε φοβηθείς (Χ 136-7).

130. ἔστι δὲ κἀκεῖνο δῆλον, ὅτι τὰ πάθη περὶ τὴν καρδίαν συνίστησιν· ὀργὴν μὲν οὕτως

κραδίη δέ οἱ ἔνδον ὑλάκτει (υ 13),

λυπὴν δὲ

τέο μέχρις ὀδυρόμενος καὶ ἀχεύων

σὴν ἔδεαι κραδίην (Ω 128-9);

τὸν δὲ φόβον

κραδίη δέ μοι ἔξω

στηθέων ἐκθρῴσκει, τρομέει δ' ὑπὸ φαίδιμα γυῖα (Κ 94-5).

κατὰ τὸν αὐτὸν δὲ λόγον, ὥσπερ τὸν φόβον, οὕτω καὶ θάρσος περὶ καρδίαν ἀποφαίνει

⟨ἐν δὲ σθένος ὦρσεν ἑκάστῳ⟩

> You seem to have spoken all this fittingly,
> but I am near bursting with bitterness whenever I think
> of that man who has degraded me among the Greeks
> [Il. 9.645-47].

There are also times when reason stands aside because of fear, as when Hector is determined to face the fight with Achilles and says,

> Better to come together in battle as soon as possible.
> Let us see to whom the Olympian will give the boast
> [Il. 22.129-30],

but then gives way when Achilles comes near:

> Fear gripped Hector when he saw him and he could not bear
> to stand still. He left the gates behind and fled in terror
> [Il. 22.136-37].

130. It is also clear that he places the emotions in the region of the heart, first anger:

> His heart within him barked
> [Od. 20.13],

then grief,

> how long with weeping and crying
> will you eat out your heart?
> [Il. 24.128-29],

and fear,

> my heart leaps
> from my breast and my strong limbs quake
> [Il. 10.94-95].

In the same way, he shows that bravery, like fear, is related to the heart:

> He stirred up strength in the heart

καρδίη, ἄλληκτον πολεμίζειν ἠδὲ μάχεσθαι (Β 451-2).
ἐκ δὲ τῶν εἰρημένων ἔδοξε τοῖς Στωικοῖς τὸ ἡγεμονικὸν εἶναι περὶ καρδίαν. τὸ δὲ ἐπιθυμητικὸν ὅπως περὶ γαστέρα ἐν πολλοῖς διασαφεῖ καὶ ἐν τούτοις·

ἀλλά με γαστὴρ
ὀτρύνει κακοεργός (σ 53-4),

καὶ

γαστέρα δ' οὔ πως ἔστιν ἀποκρύψαι μεμαυῖαν (ρ 286).

131. καὶ τὰς αἰτίας δὲ τῶν περὶ τὸ θυμικὸν μέρος τῆς ψυχῆς φύσει συμβαινούσας κατεῖδε, τὴν μὲν ὀργὴν ὑπὸ λύπης ἐγγινομένην, ζέσιν δέ τινα τοῦ αἵματος καὶ τοῦ ἐν αὐτῷ πνεύματος οὖσαν ἐμφαίνων, ὡς ἐν τούτοις·

ἀχνύμενος· μένεος δὲ μέγα φρένες ἀμφὶ μέλαιναι
πίμπλαντ', ὄσσε δέ οἱ πυρὶ λαμπετόωντι εἴκτην (Α 103-4 = δ 661-2).

μένος γὰρ τὸ πνεῦμα προσαγορεύειν ἔοικε, τοῦτο δὲ ἐκτείνεσθαι καὶ φλέγεσθαι ἐπὶ τῶν θυμουμένων οἴεται. πάλιν δὲ αὖ τὸ τῶν φοβουμένων πνεῦμα συγχεόμενον καὶ καταψυχόμενον τὰς φρίκας καὶ τοὺς τρόμους ποιεῖ καὶ τὰς ὠχριάσεις ἐν τοῖς σώμασι. πάντα γὰρ ταῦτα συμβαίνει ὑπὸ ψύξεως, ἡ μὲν ὠχρότης ὅτι τοῦ θερμοῦ συντρέχοντος εἰς τὰ μέσα τὸ ἔρευθος ἀπολείπει τὴν ἐπιφάνειαν, ὁ δὲ τρόμος ὅτι ἐντὸς συνειλούμενον τὸ πνεῦμα ἀράσσει τὸ σῶμα· ἡ δὲ φρίκη ὅτι πηγνυμένου τοῦ ὑγροῦ αἱ τρίχες πιεζόμεναι ἀνίστανται. πάντα οὖν ταῦτα σαφῶς σημαίνει Ὅμηρος· φησὶ γὰρ

χλωροὶ ὑπαὶ δείους (Ο 4)

of each, to fight unceasingly and do battle
[Il. 2.451-52].

From the sayings of Homer the Stoics likewise derived the idea that the seat of the ruling principle [τὸ ἡγεμονικόν] is in the region of the heart.

That the appetitive part of the soul is likewise in the region of the stomach he shows in numerous passages, including these:

> but my damned stomach drives me on
> [Od. 18.53-54],

and

> There is no suppressing the cravings of the stomach
> [Od. 17.286].

131. He likewise understood the causes of those things that are the consequences of the nature of the passionate part of the soul: he shows anger, which arises from pain, to be a sort of boiling of the blood and of the spirit in it, as in these verses:

> in a rage—his darkened mind was filled
> with anger and his eyes gleamed like fire
> [Il. 1.103-04 = Od. 4.661-62].

With the word "anger" [μένος], he seems to be designating the spirit and he believes that this is extended and bursts into flame when a person is angered. The spirit of those who are experiencing fear, on the contrary, is contracted and cool, producing goosepimples and shaking and paleness of the body, for all these phenomena are produced by cooling: paleness, because when the warmth retires inward the redness leaves the surface; shaking, because the confined spirit shakes the body; and the goosepimples because as the moist humors are chilled and thicken there is pressure on the hairs and they stand up. Homer clearly indicates all of this, for he says,

> green with fear [Il. 15.4]

καὶ
>>χλωρὸν δέος ᾕρει (Η 479 al.)

καὶ
>>τρομέει δ' ὑπὸ φαίδιμα γυῖα (Κ 95)

καὶ
>>ὣς φάτο· σὺν δὲ γέροντι νόος χύτο, δείδιε δ' αἰνῶς·
>>ὀρθαὶ δὲ τρίχες ἔσταν ἐνὶ γναμπτοῖσι μέλεσσι (Ω 358-9).

κατὰ ταῦτα οὖν καὶ τὸ ἐφοβήθη ῥίγησε (Γ 259 al.) λέγει καὶ τὸν φόβον κρυόεντα (Ι 2) προσαγορεύει, ἐκ δὲ τοῦ ἐναντίου θαλπωρὴν (Ζ 412 al.) τὸ θάρσος καὶ τὴν ἀγαθὴν ἐλπίδα. τὰ μὲν οὖν φαῦλα πάθη τοῦτον τὸν τρόπον διαιρεῖ.

132. πάλιν δὲ τῶν περὶ Ἀριστοτέλην ἀστεῖα πάθη ἡγουμένων τὴν νέμεσιν καὶ τὸν ἔλεον (τοὺς γὰρ ἀγαθοὺς δάκνεσθαι ἐπὶ τοῖς πλησίον, εἰ παρ' ἀξίαν εὐτυχοῦσιν, ὅπερ νέμεσις καλεῖται, ἢ παρ' ἀξίαν δυστυχοῦσιν, ὃ δὴ λέγεται ἐλεεῖν) ταῦτα καὶ Ὅμηρος προσήκειν τοῖς ἀγαθοῖς νομίζει, ὅπου καὶ τῷ Διῒ ἀνατίθησιν αὐτά· ποιεῖ γὰρ ἄλλα τε καὶ ταῦτα

>>Αἴαντος δ' ἀλέεινε μάχην Τελαμωνιάδαο·
>>Ζεὺς γάρ οἱ νεμεσᾶθ' ὅτ' ἀμείνονι φωτὶ μάχοιτο (Λ 542-3).

καὶ ἐν ἄλλοις πάλιν οἰκτείρει τὸν αὐτὸν [τρόπον]
>>διωκόμενον περὶ τεῖχος (Χ 168).

and

> green fear seized them [Il. 7.479, etc.]

and

> [my] strong limbs quake [Il. 10.95],

and

> So he spoke, and the old man's mind was confounded in terror—
> the hair stood straight up on his bent limbs
> [Il. 24.358-59].

For this reason he also says "he was cold" for "he was afraid" and calls fear "icy" and conversely, courage and good hope "warming." This is the manner in which he distinguishes the baser emotions.

132. Aristotle and his school consider indignation and pity to be refined emotions,[1] for good men are annoyed if they see those around them enjoying good fortune they do not deserve, and this is called "indignation" [νέμεσις] or, on the other hand, they experience what is called "pity" [ἐλεεῖν] when they see others experiencing bad fortune they do not deserve. Homer as well considers these emotions appropriate to good men and so attributes them even to Zeus. Here is one example:

> He shrank from fighting Telamonian Ajax,
> for Zeus was indignant that he should fight a better man
> [Il. 11.542-43].

Elsewhere, he takes pity on the same man,

> chased around the walls [Il. 22.168].

---

[1] The term (ἀστεῖα πάθη) is foreign to Aristotle, but the clear reference here is to *Rhetoric* 1386b (2.9.1-2). Cf. *Poetics* 1452b-53b, where pity (ἔλεος) and fear (φόβος) are privileged, and discussed along with the elusive φιλάνθρωπον (1453a1), which may correspond to νέμεσις here.

133. περὶ δὲ ἀρετῆς καὶ κακίας ψυχῆς ἣν ἔχει δόξαν ὁ ποιητὴς ἐν πολλοῖς παρίστησιν. ἐπεὶ γὰρ τὸ μέν τι τῆς ψυχῆς νοερὸν καὶ λογικόν ἐστι τὸ δὲ ἄλογον καὶ ἐμπαθές, καὶ διὰ τοῦτο μέσος θεοῦ καὶ θηρίου γέγονεν ἄνθρωπος, τὴν μὲν ἄκραν ἀρετὴν θείαν ἡγεῖται τὴν δὲ ἄκραν κακίαν θηριωδίαν, ὡς ὕστερον Ἀριστοτέλης (ΝΕ 1145 Α 24) ἐνόμισε. καὶ ταῦτα ἐμφανίζει ἐν ταῖς ὁμοιώσεσιν· ἀεὶ γὰρ ἀγαθοὺς ὀνομάζει θεοειδεῖς (Β 623 al.) καὶ

Διὶ μῆτιν ἀτάλαντον (Β 169 al.)·

τῶν δὲ φαύλων τοὺς μὲν δειλοὺς φυζακινοῖς ἐλάφοισιν (Ν 102) εἴκασε καὶ προβάτοις ἀσημάντοις καὶ λαγωοῖς διωκομένοις· ἐπὶ δὲ τῶν προπετῶς καὶ ἀνοήτως ὑπὸ ὀργῆς φερομένων φησὶ

οὔτ' οὖν πορδάλιος τόσσον μένος οὔτε λέοντος
οὔτε συὸς κάπρου τ' ὀλοόφρονος οὔ τε μέγιστος
θυμὸς ἐνὶ στήθεσσι περὶ σθένεϊ βλεμεαίνει
ὅσσον Πάνθου υἷες ἐυμμελίαι φρονέουσιν (Ρ 20-3).

τοὺς δὲ λυπουμένων ἐμπαθέστερον ὀδυρμοὺς ἀηδόνων φωναῖς ἀπεικάζει

⟨οἷσί τε⟩ τέκνα

ἀγρόται ἐξείλοντο πάρος πετεηνὰ γενέσθαι (π 217-8).

134. οἱ μὲν οὖν Στωικοὶ τὴν ἀρετὴν τίθενται ἐν τῇ ἀπαθείᾳ, ἐκείνοις ἑπόμενοι, ἐν οἷς πᾶν πάθημα ἀναιρεῖ, λέγων περὶ μὲν λύπης

ἀλλὰ χρὴ τὸν μὲν καταθάπτειν ὅς κε θάνῃσι,
νηλέα θυμὸν ἔχοντας, ἐπ' ἤματι δακρύσαντας (Τ 228-9)

καὶ

τίπτε δεδάκρυσαι, Πατρόκλεις, ἠΰτε κούρη (Π 7);

133.	The poet demonstrates his belief concerning the virtue and vice of the soul in many passages. Since one part of the soul is intellectual and rational and the other irrational and emotional and for this reason man is something midway between a god and a beast, Homer calls the extreme of virtue "divine" and the extreme of vice "bestiality," a position later adopted by Aristotle.[1] Homer's belief is revealed in the comparisons, for he is always calling the good "godlike" and "like Zeus in judgment," while among the inferior, the cowardly were like "fleeing deer" [Il. 13.102], and sheep without a shepherd and hunted hares. Concerning those who are impetuously and mindlessly carried away by rage he says,

> A leopard does not have such rage, nor a lion,
> nor a terrible wild boar (whose great raging heart
> is the mightiest of all) as the sons of Panthoos
> of the good ash spear are harboring in their minds
> [Il. 17.20-23],

and he compares the wailings of those who are weeping very emotionally to the song of nightingales,

> whose young
> the peasants have taken, before they were feathered
> [Od. 16.217-18].

134.	The Stoics take virtue to lie in freedom from emotion [ἀπάθεια][2] taking their lead from those passages in which Homer does away with all emotion, saying with regard to grief,

> but whoever dies must be buried
> with a firm heart, after a day's weeping
> [Il. 19.228-29],

and [when Achilles says],

> Why are you weeping, Patroclus, like a girl?
> [Il. 16.7]

---

[1] *Nicomachean Ethics*, 1145a
[2] See Diogenes Laertius 7.117 (Zeno), and ch. 189, below.

περὶ δὲ ὀργῆς

>ὡς ἔρις ἔκ τε θεῶν ἔκ τ' ἀνθρώπων ἀπόλοιτο (Σ 107),

περὶ δὲ τοῦ φόβου

>μή τι φόβον δ' ἀγόρευ', ἐπεὶ οὐδέ σε πεισέμεν ὀΐω (Ε 252)

καὶ

>ὃς δέ κεν ὑμέων
>βλήμενος ἠὲ τυπεὶς θάνατον καὶ πότμον ἐπίσπῃ,
>τεθνάτω (Ο 494-6).

οὕτως καὶ προκαλούμενοι εἰς μονομαχίαν ἀφόβως ὑπακούουσι καὶ πλείους ἀνθ' ἑνὸς ἀνίστανται· καὶ ὁ τετρωμένος οὐδὲν ἧσσον ἔχει τὸ θάρσος παραμένον, ὥς πού φησι

>νῦν δέ μ' ἐπιγράψας ταρσὸν ποδὸς εὔχεαι αὔτως (Λ 388).

καὶ πᾶς ὁ γενναῖος ἀπεικάζεται λέοντι ἢ κάπρῳ ἢ χειμάρρῳ ἢ λαίλαπι.

135. οἱ δὲ ἐκ τοῦ Περιπάτου τὴν ἀπάθειαν ἀνέφικτον ἀνθρώπῳ νομίζουσι, τὴν δὲ μετριοπάθειαν εἰσάγοντες, τῷ τὴν ὑπερβολὴν τῶν παθῶν ἀναιρεῖν, μεσότητι τὴν ἀρετὴν ὁρίζονται. καὶ Ὅμηρος ἀεὶ παράγει τοὺς ἀρίστους οὔτε ἀγεννεῖς οὔτε μὴν ἀφόβους ἢ ἀλύπους παντελῶς, ἐν τῷ μὴ ἄγαν δὲ τοῖς πάθεσι κρατεῖσθαι τῶν φαύλων διαφέροντας. φησὶ γάρ

>τοῦ μὲν γάρ τε κακοῦ τρέπεται χρὼς ἄλλυδις ἄλλῃ,
>οὐδέ οἱ ἀτρέμας ἧσθαι ἐρήτυετ' ἐν φρεσὶ θυμός·
>ἐν δέ τέ οἱ κραδίη μεγάλα στέρνοισι πατάσσει

and with regard to anger:

> Would that strife might disappear from gods and men!
> [Il. 18.107]

and to fear,

> Do not speak of fear, for you will not persuade me
> [Il. 5.252],

and

> whichever of you
> is struck or wounded and meets death and fate,
> let him die   [Il. 15.494-96],

and although it is in this manner that they are called to the fight, they obey fearlessly and not one but many jump up. Moreover, those who are wounded retain all their bravery, as one of them says,

> So now you've scratched the sole of my foot—is
> that your boast?   [Il. 11.388].

Finally, each noble character is compared to a lion, a wild boar, a torrent, or a storm.

135.   The Peripatetics consider freedom from emotion [ἀπάθεια] unattainable for man and introduce the notion of moderation of emotion [μετριοπάθεια],[1] defining virtue in terms of moderation and eliminating excess emotion. Likewise, Homer shows the greatest heroes as by no means lacking in nobility, but at the same time not totally free of fear or grief, but differing from the cowards in not being excessively ruled by emotion. He says,

> The color of a base man is always changing,
> and his heart is not fixed and unshaking within him.
> His great heart pounds within him at the thought

---

[1] The term is foreign to Aristotle, but precisely this distinction is attributed to Aristotle by Diogenes Laertius (5.31).

κῆρας οἰομένῳ· πάταγος δέ τε γίγνετ' ὀδόντων·
τοῦ δ' ἀγαθοῦ οὔτ' ἄρ τρέπεται χρὼς οὔτε τι λίην
ταρβεῖ (Ν 279-80, 282-5).

εὔδηλον γὰρ ὅτι τοῦ ἀγαθοῦ τὸ λίαν φοβεῖσθαι ὑφελὼν τὸ μέτριον κατέλιπε. τοῦτο δὲ καὶ ἐπὶ τῶν ὁμοίων, λύπης τε καὶ ὀργῆς, χρὴ νοεῖν. τοιοῦτόν ἐστι κἀκεῖνο·

Τρῶας μὲν τρόμος αἰνὸς ὑπήλυθε γυῖα ἕκαστον,
Ἕκτορί τ' αὐτῷ θυμὸς ἐνὶ στήθεσσι πάτασσεν (Η 215-6).

οἱ μὲν γὰρ ἄλλοι καὶ ὁρῶντες ἔτρεμον, ὁ δὲ ἐν τῷ κινδύνῳ καθεστὼς ἀνδρεῖος ὢν μόνον ἠγωνία. ὅθεν ἄλλως μὲν ποιεῖ τὸν Δόλωνα καὶ τὸν Λυκάονα φοβουμένους, ἄλλως δὲ τὸν Αἴαντα καὶ τὸν Μενέλαον, ἐντροπαλιζομένους καὶ βάδην ὑποχωροῦντας, ὥσπερ ἀπωσμένους σταθμοῦ λέοντας. ὡσαύτως δὲ καὶ λυπουμένων διαφορὰς ἐπιδείκνυσι καὶ ἡδομένων ὁμοίως· ὥσπερ ὁ μὲν Ὀδυσσεὺς διηγούμενος ὃν τρόπον τοὺς Κύκλωπας ἐξηπάτησεν ἔφη

ἐμὸν δ' ἐγέλασσε φίλον κῆρ (ι 413).

οἱ δὲ μνηστῆρες πεσόντα τὸν πτωχὸν ἰδόντες
χεῖρας ἀνασχόμενοι γέλῳ ἔκθανον (σ 100).

φαίνεται δὲ ἐν ἑκατέροις ἡ τοῦ μετρίου διαφορά. καὶ ὁ μὲν Ὀδυσσεὺς τῆς ἑαυτοῦ γυναικὸς ἐρῶν καὶ κλαίουσαν ἐπ' αὐτῷ ὁρῶν φέρει

ὀφθαλμοὶ δ' ὡς εἰ κέρας ἕστασαν ἠὲ σίδηρος (τ 211).

τῶν δὲ μνηστήρων τῆς αὐτῆς ἐρώντων, θεασαμένων αὐτὴν

of death, and his teeth chatter—
but the good man's color does not change, nor is he
excessively afraid [Il. 13.279-80, 282-85].

It is clear that when he denies excessive fear to the good man, what is left is moderation, and we must conclude that this is true for the comparable emotions of grief and anger as well. This is of the same sort:

A terrible trembling came on the limbs of every Trojan
and even the heart of Hector was stirred in his chest
[Il. 7.215-16].

The others trembled merely at the sight, but he, though he was in peril, was brave and experienced only anguish. There is a similar difference between Homer's portrayal of Dolon and Lycaon in their terror and that of Ajax and Menelaus, who turn from side to side and give ground gradually, like lions driven from the sheep pen. He also presents differences among people who grieve and among people who are happy. Odysseus, describing how he tricked the Cyclopes, said,

My heart laughed within me
[Od. 9.413],

but the suitors, when they saw the beggar down,

were waving their arms in the air, dying with laughter
[Od. 18.100].

In the following set of passages as well, the difference between the moderate man [and the immoderate] appears. Odysseus, while he loves his wife, endures seeing her weep over him:

His eyes were fixed as if they were horn or iron
[Od. 19.211].

But when the suitors, who were in love with the same woman, caught a glimpse of her,

λύτο γούνατ', ἔρως δ' ἄρα θυμὸν ἔθελγε,

πάντες δ' ἠρήσαντο παραὶ λεχέεσσι κλιθῆναι (σ 212-3).

τοιαῦτα μέν ἐστι τὰ παρὰ τῷ ποιητῇ περὶ ψυχῆς δυνάμεων καὶ παθῶν.

136. περὶ δὲ ἀγαθῶν καὶ εὐδαιμονίας πολλῶν εἰρημένων παρὰ τοῖς φιλοσόφοις, τὸ μὲν τὴν ἀρετὴν τῆς ψυχῆς μέγιστον εἶναι τῶν ἀγαθῶν κατὰ πάντας συνέστηκεν. ἀλλ' οἱ μὲν Στωικοὶ τὴν ἀρετὴν αὐτάρκη ἡγοῦνται πρὸς εὐδαιμονίαν, λαβόντες τὸ ἐνδόσιμον ἐκ τῶν Ὁμηρικῶν τούτων, ἐν οἷς τὸν σοφώτατον καὶ φρονιμώτατον πεποίηκεν ὑπὲρ εὐκλείας πόνου καταφρονοῦντα καὶ ἡδονῆς ὑπερορῶντα· τὸ μὲν πρότερον οὕτως·

ἀλλ' οἷον τόδ' ἔρεξε καὶ ἔτλη καρτερὸς ἀνήρ·

αὐτόν μιν πληγῇσιν ἀεικελίῃσι δαμάσσας,

σπεῖρα κάκ' ἀμφ' ὤμοισι βαλών, οἰκῆι ἐοικώς,

ἀνδρῶν δυσμενέων κατέδυ πτόλιν (δ 242, 244-6).

τὸ δεύτερον δ' οὕτως

ἢ μέν μ' αὐτόθ' ἔρυκε Καλυψώ, δῖα θεάων.

ὣς δ' αὔτως Κίρκη κατερήτυεν ἐν μεγάροισιν

Αἰαίη δολόεσσα, λιλαιομένη πόσιν εἶναι·

ἀλλ' ἐμὸν οὔ ποτε θυμὸν ἐνὶ στήθεσσιν ἔπειθεν (ι 29, 31-3).

μάλιστα δὲ ἐν τούτοις τὴν τῆς ἀρετῆς δόξαν συνίστησιν, ἐν οἷς τὸν μὲν Ἀχιλλέα ποιεῖ οὐ μόνον ἀνδρεῖον ἀλλὰ καὶ κάλλιστον τὸ εἶδος καὶ ποδωκέστατον καὶ εὐγενέστατον καὶ πατρίδος ἐπιφανοῦς καὶ ὑπὸ τοῦ μεγίστου τῶν θεῶν βοηθούμενον, τὸν δὲ Ὀδυσσέα συνετὸν μὲν καὶ καρτερὸν τῇ ψυχῇ τὰ δὲ ἄλλα οὐχ ὁμοίᾳ τύχῃ κεχρημένον, ἡλικίας τε καὶ ὄψεως οὐκ ἴσης καὶ γονέων οὐ πάντη ὀνομαστῶν καὶ πατρίδος ἀδόξου καὶ ἀπεχθόμενον ἑτέρῳ θεῷ, ὧν

their limbs went slack, desire bewitched their hearts
and they all swore they would lie beside her
[Od. 18.212-13].

These are the sorts of things the poet says about the faculties of the soul and the passions.

136. Concerning good things [ἀγαθά] and happiness or success [εὐδαιμονία], the philosophers have said a great deal, but all agree that the virtue [ἀρετή] of the soul is the greatest of good things. The Stoics believe that virtue is sufficient for happiness,[1] taking their lead from those Homeric passages in which he shows the wisest and most reasonable of men thinking nothing of toil endured for the sake of fame and showing contempt for pleasure. The first of these qualities appears here:

The powerful hero took this upon him and accomplished it;
covering himself with terrible wounds
and throwing a foul rag around his shoulders,
he entered the city full of his enemies, disguised as a slave
[Od. 4.242, 244-46],

and the second here:

Calypso, brilliant among goddesses, held me back
just as Aiaian Circe forced me to stay
in her halls, the witch, wanting me for her husband,
but she did not persuade the heart within my chest
[Od. 9.29, 31-33].

The doctrine concerning virtue appears even more clearly in those passages in which Homer makes Achilles not only brave but physically very beautiful, swift of foot, noble, sprung from a glorious land, and helped by the greatest of the gods—Odysseus, on the other hand, who is wise and strong of spirit is not shown as equally fortunate in other things, for he does not have the advantages of age and appearance, his family is undistinguished, his homeland obscure, and he is hated by

---

[1] Diogenes Laertius (7.127 [Zeno]) attributes this belief to Zeno, Chrysippus, and Hecaton. Similar claims are frequent in the doxographers. See SVF III, nos. 49-67.

οὐδὲν ἐκώλυεν αὐτὸν εἶναι εὐκλεᾶ, τὴν τῆς ψυχῆς ἀρετὴν κεκτημένον.

137. οἱ δὲ ἐκ τοῦ Περιπάτου πρωτεύειν μὲν τὰ τῆς ψυχῆς ἀγαθὰ νομίζουσιν, οἷον φρόνησιν, ἀνδρείαν, σωφροσύνην, δικαιοσύνην· δεύτερα δὲ εἶναι τὰ τοῦ σώματος, οἷον ὑγίειαν, ἰσχὺν, κάλλος, τάχος· τρίτα δὲ τὰ ἐκτός, οἷον εὐγένειαν, εὐδοξίαν, πλοῦτον. ἐπαινετὸν μὲν γὰρ εἶναι καὶ θαυμαστὸν τὸ ἐν ἀλγηδόσι καὶ νόσῳ καὶ ἀπορίᾳ καὶ συμφοραῖς ἀβουλήτοις χρῆσθαι τῇ ἀρετῇ τῆς ψυχῆς ἀντεχούσης τοῖς κακοῖς, οὐ μέντοι αἱρετὸν οὐδὲ μακάριον· τὸ δὲ ἐν ἀγαθοῖς νοῦν ἔχειν τῷ ὄντι εὔδαιμον, οὐδὲ γὰρ τὴν κτῆσιν μόνην τῆς ἀρετῆς ἀλλὰ καὶ τὴν χρῆσιν καὶ τὴν ἐνέργειαν εἶναι καλόν. ταῦτα δὴ καὶ Ὅμηρος δείκνυσιν ἄντικρυς· τοὺς μὲν γὰρ θεοὺς ἀεὶ ποιεῖ δωτῆρας ἐάων (θ 325) τουτέστι τῶν ἀγαθῶν, ἃ καὶ εὔχονται οἱ ἄνθρωποι παρέχειν αὐτοῖς τοὺς θεούς, οὐκ ἀνωφελῆ δηλονότι ὄντα αὐτοῖς οὐδ' ἀδιάφορα ἀλλὰ πρὸς εὐδαιμονίαν χρήσιμα.

138. τίνα οὖν ἐστι τὰ ἀγαθὰ ὧν ἐφίενται οἱ ἄνθρωποι καὶ δι' ἃ μακαρίζονται ἐν πολλοῖς διασαφεῖ, ἅμα μὲν πάντα ἐπὶ τοῦ Ἑρμοῦ
    οἷος δὴ σὺ δέμας καὶ εἶδος ἀγητός,
πέπνυσαι δὲ νόῳ, μακάρων δ' ἔξ ἐσσι τοκήων (Ω 376-7).
μαρτυρεῖ γὰρ αὐτῷ κάλλος σώματος καὶ φρόνησιν καὶ εὐγένειαν. τὰ δὲ κατὰ μέρος
    τῷ δὲ θεοὶ κάλλος τε καὶ ἠνορέην ἐρατεινὴν

another god [Poseidon]. Yet none of these things prevented his being famous, since he possessed virtue of the soul.

137.   The Peripatetics [make a classification of good things.[1] They] consider primary those belonging to the soul: rationality, bravery, self-restraint, justice—secondary, those of the body, such as health, strength, beauty, speed—and the externals, such as nobility, fame, and wealth, they call tertiary. They consider it admirable and wonderful for someone to maintain the virtue of the soul in the face of pain and sickness, of poverty and unwished-for distress, but at the same time they do not consider this something to be sought after or considered fortunate. They take true happiness to lie in acting with wisdom and restraint while enjoying good things.[2] They believe, moreover, that that which is truly fine is not simply the possession of virtue, but this combined with its use and realization in action.[3] Homer on his side demonstrates this, for he makes the gods to be always

> granters of benefices [ἐάων]   [Od. 8.325],

that is, of "good things" [ἀγαθῶν], which men pray they may receive and which are clearly not useless to them, or indifferent, but useful for happiness.

138.   In many passages Homer indicates which are the good things that men desire and through which they are considered blessed, but he gives a general summary [in what Priam says] with regard to the disguised Hermes:

> so noble you are in face and form,
> wise in mind, and sprung from noble parents
> [Il. 24.376-77],

pointing to his beauty of body, rationality, and nobility. He also mentions these individually:

> The gods granted him beauty and admirable

---

[1] See e.g. *Eudemian Ethics* 1217b-18b, 1235b-36a; *Magna Moralia* 2.9 (1207b).
[2] See e.g. *Nicomachean Ethics*, 1178b-79a.
[3] See e.g. *Eudemian Ethics* 1219a, esp. 33-39.

ὤπασαν (Ζ 156-7)
καὶ
θεσπέσιον πλοῦτον κατέχευε Κρονίων (Β 670).
δῶρον γάρ ἐστι καὶ τοῦτο τοῦ θεοῦ
Ζεὺς δ' αὐτὸς νέμει ὄλβον Ὀλύμπιος ἀνθρώποισι (ζ 188).

139. ποτὲ δὲ καὶ τὴν τιμὴν ἡγεῖται καλὸν
τιοίμην δ' ὡς τίετ' Ἀθηναίη καὶ Ἀπόλλων (Θ 540 = Ν 827),
ποτὲ δὲ τὴν εὐπαιδίαν
ὡς ἀγαθὸν καὶ παῖδα καταφθιμένοιο λιπέσθαι (γ 196),
ποτὲ δὲ τὴν τῶν οἰκείων ἀπόλαυσιν
πέμπετέ με σπείσαντες ἀπήμονα, χαίρετε δ' αὐτοί·
ἤδη γὰρ τετέλεσται ἅ μοι φίλος ἤθελε θυμός,
πομπὴ καὶ φίλα δῶρα, τά μοι θεοὶ οὐρανίωνες
ὄλβια ποιήσειαν· ἀμύμονα δ' οἴκοι ἄκοιτιν
νοστήσας εὕροιμι σὺν ἀρτεμέεσσι φίλοισιν.
ὑμεῖς δ' αὖθι μένοντες εὐφραίνοιτε γυναῖκας
κουριδίας καὶ τέκνα· θεοὶ δ' ἀρετὴν ὀπάσειαν
παντοίην, καὶ μή τι κακὸν μεταδήμιον εἴη (ν 39-46).

140. ὅτι δὲ ἐν τῇ τῶν ἀγαθῶν συγκρίσει τοῦ πλούτου κρεῖσσόν ἐστιν αὐτὸ τὸ δύνασθαι δηλοῖ διὰ τούτων
ὃς καὶ χρυσὸν ἔχων πόλεμόνδ' ἴεν ἠΰτε κούρη,
νήπιος, οὐδέ τί οἱ τόδ' ἐπήρκεσε λυγρὸν ὄλεθρον (Β 872-3)

> courage [Il. 6.156-57],

and

> Zeus poured marvelous wealth upon them
> [Il. 2.670],

for this as well is a gift of the gods:

> Zeus himself, the Olympian, deals out wealth to men
> [Od. 6.188].

139.   In some places he also considers honors a fine thing:

> I would be honored as Athena and Apollo are honored
> [Il. 8.540 = 13.827],

sometimes offspring:

> What a good thing, on dying, to leave a son behind
> [Od. 3.196],

sometimes enjoyment of one's neighbors:

> Pour libations and send me away safe, and so farewell!
> What my heart desired is as good as accomplished,
> a journey home and gifts—may the heavenly gods
> deliver these riches and may I find my beautiful wife
> at home and my friends safe.
> And may you who remain here be a joy to your wives
> and children, and may the gods give every kind
> of goodness and let no evil enter your city
> [Od. 13.39-46].

140.   He shows in the following lines that when good things are compared, strength is greater than wealth:

> Adorned with gold, like a girl, he went off to war,
> —fool—it didn't save him from bitter death
> [Il. 2.872-73],

καὶ

ὡς οὔ τοι χαίρων τοῖσδε κτεάτεσσιν ἀνάσσω (δ 93)
καὶ ὅτι ἀεὶ τοῦ δύνασθαι τὸ φρονεῖν ἄμεινον,

ἄλλος μὲν γάρ τ' εἶδος ἀκιδνότερος πέλει ἀνήρ,
ἀλλὰ θεὸς μορφὴν ἔπεσι στέφει (θ 169-70).

141. δῆλον μὲν οὖν ὅτι καὶ τὰ περὶ σῶμα καὶ τὰ ἐκτὸς εὐτυχούμενα ἀγαθὸν νομίζει· ὅτι δὲ ἄνευ τούτων οὐκ ἔστιν αὐτάρκης ἡ ἀρετὴ μόνη πρὸς εὐδαιμονίαν ἐν ἐκείνοις παρίστησι· δύο γὰρ ἄνδρας εἰς τέλος ἀρετῆς ἥκοντας ὑποθέμενος, τὸν Νέστορα καὶ τὸν Ὀδυσσέα, καὶ τῶν μὲν ἄλλων διαφέροντας, ἀλλήλοις δὲ ὁμοίους φρονήσει καὶ ἀνδρείᾳ καὶ λόγων δυνάμει, οὐκέτι ὁμοίους ἐν ταῖς τύχαις πεποίηκεν, ἀλλὰ τῷ μὲν Νέστορι τοὺς θεοὺς

ὄλβον ἐπικλῶσαι γαμέοντί τε γεινομένῳ τε·
αὐτὸν μὲν λιπαρῶς γηρασκέμεν ἐν μεγάροισιν,
υἱέας αὖ πινυτούς τε καὶ ἔγχεσιν εἶναι ἀρίστους (δ 208, 210-11).

τὸν δὲ Ὀδυσσέα, καίπερ ἐπητὴν ὄντα καὶ ἀγχίνοον καὶ ἐχέφρονα, ἀποκαλεῖ δύστηνον πολλάκις. καὶ γὰρ τὸν μὲν ἐς τὴν ἀνακομιδὴν πλεῦσαι ταχέως καὶ ἀσφαλῶς, τὸν δὲ πλανηθῆναι χρόνῳ πολλῷ καὶ πόνους καὶ κινδύνους ὑπομένειν ἀεὶ μυρίους. οὕτως αἱρετὸν καὶ μακάριόν ἐστιν ὅταν τῇ ἀρετῇ συναιρομένη καὶ μὴ ἀντιπράττουσα ἡ τύχη παρῇ.

142. πῶς δὲ ἡ κτῆσις τῆς ἀρετῆς οὐδὲν ἔστ' ὄφελος, ἂν μὴ καὶ ἐνεργῇ, φανερὸν ἐκ τούτων, ὅπου ὁ μὲν Πάτροκλος ἐπιπλήσσων τῷ Ἀχιλλεῖ λέγει

αἰναρετή· τί σευ ἄλλος ὀνήσεται ὀψίγονός περ,
αἴ κε μὴ Ἀργείοισιν ἀεικέα λοιγὸν ἀμύνῃς (Π 31-2);

and
> so I rule here, taking no joy in my possessions
> [Od. 4.93].

Likewise, he shows that intelligence is always better than strength:

> The other is a weaker man in looks,
> but some god crowns his appearance with words
> [Od. 8.169-70].

141. It is clear that Homer also includes among the good things those positive factors that relate to the body and to externals. He believes, moreover, that without these virtue alone is insufficient for happiness, and demonstrates this as follows. He shows two men, Nestor and Odysseus, at the pinnacle of virtue, surpassing all other men but equal to each other in reasonableness and bravery and power of speech, yet he does not portray them as equal in their fortunes. Rather, the gods made Nestor

> happy in marrying and begetting
> and granted him a rich old age in his halls
> and sons who were wise and masters of the spear
> [Od. 4.208, 210-11],

but Odysseus, though he is "gentle," "shrewd," and "reasonable," is often called "unfortunate." The one sails swiftly and safely home while the other wanders for a long time and goes on enduring countless toils and dangers. Thus the situation to be chosen and considered truly blessed is that in which fortune works with virtue and not against it.

142. In the following passage, where Patroclus is chastising Achilles, Homer indicates that the possession of virtue is useless unless that virtue is active:[1]

> Your damned courage—what good will it ever do anyone,
> if you do not keep the Greeks from terrible destruction?
> [Il. 16.31-32]

---

[1] See ch. 137, above.

οὕτω γὰρ προσεῖπε τὸν τῇ ἀπραξίᾳ ἀνωφελῆ ποιοῦντα τὴν ἀρετήν. ὁ δὲ Ἀχιλλεὺς τὴν ἀπραξίαν ταύτην ὀδυρόμενός φησιν

>ἀλλ' ἧμαι παρὰ νηυσὶν ἐτώσιον ἄχθος ἀρούρης,
>
>τοῖος ἐὼν οἷος οὔ τις Ἀχαιῶν χαλκοχιτώνων (Σ 104-5).

ἄχθεται γὰρ ὅτι τὴν ἀρετὴν κεκτημένος οὐ κέχρηται αὐτῇ, ἀλλὰ μηνίων τοῖς Ἀχαιοῖς

>οὔτε ποτ' εἰς ἀγορὴν πωλέσκετο κυδιάνειραν,
>
>... ἀλλὰ φθινύθεσκε φίλον κῆρ
>
>αὖθι μένων, ποθέεσκε δ' αὐτήν τε πόλεμόν τε (Α 490-2).

καὶ γὰρ οὕτως ὁ Ποῖνιξ ἐπαίδευε

>μύθων τε ῥητῆρ' ἔμεναι πρηκτῆρά τε ἔργων (Ι 443).

ὅθεν καὶ τεθνεὼς ἄχθεται τῇ ἀπραξίᾳ λέγων

>βουλοίμην κ' ἐπάρουρος ἐὼν θητευέμεν ἄλλῳ
>
>ἀνδρὶ παρ' ἀκλήρῳ, ᾧ μὴ βίοτος πολὺς εἴη,
>
>ἢ πᾶσιν νεκύεσσι καταφθιμένοισιν ἀνάσσειν (λ 489-91),

καὶ ἐπιφέρει τὴν αἰτίαν

>οὐ γὰρ ἐγὼν ἐπαρωγὸς ὑπ' αὐγὰς ἠελίοιο
>
>τοῖος ἐών, οἷός ποτ' ἐνὶ Τροίῃ εὐρείῃ (λ 498-9)

for this is how he addressed Achilles, who was rendering his bravery ineffective by inactivity. Achilles himself, lamenting his own inactivity, says,

> but I sit beside the ships, a useless weight on the earth,
> though I am capable of more than any of the other Greeks
> [Il. 18.104-05].

It pains him that he has virtue but makes no use of it, but in his anger at the Greeks,

> he never frequented the assembly where men win fame,
> ... but wore away his heart
> staying away, though he craved the fight and the battle cry
> [Il. 1.490-92].

Phoenix had taught him

> to be a speaker of words and a doer of deeds
> [Il. 9.443],

so that even when he is dead, inactivity weighs upon him, since he says,

> I would rather be a servant
> to an insignificant man with no wealth
> than be lord over all the dead
> [Od. 11.489-91]

and he adds the reason:

> for I am not a fighting man under the sun
> such as I once was at wide Troy
> [Od. 11.498-99].

143. ἔτι τοίνυν οἱ Στωικοὶ φίλους θεῶν τοὺς ἀγαθοὺς ἄνδρας ἀποφαίνοντες παρ' Ὁμήρου καὶ τοῦτο ἔλαβον, λέγοντος ἐπὶ τοῦ Ἀμφιαράου

ὃν περὶ κῆρι φίλει Ζεὺς αἰγίοχος καὶ Ἀπόλλων (ο 245)

καὶ ἐπὶ τοῦ Ὀδυσσέως

χαῖρε δ' Ἀθηναίη πεπνυμένῳ ἀνδρὶ δικαίῳ (γ 52).

144. ἔστι δὲ τῶν αὐτῶν φιλοσόφων δόγμα καὶ τὸ διδακτὴν εἶναι τὴν ἀρετὴν, ἔχουσαν μὲν ἀρχὴν τὴν εὐγένειαν· ὃ καὶ Ὅμηρός φησι

τοίου γὰρ ... πατρός, ὃ καὶ πεπνυμένα βάζεις (δ 206).

ὑπὸ δὲ παιδείας εἰς τὸ τέλειον προαγομένην. ἔστι γὰρ ἀρετὴ ἐπιστήμη τοῦ ὀρθῶς βιοῦν, τουτέστιν ὧν τοὺς εὖ βιωσομένους πράσσειν προσήκει. λέγει γὰρ

νήπιον. οὔ πω εἰδόθ' ὁμοιίου πολέμοιο

οὐδ' ἀγορέων (Ι 440-1)

καὶ ἐν ἄλλοις

οὐδέ με θυμός ἄνωγεν, ἐπεὶ μάθον ἔμμεναι ἐσθλός (Ζ 444)

καὶ ὁ Φοῖνιξ φησιν ἐπὶ τοῦ Ἀχιλλέως

143. Moreover the Stoics, who indicate that good men are the friends of the gods,[1] took this from Homer as well, where he describes Amphiareus as a man

> whom aegis-bearing Zeus and Apollo love greatly
> [Od . 15.245]

and says of Odysseus,

> Athena was pleased with the wise, just man
> [Od. 3.52].

144. The same philosophers also maintain the position that virtue can be taught,[2] and that it has its roots in noble birth.[3] Homer says this as well:

> of such a father, for you speak wisely
> [Od. 4.206].

They believe virtue is brought to perfection through education, for virtue is knowledge of how to live correctly—that is, of those things that are fitting for those who are going to live well. This, too, is in Homer, for he says [of Achilles that he was]

> a mere infant, with no experience of war
> or of speaking   [Il. 9.440-41],

and elsewhere [Hector says],

> my heart does not urge me to flee, for I have learned to be noble
> [Il. 6.444].

Phoenix says of Achilles [referring to Peleus]:

---

[1] SVF I, no. 216 (Zeno); III, no. 584.
[2] Diogenes Laertius (7.91) attributes this opinion to Chrysippus, Cleanthes, and Posidonius.
[3] This "Stoic" position is less easily documented, and if anything the Stoics seem to have had little concern for birth. At any rate, εὐγένεια was grouped with the "indifferent" things (οὐδέτερα or ἀδιάφορα, Diogenes Laertius 7.102).

τούνεκά με προέηκε διδασκέμεναι τάδε πάντα,

μύθων τε ῥητῆρ' ἔμεναι πρηκτῆρά τε ἔργων (Ι 442-3).

ἐπεὶ γὰρ ὁ βίος ἐκ πράξεων καὶ λόγων συνέστηκε, τούτων φησὶ διδάσκαλον ἑαυτὸν τοῦ νεανίσκου γεγονέναι. ἐκ δὲ τῶν εἰρημένων δῆλον ὅτι πᾶσαν ἀρετὴν ἀποφαίνει διδακτήν. οὕτω μὲν οὖν πρῶτος Ὅμηρος ἔν τε ἠθικοῖς καὶ φυσικοῖς φιλοσοφεῖ.

145. ἔχεται δὲ τῆς αὐτῆς θεωρίας καὶ ἀριθμητικὴ καὶ μουσική, ἃς καὶ Πυθαγόρας διαφερόντως ἐτίμησεν. ἴδωμεν οὖν εἰ καὶ τούτων ἐστὶ παρὰ τῷ ποιητῇ λόγος. ἀλλὰ μὴν πλεῖστος· ὀλίγα δὲ ἐκ πολλῶν παρατεθέντα ἐξαρκέσει. ὁ γὰρ Πυθαγόρας τοὺς ἀριθμοὺς μεγίστην δύναμιν ἔχειν ἡγούμενος καὶ πάντα εἰς ἀριθμοὺς ἀναφέρων, τῶν τε ἄστρων τὰς περιόδους καὶ τῶν ζῴων τὰς γενέσεις, δύο τὰς ἀνωτάτω ἀρχὰς ἐλάμβανε, τὴν μὲν ὡρισμένην μονάδα, τὴν δὲ ἀόριστον δυάδα καλῶν, τὴν μὲν ἀγαθῶν, τὴν δὲ κακῶν οὖσαν ἀρχήν· ἡ μὲν γὰρ τῆς μονάδος φύσις ἐγγενομένη τῷ μὲν περιέχοντι εὐκρασίαν, ψυχαῖς δὲ ἀρετήν, σώμασι δὲ ὑγίειαν, πόλεσι δὲ καὶ οἴκοις εἰρήνην καὶ ὁμόνοιαν παρέσχε. πᾶν γὰρ ἀγαθὸν συμφωνίας οἰκεῖόν ἐστιν. ἡ δὲ τῆς δυάδος πᾶν τοὐναντίον, ἀέρι χειμῶνα, ψυχαῖς κακίαν, σώμασι νόσους, πόλεσι δὲ καὶ οἰκίαις στάσεις καὶ ἔχθρας ἐγέννησε. πᾶν γὰρ κακὸν ἐκ διαστάσεως καὶ διαφορᾶς γίνεται. ὅθεν καὶ τῶν ἐφεξῆς ἀριθμῶν τὸν μὲν ἄρτιον ἐνδεᾶ καὶ ἀτελῆ, τὸν δὲ περισσὸν πλήρη τε καὶ τέλειον ἀπέφηνεν, ὅτι μιγνύμενός τε πρὸς τὸν ἄρτιον ἀεὶ τὴν ἑαυτοῦ δύναμιν διασῴζει, τοῦ περισσοῦ καὶ ἐν τούτοις ἐπικρατοῦντος· ἑαυτῷ τε συντιθέμενος γεννᾷ τὸν ἄρτιον· γόνιμος γάρ ἐστι καὶ ἔχει δύναμιν ἀρχῆς καὶ διαίρεσιν οὐκ ἐπιδέχεται, ἀεὶ τῆς μονάδος ἐν αὐτῷ περιούσης. ὁ δὲ ἄρτιος οὔτε γεννᾷ ποτε τὸν περισσὸν συντιθέμενος ἑαυτῷ οὔτε ἐστὶν ἀδιαίρετος. καὶ Ὅμηρος τοίνυν τήν τε τοῦ ἑνὸς φύσιν ἐν τῇ τοῦ ἀγαθοῦ μοίρᾳ καὶ τὴν τῆς δυάδος ἐν τῇ ἐναντίᾳ τιθεὶς φαίνεται πολλάκις, ἐνηέα (Ρ 204

[Plutarch] 54B *The Essay on the Life and Poetry of Homer* 229

> Therefore he set me to teach you all these things:
> to be a speaker of words and a doer of deeds
> [Il. 9.442-43],

for since life is made up of actions and words he says that he was a teacher of these things for the young man. From this it is clear that Homer shows all virtue to be teachable.

Thus Homer was the first to philosophize in the areas of ethics and physics.

145. Arithmetic and music,[1] which Pythagoras held in particular honor, belong to the same area of speculation. Let us examine whether or not there is an account of these things in the Poet. Why, there is a very substantial account, indeed! It will suffice to set out a few examples from the many available. Pythagoras believed that numbers have enormous power and referred everything to number, including the rotations of the heavenly bodies and the births of living creatures. He took there to be two highest principles, the one finite, which he called the monad, and the other infinite, which he called the dyad. The first was the principle of good things, the second, that of evil. The nature of the monad, when it is present, produces mildness in the environment, excellence in souls, health in bodies and peace and concord in cities and households. Everything that is good is related to harmony. The nature of the dyad is just the opposite, producing storms in the atmosphere, baseness in souls, diseases in bodies and rebellion and hatred in cities and households. All evil comes from division and difference.

Thus among the rest of the numbers he showed that the even were imperfect and incomplete, the odd complete and perfect, because when the odd is added to the even it always retains its own force,[2] and the odd is dominant here as well. If odd is added to odd it produces even, for it is productive and retains the force of a first principle: it does not tolerate division in half, since a monad always remains.[3] The even added to itself never produces the odd, nor is it indivisible.

Homer often places the nature of the "one" in the sphere of the good and that of the dyad in the opposite sphere. He often calls a good

---

[1] A similar account of Pythagorean arithmology can be found in Stobaeus, 1.1.10 (Dox Gr 96-97). Cf. Stobaeus 1.1.2. On the inconsistencies with the Aristotelian account of Pythagoreanism, see Burkert (1972), 61 with n. 44.
[2] I.e. odd + even = odd.
[3] I.e. if you try to divide an odd number in two, there is always a "one" left over.

al.) τὸν ἀγαθὸν λέγων πολλάκις καὶ ἐνηείην (Ρ 670) τὴν τοιαύτην διάθεσιν, δύην (Ξ 215 al.) δὲ τὴν κάκωσιν· καὶ ὅτι

  οὐκ ἀγαθὸν πολυκοιρανίη· εἷς κοίρανος ἔστω (Β 204)
καὶ

  μήτ' ἐν πολέμοις δίχα βάζειν μήτ' ἐνὶ βουλῇ,
  ἀλλ' ἕνα θυμὸν ἔχοντε νόῳ καὶ ἐπίφρονι βουλῇ (γ 127-8).
ἀεὶ δὲ τῷ περισσῷ ἀριθμῷ χρῆται ὡς κρείσσονι· καὶ γὰρ τὸν σύμπαντα κόσμον πέντε μοίρας ἔχοντα ποιῶν τὰς τρεῖς τούτων οὔσας μέσας διαιρεῖ,

  τριχθὰ δὲ πάντα δέδασται, ἕκαστος δ' ἔμμορε τιμῆς (Ο 189).
διὸ καὶ Ἀριστοτέλης (De mundo 393A1) πέντε εἶναι τὰ στοιχεῖα ἐνόμισεν, ὡς τοῦ περισσοῦ καὶ τελείου ἐν παντὶ τὸ κράτος ἔχοντος. καὶ τοῖς μὲν οὐρανίοις δαίμοσι τὰ περισσὰ ἀπονέμει. ὅ τε γὰρ Νέστωρ τῷ Ποσειδῶνι θύει ἐννεάκις ἐννέα ταύρους καὶ τὸν Ὀδυσσέα θύειν κελεύει ὁ Τειρεσίας

  ἀρνειὸν ταῦρόν τε συῶν τ' ἐπιβήτορα κάπρον (λ 131 = ψ 278).
ὁ δὲ Ἀχιλλεὺς τῷ Πατρόκλῳ ἐναγίζει πάντα ἄρτια, ἵππους μὲν τέσσαρας

  δώδεκα δὲ Τρώων μεγαθύμων υἱέας ἐσθλούς (Ψ 175).

man "gentle" [ἐνηής]¹ and the corresponding condition "gentleness" [ἐνηείη], while he calls misfortune "misery" [δύη].² And he says,

> It is no good for many to rule: let there be one chief
> [Il. 2.204],

and

> not to be divided in war or in counsel,
> but to be of one mind, with one sound opinion
> [cf. Od. 3.127-28].

Homer always takes the odd number as better, for he depicts the entire universe as divided into five parts and then further distinguishes the middle three:

> The universe was divided in three and each had his share of honor [Il 15.189].

For this reason, Aristotle held the opinion that there were five elements since the odd in its perfection has power in everything.³ He also assigns the odd to the celestial gods, for Nestor sacrifices nine times nine bulls to Poseidon and Tiresias tells Odysseus to sacrifice

> a ram, an ox, and a boar that mounts the sows
> [Od. 11.131 = 23.278],

but Achilles in his sacrifices for Patroclus⁴ uses even numbers of victims, four horses,

> and twelve noble sons of the great-hearted Trojans
> [Il. 23.175],

---

[1] The author relates ἐνηής "gentle" and ἐνηείη "gentleness" to the similar-sounding ἕν "one."
[2] As if from δύο, "two."
[3] [Aristotle], *On the Universe* 393a.
[4] Cf. ch. 190, below, on the assessment of Achilles' funerary sacrifice for Patroclus.

καὶ ἐννέα κυνῶν ὄντων τοὺς δύο ἐμβάλλει τῇ πυρᾷ, ἵνα τοὺς ἑπτὰ ἑαυτῷ ἀπολίπηται. καὶ ἐν πολλοῖς τῷ τῶν τριῶν καὶ πέντε καὶ ἑπτὰ ἀριθμῷ χρῆται, μάλιστα δὲ τῷ τῶν ἐννέα·

 ὣς νείκεσσ᾽ ὁ γέρων· τοί δ᾽ ἐννέα πάντες ἀνέσταν (H 161)

καὶ

 ἐννέωροι γάρ τοί γε καὶ ἐννεαπήχεες ἦσαν
 εὖρος· ἀτὰρ μῆκός γ᾽ ἐγενέσθην ἐννεόργυιοι (λ 311-2)

καὶ

 ἐννῆμαρ μὲν ἀνὰ στρατὸν ᾤχετο κῆλα θεοῖο (A 53)

καὶ

 ἐννῆμαρ ξείνισσε καὶ ἐννέα βοῦς ἱέρευσε (Z 174).

τί δήποτε οὖν ἐστιν ὁ τῶν ἐννέα ἀριθμὸς τελειότατος; ὅτι ἐστὶν ἀπὸ τοῦ πρώτου περισσοῦ τετράγωνος καὶ περισσάκις περισσός, εἰς τρεῖς διαιρούμενος τριάδας, ὧν ἑκάστη πάλιν εἰς τρεῖς μονάδας διαιρεῖται.

146. οὐ μόνον δὲ τὴν δύναμιν τῶν ἀριθμῶν ἀλλὰ καὶ τὴν λογιστικὴν μέθοδον ὑπέδειξεν, ἐν μὲν τῷ καταλόγῳ ποιήσας

 τῶν μὲν πεντήκοντα νέες κίον, ἐν δὲ ἑκάστῃ
 κοῦροι Βιωτῶν ἑκατὸν καὶ εἴκοσι βαῖνον (B 509-10)

καὶ πάλιν

 πεντήκοντ᾽ ἔσαν ἄνδρες (Π 170).

ἐξ ὧν λογίζεσθαι πάρεστιν ὅτι τῶν νεῶν πασῶν οὐσῶν ἐγγὺς χιλίων διακοσίων καὶ ἐχουσῶν ἑκάστης ἑκατὸν ἄνδρας ὁ σύμπας ἀριθμὸς δώδεκά που μυριάδων

and of the nine dogs he throws two into the flames so that he has seven left. Homer often uses the numbers 3, 5, 7, and most particularly, 9:

> Thus the old man rebuked them and the nine men sprang up
> [Il. 7.161],

and

> When they were nine years old they were nine cubits across the shoulders, and their height was nine fathoms
> [Od. 11.311-12],

and

> The god's shafts went nine days through the camp
> [Il. 1.53],

and

> He entertained him for nine days and sacrificed nine oxen
> [Il. 6.174].

Why, in fact, is the number 9 the most perfect? It is that it is the square of the first odd number and odd several times over, since it may be divided into three triads, each of which may be divided into three monads.

146. Homer demonstrates not only the power of numbers but also the technique of calculation, saying in the catalogue,

> From these came fifty ships, and in each
> were a hundred and twenty Boeotian young men
> [Il. 2.509-10],

and again [in each of Philoctetes' ships], "there were fifty men" [Il. 16.170], from which it is possible to calculate that since there are

γίνεται. πάλιν δὲ ἐπὶ τῶν Τρώων φήσας

    χίλι' ἄρ' ἐν πεδίῳ πυρὰ καίετο, πὰρ δὲ ἑκάστῳ

    πεντήκοντ' ἔσαν ἄνδρες (Θ 562-3),

παρέχει λογίζεσθαι ὅτι ἦσαν πεντάκις μύριοι ἄνευ τῶν συμμάχων.

147. τὴν δὲ μουσικήν, οἰκειοτάτην οὖσαν τῇ ψυχῇ, καθότι ἐστὶν ἁρμονία κεκραμένη ἐκ διαφόρων ἀρχῶν, καὶ τοῖς μέλεσι καὶ ῥυθμοῖς τό τε ἐκλελυμένον αὐτῆς ἐπιτείνουσαν καὶ τὸ σφοδρὸν ἀνιεῖσαν, οἵ τε Πυθαγορικοὶ διὰ σπουδῆς εἶχον καὶ πρὸ αὐτῶν Ὅμηρος. καὶ ἐγκώμιον μὲν αὐτῆς ἐπὶ τῶν Σειρήνων διεξέρχεται, ᾧ καὶ ἐπιλέγει

    ἀλλ' ὅ γε τερψάμενος νεῖται καὶ πλείονα εἰδώς (μ 188).

ἄλλοτε δὲ ἐν ταῖς εὐωχίαις τὴν κιθάραν παραλαμβάνει, ὡς καὶ παρὰ τοῖς μνηστῆρσι

                                      φόρμιγξ,

    ...ἣν ἄρα δαιτὶ θεοὶ ποίησαν ἑταίρην (ρ 270-1),

καὶ παρ' Ἀλκινόῳ ὁ κιθαρῳδὸς

                      ἀνεβάλλετο καλὸν ἀείδειν (θ 266)

καὶ ἐν γάμοις

    αὐλοὶ φόρμιγγές τε βοὴν ἔχον (Σ 495)

καὶ ἐν ἔργοις, ὅπου τρυγωμένης ὀπώρας

nearly 1,200 ships in all, and each had a hundred men, the total number of the Greeks comes to about 120,000.[1]

On the other hand when he says with regard to the Trojans,

> A thousand fires burned in the plain and beside each
> lay fifty men
> [Il. 8.562-63],

he permits us to calculate that they numbered 50,000, not counting the allies.

147. The Pythagoreans and Homer before them held music in high esteem, as intimately related to the soul, since it is a harmony mixed from various sources, using melody and rhythm to draw the soul taut when it is slack and relax it when it is excessively strained. Homer praises music when he is discussing the Sirens and says,

> but when he has enjoyed it he goes away wiser
> [Od. 12.188].

Sometimes in feasts he includes the lyre, so that even among the suitors [we find]:

> the lyre,
> ... which the gods made to be a companion for feasting
> [Od. 17.270-71].

Likewise, the kitharode in Alcinous' halls

> began a beautiful song   [Od. 8.266].

In weddings,

> flutes and lyres sounded   [Il. 18.495]

and at the fall harvest, while they worked,

---

[1] The calculation is done along the same lines by Thucydides (1.10).

πάις φόρμιγγι λιγείη

ἱμερόεν κιθάριζε, λίνον δ' ὑπὸ καλὸν ἄειδεν (Σ 569-70)

καὶ ἐν πολέμῳ

αὐλῶν συρίγγων τ' ἐνοπήν (Κ 13)

ἀκούεσθαι λέγει. οὐδὲν δὲ ἧσσον καὶ εἰς πένθη παραλαμβάνει τὴν μουσικήν,

θρήνων ἐξάρχους (Ω 721)

ἀοιδοὺς ποιῶν, ὡς τῇ λειότητι τῶν μελῶν τὴν τραχύτητα τῆς ψυχῆς καταστέλλοντας.

148. οὐκ ἄδηλον δὲ ὅτι διττή ἐστιν ἡ μελῳδία, ἡ μὲν ἐν τῇ φωνῇ ἡ δὲ ἐν ὀργάνοις, τοῖς τε ἐμπνευστοῖς τοῖς τε ἐντατοῖς· τῶν δὲ ἐν αὐτῇ φθόγγων ὁ μέν ἐστι βαρὺς ὁ δὲ ὀξύς, καὶ τούτων δὲ τὰς διαφορὰς Ὅμηρος ἔγνω, ὃς γυναῖκας μὲν καὶ παῖδας καὶ γέροντας ὀξυφώνους ποιεῖ διὰ τὸ λεπτὸν τοῦ πνεύματος, τοὺς δὲ ἄνδρας βαρυφώνους ἔν τε ἄλλοις καὶ ἐν τούτοις·

τῷ δὲ βαρὺ στενάχοντι παρίστατο πότνια μήτηρ,

ὀξὺ δὲ κωκύσασα κάρη λάβε παιδὸς ἑοῖο (Σ 70-1)

καὶ πάλιν

ὣς ὁ βαρὺ στενάχων ἔπε' Ἀργείοισι μετηύδα (Ι 16).

οἱ δὲ γέροντες

τέττιξιν ἐοίκοτες (Γ 151)

ζῴοις ὀξυφώνοις ἰσάζονται. καὶ ἐν τοῖς ὀργάνοις δὲ αἱ χορδαὶ ὅσαι λεπταί εἰσι καὶ συντόνως κινούμεναι ῥᾳδίως τέμνουσι τὸν ἀέρα, ὅθεν τὸν ὀξὺν φθόγγον ἀποτελοῦσιν· αἱ δὲ παχεῖαι βραδεῖαν ἔχουσαι τὴν κίνησιν ἠχοῦσι βαρύ· καθ' ὃν λόγον καὶ Ὅμηρος τὴν μάστιγα λιγυρὴν (Λ 532) προσηγόρευσεν, ἐπεὶ λεπτὴ οὖσα ὀξὺν ἦχον ἀποδίδωσι· ταῦτα μὲν οὖν περὶ τῆς παρ' Ὁμήρῳ μουσικῆς.

> A boy played beautifully
> on the joyful lyre and sang the Linus song
> [Il. 18.569-70].

Likewise in war, he says that

> a sound of flutes and pipes   [Il. 10.13]

is heard. He even makes music the companion of grief and makes bards

> the leaders of the lamentation [Il. 24.721],

moderating the violence of the grieving soul by the smooth sound of the melodies.

148. Clearly there are two kinds of music, that of the voice and that of instruments, the latter further divided into wind and string instruments. Pitch is likewise divided into low and high. Homer recognized these distinctions and made women, children, and old men high-voiced, because of the delicacy of their spirit, and mature men deep-voiced, in such passages as,

> As he moaned deeply his mother came to him
> and, with a piercing wail, grasped her son's head
> [Il. 18.70-71],

and again,

> Groaning deeply he addressed the Greeks
> [Il. 9.16],

and where he says the old men were "like cicadas" [Il. 3.151], comparing them to high-voiced creatures.

Likewise in instruments, strings which are fine and vibrate tightly and rapidly cut the air easily and so produce a high sound; thick strings with slow motion sound low and it is for this reason that Homer calls the whip "shrill," since it gives off a high sound by virtue of being fine.

This will suffice on Homer's treatment of music.

149. ἐπεὶ δὲ ἐν τούτοις καὶ Πυθαγόρου ἐμνημονεύσαμεν, ᾧ μάλιστα ἤρεσκεν ἡ ἐχεμυθία καὶ τὸ σιγᾶν ἃ μὴ χρὴ λέγειν, θεασώμεθα εἰ καὶ Ὅμηρος ταύτην ἔσχε τὴν γνώμην. ἐπί τε γὰρ τῶν παροινούντων ἔφη

καί τι ἔπος προέηκεν ὅπερ τ' ἄρρητον ἄμεινον (ξ 466)·

καὶ τῷ Θερσίτῃ ἐπιπλήττει

Θέρσιτ' ἀκριτόμυθε, λιγύς περ ἐὼν ἀγορητής·

ἴσχεο (Β 246-7)·

καὶ τοῦ Ἰδομενέως καθαπτόμενος ὁ Αἴας λέγει

αἰεὶ μύθοις λαβρεύεαι· οὐδέ τί σε χρὴ

λαβραγόρην ἔμεναι (Ψ 478-9)·

καὶ τῶν στρατευμάτων εἰς μάχην συνιόντων

Τρῶες μὲν κλαγγῇ τ' ἐνοπῇ τ' ἴσαν, ὄρνιθες ὥς·

οἱ δ' ἄρ' ἴσαν σιγῇ μένεα πνείοντες Ἀχαιοί (Γ 2, 8).

βαρβαρικὸν γὰρ ἡ κραυγή, Ἑλληνικὸν δὲ ἡ σιωπή· διὸ καὶ τοὺς φρονιμωτάτους ἐγκρατεστάτους γλώσσης πεποίηκε· καὶ τὸν Ὀδυσσέα τῷ υἱῷ διακελευόμενον

εἰ ἐτεόν γ' ἐμός ἐσσι, ἐμοὶ δέ σε γείνατο μήτηρ,

μήτε τι Λαέρτης ἴστω τόδε μήτε συβώτης

μήτε τις οἰκείων μήτ' αὐτὴ Πηνελόπεια (π 300, 302-3)·

149.[1] Since in this context we have mentioned Pythagoras, who put great value on silence and on keeping silent that which must not be spoken, let us consider whether Homer as well had this opinion. He says about drunkards:

> and he spoke words which would better have remained unspoken [Od. 14.466],

and he rebukes Thersites saying,

> Silence, Thersites—you speak thoughtlessly,
> shrill speaker though you are
> [Il. 2.246-47].

Ajax says, silencing Idomeneus,

> You are always speaking rashly—you must not be a braggart [Il. 23.478-79],

and when the armies enter the battle,

> The Trojans went with noise and shouting like birds
> but the Greeks went silently, breathing might
> [Il. 3.2, 8],

for crying out is barbaric and silence is Greek, and for this reason he has made the most reasonable men those who are best able to restrain their tongues. Odysseus tells his son,

> If you are mine and your mother bore you to me,
> do not let Laertes or the swineherd know our secret
> nor any of the servants, nor Penelope herself
> [Od. 16.300, 302-03],

---

[1] This chapter resembles Plutarch fr. 207 (incert. lib.) Sandbach (= Stobaeus 3.33.16). See Dox Gr, 97-99. Wyttenbach (in his edition, 1800) attributed it to Plutarch's *Homeric Studies*, Diels (Dox Gr, 97-99) to an early pseudo-Plutarchan work subsequently mined in the present text, and Della Corte (1938) to a lost Plutarchan work. See Sandbach *ad loc.* in his Loeb edition of the fragments (= Plutarch, *Moralia* 15, 380, note b).

καὶ πάλιν αὐτῷ παραινεῖ

σίγα καὶ κατὰ σὸν νόον ἴσχανε μηδ' ἐρέεινε (τ 42).

τοιαῦτα μὲν δὴ τὰ τῶν ἐνδόξων φιλοσόφων δόγματα ἅπερ ἐξ Ὁμήρου τὴν ἀρχὴν ἔχει.

150. εἰ δὲ δεῖ καὶ τῶν ἰδίας τινὰς αἱρέσεις ἑλομένων μνημονεῦσαι, εὕροιμεν ἂν κἀκείνους παρ' Ὁμήρου τὰς ἀφορμὰς λαβόντας. Δημόκριτον μὲν τὰ εἴδωλα ποιήσαντα ἐξ ἐκείνων·

αὐτὰρ ὁ εἴδωλον τεῦξ' ἀργυρότοξος Ἀπόλλων (Ε 449),

ἄλλους δὲ πλανηθέντας οἷς ἐκεῖνος οὐχ ἑπόμενος ἀλλὰ πρὸς τὸν παραπίπτοντα καιρὸν ἁρμοζόμενος περιέθηκεν. ἐπεὶ γὰρ ὁ Ὀδυσσεὺς παρ' Ἀλκινόῳ κατεχόμενος, ἡδυπαθείᾳ καὶ τρυφῇ κεχρημένῳ, πρὸς χάριν αὐτῷ διαλεγόμενος ἔφη

οὐ γὰρ ἐγώ γέ τί φημι τέλος χαριέστερον εἶναι
ἢ ὅταν εὐφροσύνη μὲν ἔχῃ κατὰ δῆμον ἅπαντα,
δαιτυμόνες δ' ἀνὰ δώματ' ἀκουάζωνται ἀοιδοῦ,
ἥμενοι ἑξείης, παρὰ δὲ πλήθωσι τράπεζαι
σίτου καὶ κρειῶν, μέθυ δ' ἐκ κρητῆρος ἀφύσσων
οἰνοχόος φορέῃσι καὶ ἐγχείῃ δεπάεσσι.
τοῦτό τί μοι κάλλιστον ἐνὶ φρεσὶν εἴδεται εἶναι (ι 5-11).

τούτοις παραχθεὶς καὶ Ἐπίκουρος τὴν ἡδονὴν τέλος εὐδαιμονίας ἐνόμισε. καὶ ἐπεὶ αὐτὸς οὗτος ὁ Ὀδυσσεὺς ποτὲ μὲν οὔλῃ καὶ ἀπαλῇ χλανίδι ἠμπίσχετο, ποτὲ δὲ ῥακίοις καὶ πήραις, καὶ νῦν μὲν τῇ Καλυψοῖ συνανεπαύετο νῦν δὲ ὑπὸ Ἴρου καὶ Μελανθίου περιυβρίζετο, ταύτην εἰκόνα τοῦ βίου παραλαβὼν Ἀρίστιππος

and again admonishes him,

> Silence! Restrain yourself and do not ask.
> [Od. 19.42].

These are the sorts of doctrines of the esteemed philosophers that have their source in Homer.

150.   If we were now to consider those who have founded their own schools, we would find them as well getting their impulse from Homer. Democritus, who speaks of "images" [εἴδωλα][1] starts from

> but Apollo of the silver bow made an image [of Aeneas]
> [Il. 5.449].

Others went astray over passages that Homer himself did not present with approval, but adapted to the conditions of his narrative. When Odysseus is detained by Alcinous, who is accustomed to pleasure and feasting, he says, to please him,

> I say there is no more pleasing end
> than when good cheer holds the entire company
> and the diners down the hall listen to a bard,
> reclining in a row. The tables are full beside them
> with grain and meat; the server pours the wine from the bowl
> and bring it around to serve in cups.
> This seems to my mind to be the best of things.
> [Od. 9.5-11].

However, misled by these lines, Epicurus got the idea that pleasure is the goal of the fortunate life [εὐδαιμονία].[2] And since this same Odysseus at one time wears a rich and delicate shawl and at another rags and a pack, at one moment is entertained by Calypso and at the next abused by Irus and Melanthius, Aristippus[3] took this as a model

---

[1] The term is used very frequently by the atomists, including Democritus. E.g. Democritus frs. A1, A121, A135 DK.
[2] A notion widely attributed to Epicurus. E.g. in the *Life* ("Epistle to Pythocles") = Epicurus 1, 120b-121a (Arrighetti).
[3] Fr. 30 (Mannebach). Cf. Diogenes Laertius 2.66.

(fr. 30 Mannebach) καὶ πενίᾳ καὶ πόνοις συνηνέχθη ἐρρωμένως καί ἡδονῇ ἀφειδῶς ἐχρήσατο.

151. τῆς δὲ Ὁμήρου σοφίας κἀκεῖνα καταμαθεῖν ἔστι δείγματα, ὅτι καλὰ καὶ πολλὰ σοφῶν ἀνδρῶν ἀποφθέγματα προανεφώνησεν, οἷον τὸ ἕπου θεῷ·

ὅς κε θεοῖς ἐπιπείθηται, μάλα δ' ἔκλυον αὐτοῦ (Α 218)
καὶ μηδὲν ἄγαν·

καὶ δ' ἄλλῳ νεμεσῶ, ὅς κ' ἔξοχα μὲν φιλέῃσιν,
ἔξοχα δ' ἐχθαίρῃσιν· ἀμείνω δ' αἴσιμα πάντα (ο 70-71)
καὶ ἐγγύα, πάρα δ' ἄτα·

δειλαί τοι δειλῶν γέ καὶ ἐγγυάασθαι (θ 351)
καὶ τὸ τοῦ Πυθαγόρου πρὸς τὸν πυθόμενον τί ἐστι φίλος ῥηθὲν ἄλλος ἐγώ·

ἶσον ἐμῇ κεφαλῇ (Σ 82).

152. ἔστι δὲ τῆς αὐτῆς ἰδέας τῶν ἀποφθεγμάτων καὶ ἡ καλουμένη γνώμη, ἥπερ ἐστὶν ἀπόφασις καθολικὴ περὶ τῶν κατὰ τὸν βίον λόγῳ συντόμῳ· καὶ τούτῳ δὴ χρησαμένων πάντων τῶν ποιητῶν καὶ φιλοσόφων καὶ

life and not only vigorously espoused poverty and toil, but also indulged lavishly in pleasure.

151.   Demonstrations of Homer's wisdom can also be found in the fact that he was the first to enunciate many of the beautiful sayings of the sages, as for example, "Follow god":[1]

> Whoever obeys the gods has their ear
> [Il. 1.218],

and "Nothing in excess":[2]

> I hate the man who loves too much
> or hates too much: moderation is always better
> [cf. Od. 15.70-71],

and "Pledges are haunted by trouble":[3]

> Useless as security are the pledges of useless men
> [Od. 8.351],

and finally Pythagoras' answer to the question "What is a friend?"—"Another self,"[4] [is found in the speech of Achilles, where he says of Patroclus that he was as dear]

> as my own head   [Il. 18.82].

152.   The so-called *gnome* or maxim belongs to the same class of utterances, constituting a general and concise statement about human life. All the poets and philosophers and writers make use of this sort of

---

[1] See the fifth of the Pythagorean *symbola* listed by Iamblichus (Protr. 21 = DK 58 [Pythagoreische Schule] fr. C6, I, 466, 20-21).
[2] A Delphic maxim (Plato *Protagoras* 343A), attributed to Solon (DK 10 [Die Sieben Weisen] fr. 3β1) as well as Chilon (DK 11 [Thales] fr. A2). Cf. Plutarch *Banquet of the Seven Sages* 164B.
[3] Attributed to Chilon (DK 11 [Thales] fr. A2 and to Thales (DK 10 [Die Sieben Weisen] fr. 3δ1. It is discussed in Plutarch's *Banquet of the Seven Sages* (164B-C), where the same Homeric line is cited for comparison.
[4] Cited as proverbial by Aristotle (*Eudemian Ethics* 1245a29), and widely attributed to "the Pythagoreans," e.g. by the scholiasts on Il. 18.82, who make the same comparison as our text.

λογογράφων καὶ γνωμικῶς τινα ἀποφαίνεσθαι ἐπιτηδευσάντων πρῶτος Ὅμηρος πολλὰς καὶ ἀγαθὰς γνώμας ἐξήνεγκε δι' ὅλης τῆς ποιήσεως· τοῦτο μὲν ἀποφαινόμενος οἷόν ἐστιν ὃ βούλεται παραστῆσαι, ὡς ὅταν εἴπῃ

κρείσσων γὰρ βασιλεύς, ὅτε χώσεται ἀνδρὶ χέρηι (Α 80).

τοῦτο δὲ ὡς δέον πράσσειν τι, οἷον

οὐ χρὴ παννύχιον εὕδειν βουληφόρον ἄνδρα (Β 24 = 61).

153. πολλὰς δὲ γνώμας καὶ παρανέσεις ἀγαθὰς Ὁμήρου ἐξενεγκόντος παρέφρασαν οὐκ ὀλίγοι τῶν μετ' αὐτόν, ὧν τινα παραδείγματα οὐκ ἄκαιρόν ἐστι παραθέσθαι, οἷόν ἐστι τὸ Ὁμήρου

νήπιοι, οἳ Ζηνὶ μενεαίνομεν ἀφρονέοντες·

ἢ ἔτι μιν μέμαμεν καταπαυσέμεν ἆσσον ἰόντες

ἢ ἔπει ἠὲ βίῃ· ὁ δ' ἀφήμενος οὐκ ἀλεγίζει

οὐδ' ὄθεται· φησὶν γὰρ ἐν ἀθανάτοισι θεοῖσι

κάρτεΐ τε σθένεΐ τε διακριδὸν εἶναι ἄριστος.

τῷ ἔχεθ' ὅττι κεν ὔμμι κακὸν πέμπῃσιν ἑκάστῳ (Ο 104-9).

παρὰ τοῦτο δέ ἐστι τὸ Πυθαγορικὸν

ὅσσα τε δαιμονίαισι τύχαις βροτοὶ ἄλγε' ἔχουσιν,

ἣν ἂν μοῖραν ἔλῃς, ταύτην φέρε μηδ' ἀγανάκτει. (Carm. Aur. 17-8)

καὶ ἐπὶ τούτοις τὸ Εὐριπίδου

τοῖς πράγμασιν γὰρ οὐχὶ θυμοῦσθαι χρεών·

μέλει γὰρ αὐτοῖς οὐδέν· ἀλλ' ὁ(ὑν)τυγχάνων

τὰ πράγματ' ὀρθῶς ἂν τιθῇ, πράσσει καλῶς (fr. 287 Nauck).

154. πάλιν Ὅμηρος μέν φησι

statement and express themselves in maxims to a certain extent, but Homer was the first to introduce an abundance of excellent maxims throughout his poetry. Some are descriptive, as when he says,

> When a king is angry at a lesser man, he is the stronger
> [Il. 1.80],

and some prescriptive, as

> A leader in counsel must not sleep through the night
> [Il. 2.24 = 61].

153. A number of those who came after Homer paraphrased the many excellent maxims and admonitions he invented, and a few examples will not be out of place here. Homer says,

> We are fools to rage mindlessly against Zeus.
> We long to go to him and make him stop,
> either by word or action, but he will not relent
> or pay attention, for he claims that among the immortal gods
> he is the greatest by far in strength and might.
> Whatever evil he sends each of you, accept it
> [Il. 15.104-09].

Parallel to these are the Pythagorean verses,

> Whatever evils humans receive by the allocation of the gods,
> whatever your portion, bear it, and do not complain,
> [*Carm. aur.* (after Hierocles), 17-18]

and along with this consider Euripides' lines,

> Not by raging at events—they
> don't care—but by keeping things on an
> even keel, whatever happens: that's how you do well
> [fr. 287, Nauck].

154. Again, Homer says:

τέκνον ἐμόν, τέο μέχρις ὀδυρόμενος καὶ ἀχεύων

σὴν ἔδεαι κραδίην (Ω 128-9);

ὁ δὲ Πυθαγόρας

φείδεο τῆς ζωῆς, μή μιν καταθυμοβορήσῃς (fr. 16 Nauck).

155. ἔτι Ὁμήρου εἰπόντος

τοῖος γὰρ νόος ἐστὶν ἐπιχθονίων ἀνθρώπων,

οἷον ἐπ᾽ ἦμαρ ἄγησι πατὴρ ἀνδρῶν τε θεῶν τε (σ 136-7),

Ἀρχίλοχος τά τε ἄλλα αὐτοῦ μιμούμενος καὶ τοῦτο μὲν παρέφρασεν, εἰπών

τοῖος ἀνθρώποισι θυμός, Γλαῦκε, Λεπτίνεω πάι,

γίνεται θνητοῖς, ὁποίην Ζεὺς ἐφ᾽ ἡμέρην ἄγῃ (fr. 131 West).

156. καὶ ἐν ἄλλοις Ὁμήρου εἰπόντος

ἄλλῳ μὲν γὰρ ἔδωκε θεὸς πολεμήια ἔργα,

ἄλλῳ δ᾽ ἐν στήθεσσι τιθεῖ νόον εὐρύοπα Ζεὺς

ἐσθλόν, τοῦ δέ τε πολλοὶ ἐπαυρίσκοντ᾽ ἄνθρωποι,

καί τε πόλεις ἐσάωσε, μάλιστα δέ καὐτὸς ἀνέγνω (Ν 730, 732-4).

Εὐριπίδης παρὰ τοῦτο ἐποίησε

γνώμαις γὰρ ἀνδρὸς εὖ μὲν οἰκοῦνται πόλεις,

εὖ δ᾽ οἶκος, εἰς δ᾽ αὖ πόλεμον ἰσχύει μέγα·

σοφὸν γὰρ ἓν βούλευμα τὰς πολλὰς χέρας

νικᾷ, σὺν ὄχλῳ δ᾽ ἀμαθία πλεῖστον κακόν (fr. 200 Nauck).

> My child, how long with weeping and crying
> will you eat out your heart?   [Il. 24.128-29],

and Pythagoras,

> Spare your life, do not eat out your heart
> [fr. 16, Nauck].

155.   And again, Homer says,

> The mind of mortal men is such
> as the father of gods and men gives, day by day
> [Od. 18.136-37],

and Archilochus, who imitated him in other things as well, paraphrases this when he says,

> The heart of man, Glaucus son of Leptines,
> is whatever Zeus makes it on a given day
> [fr. 131, West].

156.   Elsewhere, Homer says,

> god gives the arts of war to one...
> and far-seeing Zeus puts a mind in the other's breast,
> a noble mind, and many men profit from it:
> he saves cities, and his knowledge is beyond that of other men
> [Il. 13.730, 732-34],

and parallel to this Euripides wrote,

> Cities and homes are well ruled by the wisdom
> of man, and such things prevail in war.
> A single wise counsel defeats a host of strong
> arms. Along with the mob, the greatest evil is ignorance
> [fr. 200, Nauck].

157. ἃ δὲ παρακελευόμενον τῷ ἑταίρῳ τὸν Ἰδομενέα πεποίηκεν

ὦ πέπον, εἰ μὲν δὴ πόλεμον περὶ τόνδε φυγόντες
αἰεὶ δὴ μέλλοιμεν ἀγήρω τ' ἀθανάτω τε
ἔσσεσθ', οὔτε κεν αὐτὸς ἐνὶ πρώτοισι μαχοίμην
οὔτε κέ σε στέλλοιμι μάχην εἰς κυδιάνειραν·
νῦν δ' ἔμπης γὰρ κῆρες ἐφεστᾶσιν θανάτοιο
μυρίαι, ἃς οὔκ ἔστι φυγεῖν βροτὸν οὐδ' ὑπαλύξαι
ἴομεν, ἠέ τῳ εὖχος ὀρέξομεν ἠέ τις ἡμῖν (Μ 322-8).

Αἰσχύλος μὲν δεύτερος λέγων οὕτως ἔφη

ἀλλ' οὔτε πολλὰ τραύματ' ἐν στέρνοις λαβὼν
θνῄσκει τις, εἰ μὴ τέρμα συντρέχοι βίου·
οὔτ' ἐν στέγῃ τις ἥμενος παρ' ἑστίᾳ
φεύγει τι μᾶλλον τὸν πεπρωμένον μόρον (fr. 362 Radt).

ἐν δὲ πεζῇ λέξει Δημοσθένης οὕτως·

πέρας μὲν γὰρ ἐστι ἅπασιν ἀνθρώποις τοῦ βίου θάνατος, κἂν ἐν οἰκίσκῳ τις αὐτὸν καθείρξας τηρῇ· δεῖ δὲ τοὺς ἀγαθοὺς ἄνδρας ἐγχειρεῖν μὲν ἅπασιν ἀεὶ τοῖς καλοῖς, φέρειν δ' ὅ τι ἂν ὁ θεὸς διδῷ γενναίως (18.97).

158. πάλιν δὲ τὸ Ὁμήρου

οὔ τοι ἀπόβλητ' ἐστὶ θεῶν ἐρικυδέα δῶρα (Γ 65)

Σοφοκλῆς παρέφρασεν εἰπὼν

157. This is Homer's version of his companion's advice to Idomeneus:[1]

> Friend, if we could flee this war
> and live forever and never grow old,
> then I would not fight among the first
> nor would I send you into battle where men win glory.
> But now, since death is thick around us,
> that no mortal escapes,
> let us give someone reason to boast, or win it for ourselves
> [Il. 12.322-28],

and Aeschylus said later,

> If he had not reached the end of his life
> a man would not die even if he had many wounds in his chest,
> but not even a man sitting at home by the fire
> can escape his destined end   [fr. 362, Radt].

And in prose, Demosthenes wrote as follows:

> Death is the end of every man's life, even if, to protect himself, a man shuts himself up in a little room. Good men must always involve themselves in every noble course, holding good hope before them as a shield, and bear in a noble spirit whatever the god sends. [*On the Crown*, 97].

158. Again, Homer says,

> The gifts with which the gods honor us are not to be rejected
> [Il. 3.65],

and Sophocles paraphrased this when he said,

---

[1] The passage is in fact spoken by Glaucus to Sarpedon.

θεοῦ τὸ δῶρον τοῦτο· χρὴ δ' ὅσ' ἂν θεοὶ
διδῶσι, φεύγειν μηδέν', ὦ τέκνον, ποτέ (fr. 964 Radt).
159. παρ' ἐκείνου δὲ
τοῦ καὶ ἀπὸ γλώσσης μέλιτος γλυκίων ῥέεν αὐδή (Α 249)
Θεόκριτος εἶπεν
οὕνεκά οἱ γλυκὺ Μοῦσα κατὰ στόματος χέε νέκταρ (7.82).

160. † πῶς δὲ † καὶ Ἄρατος παρέφρασε τὸ μὲν
οἴη δ' ἄμμορός ἐστι λοετρῶν Ὠκεανοῖο (Σ 489)
εἰπὼν
ἄρκτοι κυανέου πεφυλαγμέναι ὠκεανοῖο (*Phaen.* 48),
τὸ δὲ
τυτθὸν γὰρ ὑπὲκ θανάτοιο φέρονται (Ο 628)
εἰπὼν
ὀλίγον δὲ διὰ ξύλον Ἄιδ' ἐρύκει (*Phaen.* 299).
καὶ περὶ μὲν τούτων ἅλις.

161. ὁ δὲ πολιτικὸς λόγος ἐστὶν ἐν τῇ ῥητορικῇ τέχνῃ, ἧς ἐντὸς Ὅμηρος πρῶτος γέγονεν, ὡς φαίνεται. εἰ γάρ ἐστιν ἡ ῥητορικὴ δύναμις τοῦ πιθανῶς λέγειν, τίς μᾶλλον Ὁμήρου ἐν τῇ δυνάμει ταύτῃ καθέστηκεν, ὃς τῇ τε μεγαλοφωνίᾳ πάντας ὑπεραίρει ἔν τε τοῖς διανοήμασι τὴν ἴσην τοῖς λόγοις ἰσχὺν ἐπιδείκνυται;

> This is a gift of a god, and whatever the gods give,
> my child, one must never try to avoid
> [fr. 964, Radt].

159. Based on this Homeric line,

> The voice flowed from his tongue sweeter than honey
> [Il. 1.249],

Theocritus said,

> And so the Muse poured sweet nectar in his mouth
> [7.82].

160. Aratus also paraphrased this line,

> who alone has no part in the baths of Ocean
> [Il. 18.489],

when he said,

> the Bears, avoiding blue Ocean   [*Phaenomena*, 48],

and this,

> For a moment they are suspended over death
> [Il. 15.628]

when he said,

> A bit of wood holds back death from them
> [*Phaenomena*, 299],

But enough of these things.

161. Political discourse is a function of the craft of rhetoric, which Homer seems to have been the first to understand, for if rhetoric is the power to speak persuasively, who more than Homer has established his preeminence in this? He surpasses all others in grandiloquence and his thought displays the same power as his diction.

162. καὶ πρῶτόν ἐστι τῆς τέχνης ἡ οἰκονομία, ἣν δι' ὅλης τῆς ποιήσεως παρίστησι, καὶ μάλιστα ἐν ταῖς ἀρχαῖς τῶν πραγμάτων. οὐ γὰρ πόρρωθεν ἐμβαλὼν τὴν ἀρχὴν τῆς Ἰλιάδος ἐποιήσατο ἀλλὰ καὶ καθ' ὃν χρόνον αἱ πράξεις ἐνεργότεραι καὶ ἀκμαιότεραι κατέστησαν· τὰ δὲ τούτων ἀργότερα, ὅσα ἐν τῷ παρελθόντι χρόνῳ ἐγένοντο, συντόμως ἐν ἄλλοις τόποις παραδιηγήσατο. τὸ δὲ αὐτὸ καὶ ἐν τῇ Ὀδυσσείᾳ πεποίηκεν, ἀρξάμενος μὲν ἀπὸ τῶν τελευταίων τῆς πλάνης τοῦ Ὀδυσσέως χρόνων, ἐν οἷς καιρὸς ἦν ἤδη καὶ τὸν Τηλέμαχον εἰσάγειν καὶ τὴν τῶν μνηστήρων ὕβριν ἐμφανίζειν· τὰ δὲ πρὸ τούτων, ὅσα τῷ Ὀδυσσεῖ ἀλωμένῳ συνέπεσεν, αὐτὸν παράγει διηγούμενον, ἃ καὶ δεινότερα καὶ πιθανώτερα ἔμελλε φαίνεσθαι, ὑπὸ αὐτοῦ τοῦ παθόντος λεγόμενα.

163. ἀεὶ τοίνυν χρωμένων τῶν ῥητόρων πάντων τοῖς προοιμίοις ὑπὲρ τοῦ προσεκτικώτερον ἢ εὐνούστερον ποιεῖν τὸν ἀκροατήν, αὐτὸς μὲν ὁ ποιητὴς κέχρηται προοιμίοις τοῖς μάλιστα κινῆσαι καὶ παράγεσθαι πρὸς τὴν ἀκρόασιν δυναμένοις ἔν τε τῇ Ἰλιάδι προαναφωνῶν ὅτι μέλλει λέγειν ὅσα διὰ τὴν Ἀχιλλέως ὀργὴν καὶ τὴν Ἀγαμέμνονος ὕβριν κακὰ τοῖς Ἕλλησι συνέβη, καὶ ἐν τῇ Ὀδυσσείᾳ ὅσοις πόνοις καὶ κινδύνοις περιπεσὼν ὁ Ὀδυσσεὺς πάντων τῇ τῆς ψυχῆς συνέσει καὶ καρτερίᾳ περιεγένετο. καὶ ἐν ἑκατέρῳ τῶν προοιμίων τὴν Μοῦσαν παρακαλεῖ, ἵνα θειοτέραν καὶ μείζονα τὴν δόξαν τῶν λεγομένων παραστήσῃ.

164. πολλὰ δὲ τῶν εἰσαγομένων ὑπ' αὐτοῦ προσώπων λέγοντα ποιῶν ἢ πρὸς οἰκείους ἢ φίλους ἢ ἐχθροὺς ἢ δήμους ἑκάστῳ τὸ πρέπον εἶδος τῶν λόγων ἀποδίδωσιν, ὥσπερ ἐν ἀρχῇ πεποίηται αὐτῷ ὁ Χρύσης ἐν τοῖς πρὸς τοὺς Ἕλληνας λόγοις χρησιμωτάτῳ προοιμίῳ κεχρημένος· συνεύχεται γὰρ αὐτοῖς πρότερον κρατῆσαι τῶν πολεμίων καὶ οἴκαδε ἀναστρέψαι, ἵνα τὴν παρ' αὐτῶν εὔνοιαν ἐπισπάσηται· ἔπειτα οὕτως ὑπὲρ τῆς παιδὸς παρακαλεῖ. ὁ δὲ Ἀχιλλεὺς ἐπὶ τῇ ἀπειλῇ τοῦ Ἀγαμέμνονος θυμούμενος μιγνύει τὸν ὑπὲρ αὑτοῦ καὶ τῶν

162. The first element of this craft is economy or organization [οἰκονομία],[1] which he demonstrates in all his poetry, but particularly at the outset. For he did not start off the *Iliad* in the remote past, but began at a time when the action had reached a peak of intensity. Those things which had happened before were less significant and he summarized them in various places. He did the same in the *Odyssey*, starting with the very last part of the wanderings of Odysseus, at the point at which it was possible to bring in Telemachus and to reveal the arrogance of the suitors. That which had gone before and all that had happened to Odysseus in his wanderings, he has Odysseus himself tell, and even these things seem more ingenious and more credible narrated by the man who actually experienced them.

163. Speakers always use prologues,[2] to make their audiences more attentive or better disposed, and the poet himself uses prologues with tremendous power, to move the audience and dispose them to listen. In the prologue of the *Iliad*, he says that he is going to tell all the evils that came upon the Greeks through the anger of Achilles and the arrogance of Agamemnon—in that of the *Odyssey*, what toil and danger Odysseus fell into, and yet overcame it all through the wisdom and strength of his soul. In both prologues, he calls on the Muses in order to enhance the glory of what he says and to make it more divine.

164. Many of the characters he introduces he causes to speak, whether to relatives or friends or enemies or to the people, and he gives to each the appropriate form of speech.[3] Thus in the beginning of the *Iliad* he depicted Chryses making a very appropriate introduction to his speech to the Greeks. First, he prays that they may defeat their enemies and return home—this, in order to secure their goodwill—and only then asks for his child. Achilles, angered at Agamemnon's threat, talks about himself and about the rest of the Greeks in the speech he makes on this matter, in order to make the others well disposed toward

---

[1] On οἰκονομία as an equivalent to *dispositio*, or more specifically, the *ordo artificialis*, or narration *more Homerico*, see Lausberg (1990), pars. 317, 443, 452.
[2] Aristotle, *Rhetoric* 1414b19.
[3] Such "appropriateness" in the portrayal of characters is stressed by (among others) Hermogenes (*Progymnasmata*, 9). Cf. ch. 172, below.

Ἑλλήνων λόγον, ἵνα κἀκείνους ἀκούσαντας εὐνουστέρους καταστήσῃ· πάντας γὰρ ἐπὶ τὸν πόλεμον ἐστάλθαι οὐκ ἰδίας τινὸς ἀπεχθείας ἕνεκα, ἀλλὰ εἰς χάριν αὐτοῦ τοῦ Ἀγαμέμνονος καὶ τοῦ ἀδελφοῦ αὐτοῦ· καὶ πολλὰ μὲν πεποιηκέναι ἑαυτόν, τὸ δὲ γέρας οὐ παρὰ τούτων ἀλλὰ παρὰ τοῦ κοινοῦ τῶν Ἑλλήνων εἰληφέναι. οἷς ἀντιλέγων ὁ Ἀγαμέμνων οὐκ ἀπορεῖ ὅπως καὶ αὐτὸς θεραπεύσει τὸ πλῆθος· φήσαντος γὰρ τοῦ Ἀχιλλέως ἀπελεύσεσθαι εἰς τὴν πατρίδα δι' ἣν ἔπαθεν ὕβριν οὐκ εἶπεν ἄπιθι ἀλλὰ φεῦγε (Α 173), τὸ ἁπλῶς ῥηθὲν εἰς τὸ ἀδοξότερον μεταβαλών· καὶ ὅτι οὐ παρακαλῶ σε μένειν· πάρεισι γὰρ καὶ ἄλλοι, οἳ τιμῆς ἀξιώσουσί με (Α 173-5)· ἦν δὲ καὶ τοῦτο τοῖς ἀκούουσι κεχαρισμένον.

165. καὶ ἐπὶ τούτοις εἰσάγεται ῥήτωρ ὁ Νέστωρ, ὃν ἡδυεπῆ καὶ λιγὺν ἀγορητὴν (Α 248) προσεῖπε,

τοῦ καὶ ἀπὸ γλώσσης μέλιτος γλυκίων ῥέεν αὐδή (Α 249),

οὗ μεῖζον ἐγκώμιον οὐκ ἂν γένοιτο ῥήτορος. τί δὲ οὗτος διαπράσσεται τῷ λόγῳ; ἄρχεται μὲν ἀπὸ προοιμίου, δι' οὗ μετάγνωσιν ἐμποιεῖν πειρᾶται τοῖς διαφερομένοις ἀριστεῦσιν, ἐννοεῖν αὐτοὺς παρασκευάζων, ὅτι μαχόμενοι παρέξουσιν ἀφορμὴν χαρᾶς τοῖς πολεμίοις· πρόεισι δὲ νουθετῶν ἑκάτερον καὶ πείθεσθαι ἑαυτῷ ὡς πρεσβυτέρῳ παραινῶν· καὶ ἐν τῷ σωφρονίζειν τὸν ἕτερον κεχαρισμένα τῷ ἑτέρῳ λέγει· τῷ μὲν γὰρ Ἀγαμέμνονι παραινεῖ μὴ ἀφαιρεῖσθαι τὸ δοθὲν τῷ πολλὰ κεκμηκότι γέρας, τῷ δὲ Ἀχιλλεῖ μὴ ἐρίζειν τῷ βασιλεύειν προκρινομένῳ· καὶ πρέποντα ἑκατέρῳ ἔπαινον ⟨διδοὺς⟩, τῷ μὲν ὡς πλειόνων βασιλεύοντι, τῷ δὲ ὡς πλέον ἰσχύοντι, τοῦτον τὸν τρόπον πραΰνειν αὐτοὺς ἐπιχειρεῖ.

166. τί δέ; οὐχὶ καὶ ἐν τοῖς ἑξῆς, ὁπότε εἶδε τὸν ὄνειρον ὁ Ἀγαμέμνων ἐλπίδας ἀγαθὰς αὐτῷ φέροντα παρὰ τοῦ Διὸς καὶ ὁπλίζειν τοὺς Ἕλληνας παρακελευόμενον, ῥητορικῇ χρῆται τέχνῃ, τοὐναντίον οἷς βούλεται πρὸς τοὺς πολλοὺς λέγων, ἵνα πεῖραν τῆς ὁρμῆς αὐτῶν λάβῃ καὶ μὴ ἐπαχθὴς ᾖ πολεμεῖν

him as they listened. He says they all went off to war not on account of their own hatred, but to please Agamemnon himself and his brother, and that he himself has done a great deal and that he holds his gift not from the sons of Atreus but from the common store of the Greeks. Agamemnon is not at a loss to answer: he says that he as well serves the whole army, and when Achilles has said he is going home because of the offense he has suffered, Agamemnon says to him not "Go away," but "Run away"—changing the neutral statement into something more shameful—and "I will not ask you to stay, for there are others here who will deem me worthy of honor" [cf. Il. 1.173-75], and this last as well was to please the audience.

165. At this point Nestor is introduced, whom he calls "sweet-voiced" and "fine speechmaker" [Il. 1.248]:

> The voice flowed from his tongue sweeter than honey
> [Il. 1.249].

There could be no greater praise for a speaker. And what will this man accomplish in his speeches? He begins with an introduction, in which he tries to make the quarreling lords relent, impressing upon them that by arguing they are giving the enemy reason to be pleased. He goes on, rebuking each of them and calling on each to give in to him, as an elder. Each time he tells the one to be reasonable he pleases the other. He tells Agamemnon not to take away the gift given to one who has worked hard, and Achilles not to attack the man who has been chosen to rule. Thus he gives to each the appropriate praise—to Agamemnon as the greater ruler and to Achilles as the stronger man—and in this way he undertakes to mollify them.

166. Then what? In what follows, when Agamemnon has the dream that brings him hopes from Zeus and orders him to arm the Greeks, does he not use the rhetorical craft, saying to the crowd just the opposite of what he actually thinks, to test their motivation, rather than impose

ἀναγκάζων ὑπὲρ ἑαυτοῦ; ἀλλ' αὐτὸς μὲν πρὸς χάριν λέγει, ἄλλος δέ τις τῶν πείθειν αὐτοὺς δυναμένων ἐπιστρέψει μένειν, ὡς τοῦτο τῇ ἀληθείᾳ τοῦ βασιλέως θέλοντος. καὶ γὰρ ἐν οἷς δημηγορεῖ ἐμφαίνει ὅτι τοὐναντίον βούλεται· ὁ δὲ δεχόμενος τοὺς λόγους τούτους ἐστὶν Ὀδυσσεύς, παρρησίᾳ τῇ πρεπούσῃ χρώμενος καὶ τοὺς μὲν ἀρίστους λόγοις προσηνέσι πείθων, τοὺς δὲ ὑποδεεστέρους καταπληκτικῶς ὑπακούειν τοῖς κρείττοσι ἀναγκάζων· καὶ τὸ ἄτακτον καὶ θορυβῶδες τῶν πολλῶν καταπαύσας ἅμα πάντας πείθει λόγοις ἔμφροσι, μετρίως μὲν ὀνειδίσας, διότι οὐκέτι τελοῦσιν ἃ ὑπέσχοντο, καὶ ἅμα συγγνώμης ἀξιώσας, ὅτι πολὺν χρόνον ἄπρακτοι μένοντες τῶν φιλτάτων ἐστέρηνται, παρακλήσει δὲ καὶ ἐλπίδι τῇ ἐκ τῶν μαντειῶν συμπείθων μένειν.

167. ὁμοίως δὲ καὶ ὁ Νέστωρ λόγους ἐξηλλαγμένους μὲν εἰς ταὐτὸ δὲ τείνοντας ποιούμενος καὶ πλείονι παρρησίᾳ πρὸς τοὺς ἤδη μεμαλαγμένους χρώμενος πείθει τὸ πλῆθος· καὶ τὴν αἰτίαν τῆς ὀλιγωρίας εἰς ὀλίγους τοῦ μηδενὸς ἀξίους ἀναφέρων τοὺς πολλοὺς ἐντρέπει· προστίθησι δὲ καὶ ἀπειλὴν τοῖς ἀπειθοῦσι καὶ εὐθέως συμβουλεύει τῷ βασιλεῖ, ὅπως χρὴ καταλέγειν τὰ στρατιωτικὰ τάγματα.

168. πάλιν δὲ ἐν ταῖς κατὰ τὸν πόλεμον πράξεσι τῶν Ἑλλήνων τὰ μὲν εὐτυχησάντων τὰ δὲ πταισάντων καὶ ἐν φόβῳ καταστάντων, ὁ μὲν Διομήδης, ἅτε τὸ ἐκ τῆς νεότητος θράσος καὶ τὴν ἐκ τῆς ἀριστείας παρρησίαν ἔχων, πρὸ τοῦ ἐπιδείξασθαι τὴν ἀνδραγαθίαν σιωπῆς ἀξιώσας τὸ παρὰ τοῦ βασιλέως ὄνειδος, τότε ἐπιπλήσσει τῷ Ἀγαμέμνονι ὡς ὑπὸ ἀνανδρίας συμβουλεύοντι φεύγειν· φησὶ γὰρ

Ἀτρείδη, σοὶ πρῶτα μαχέσσομαι ἀφραδέοντι,
ᾗ θέμις ἐστίν, ἄναξ, ἀγορῇ· σὺ δὲ μή τι χολωθῇς (Ι 32-3),

upon them by forcing them to fight on his behalf? He himself in fact speaks in a manner that pleases them, but someone else who has power to persuade them will turn them back to stay and fight, since this is in fact what the king had wanted all along. When he speaks to the people, however, he indicates that he wants just the opposite. Odysseus takes up the task and speaks with appropriate directness, winning over the leaders with gentle words and forcing the underlings in their confusion to obey the leaders. After he has put an end to the riot and disorder of the crowd, then he wins them all over with ingenious speeches, rebuking them with moderation for not completing what they promised to complete and, at the same time, excusing them because they have been away from their families for a long time without accomplishing anything. Finally, by means of entreaty and the hope held out by the prophecies, he persuades them to remain.

167. Then Nestor speaks, using different words but tending toward the same goal. He is more outspoken, now that the audience has been softened [by Odysseus], and persuades the crowd. He focuses the blame for the insubordination on a few worthless characters and turns the majority around. He even adds a threat to the disobedient and goes right on to advise the king to tally up the military divisions.[1]

168. When the fighting resumes, the Greeks oscillate between success and failure, accompanied by crippling fear. Diomedes, with the boldness of youth and the outspokenness to which he has a right because of his recent display of excellence as a fighter—before demonstrating his own bravery, he had passed over in silence a rebuke from the king—rebukes Agamemnon for having counseled flight and cowardice.[2] He says,

> Son of Atreus, I shall contend first with you in your folly,
> as is right, with words—and king, be not angered
>   [Il. 9.32-33],

---

[1] Il. 2.434-40, where Nestor advises Agamemnon to draw up each component of the army, thus providing the context for the Catalogue of Ships.
[2] The same points about Diomedes' new rhetorical mode "after his *aristeia*" are made by the scholiasts *ad loc.* (schol in Il. 9.31).

ἐν οἷς ἅμα μὲν νουθετεῖν αὐτὸν ἐπιχειρεῖ, ἅμα δὲ τὴν παρ' αὐτοῦ ὀργὴν παραιτεῖται. καὶ τὰ μὲν φθάνοντα διαπεπρᾶχθαι ἑαυτῷ ἀνεπαχθῶς ὑπομιμνήσκει, λέγων

ταῦτα δὲ πάντα

ἴσασ' Ἀργείων ἠμὲν νέοι ἠδὲ γέροντες (Ι 35-6).
εἰς δὲ τὰ ἑξῆς προτρέπει τοὺς Ἕλληνας, τεχνικῶς ἐγκωμιάζων αὐτοὺς

δαιμόνι', οὕτω που μάλα ἔλπεαι υἷας Ἀχαιῶν

ἀπτολέμους τ' ἔμεναι καὶ ἀνάλκιδας, ὡς ἀγορεύεις (Ι 40-1);
καὶ αὐτὸν τὸν Ἀγαμέμνονα δυσωπεῖ, συγχωρῶν αὐτῷ εἰ βούλεται ἀπιέναι· τοὺς γὰρ ἄλλους ἐξαρκέσειν ἤ, κἂν πάντες φύγωσιν, αὐτόν γε σὺν τῷ ἑταίρῳ μένειν καὶ μάχεσθαι, εἰπών

νῶι δ', ἐγὼ Σθένελός τε, μαχησόμεθα (Ι 48).
ὁ δὲ Νέστωρ τούτῳ μὲν γνώμης τε καὶ πράξεως ἀρετὴν μαρτυρεῖ, ὅσα δὲ εἰς τέλος τῆς συμβουλῆς διαφέρει, ἑαυτὸν ὡς πρεσβύτερον δεῖν παραινεῖν ἀξιοῖ· καὶ ἐπέξεισι τῷ λόγῳ τὴν πρὸς Ἀχιλλέα πρεσβείαν παρασκευάζειν ἐπιχειρῶν.

169. καὶ ἐν αὐτῇ δὲ τῇ πρεσβείᾳ ποικίλαις τέχναις ποιεῖ χρωμένους τοὺς ῥήτορας· ὁ μὲν γὰρ Ὀδυσσεὺς ἀρχόμενος τοῦ λόγου (Ι 225) οὐκ εὐθέως ἔφη ὅτι Ἀγαμέμνων μετεγνωκὼς ἐπὶ τῇ τῆς Βρισηίδος ἀφαιρέσει τήν τε κόρην ἀποδίδωσι καὶ δῶρα τὰ μὲν παραυτίκα πέμπει τὰ δὲ ὕστερον ἐπαγγέλλεται· οὐ γὰρ ἦν χρήσιμον, οἰδοῦντος ἔτι τοῦ θυμοῦ, ταῦτα ὑπομιμνήσκειν· ἀλλὰ πρῶτον ἠθέλησεν ἐμβαλεῖν τὸν Ἀχιλλέα εἰς οἶκτον τῶν Ἑλληνικῶν ἀτυχημάτων· εἶτα εἰπὼν ὡς ὕστερον βουληθεὶς ἐπανορθώσασθαι τὰς συμφορὰς οὐκέτι δυνήσεται, μετὰ ταῦτα τῶν Πηλέως παραινέσεων ἀνέμνησεν, ἑαυτοῦ μὲν ἀφαιρῶν τὸ ἐπαχθὲς τῷ δὲ μᾶλλον ἐντρέπειν δυναμένῳ προσώπῳ τῷ τοῦ πατρὸς περιθεὶς τὸν λόγον· καὶ ὅτε ἐδόκει πραότερον αὐτὸν εἶναι τότε καὶ τῶν

undertaking on the one hand to correct him and at the same time to avoid his wrath. Likewise, without taking offense, he recalls how he was treated earlier, saying,

> all this
> the Greeks know well, both young and old
> [Il. 9.35-36].

Then he urges the Greeks on to what lies before them by skillfully praising them:

> Madman! Do you really think that the sons of the Achaeans
> are unwarlike, weaklings, as you are saying?
> [Il. 9.40-41]

and he shames Agamemnon himself, telling him to leave if he wants, for the others are sufficient without him—or, even if everyone leaves, he is staying with his companion and fighting on:

> We two, Sthenelus and I, will go on fighting
> [Il. 9.48].

Nestor confirms the excellence of his thought and his deeds but says that he himself, since he is older, must take precedence with regard to the purpose of the present council, and he goes on to persuade the Greeks to prepare the embassy to Achilles.

169.   Furthermore, Homer shows the orators in the embassy itself using various techniques.

Odysseus, starting his speech [Il.. 9.225], did not immediately say that Agamemnon had repented of the seizure of Briseis and was giving the girl back and sending gifts and promising more later; [he saves this for last, because] Achilles is still swollen with anger over the matter and it would not have been helpful to bring it up at the start. His first goal was rather to inspire Achilles with pity for the misfortune of the Greeks. Then, saying that when he wished to correct the disaster after the fact he would be unable to do so, he recalled the injunction of Peleus, diverting the anger Achilles feels toward the speaker and placing the words rather in the more persuasive mouth of his father. Then, when he thought Achilles had been softened, he

Ἀγαμέμνονος δώρων ἐμνημόνευσε· καὶ πάλιν εἰς τὰς ὑπὲρ τῶν Ἑλλήνων δεήσεις μετέβαλε τὸν λόγον ὅτι, εἰ καὶ δικαίως Ἀγαμέμνονι μέμφεται, καλὸν γοῦν σῶσαι τοὺς μηδὲν εἰς αὐτὸν ἐξημαρτηκότας, ἐχρῆν γὰρ καὶ τὸν ἐπίλογον μηδὲν ἔχειν τῶν λυπούντων τὸν ἀκούοντα, ἐπεὶ καὶ μάλιστα μνημονεύεται τὰ τέλη τῶν λόγων. ἡ δὲ τελευταία παράκλησις ἔχει τι καὶ διεγερτικὸν ἐπὶ τοὺς πολεμίους ὡς καὶ αὐτοῦ καταφρονοῦντας· "νῦν γὰρ ἄν," φησίν, "ἕλοις τὸν Ἕκτορα, εἴ σου κατεναντίον σταίη, ἐπεὶ οὐδένα τῶν Ἑλλήνων ἑαυτῷ φησιν εἶναι ὅμοιον" (cf. I 304). ὁ δὲ Φοῖνιξ, δεδοικὼς μὴ ἐνδεέστρον ἢ προσῆκε χρῆται τῇ δεήσει, δάκρυα προΐεται· καὶ πρῶτον μὲν τῇ ὁρμῇ αὐτοῦ συντίθεται, φήσας μὴ ἀπολειφθήσεσθαι αὐτοῦ, εἰ ἀποπλέοι· τοῦτο γὰρ ἦν αὐτῷ κεχαρισμένον· εἶτα καὶ τὴν αἰτίαν λέγει, ὅπως τρέφειν αὐτὸν ἐπιστεύθη παρὰ τοῦ Πηλέως νήπιον παραλαβών, καὶ διδάσκαλος ἔργων καὶ λόγων εἶναι ἠξιώθη. παραδιηγεῖται δὲ καὶ τὰς ἐπὶ τῆς νεότητος ἁμαρτίας αὐτοῦ, ἐμφαίνων ὡς ἄβουλον ἡ τοιαύτη ἡλικία· καὶ προϊὼν οὐδὲν τῶν εἰς προτροπὴν παραλείπει, πᾶσι τοῖς κεφαλαίοις ῥητορικῶς χρώμενος, ὅτι διηλλάχθαι καλὸν τῷ ἱκετεύοντι καὶ δῶρα πέμποντι καὶ πρέσβεις τοὺς ἀρίστους κἀκείνῳ τιμιωτάτους ἀπεσταλκότι· καὶ ὅτι καὶ αὐτὸς δίκαιός ἐστιν ὧν ἀξιοῖ τυγχάνειν, τροφεύς γε ὢν καὶ διδάσκαλος· καὶ ὅτι μεταγνώσεται προέμενος τὸν παρόντα καιρόν· καὶ παραδείγματι χρῆται τῷ κατὰ Μελέαγρον διηγήματι, ὅτι κἀκεῖνος παρακαλούμενος ὑπὸ τῶν οἰκείων βοηθεῖν τῇ πατρίδι οὐ συγκατέθετο, ἕως ὑπὸ τῆς ἀνάγκης τῶν καταλαβουσῶν τὴν πόλιν συμφορῶν ἐπὶ τὸ ἀμύνειν ἐτράπετο. Αἴας δὲ οἴκτου μὲν καὶ ἱκεσίας οὐδὲν ἐδεήθη, παρρησίᾳ δὲ χρησάμενος καθελεῖν τὸ φρόνημα τοῦ Ἀχιλλέως διέγνω, τὰ μὲν εὐκαίρως ἐπιπλήττων τὰ δὲ εὐγενῶς παρακαλῶν, ἵνα μὴ τελέως παροξύνῃ· οὕτω γὰρ ἥρμοζε τῷ τῆς ἀρετῆς μετειληφότι. πρὸς δὲ τούτων ἕκαστον ὁ Ἀχιλλεὺς ἀποκρινόμενος ἦθος γενναῖον ἅμα καὶ ἁπλοῦν ἐμφαίνει. τοῖς μὲν γὰρ ἄλλοις ἐλεγκτικῶς ἅμα καὶ μεγαλοφρόνως ἀντιλέγει, αἰτίας εὐλόγους τῆς ὀργῆς παριστάς, Αἴαντι δὲ

brought up Agamemnon's gifts, then again changed the subject back to the prayers of the Greeks, saying that even if he is entirely justified in his rage at Agamemnon, it is still a good thing to save those who have done him no harm—the epilogue likewise must contain nothing to cause pain to the listener, since indeed it is the last words that are best remembered.[1] The final exhortation has something in it to rouse Achilles against the enemy: a suggestion that they are contemptuous of him. "For," he says, "now you could take Hector if he stood up to you, since he brags that none of the Greeks is his equal" [cf. Il. 9.304].

Phoenix, fearing prayers will be inadequate, weeps, and at first associates himself with Achilles' plan, saying that he will not be left behind there if Achilles sails home—this was gratifying to him. Then he explains the reason, how he was entrusted by Peleus with the task of raising the boy and he took him as a child and was responsible for teaching him to speak and to act. He goes on to mention his childhood mistakes, indicating the lack of judgment of the very young. As he proceeds he leaves out nothing that might persuade him, rhetorically summarizing all the main points: that it is a noble thing to give in when approached by a suppliant who both offers gifts and sends as ambassadors the leaders of the Greeks, and specifically those whom Achilles most respects; that it is right that he heed him since he raised him and instructed him, and that he will regret it if he does not take advantage of the present moment. As an illustration, he tells the story of Meleager who was likewise called upon by his people to defend the land but refused until he was brought to defend it by necessity, when disaster was upon it.

Ajax needed neither compassion nor prayer but only outspokenness, and decided to break Achilles' determination by tactful rebukes mixed with polite requests, added in order to avoid angering him in the end. This behavior was appropriate to one who had military prowess.

Achilles in his answers to each of these reveals his nobility and integrity. He answers the others in a manner that is simultaneously critical and generous, bringing forward the reasonable causes for his anger, but to Ajax he justifies himself. He has told Odysseus he is

---

[1] Quintilian (10.1.50) makes similar points about the use of the epilogue, and likewise points to Homer as the master of the art, but his example is not this speech but rather Priam's to Achilles in the final book.

ἀπολογεῖται. καὶ Ὀδυσσεῖ μὲν ἔφη ἀποπλεύσεσθαι τῇ ὑστεραίᾳ, καμπτόμενος δέ πως ταῖς Φοίνικος δεήσεσι βουλεύσεσθαί φησι περὶ τοῦ ἀπόπλου· ἐκνικηθεὶς δὲ ὑπὸ τῆς Αἴαντος παρρησίας ἐξομολογεῖται πᾶν ὃ μέλλει ποιήσειν, ὅτι οὐ πρότερον ἔξεισιν ἐπὶ τὸν πόλεμον πρὶν ἂν ὁ Ἕκτωρ ἐπὶ τὰς σκηνὰς αὐτοῦ καὶ τὰς ναῦς ἀφίκηται, τοὺς πολλοὺς τῶν Ἑλλήνων ἀπεκτονώς· ἔνθα φησὶν ὅτι καίπερ ἐκθύμως μαχόμενον τὸν Ἕκτορα παύσεσθαι νομίζω· καὶ γὰρ καὶ τοῦτο πρὸ(ς τὸ) εἰρημένον πρόσθεν ὑπὸ τοῦ Ὀδυσσέως περὶ τοῦ ἐνστῆναι τῇ ὁρμῇ τοῦ Ἕκτορος ἀντέθηκεν.

170. ἐν δὲ τοῖς τοῦ Φοίνικος λόγοις κἀκεῖνο παρίστησιν, ὅτι τέχνη ἐστὶν ἡ ῥητορική· φησὶ γὰρ τῷ Ἀχιλλεῖ, διότι παρέλαβόν σε

νήπιον, οὔ πω εἰδόθ᾽ ὁμοιίου πολέμοιο

οὐδ᾽ ἀγορέων, ἵνα τ᾽ ἄνδρες ἀριπρεπέες τελέθουσι·

τοὔνεκά με προέηκε διδασκέμεναι τάδε πάντα,

μύθων τε ῥητῆρ᾽ ἔμεναι πρηκτῆρά τε ἔργων (Ι 440-3).

ἐν οἷς καὶ τοῦτο δείκνυσιν, ὅτι ἡ τῶν λόγων δύναμις μάλιστα τοὺς ἄνδρας εὐκλεεῖς ἀπεργάζεται.

171. ἔστι δὲ καὶ ἐν ἄλλοις πολλοῖς τῆς ποιήσεως τόποις εὑρεῖν λόγους τῆς ῥητορικῆς τέχνης ἐχομένους· καὶ κατηγορίας καὶ ἀπολογίας ὑποδείκνυσι τρόπον ἔν τε ἄλλοις καὶ ἐν οἷς ὁ Ἕκτωρ καθάπτεται τοῦ ἀδελφοῦ, ὀνειδίζων αὐτῷ δειλίαν καὶ ἀκολασίαν· καὶ ὅτι τοιοῦτος ὢν ἠδίκει τοὺς πόρρω ἀπῳκισμένους ἔπλευσεν ὅθεν αἴτιος κακῶν τοῖς οἰκείοις ἐγένετο. καὶ ὁ Ἀλέξανδρος ἐκλύει τὸν θυμὸν τοῦ ἀδελφοῦ, δικαίως ἐπιπλήσσεσθαι συγκατατιθέμενος καὶ τῷ ὑποσχέσθαι τὴν πρὸς τὸν Μενέλαον μάχην ἀπολυόμενος τὸ ἔγκλημα τῆς δειλίας. καὶ ὅτι μὲν τεχνίτης λόγων Ὅμηρος οὐκ ἂν ἄλλως τις εἴποι εὖ φρονῶν· δῆλα γὰρ καὶ τὰ ἄλλα ἐξ αὐτῆς τῆς ἀναγνώσεως.

172. οὐκ ἠμέλησε δὲ οὐδὲ χαρακτηρίσαι τοὺς ῥήτορας. τὸν μὲν γὰρ Νέστορα ἡδὺν καὶ προσηνῆ τοῖς ἀκούουσιν εἰσάγει, τὸν δὲ Μενέλαον

leaving the next day, but giving in to the prayers of Phoenix he says that he will think further about his departure. Prevailed upon by the frankness of Ajax, he admits all he plans to do: that he will not go out to fight until Hector reaches his tents and ships and has killed many of the Greeks. There, he says, "I intend to stop Hector, however fiercely he fights" [cf. Il. 9.655]. This responds to what Odysseus had said earlier about standing up to the onslaught of Hector.

170. In Phoenix' speech Homer also indicates that rhetoric is an art, for Phoenix says to Achilles, "I took you up,

> a mere infant with no experience of war
> or of speaking, where men excel.
> Therefore he set me to teach you all these things:
> to be a speaker of words and a doer of deeds
>   [Il. 9.440-43]."

Here Homer indicates that it is preeminently the power of eloquence that makes men great.

171. It is possible to find many other places in the poems where speeches illustrate the art of rhetoric. Among the many passages in which he demonstrates the modes of accusation and response is that where Hector rebukes his brother, calling him cowardly and lacking in restraint, and saying that because of these faults he has committed a crime against people living far away and thus become a cause of suffering for his own people. Paris calms his brother's anger by agreeing that the rebuke is justified, but undertakes to clear himself of the charge of cowardice by promising to duel with Menelaus.

    No reasonable person will deny that Homer was an artificer of discourse, for this much and more is clear simply from reading him.

172. He was concerned to give each orator a particular character,[1] and makes Nestor sweet and saying things pleasing to the listeners, Menelaus brief and winning, coming right to the point, and Odysseus

---

[1] Cf. ch. 164, above, with note.

βραχυλόγον καὶ εὔχαριν καὶ τοῦ προκειμένου τυγχάνοντα, τὸν δὲ Ὀδυσσέα πολλῇ καὶ πυκνῇ ⟨καὶ⟩ πληκτικῇ τῇ δεινότητι τῶν λόγων κεχρημένον· ταῦτα γὰρ τοῖς δυσὶ τούτοις ἥρωσιν ὁ Ἀντήνωρ μαρτυρεῖ, ἀκούσας αὐτῶν, ὁπότε πρεσβεύοντες ἀφίκοντο εἰς τὴν Ἴλιον. καὶ ταύτας τὰς ἰδέας τῶν λόγων Ὅμηρος παρίστησιν αὐτός, ἐν τῇ ποιήσει δείξας ἁπάσῃ.

173. οἶδε δὲ καὶ τὴν ἀντίθεσιν τῶν λόγων, ἀεὶ τῶν ἐναντίων ἐπὶ παντὸς πράγματος τιθεμένων καὶ τὸ αὐτὸ κατασκευαζόντων καὶ ἀναιρούντων διὰ τὴν εὐπορίαν τῆς λογικῆς ἕξεως· φησὶ γὰρ

στρεπτὴ δὲ γλῶσσ' ἐστὶ βροτῶν, πολέες δ' ἔνι μῦθοι
παντοῖοι, ἐπέων δὲ πολὺς νομὸς ἔνθα καὶ ἔνθα.
ὁπποῖόν κ' εἴπησθα ἔπος, τοῖόν κ' ἐπακούσαις (Υ 248-50).

174. ἐπίσταται δὲ τὰ αὐτὰ καὶ διὰ πολλῶν λέγειν καὶ δι' ὀλίγων ἐπαναλαμβάνειν, ὅπερ καλεῖται ἀνακεφαλαίωσις, καὶ ἔστιν ἐν χρήσει παρὰ τοῖς ῥήτορσιν, ὁπόταν δέῃ πολλὰ πράγματα εἰρημένα ἀναμνῆσαι συντόμως· ἃ γὰρ διηγήσατο ὁ Ὀδυσσεὺς παρὰ τοῖς Φαίαξιν ἐν τέτταρσι ῥαψῳδίαις, ταῦτα πάλιν βραχέως διέξεισιν ἐν τούτοις·

ἤρξατο δ' ὡς πρῶτον Κίκονας δάμασ', αὐτὰρ ἔπειτα (ψ 310)
καὶ τὰ ἑξῆς.

175. τοῦ δὲ πολιτικοῦ λόγου ἔχεται καὶ ἡ τῶν νόμων ἐπιστήμη καὶ οὐδὲ ταύτης ἐκτὸς τὸν Ὅμηρον εὕροιμεν ἄν. εἰ μὲν οὖν καὶ τοὔνομα τοῦ νόμου ἦν κατ' αὐτὸν ἐν χρήσει, οὐκ ἔστι σαφῶς διορίσασθαι. οἱ μὲν γάρ φασι δῆλον αὐτὸν εἶναι εἰδότα τοὔνομα τοῦ νόμου ἐν τῷ εἰπεῖν

ἀνθρώπων ὕβριν τε καὶ εὐνομίην ἐφορῶντες (ρ 487).

using many complex ingenuities of language. Antenor is the witness to these qualities in the two heroes, whom he heard when they came to Troy as ambassadors, and Homer demonstrates these modes of discourse himself, inserting them everywhere into his poetry.

173. Homer is also acquainted with rhetorical antithesis,[1] a form of discourse that introduces the opposite of everything said, simultaneously proving and disproving the same thing through the faculty of agile reasoning, for he says,

> The tongue of man is flexible and tells many stories
> of all sorts—the field of discourse is immense.
> The kind of thing you say determines the kind of response you
> get   [Il. 20.248-50].

174. He also understands the technique—called anacephalaeosis, or recapitulation[2]—of saying something with many words and then repeating it with a few, a technique also in use among the rhetors in situations where many things have been said and must be recalled succinctly. What it took Odysseus four entire books to describe to the Phaeacians he resumes briefly in the passage that begins,

> He started with how he defeated the Cicones, and then. . .
> [Od. 23.310]

and so on.

175. Knowledge of law is also part of political discourse and we would find that Homer was no stranger to this. It is impossible to say with certainty whether or not the word "law" [νόμος][3] was in use in his time, for some claim that it is obvious that he was acquainted with the word from the fact that he says,

> see both the crimes and the lawfulness [εὐνομία] of men
> [Od. 17.487],

---

[1] See, e.g. Rhet. ad Alex. 26, 1435b25-30.
[2] Widely discussed in the rhetorical writers, including Hermogenes (περὶ μεθόδου δεινότητος, 12).
[3] The word νόμος does not occur in the Homeric corpus. See e.g. schol in Il. 9.99: "They did not yet have written laws, but rather everything was in the hands of the powerful."

Ἀρίσταρχος δὲ ᾠήθη τὴν εὐνομίαν εἰρῆσθαι παρὰ τὸ εὖ νέμεσθαι. καίτοι καὶ ὁ νόμος λέγεσθαι ἔοικεν ἀπὸ τὸ νέμειν τὰ ἴσα πᾶσιν ἢ τὸ κατ' ἀξίαν ἑκάστῳ. ὅτι δὲ τὴν δύναμιν τῶν νόμων οἶδεν, εἰ μὴ καὶ ἐν γραφαῖς ἀλλ' ἐν ταῖς γνώμαις τῶν ἀνθρώπων φυλασσομένην, ἐν πολλοῖς παρίστησι· τὸν γὰρ Ἀχιλλέα ποιεῖ ὑπὲρ τοῦ σκήπτρου λέγοντα

νῦν αὖτέ μιν υἷες Ἀχαιῶν

ἐν παλάμαις φορέουσι δικασπόλοι, οἵ τε θέμιστας

πρὸς Διὸς εἰρύαται (Α 237-9).

θέμιστες γὰρ καὶ θεσμοὶ οἱ νόμοι, ὧν τὸν Δία εἰσηγητὴν παραδίδωσιν, ᾧ καὶ τὸν Μίνωα τὸν τῶν Κρητῶν βασιλέα φησὶν ὁμιλεῖν· ἡ δὲ ὁμιλία νόμων μάθησις ἦν, ὡς καὶ Πλάτων (*Min.* 319C) μαρτυρεῖ. σαφῶς δὲ καὶ ἐν ἐκείνοις δηλοῖ ὅτι χρὴ τοῖς νόμοις ἕπεσθαι καὶ μὴ ἀδικεῖν

τῷ μή τίς ποτε πάμπαν ἀνὴρ ἀθέμιστος εἴη,

ἀλλ' ὅ γε σιγῇ δῶρα θεῶν ἔχοι, ὅττι διδοῖεν (σ 141-2).

176. πρῶτος τοίνυν Ὅμηρος τὰ τῆς πολιτείας διεῖλεν· ἐν γὰρ τῇ ἀσπίδι ἣν τοῦ κόσμου παντὸς μίμημα κατεσκεύασεν Ἥφαιστος—τουτέστιν ἡ πνευματικὴ δύναμις—ἐμπεριεχομένας ἐποίησε δύο πόλεις, τὴν μὲν ἐν εἰρήνῃ καὶ εὐφροσύνῃ διάγουσαν τὴν δὲ ἐν πολέμῳ σχολάζουσαν· καὶ παραθεὶς τὰ ἑκατέρᾳ πρόσφορα παρίστησιν ὅτι ὁ μὲν πολιτικός ἐστι βίος ὁ δὲ στρατιωτικός. οὐ παρεῖδε δὲ οὐδὲ τὸν τρίτον τὸν γεωργικόν· ἀλλὰ καὶ τοῦτον ἔδειξεν, ἐνάργειαν ἅμα καὶ κάλλος περιθεὶς τοῖς λόγοις.

177. ὃ δὲ ἐν πάσῃ πόλει νενομοθέτηται, τὸ εἶναι συνέδριον βουλῆς καὶ τοῦτο προβουλεύεσθαι πρὸ τοῦ τὸν δῆμον συνιέναι, πρόδηλον ὅτι ἐστὶν ἐκ τῶν Ὁμηρικῶν τούτων

βουλὴν δὲ πρῶτον μεγαθύμων ἷζε γερόντων (Β 53)·

συνάγει γὰρ Ἀγαμέμνων τοὺς γέροντας καὶ σκέπτεται μετ' αὐτῶν, ὅπως ὁπλίσῃ τὸ πλῆθος πρὸς τὴν μάχην.

but Aristarchus maintained that εὐνομία was derived from εὖ νέμεσθαι [i.e. their receiving their just portions]. Moreover, νόμος seems to come from "distribute [νέμειν] equal portions to all, or portions according to their own deserts." That he knew the force of laws, though preserved not in writing but in the maxims of men, he demonstrates in many passages. He depicts Achilles saying about the scepter:

> Now, however, the sons of the Achaeans
> hold it in their hands when they act as judges, maintaining
> rulings
> that come from Zeus   [Il. 1.237-39],

for "laws" [νόμοι] include "rulings" and "rules," which, he says, Zeus introduced, for Zeus spoke with Minos the king of the Cretans, and their conversation, as Plato testifies [*Minos* 319c], was a teaching of laws. He also shows clearly in the following passage that one must follow the laws and not commit crimes:

> Therefore let no man ever be unruly,
> but quietly accept the gifts of the gods, whatever they give
> [Od. 18.141-42].

176. Homer was the first to speak analytically about the state, for in the shield which Hephaestus (that is, the power of the spirit) made as an image of the entire universe, he included two states, the one living in peace and happiness and the other occupied with war. He elaborated material appropriate to each, indicating that there is on the one hand a civic life and on the other a military life—nor does he overlook the third possibility, the farming life, but describes this as well, with vivid and beautiful language.

177. It is clear that what has been instituted in every city, namely that there be a deliberative council that meets before the people is assembled, emerges from this Homeric passage:

> He first called the great-hearted elders to council
> [Il. 2.53],

for Agamemnon calls the elders together and considers with them how to arm the troops for battle.

178. καὶ ὅτι δεῖ τὸν ἄρχοντα πρὸ τῶν ἄλλων πεφροντικέναι τῆς πάντων σωτηρίας ἐν τῷ αὐτῷ προσώπῳ διδάσκει, ᾧ καὶ παραινεῖ

οὐ χρὴ παννύχιον εὕδειν βουληφόρον ἄνδρα (Β 24 = 61)·

καὶ ὅτι δεῖ τῷ ἡγουμένῳ πείθεσθαι τοὺς ὑποτεταγμένους καὶ ὅπως ἑκάστῳ προφέρεσθαι τὸν προτεταγμένον ὁ Ὀδυσσεὺς ὑποδείκνυσι, τοὺς μὲν ἐντίμους λόγοις προσηνέσι πείθων, τοῖς δὲ ἐκ τοῦ ὄχλου πικρότερον ἐπιπλήσσων.

179. ἀλλὰ καὶ τὸ ὑπανίστασθαι τοῖς ἀμείνοσι παρὰ πᾶσι νενόμισται· ὃ καὶ αὐτοὶ οἱ θεοὶ ποιοῦσιν ἐπὶ τοῦ Διὸς

οὐδέ τις ἔτλη

μεῖναι ἐπερχόμενον, ἀλλ' ἀντίοι ἔσταν ἅπαντες (Α 534-5).

180. νόμος παρὰ τοῖς πλείστοις τὸν πρεσβύτατον λέγειν· ὁ δὲ Διομήδης ὑπὸ ἀνάγκης τοῦ πολέμου πρῶτος θαρσήσας λέγειν συγγνωστὸς εἶναι ἀξιοῖ

καὶ μή τι κότῳ ἀγάσησθε ἕκαστος,

οὕνεκα δὴ γενεῆφι νεώτατός εἰμι μεθ' ὑμῶν (Ξ 111-2).

181. κἀκεῖνο δὲ παρὰ πᾶσι νενόμισται, τὸ κολάζεσθαι τὰ ἑκούσια ἁμαρτήματα, τὰ δὲ ἀκούσια συγγνώμης τυγχάνειν. τοῦτο πάλιν δείκνυσιν ὁ ποιητής, ἐν οἷς φησιν ὁ ἀοιδὸς παρ' αὐτῷ

καί κεν Τηλέμαχος τάδε γ' εἴποι, σὸς φίλος υἱός,

ὡς ἐγὼ οὔ τι ἑκὼν ἐς σὸν δόμον οὐδὲ χατίζων

πωλεύμην μνηστῆρσιν ἀεισόμενος μετὰ δαῖτας,

ἀλλὰ πολὺ πλέονες καὶ κρείσσονες ἦγον ἀνάγκῃ (χ 350-3).

182. τριῶν δὲ οὐσῶν πολιτειῶν πρὸς δικαιοσύνην καὶ εὐνομίαν, βασιλείας τε καὶ ἀριστοκρατίας καὶ δημοκρατίας, καὶ ταύταις πάλιν ἀντικειμένων τριῶν πρὸς ἀδικίαν καὶ παρανομίαν, τυραννίδος, ὀλιγαρχίας,

178. In this same character, he shows that the king must be the first to be concerned for the safety of all, for [Agamemnon] is advised,

> A leader in counsel must not sleep through the night
> [Il. 2.24 = 61].

Odysseus demonstrates that underlings must obey the leader, and likewise shows how leaders must deal with each individual, winning over the people of rank with gentle words but berating those in the crowd more severely.

179. It is universally accepted that people must stand to show respect to their superiors, as even the gods themselves do for Zeus:

> nor did any dare to sit as he approached
> but all stood up to greet him   [Il. 1.534-35].

180. It is the custom among most peoples that the oldest speaks. When Diomedes presumes to speak first, because of the compelling necessity of war, he excuses himself:

> Let no one be angered at my speaking,
> simply because I am younger than the rest of you
> [Il. 14.111-12].

181. It is also the law among all peoples for deliberate crimes to be punished and for unintentional ones to be pardoned. The poet again teaches this when he has Phemius the bard say to Odysseus,

> Telemachus your own son would tell you the same thing,
> how I used to go neither willingly nor for gain
> to your great house to sing at the suitors' feasts,
> but in their numbers and their strength they forced me
> [Od. 22.350-53].

182. There are three kinds of governments that tend toward justice and lawfulness: monarchy, aristocracy, and democracy—and opposite these there are three that tend toward injustice and lawlessness:

ὀχλοκρατίας, οὐδὲ ταύτας Ὅμηρος ἀγνοεῖν ἔοικε, τὴν μὲν βασιλείαν δι' ὅλης τῆς ποιήσεως ὀνομάζων καὶ ἐγκωμιάζων, ὡς ἐν τούτοις·

θυμὸς δὲ μέγας ἐστὶ διοτρεφέων βασιλήων·
τιμὴ δ' ἐκ Διός ἐστι, φιλεῖ δέ ἑ μητίετα Ζεύς (Β 196-7).
καὶ ὁποῖον δεῖ εἶναι τὸν βασιλέα, σαφῶς δηλοῖ
λαῶν δ' οἷσιν ἄνασσε, πατὴρ δ' ὣς ἤπιος ἦεν (β 234 = ε 12)

καὶ

οὔτε τινὰ ῥέξας ἐξαίσιον οὔτε τι εἰπὼν
ἐν δήμῳ, ἥ τ' ἐστὶ δίκη θείων βασιλήων (δ 690-1).
τὴν δὲ ἀριστοκρατίαν, ἐν οἷς Βοιωτῶν βασιλέας πέντε καταριθμεῖ (Β 494-5), καὶ παρὰ τοῖς Φαίαξι

δώδεκα γὰρ κατὰ δῆμον ἀριπρεπέες βασιλῆες
ἀρχοὶ κρίνουσι, τρισκαιδέκατος δ' ἐγὼ αὐτός (θ 390-1).
δημοκρατίας δὲ εἰκόνα ἐναργῶς ἐν τῇ κατασκευῇ τῆς ἀσπίδος δεικνύει, ἐν ᾗ δύο ποιήσας πόλεις τὴν ἑτέραν δημοκρατεῖσθαί φησι μηδενὸς ἡγουμένου, πάντων δὲ πρὸς τὴν ἑαυτῶν βούλησιν κατὰ νόμους βιούντων· ἔνθα καὶ δικαστήριον εἰσάγει καὶ ἐν ἐκείνῃ γε τὴν δημοκρατίαν παρίστησιν, ἐν οἷς φησι

δῆμον ὑποδδείσας· δὴ γὰρ κεχολώσατο λίην
οὕνεκα ληιστῆρσιν ἐπισπόμενος Ταφίοισιν

tyranny, oligarchy, and mob rule.[1] Homer seems to have been acquainted with all of these, for he mentions monarchy throughout his poetry with praise, as in

> Terrible is the wrath of Zeus-nurtured kings:
> their honor comes from Zeus and Zeus the counselor loves them
> [Il. 2.196-97].

He shows clearly the qualities the king should have:

> like a gentle father to the people he rules
> [Od. 2.234 = 5.12],

and

> He neither said not did anything unfair
> among the people—and that is the right of divine kings
> [Od. 4.690-91].

He portrays aristocracy when he speaks of five kings among the Boeotians [Il. 2.494-95], and in the description of the Phaeacians as well. [As Alcinous says,]

> There are twelve glorious kings to give judgment
> among the people, and I myself am the thirteenth
> [Od. 8.390-91].

He draws a vivid portrait of democracy in the making of the shield, in which he puts two cities, the one of which he says is democratic, for it has no leader and everyone lives as he likes under the law. There he has a lawcourt as well. He also portrays democracy in this city, where [according to Penelope Antinous' father took refuge]:

> fearing the people, for indeed they were angered
> that he had joined the Taphian pirates and brought

---

[1] This is essentially the same classification found in Aristotle (*Politics* 1279a-b), though Aristotle uses the general term for "constitution" or "government," πολιτεία, to designate the successful democracy, and reserves δημοκρατία for the "deviation" from good government to rule "in the interest of the poor" (1279b8-9).

ἤκαχε Θεσπρωτούς· οἱ δ' ἡμῖν ἄρθμιοι ἦσαν (π 425-7).

183. τὸν δὲ βιαίως καὶ παρανόμως ἄρχοντα τύραννον μὲν οὐ καλεῖ· νεώτερον γὰρ τὸ ὄνομα. οἷος δὲ τοῖς ἔργοις γίνεται, δείκνυσιν ἐν τούτοις

εἰς Ἔχετον βασιλῆα, βροτῶν δηλήμονα πάντων,

ὅς κ' ἀπὸ ῥῖνα τάμῃσι καὶ οὔατα νηλέι χαλκῷ (σ 85-6).

καὶ τὸν Αἴγισθον δὲ τυραννικὸν ἀποφαίνει, ὃς ἀποκτείνας τὸν Ἀγαμέμνονα ἐκράτει τῶν Μυκηναίων· "καὶ ὁπότε ἀνῃρέθη," φησίν ὅτι "οὐκ ἂν ἔτυχε ταφῆς, εἴπερ Μενέλαος παρῆν"· τοῦτο γὰρ ἐπὶ τῶν τυράννων νενόμισται·

τῷ ... οὐδὲ θανόντι χυτὴν ἐπὶ γαῖαν ἔχευαν,

ἀλλ' ἄρα τόν γε κύνες τε καὶ οἰωνοὶ κατέδαψαν

κείμενον ἐν πεδίῳ· μάλα γὰρ μέγα μήσατο ἔργον (γ 258-60α, 261β).

ὀλιγαρχίαν δὲ δηλοῦν δοκεῖ διὰ τῆς τῶν μνηστήρων πλεονεξίας, περὶ ὧν φησιν

ἠδ' ὅσσοι κραναὴν Ἰθάκην κάτα κοιρανέουσι (α 247 = π 124).

τὴν δὲ ὀχλοκρατίαν ἐν τῇ τῶν Τρώων πολιτείᾳ παραδίδωσιν, ἐν ᾗ καὶ συναράμενοι πάντες Ἀλεξάνδρῳ κακοῖς περιέπεσον καὶ ὁ Πρίαμος λοιδορεῖται τοῖς παισὶν ὡς τούτων αἰτίοις

σπεύσατέ μοι, κακὰ τέκνα, κατηφόνες (Ω 253)

καὶ ἄλλος δέ τις τῶν Τρώων, ὁ Ἀντίμαχος,

χρυσὸν Ἀλεξάνδροιο δεδεγμένος, ἀγλαὰ δῶρα,

οὐκ εἴασχ' Ἑλένην δόμεναι ξανθῷ Μενελάῳ (Λ 124-5).

> woe to the Thesprotians, who were on our side
> [Od. 16.425-27].

183.   He does not use the word "tyrant" [τύραννος] for one who rules illegally and by force, for the word has been introduced since his time, but he shows how such a man acts in these lines: [We'll send you]

> to King Echetus, cruelest of all men,
> who'll cut off your nose and your ears with a sharp knife!
> [Od. 18.85-86].

He also portrays Aegisthus as a tyrant, since he killed Agamemnon and then ruled the Mycenaeans. When he was killed, the poet says, he would have had no gravestone if Menelaus had been present. For this is customary for tyrants:

> They did not even pile the earth over his corpse
> but the dogs and birds devoured him,
> lying on the plain, for his crime was a huge one
> [cf. Od. 3.258-60, 261].

He seems to be describing oligarchy in the ambitious greed of the suitors, of whom he says [that they included]

> all those who were chiefs of rocky Ithaca
> [Od. 1.247 = 16.124].

He shows mob rule in the Trojan state, where all are accomplices of Paris and so come on evil times, and Priam reviles his sons as responsible for the situation:

> Exert yourselves, you useless children who bring shame upon me
> [Il. 24.253],

and another of the Trojans, Antimachus,

> corrupted by dazzling gifts of gold from Paris,
> was against returning Helen to blond Menelaus
> [Il. 11.124-25].

184. ἐπεὶ δὲ τὸ παρὰ ἀνθρώποις δίκαιον τοῦτο νομίζεται, τὸ ἀπονεμητικὸν ἑκάστῳ τοῦ κατ' ἀξίαν, ἐν ᾧ μάλιστά ἐστι τὸ θεοὺς σέβειν, γονέας καὶ οἰκείους τιμᾶν, τὴν μὲν εἰς θεοὺς εὐσέβειαν ἐν πολλοῖς διδάσκει, εἰσάγων τοὺς ἥρωας θύοντας καὶ εὐχομένους καὶ δῶρα ἀνατιθέντας τοῖς θεοῖς καὶ ὕμνοις γεραίροντας αὐτούς, καὶ τῆς εὐσεβείας ἀμοιβὴν ἀπολαμβάνοντας τὴν παρὰ τῶν θεῶν ἐπικουρίαν.

185. τὴν δὲ πρὸς τοὺς γειναμένους τιμὴν ἐν τῷ Τηλεμάχου προσώπῳ μάλιστα δείκνυσι καὶ ἐν οἷς ἐπαινεῖ τὸν Ὀρέστην

οὐκ ἀίεις οἷον κλέος ἔλλαβε δῖος Ὀρέστης

πάντας ἐπ' ἀνθρώπους, ἐπεὶ ἔκτανε πατροφονῆα (α 298-9);
καὶ ὅτι τὸ γηροτροφεῖσθαι τοὺς γονέας ὑπὸ τῶν παίδων φύσει δίκαιον καὶ ἐξ ἀμοιβῆς ὀφειλόμενον, διὰ μιᾶς λέξεως ἐδήλωσεν εἰπών

οὐδὲ τοκεῦσι

θρέπτρα φίλοις ἀπέδωκεν (Δ 477-8 = Ρ 301-2).
ἀδελφῶν δὲ εὔνοιαν καὶ πίστιν πρὸς ἀλλήλους ἐν τῷ Ἀγαμέμνονι καὶ Μενελάῳ, φίλων δὲ ἐν Ἀχιλλεῖ καὶ Πατρόκλῳ δείκνυσι, γυναικὸς δὲ σωφροσύνην καὶ φιλανδρίαν ἐν τῇ Πηνελόπῃ, ἀνδρὸς δὲ πόθον τῆς αὐτοῦ γυναικὸς ἐν τῷ Ὀδυσσεῖ παρίστησιν.

186. ὅπως δὲ καὶ ὑπὲρ τῆς πατρίδος χρὴ πράσσειν ἐν τούτῳ μάλιστα ἐδήλωσεν·

εἷς οἰωνὸς ἄριστος ἀμύνεσθαι περὶ πάτρης (Μ 243).
καὶ πάλιν ὅπως τοὺς τῆς πολιτείας κοινωνοῦντας φιλίας ἔχειν δεῖ·

184. Since the disposition to give everyone his due is traditionally equated with justice among men, and since one's first obligation is to revere the gods, and to honor parents and family,[1] Homer teaches reverence for the gods in many passages, showing the heroes offering sacrifices and praying and dedicating gifts to the gods and celebrating them with hymns—and, in exchange for their reverence, receiving the help of the gods.

185. He shows honor for parents primarily in the character of Telemachus and where he praises Orestes:

> Haven't you heard how brilliant Orestes won fame
> among all men, when he killed his father's murderer?
> [Od. 1.298-99].

Likewise he showed in a single phrase that it is right for parents to be supported in their old age by their children, for they owe it to them in exchange for their upbringing:

> nor did he repay his parents
> for his upbringing
> [Il. 4.477-78 = 17.301-02].

The goodwill and good faith of brothers for one another he shows in Agamemnon and Menelaus, that of friends in Achilles and Patroclus; a woman's self-restraint and love for her husband he shows in Penelope and a man's desire for his own wife in Odysseus.

186. Here, in particular, he shows how one must act toward one's country:

> There is one omen that is best: to guard the state
> [Il. 12.243],

and furthermore he shows that the members of the community must share in friendship:

---

[1] This passage on basic obligations makes particularly clear the pedagogical thrust of the *Essay*.

ἀφρήτωρ ἀθέμιστος ἀνέστιός ἐστιν ἐκεῖνος

ὃς πολέμου ἔραται ἐπιδημίου ὀκρυόεντος (Ι 63-4).

ὅπως δὲ τὸ ἀληθεύειν τίμιον τὸ δὲ ἐναντίον φευκτόν·

ἐχθρὸς γάρ μοι κεῖνος ὁμῶς Ἀίδαο πύλῃσιν,

ὅς χ' ἕτερον μὲν κεύθ' ἐνὶ φρεσίν, ἄλλο δὲ εἴπῃ (Ι 312-3)

καὶ

οἵ τ' εὖ μὲν βάζουσι, κακῶς δ' ὄπιθεν φρονέουσι (σ 168).

187. τῶν δὲ οἴκων μάλιστα σῳζομένων ὁπόταν γυνὴ μήτε τὰς ἀπορρήτους διανοίας τοῦ ἀνδρὸς πολυπραγμονῇ μήτε ἄνευ τῆς γνώμης αὐτοῦ πράσσειν τι ἐπιχειρῇ, ἑκάτερον ἐκ τῆς Ἥρας ὑπέδειξε, τὸ μὲν πρότερον τῷ Διὶ λέγοντι περιθείς

Ἥρη, μὴ δὴ πάντας ἐμοὺς ἐπιέλπεο μύθους

εἰδήσειν (Α 545-6),

τὸ δὲ ἕτερον τῇ Ἥρᾳ

μή πώς μοι μετέπειτα χολώσεαι, αἴ κε σιωπῇ

οἴχωμαι πρὸς δῶμα βαθυρρόου Ὠκεανοῖο (Ξ 310-11).

188. τὸ δὲ καὶ τοὺς ἐξιόντας ἐπὶ πόλεμον ἢ ἐν κινδύνῳ καθεστῶτας ἐντέλλεσθαί τι τοῖς οἰκείοις εἰθισμένον παρὰ πᾶσιν οὐκ ἠγνόησεν ὁ ποιητής. ἡ μὲν γὰρ Ἀνδρομάχη στένουσα τὸν Ἕκτορά φησιν

οὐ γάρ μοι θνῄσκων λεχέων ἐκ χεῖρας ὄρεξας,

οὐδέ τί μοι εἶπας πυκινὸν ἔπος, οὗ τέ κεν αἰεὶ

μεμνῄμην νύκτας τε καὶ ἤματα δάκρυ χέουσα (Ω 743-5).

> Tribeless, outlawed, homeless is he
> who loves domestic strife in all its horror
> [Il. 9.63-64].

He shows that telling the truth is honorable and the opposite to be avoided:

> Hateful to me as the gates of Hades
> is the man who hides one thing in his mind and says another
> [Il. 9.312-13],

and [he speaks of]

> those who speak kindly now, but plan evil later
> [Od. 18.168].

187. He shows in Hera that that home is safest in which the wife neither meddles in the secret thoughts of her husband nor undertakes anything without his knowledge. The first point is made when Zeus says to her,

> Hera, do not try to know all my thoughts [Il. 1.545-46],

the second by Hera herself: [I have come to tell you,]

> lest you be angry afterwards if without saying anything
> I should go off to the house of deep-flowing Ocean
> [Il. 14.310-11].

188. The poet was not unaware that those going off to war or in dangerous situations customarily make certain demands of their families. Andromache, moaning for Hector, says,

> You did not die stretching out your hand to me from your bed,
> nor did you give me any instructions that I might always
> remember in my nights and days of weeping
> [Il. 24.743-45].

ἡ δὲ Πηνελόπη τῶν τοῦ Ὀδυσσέως ἐντολῶν μνημονεύει, φήσαντος ὁπότε ἐξῄει
>τῷ οὐκ οἶδ᾽ εἴ κέν μ᾽ ἀνέσει θεός, ἦ κεν ἁλώω
>αὐτοῦ ἐνὶ Τροίῃ· σοὶ δ᾽ ἐνθάδε πάντα μελόντων,
>μεμνῆσθαι πατρὸς καὶ μητέρος ἐν μεγάροισιν
>ὡς νῦν, ἢ ἔτι μᾶλλον ἐμεῦ ἀπονόσφιν ἐόντος·
>αὐτὰρ ἐπειδὴ παῖδα γενειήσαντα ἴδηαι,
>γήμασθ᾽ ᾧ κ᾽ ἐθέλησθα, τεὸν κατὰ δῶμα λιποῦσα (σ 265-70).

οἶδε δὲ καὶ ἐπιτρόπους
>καί οἱ ἰὼν ἐν νηυσὶν ἐπέτρεπεν οἶκον ἅπαντα,
>πείθεσθαί τε γέροντι καὶ ἔμπεδα πάντα φυλάσσειν (β 226-7).

189. τὰ δὲ ἐπὶ τοῖς θανάτοις τῶν οἰκείων πένθη οὔτε ἄμετρα εἶναι ἀξιοῖ—ἀγεννὲς γὰρ τοῦτο—οὔτε παντελῶς ἐκκεκόφθαι ἐᾷ—ἀδύνατον γὰρ τὸ ἀπαθὲς ἐπὶ ἀνθρώπων. ὅθεν λέγει τὰ τοιαῦτα·

>ἀλλ᾽ ἦ τοι κλαύσας καὶ ὀδυρόμενος μεθέηκεν·
>τλητὸν γὰρ Μοῖραι θυμὸν θέσαν ἀνθρώποισιν (Ω 48-9).

ἔν ἄλλοις δέ φησιν
>ἀλλὰ χρὴ τὸν μὲν καταθάπτειν ὅς κε θάνῃσι,
>νηλέα θυμὸν ἔχοντας, ἐπ᾽ ἤματι δακρύσαντας (Τ 228-9).

190. ἔγνω δὲ κἀκεῖνα ἃ καὶ νῦν ἐν ταῖς ταφαῖς νομίζεται ἔν τε ἄλλοις καὶ ἐν τούτοις·

>ἔνθα ἑ ταρχύσουσι κασίγνητοί τε ἔται τε

Penelope recalls Odysseus' commands when he went off to war:

> Thus I know not whether god will send me back or I shall be killed
> there in Troy. Let everything here be in your hands—
> be mindful of my father and mother here at home
> as now—or moreso—in my absence.
> But when our son is grown to manhood,
> marry whom you like and leave your home behind
> [Od. 18.265-70].

Homer also knows about overseers [as is seen in this passage concerning Mentor]:

> As he went aboard he turned over his entire house
> to the old man, telling the household to obey him,
> to keep safe watch over all
> [Od. 2.226-27].

189. He believes that the grief over the death of relatives should not be excessive, for this is ignoble, but he does not let it be eliminated entirely, for freedom from emotion [τὸ ἀπαθές] is impossible for men.[1] Hence he says things of this sort:

> but he stops crying and grieving,
> for the fates have given man an enduring heart
> [Il. 24.48-49].

Elsewhere he says,

> but whoever dies must be buried
> with a firm heart, after a day's weeping
> [Il. 19.228-29].

190. In various passages including the following, he recognized burial customs like those in use today:

His brothers and friends will make him a tomb and stele,

---

[1] Cf. ch. 134, above.

τύμβῳ τε στήλῃ τε· τὸ γὰρ γέρας ἐστὶ θανόντων (Π 456-7 = 674-5)
καὶ οἷα ἡ Ἀνδρομάχη φησὶν εἰς τὸν Ἕκτορος νέκυν γυμνὸν κείμενον·

αἰόλαι εὐλαὶ ἔδονται, ἐπεί κε κύνες κορέσωνται,

γυμνόν· ἀτάρ μοι εἵματ' ἐνὶ μεγάροισι κέονται

λεπτά τε καὶ χαρίεντα, τετυγμένα χερσὶ γυναικῶν.

ἀλλ' ἦ τοι τάδε πάντα καταφλέξω πυρὶ κηλέῳ,

οὐδὲν σοί γ' ὄφελος, ἐπεὶ οὐκ ἐγκείσεαι αὐτοῖς,

ἀλλὰ πρὸς Τρώων καὶ Τρωιάδων κλέος εἶναι (Χ 509-14).

οὕτω καὶ ἡ Πηνελόπη τὴν ἐσθῆτα κατασκευάζει

Λαέρτῃ ἥρωι ταφήιον (β 99 al.).

καὶ ταῦτα μὲν μέτρια· τὰ δὲ πέρα τούτων, καὶ ζῷα ἄλλα τε καὶ ἀνθρώπους ἐπικαίειν τὸν Ἀχιλλέα τῇ τοῦ Πατρόκλου πυρᾷ, οὐκ ἐπαινῶν λέγει· διὸ καὶ ἐπιφωνεῖ

κακὰ δὲ φρεσὶ μήδετο ἔργα (Φ 19 = Ψ 176).

191. καὶ τὰ πολυάνδρια δὲ πρῶτος ἤγειρε

τύμβον δ' ἐκ πεδίου ἕνα χεύομεν ἐξαγαγόντες (Η 336)·

καὶ τοὺς ἐπιταφίους ἀγῶνας ἔδειξε πρῶτος. ταῦτα μὲν κοινὰ τῶν τε ἐν εἰρήνῃ καὶ τῶν ἐν πολέμῳ καθεστώτων.

192. τὴν δὲ περὶ τοὺς πολέμους ἐμπειρίαν, ἣν καὶ τακτικήν τινες καλοῦσιν, ἡ ποίησις ⟨παραδίδωσιν⟩ πεποικιλμένη μὲν πεζομαχίαις, τειχομαχίαις, ἐπὶ ναυσὶ μάχαις, παρὰ ποταμῷ παρατάξεσι, μονομαχίαις, πολλὰ δὲ καὶ στρατηγικὰ περιέχουσα, ὧν ὀλίγα παραθέσθαι ἐστὶν ἄξιον. ἐν

for these are gifts due to those who have died
[Il. 16.456-57 = 674-75],

and in what Andromache says to the corpse of Hector lying naked,

> The maggots will devour you when the dogs have had enough,
> lying there naked, while I have fine, pleasing cloth
> in the halls, prepared by women's hands.
> I shall surely burn it all in the flames
> since it is of no use to you and you will not lie in it—
> still, it will be an honor to you from the Trojans and their wives
> [Il. 22.509-14],

and in the same way Penelope is preparing a cloth

> to be a shroud for the hero Laertes
> [Od. 2.99, etc.].

These things are done in moderation. Achilles' excesses, burning men and animals on the pyre of Patroclus, Homer describes without praise.[1] Thus he refers to Achilles as

> pondering evil deeds in his heart
> [Il. 22.395 = 23.176].

191. Homer was the first to describe a multiple burial:

> Let us gather them and pile a single tumulus on the plain
> [cf. Il. 7.336-37],

and the first to describe funeral games. These things are the same in war and in peace.

192. The poems contain rich experience of military matters, which some call "tactics," with a variety of infantry battles, sieges, battles over the ships, battle arrays along the river, duels, and strategic matters of all sorts. A few illustrations are in place here. For example,

---

[1] Cf. ch. 145, above.

γὰρ ταῖς παρατάξεσιν ἀεὶ χρὴ προτετάχθαι τὸ ἱππικὸν καὶ ἕπεσθαι τὸ πεζόν· καὶ τοῦτο δὲ δείκνυσιν οὕτως

> ἱππῆας μὲν πρῶτα σὺν ἵπποισιν καὶ ὄχεσφι,
> πεζοὺς δ' ἐξόπιθεν στήσας πολέας τε καὶ ἐσθλούς (Δ 297-8).

193. καὶ τὸ εἶναι ἐν τοῖς στρατιώταις ἡγεμόνας κατὰ τάξεις

> ἕπτ' ἔσαν ἡγεμόνες φυλάκων, ἑκατὸν δὲ ἑκάστῳ
> κοῦροι ἅμ' ἔστειχον δολίχ' ἔγχεα χερσὶν ἔχοντες (Ι 85-6).

καὶ τῶν ἡγεμόνων τοὺς μὲν προαγωνίζεσθαι ἐν πρώτοις τεταγμένους, τοὺς δὲ κατόπιν γενομένους ἐπείγειν τοὺς λειπομένους πρὸς τὴν μάχην

> οἱ δ' ἀμφ' Ἰδομενῆα δαΐφρονα θωρήσσοντο·
> Ἰδομενεὺς μὲν ἐνὶ προμάχοις συῒ εἴκελος ἀλκήν,
> Μηριόνης δ' ἄρα οἱ πυμάτας ὤτρυνε φάλαγγας (Δ 252-4).

194. καὶ ὅτι δεῖ τοὺς δυνάμει διαφέροντας ἐν τοῖς ἔξω στρατοπεδεύειν, ὥσπερ τεῖχος τῶν λοιπῶν περιβεβλημένους, τὸν δὲ βασιλέα ἐν τῷ ἀσφαλεστάτῳ, τουτέστι τῷ μεσαιτάτῳ, κατασκηνοῦν, δείκνυσιν ἐν τῷ τοὺς μὲν γενναιοτάτους, τὸν Ἀχιλλέα καὶ τὸν Αἴαντα, ἐν τοῖς ἐσχάτοις μέρεσι τῶν νεῶν κατεσκηνωκέναι, τὸν δὲ Ἀγαμέμνονα καὶ τοὺς ἄλλους ἀρίστους ἐν τῷ μέσῳ.

195. καὶ τὸ ἐν τῷ στρατοπεδεύεσθαι χάρακάς τε περιβάλλεσθαι καὶ τάφρους ἀποσκάπτειν εἰς εὖρος καὶ βάθος καὶ σκόλοψι κύκλῳ διαλαμβάνειν, ὡς μήτε ὑπερπηδᾶν τινα διὰ πλάτος μήτε διὰ βάθος κατιέναι δύνασθαι, γίνεταί τε ἐν τοῖς πολεμίοις καὶ παρ' Ὁμήρῳ

> καὶ δὴ τεῖχος ἔδειμε, καὶ ἤλασε τάφρον ἐπ' αὐτῷ
> εὐρεῖαν μεγάλην, ἐν δὲ σκόλοπας κατέπηξεν (Ι 349-50)

καί [τὸ]

in battle arrays, the cavalry must always be placed in front and the footsoldiers behind. This he indicates as follows:

> the cavalrymen first with their horses and chariots
> and the infantrymen behind—many and noble
> [Il. 4.297-98].

193. He shows as well that there are leaders for each group of soldiers:

> There were seven watch-leaders and a hundred men
> placed under each, long spear in hand
> [Il. 9.85-86].

Some of the leaders fight out in front of the army, while some go back behind it and urge on the stragglers to fight:

> Brilliant Idomeneus and his men armed for battle
> and he, like a boar in strength, fought among the first
> while Meriones urged on the last lines for him
> [Il. 4.252-54].

194. In placing the finest fighters, Achilles and Ajax, and their tents at the greatest distance from the ships and the tents of Agamemnon and the other leaders in the middle, he demonstrates that one must place the strongest fighters at the outer limits of the camp, set there like a wall protecting the others, and the king in the safest place, which is to say, the middle.

195. Furthermore, surrounding a camp with stakes and digging a wide, deep trench and running a palisade around so that no one can leap the defenses because of their breadth, nor go down into them and climb out again because of their depth—these are things that happen in actual warfare as well as in Homer:

> and he built a wall and drove a trench around it,
> a big, wide one, and drove stakes into it
> [Il. 9.349-50]

and

ἀπὸ γὰρ δειδίσσετο τάφρος

εὐρεῖ', οὐ γὰρ ὑπερθορέειν σχεδὸν οὔτε περῆσαι

ῥηιδίη· κρημνοὶ γὰρ ἐπηρεφέες περὶ πᾶσαν

ἕστασαν ἀμφοτέρωθεν· ὕπερθεν δὲ σκολόπεσσιν

ὀξέσιν ἠρήρειστο, τοὺς ἕστασαν υἷες Ἀχαιῶν

πυκνοὺς καὶ μεγάλους, δηίων ἀνδρῶν ἀλεωρήν (Μ 52-7).

196. καὶ μαχόμενοι θνήσκουσι γενναίως οἱ τούτοις ἑπόμενοι

μὴ μὰν ἀσπουδεί γε καὶ ἀκλειῶς ἀπολοίμην,

ἀλλὰ μέγα ῥέξας τι καὶ ἐσσομένοισι πυθέσθαι (Χ 304-5)

καὶ πάλιν

ὃς δέ κεν ὑμέων

βλήμενος ἠὲ τυπεὶς θάνατον καὶ πότμον ἐπίσπῃ,

τεθνάτω· οὔ οἱ ἀεικὲς ἀμυνομένῳ περὶ πάτρης

τεθνάμεν (Ο 494-7).

197. καὶ τοῖς μὲν ἀριστεῦσι γέρα νέμεται

ἄλλα δ' ἀριστήεσσι δίδου γέρα καὶ βασιλεῦσι (Ι 334)·

τοῖς δὲ λειποτάκταις ἀπειλεῖ

ὃν δ' ἂν ἐγὼν ἀπάνευθε νεῶν ἐθέλοντα νοήσω

αὐτοῦ οἱ θάνατον μητίσομαι (Ο 348-9).

198. ἐν δὲ ταῖς μάχαις ὃν μὲν τρόπον καὶ ὅπως διαφόρως καὶ ποικίλως τοὺς ἥρωας ποιεῖ τιτρώσκοντας καὶ τιτρωσκομένους τί δεῖ λέγειν; ἐκεῖνο δὲ ὑπομνῆσαι ἄξιον, ὅτι τοὺς μὲν πρόσθεν τετρωμένους ἐνδοξοτέρους ἡγούμεθα, ἅτε τὴν ἐκ τοῦ συνεστάναι καὶ παραμένειν προθυμίαν δεικνύοντας, τοὺς δὲ τὸν

> They were stopped by the deep trench,
> not easily to be jumped or crossed,
> for its banks were steep on both sides
> and it was set with many sharp stakes from above
> which the sons of the Achaeans drove in thick and big,
> to shelter them from their enemies
> [Il. 12.52-57].

196. And those who follow the example of these die nobly in the fighting:[1]

> Let me not die without accomplishment or fame,
> but after doing some great deed to be known to men to come
> [Il. 22.304-05],

and again,

> whichever of you
> is struck or wounded and meets death and fate,
> let him die—for it is glorious to die in defense of your country
> [Il. 15.494-97].

197. Gifts are distributed to the greatest fighters:

> [Agamemnon] gave other gifts to the greatest fighters and the kings   [Il. 9.334],

and [Hector] threatens those who break ranks:

> And whomever I find away from the ships
> I plan to see dead   [Il. 15.348-49].

198. What need is there to say how in the battles he shows the heroes in a multitude of different situations, both wounding others and being wounded? This is worth mentioning, though: that we consider those wounded in front to be more glorious, since they have shown their eagerness by standing in the fore and not giving way. Those wounded in

---

[1] Either the reference is to the leaders mentioned in ch. 193, or (perhaps more likely) a few words have fallen out.

νῶτον ἢ τὸ μετάφρενον πεπληγότας ἀτιμοτέρους, ὡς ἐν τῷ φεύγειν τοῦτο πεπονθότας. καὶ ταῦτα οὖν ἑκάτερά ἐστι παρ' Ὁμήρῳ·

εἴ περ γάρ κε βλεῖο πονεύμενος ἠὲ τυπείης,
οὐκ ἂν ἐπ' αὐχέν' ὄπισθε πέσοι βέλος οὐδ' ἐνὶ νώτῳ.
ἀλλά κεν ἢ στέρνων ἢ νηδύος ἀντιάσειε
πρόσσω ἱεμένοιο μετὰ προμάχων ὀαριστύν (Ν 288-91)·

καὶ πάλιν

οὐ μέν μοι φεύγοντι μεταφρένῳ ἐν δόρυ πήξεις,
ἀλλ' ἰθὺς μεμαῶτι διὰ στήθεσφιν ἔλασσον (Χ 283-4).

χρησίμως δὲ καὶ ἐν τῇ τροπῇ τῶν πολεμίων παραινεῖ μὴ περὶ τὰ σκῦλα γίνεσθαι μηδὲ ἐνδιδόναι καιρὸν φυγῆς, ἀλλ' ἐγκεῖσθαι καὶ διώκειν

μή τις νῦν ἐνάρων ἐπιβαλλόμενος μετόπισθεν
μιμνέτω, ὥς κεν πλεῖστα φέρων ἐπὶ νῆας ἵκηται.
ἀλλ' ἄνδρας κτείνωμεν, ἔπειτα δὲ καὶ τὰ ἕκηλοι
νεκροὺς ἂμ πεδίον συλήσετε τεθνηῶτας (Ζ 68-71).

199. ἔστι δὲ παρ' αὐτῷ πάσης ἡλικίας κατορθώματα ὑφ' ὧν πᾶς ὁστισοῦν ἐπαρθείη· ὁ μὲν ἀκμάζων ὑπὸ τοῦ Ἀχιλλέως καὶ Αἴαντος καὶ Διομήδους, ὁ δὲ νεώτερος ὑπὸ τοῦ Ἀντιλόχου καὶ τοῦ Μηριόνου, ὁ δὲ μεσαιπόλιος ὑπὸ τοῦ Ἰδομενέως καὶ τοῦ Ὀδυσσέως, ὁ δὲ γέρων ὑπὸ τοῦ Νέστορος, καὶ πᾶς βασιλεὺς ὑπὸ τούτων ἁπάντων καὶ τοῦ Ἀγαμέμνονος. τοιαῦτα μὲν τῶν πολιτικῶν λόγων καὶ πράξεών ἐστι παρ' Ὁμήρῳ τὰ λήμματα.

the back are less honored since they suffered their wounds while fleeing.[1] Both of these things are in Homer. [Idomeneus says to Meriones:]

> If you should be struck or wounded in battle
> let the arrow not hit the back of your neck or your back
> but let it meet your chest or your belly
> as you move forward with those who fight in front
> [Il. 13.288-91],

and again [Hector says to Achilles],

> You won't fix your spear in my back as I flee,
> but rather drive it into my chest as I stand to fight you
> [Il. 22.283-84].

Homer also correctly advises abandoning the spoils when the enemy turns to flee and not giving him a chance to get away but rather chasing him down.

> Let no one now stay behind to busy
> himself with the spoils, in order to take a larger haul back to the ships—
> rather, let us kill men. Then at your ease
> you'll strip the corpses strewn over the plain
> [Il. 6.68-71].

199. There are in Homer examples of exemplary deeds of people of all ages, with which absolutely everyone might be encouraged: those at the peak of their powers look to Achilles, Ajax, and Diomedes; younger men to Antilochus and Meriones; mature men to Idomeneus and Odysseus; those who are old, to Nestor. Kings look to all of these and to Agamemnon.

Such are the profitable examples of political discourse and actions to be found in Homer.

---

[1] These principles were stated in a Pythagorean saying or *akousma* (Iamblichus, *Life of Pythagoras* 18.85), though our author does not identify the idea as Pythagorean.

200. θεασώμεθα δὲ καὶ περὶ τῶν ἰατρικῶν, εἰ καὶ τούτων μὴ εἶχεν ἀπείρως Ὅμηρος. καὶ ὅτι μὲν πολλοῦ ἀξίαν τὴν τέχνην ὑπελάμβανε δῆλον ἐκ τούτου·

ἰατρὸς γὰρ ἀνὴρ πολλῶν ἀντάξιος ἄλλων (Λ 514).

δοκεῖ δὲ ἡ ἰατρικὴ ἐπιστήμη εἶναι νοσερῶν καὶ ὑγιεινῶν· ἅπερ ἐκ τούτων ἄν τις μάθοι· ὅτι μὲν ἐπιστήμη

ἰητρὸς δὲ ἕκαστος ἐπιστάμενος περὶ πάντων (δ 231)·

ὅτι δὲ ὑγιεινῶν καὶ νοσερῶν

φάρμακα πολλὰ μὲν ἐσθλὰ μεμιγμένα, πολλὰ δὲ λυγρά (δ 230)

σημαίνει τούτων ἑκάτερον.

201. ἔστι δὲ τῆς ἰατρικῆς θεωρητικὸν μὲν τὸ διὰ τῶν καθολικῶν λόγων καὶ διὰ μεθόδου ἐπάγον ἐπὶ τὴν τῶν κατὰ μέρος γνῶσιν, τούτου δὲ αὖ μέρη τὸ μὲν σημειωτικὸν τὸ δὲ αἰτιολογικόν· πρακτικὸν δὲ τὸ διὰ τῆς ἐνεργείας αὐτῆς βαδίζον, τούτου δὲ μέρη τὸ μὲν διαιτητικὸν τὸ δὲ χειρουργικὸν τὸ δὲ φαρμακευτικόν. πῶς οὖν ἑκάστῳ τούτων Ὅμηρος ἐπιβέβληκεν; ὅτι μὲν γὰρ θεωρητικόν τι εἶναι ἐπίσταται ἐν τούτῳ αἰνίσσεται·

τοῖα Διὸς θυγάτηρ ἔχε φάρμακα μητιόεντα (δ 227)·

μητιόεντα γὰρ λέγει δηλονότι κατὰ τέχνην θεωρητικὴν ἐσκευασμένα.

200. Let us also examine medical matters and whether Homer was acquainted with these things, as well. That he considered the art of medicine very worthy is clear from this:

> A doctor is a man worth many other men
> [Il. 11.514].

The science of medicine is knowledge concerning the sick and the healthy, and this might be learned from the following. He indicates both of these facts: first, that it is a branch of knowledge, [speaking of Egypt, where]

> every man is a doctor, wise beyond all other men
> [Od. 4.231],

and second, that it concerns the healthy and the sick:

> many excellent drugs concocted, and many baneful ones
> [Od. 4.230].

201. There is in medicine on the one hand a theoretical part, which, from general principles and method, proceeds to the understanding of the specific instance. This part has two elements, the interpretation of symptoms and the analysis of their causes. The practical [or empirical] part, on the other hand, proceeds from the actual activity of the physician, and is divided into dietetics, surgery, and pharmaceutics.[1] How does Homer hit upon each of these? He hints that he knows of a theoretical part in this:

> such all-wise drugs had the daughter of Zeus
> [Od. 4.227],

for "all-wise" clearly means "prepared according to theoretical skill."

---

[1] Galen's essay "On the Schools [of Medicine], for Beginners" (*De sectis*) turns on a similar distinction, though Galen is concerned to describe conflicting and competing schools of medicine, rather than two complementary elements of medical science. In general, the section on medicine (chs. 201-11) here uses vocabulary and categories that may be found throughout the medical literature, from the Hippocratic Corpus to Galen and beyond, but the source or sources of this popular, elementary introduction remain obscure.

202. τὸ δὲ σημειωτικὸν ἄντικρυς ἱστορεῖ διὰ τοῦ Ἀχιλλέως. μαθητὴς γὰρ ὢν Χείρωνος πρῶτος τὴν αἰτίαν τῆς κατασχούσης τοὺς Ἕλληνας νόσου κατενόησε, συνιδὼν ὅτι τὰ ἐπιδήμια νοσήματα ἐκ τοῦ Ἀπόλλωνός ἐστιν, ὅς γε δοκεῖ εἶναι ὁ αὐτὸς τῷ Ἡλίῳ· οὗτος γὰρ τὰς ὥρας τοῦ ἔτους ἐπάγει, αἵπερ, ὅταν ὦσι δυσκράτως διακείμεναι, νοσήματος αἰτίαι καθίστανται. καὶ γὰρ τὸ ὅλον τήν τε σωτηρίαν καὶ τὸν ὄλεθρον τῶν μὲν ἀνδρῶν τῷ Ἀπόλλωνι τῶν δὲ γυναικῶν τῇ Ἀρτέμιδι—τουτέστι τῷ Ἡλίῳ καὶ τῇ Σελήνῃ—ἀνατίθησι, τοξότας μὲν αὐτοὺς ποιῶν διὰ τὴν τῶν ἀκτίνων βολήν, οὕτω δὲ διορίζων τὸ ἄρρεν καὶ τὸ θῆλυ, ἐπεὶ καὶ θερμότερον φύσει τὸ ἄρρεν γένος. διὰ ταῦτα γοῦν φησι τὸν μὲν Τηλέμαχον τηλικοῦτον εἶναι

Ἀπόλλωνός γε ἕκητι (τ 86),

τὰς δὲ Τυνδάρεω κούρας ὑπὸ Ἀρτέμιδος ηὐξῆσθαι. τοὺς δὲ θανάτους αὐτοῖς ἀνατίθησι ἔν τε πολλοῖς ἄλλοις καὶ ἐν τούτοις διορίζει

τοὺς μέν Ἀπόλλων πέφνεν ἀπ' ἀργυρέοιο βιοῖο,

χωόμενος Νιόβῃ, τὰς δ' Ἄρτεμις ἰοχέαιρα (Ω 605-6).

ὅπου δὲ καὶ τὴν τοῦ Κυνὸς ἐπιτολὴν διηγεῖται. σημεῖον καὶ αἴτιον τοῦτο ἐκκαύσεως καὶ νόσων·

λαμπρότατος μὲν ὅ γ' ἐστί, κακὸν δέ τε σῆμα τέτυκται

καί τε φέρει πολλὸν πυρετὸν δειλοῖσι βροτοῖσιν (Χ 30-31).

203. αἰτιολογεῖ δὲ ἐν οἷς λέγει περὶ τῶν θεῶν

οὐ γὰρ σῖτον ἔδουσ', οὐ πίνουσ' αἴθοπα οἶνον·

τοὔνεκ' ἀναίμονές εἰσι καὶ ἀθάνατοι καλέονται (Ε 341-2).

ἡ γὰρ τροφὴ ἥ τε ξηρὰ καὶ ὑγρὰ αἵματός ἐστι γεννητική· τοῦτο δὲ τρέφει μέν τὸ σῶμα, πλεονάσαν δὲ ἢ διαφθαρὲν νόσων αἴτιον γίνεται.

202. He describes the analysis of symptoms with reference to Achilles, for he is Chiron's pupil and is the first to diagnose the cause of the sickness that grips the Greeks, realizing that epidemic illnesses come from Apollo. Apollo, indeed, seems to be the same as the sun, for the sun leads in the seasons of the year, which cause illnesses if they are not in good temper. In general, Homer makes Apollo preside over the life and death of men, and Artemis over the same for women—that is, the sun and the moon, making them archers because of the action of their rays. The distinction between male and female is made because the male is hotter by nature. In fact, this is why he says that Telemachus reaches maturity "by the help of Apollo" [Od. 19.86] and that the daughters of Tyndareus grew by the help of Artemis.[1] He makes Apollo and Artemis responsible for deaths in many places, and [with regard to the Niobids] he distinguishes between them:

> The boys Apollo killed with his golden bow,
> angered at Niobe, and the girls, Artemis
> [Il. 24.605-06].

At one point he describes the rising of the Dog Star, a symptom and cause of extreme heat and sickness:

> This is the brightest, and an evil sign
> bringing great fevers to miserable mortals
> [Il. 22.30-31].

203. He inquires into [physiological] causes when he says about the gods,

> For they eat no grain nor do they drink bright wine
> and so are bloodless and are called immortals
> [Il. 5.341-42],

since nourishment, both dry and moist, produces blood, and this nourishes the body, but if it is superabundant or poisoned it becomes a cause of sickness.

---

[1] This is not in the received text of Homer.

204. τὸ δὲ πρακτικὸν μέρος τῆς ἰατρικῆς οὕτως ἀκριβοῖ, ἐν ᾧ ἐστι καὶ διαιτητικόν. πρῶτον μὲν γὰρ οἶδε τὰ χρόνια τῶν νοσημάτων καὶ τὰ ὀξέα, ὡς ὅταν λέγῃ

τίς νύ σε κὴρ ἐδάμασσε τανηλέγεος θανάτοιο;
ἢ δολιχὴ νόσος, ἦ Ἄρτεμις ἰοχέαιρα
οἷς ἀγανοῖσι βέλεσσιν ἐποιχομένη κατέπεφνεν; (λ 171-3)

205. φανερὸς δέ ἐστι καὶ τὴν λιτὴν δίαιταν ὑγιεινὴν ὑπολαμβάνων· πεποίηκε γὰρ τοὺς ἥρωας ὀπτοῖς κρέασι χρωμένους, περιελὼν τὴν περὶ τὰ βρώματα περιεργίαν. καὶ ἐπεὶ ἡ γαστὴρ ἀεὶ δεῖται πληρώσεως, ὅταν τὰ πρότερα σιτία καταπεφθέντα τὸ μὲν οἰκεῖον τῷ σώματι εἰς καρδίαν καὶ τὰς φλέβας ἀναπέμψῃ τὸ δὲ περισσὸν ἐκβάλῃ, τοιαῦτά φησιν·

ἀλλ᾽ ἐμὲ μὲν δορπῆσαι ἐάσατε κηδόμενόν περ.
οὐ γάρ τι στυγερῇ ἐπὶ γαστέρι κύντερον ἄλλο
ἔπλετο, ἥ τ᾽ ἐκέλευσεν ἕο μνήσασθαι ἀνάγκῃ (η 215-7)·

καὶ πάλιν

ἡ δὲ μάλ᾽ αἰεὶ
ἐσθέμεναι κέλεται καὶ πινέμεν, ἐκ δέ με πάντων
ληθάνει ὅσσ᾽ ἔπαθον, καὶ ἐνιπλήσασθαι ἀνώγει (η 219-21).

206. οἶδε δὲ καὶ οἴνου χρήσεως διαφορὰς ὅτι ὁ μὲν πολὺς ποθεὶς βλαβερός, ὁ δὲ μέτριος ὠφέλιμος. τὸ μὲν οὕτως·

οἶνός σε τρώει μελιηδής, ὅς τε καὶ ἄλλους
βλάπτει, ὃς ἄν μιν χανδὸν ἕλῃ μηδ᾽ αἴσιμον πίνῃ (φ 293-4)·

τὸ δὲ ἐκείνως·

ἀνδρὶ δὲ κεκμηῶτι μένος μέγα οἶνος ἀέξει (Ζ 261).

καὶ ὅτι δυνάμεως ποιητικός

204. He specifies the practical element of medicine, which includes dietetics, as follows. First of all, he knows the difference between chronic and acute illnesses, as in this passage:

> What sort of death overcame you—
> did long sickness kill you, or Artemis
> with her gentle arrows? [Od. 11.171-73].

205. It is clear that Homer maintains that a simple diet is conducive to good health, for he shows the heroes eating roast meat and does not show them to have any particular interest in food. Since the stomach always demands to be filled—and when the food is digested it sends that which is useful to the body into the heart and veins and excretes the excess—he says things of this sort:

> But permit me to eat, in spite of my misery,
> for there was never anything worse than the
> foul stomach that forces you to remember it
> [Od. 7.215-17],

and again,

> and it always
> demands to eat and drink—forces me to forget
> all I've suffered and pushes me to fill it
> [Od. 7.219-21].

206. He knows also the various uses of wine and that it is harmful drunk in quantity but good in moderation. He makes the first point here:

> Sweet wine has clouded your wits, as it will do
> to anyone who gulps down mouthfuls and does not drink
> moderately [Od. 21.293-94],

and the second here:

> Wine restores the strength of a tired man
> [Il. 6.261].

He says that it produces strength:

ὃς δέ κ' ἀνὴρ οἴνοιο κορεσσάμενος καὶ ἐδωδῆς

ἀνδράσι δυσμενέεσσι πανημέριος πολεμίζῃ,

θαρσαλέον νύ οἱ ἦτορ ἐνὶ φρεσίν, οὐδέ τι γυῖα

πρὶν κάμνει, πρὶν πάντας ἐρωῆσαι πολέμοιο (Τ 167-70).

καὶ τὸν μὲν ἡδὺν εἰς τὰς φιλοφροσύνας παραλαμβάνει

ὣς φάτο· Ποντόνοος δὲ μελίφρονα οἶνον ἐκίρνα (η 182 = ν 53),

τὸν δὲ σφοδρὸν καὶ καρωτικὸν τῷ Κύκλωπι ὁ Ὀδυσσεὺς ⟨παρα⟩τίθησι, τὸν δὲ στύφοντα πρὸς ἴασιν· οὗτος γάρ ἐστιν ὁ Πράμνειος ὃν τῷ Μαχάονι τετρωμένῳ δίδωσιν.

207. ὅπως δὲ καὶ γυμνασίοις χρῆσθαι παραγγέλλει φανερὸν ἐκ πολλῶν. ἀεὶ γὰρ πονοῦντας ποιεῖ τοὺς μὲν ἐν τοῖς προσήκουσιν ἔργοις, τοὺς δὲ δι' ἐπιτηδευμάτων· ὁπότε καὶ τοὺς μάλιστα τῇ ἡδυπαθείᾳ κεχρημένους Φαίακας καὶ τοὺς ἀσώτους μνηστῆρας γυμναζομένους εἰσάγει. καὶ πόνους μὲν τοὺς αὐτάρκεις αἰτίους ὑγιείας οὕτω νομίζει, τῶν δὲ καταβαρούντων τὸ σῶμα καμάτων ἴαμα τὸν ὕπνον εἶναι. φησὶ γὰρ τῷ Ὀδυσσεῖ κεκμηκότι ἀπὸ τῆς θαλάσσης ὕπνον ἐπελθεῖν

ἵνα μιν παύσειε τάχιστα

δυσπονέος καμάτοιο (ε 492-3).

ἡ γὰρ φύσις ἀπαιτεῖ τὸ κεκμηκὸς σῶμα ἀναπαύεσθαι, καὶ ἐν ᾧ ὀλίγον τὸ θερμὸν ὑπάρχει, τοῦτο ἐπεὶ οὐ δύναται πάντῃ ἐξικνεῖσθαι, ἐν τῷ βάθει μένειν. πῶς δὲ καὶ ἀναπαύεται τὸ σῶμα; ὅτι ἡ σύντασις τῆς ψυχῆς ἀνίεται καὶ τὰ μέλη τοῦ σώματος λύεται, καὶ τοῦτο ἐναργῶς εἶπεν

εὗδε δ' ἀνακλινθεῖσα, λύθεν δέ οἱ ἄψεα πάντα (δ 794 = σ 189).

> A man who is sated with wine and food
> and fights all day against enemies
> keeps his heart bold in his chest and his limbs
> do not tire before he has driven back the enemy
> [Il. 19.167-70],

and that its sweetness is conducive to friendliness:

> So he spoke, and Pontonous mixed cheerful wine
> [Od. 7.182 = 13.53].

The wine Odysseus gives to the Cyclops is strong and stupefying. Astringent wine, on the other hand, is conducive to healing. This is the quality of the Pramnian wine that [Nestor] gives to the wounded Machaon.

207. It is clear in many passages that Homer prescribes gymnastic exercise, for he shows the heroes constantly in action, both in their regular activities and also for exercise. He even shows both the Phaeacians, whose lives are largely given over to pleasure, and the profligate suitors exercising. He thus considers sufficient exercise a means to preserve health, and sleep a cure for oppressive weariness of the body. Thus he says sleep came upon Odysseus, exhausted from the sea,

> in order quickly to relieve him of his bitter exhaustion
> [cf. Od. 5.492-93],

for nature prevails upon the tired body to stop its activity and where there is a little warmth that remains in it, keeps it in the core, since it must not depart entirely. And how does the body rest? The tension of the soul is relaxed and the limbs of the body as well, as he says clearly, [speaking of Penelope]:

> She lay down to sleep and all her limbs relaxed
> [Od. 4.794 = 18.189].

τὸ δὲ ἐν τοῖς ἄλλοις ἅπασιν ἄμετρον οὐκ ὂν ὠφέλιμον καὶ ἐπὶ τοῦ ὕπνου ἀποφαίνεται, ποτὲ μὲν εἰπών

>ἀνίη καὶ πολὺς ὕπνος (ο 394),

ποτὲ δὲ

>ἀνίη καὶ τὸ φυλάσσειν

πάννυχον ἐγρήσσοντα (υ 52-3).

208. ἐπίσταται δὲ καὶ ἀέρων εὐκρασίαν ὑγιείας οὖσαν παρασκευαστικήν, ἐν οἷς φησιν

>ἀλλά σ' ἐς Ἠλύσιον πεδίον καὶ πείρατα γαίης
>ἀθάνατοι πέμψουσιν, ὅθι ξανθὸς Ῥαδάμανθυς,
>τῇ περ ῥηίστη βιοτὴ πέλει ἀνθρώποισιν·
>οὐ νιφετὸς οὔτ' ἂρ χειμὼν πολὺς οὔτε ποτ' ὄμβρος,
>ἀλλ' αἰεὶ Ζεφύροιο λιγὺ πνείοντας ἀήτας
>Ὠκεανὸς ἀνίησιν ἀναψύχειν ἀνθρώπους (δ 563-8).

ἐν οἷς δύο ταῦτα μάλιστα ὀρθῶς διεγνωκὼς φαίνεται, ὅτι τε ἡ ἀρχὴ τῶν ἀνέμων ἀπὸ τῶν ὑγρῶν γίνεται καὶ ὅτι τὸ ἔμφυτον τοῦ ζῴου θερμὸν δεῖται ἀναψύξεως.

209. καὶ ἰάματα δὲ παθημάτων οἶδε, λιποθυμίας μὲν ἀνάψυξιν, ὅπερ ἐπὶ τοῦ Σαρπηδόνος ποιεῖ

>αὖτις δ' ἀμπνύνθη, περὶ δὲ πνοιὴ Βορέαο
>ζώγρει ἐπιπνείουσα κακῶς κεκαφηότα θυμόν (Ε 697-8).

ψύξεως δὲ θέρμην, ὡς ἐπὶ τοῦ Ὀδυσσέως κεχειμασμένου, ὃς ἐν τῷ θάμνῳ κρύπτεται, ἔνθα καὶ ἀνέμων καὶ ὄμβρων ἦν ἐν σκέπῃ καὶ τῇ παρούσῃ ὕλῃ καλύπτεται· κόπου δὲ λουτρὰ καὶ χρίσματα, ὡς ἐπὶ τοῦ Διομήδους καὶ τοῦ

Nevertheless, the universal principle that the excessive is not advantageous applies to sleep as well, as Homer indicates when he says in one place,

> Too much sleep is no good   [Od. 15.394],

and in another,

> it's no good to spend
> the night awake, on watch   [Od. 20.52-53].

208. He also knows that temperate air is conducive to health, when he says,[1]

> The immortals will send you to the Elysian Plain
> at the ends of the earth, to blond Rhadamanthys
> and there is found the easiest life for men,
> for there is no snow, no great storms or rain,
> but the gentle breezes of the West Wind blow always,
> sent by Ocean to bring coolness to men
>   [Od. 4.563-68].

Here it appears that he knew two general principles: that moisture is the source of winds and that the intrinsic heat of living creatures requires cooling.

209. He also knows cures for various complaints: those who are unconscious require cool air, as when he writes of Sarpedon,

> Again he got his breath and around him the breath of Boreas
> revived him, breathing spirit into him even as he was dying
>   [Il. 5.697-98].

On the other hand, warmth is a cure for chilling as he shows with reference to the storm-tossed Odysseus, who hides in the thicket where he is protected from wind and showers and hidden by the vegetation around him. Baths and oil cure fatigue, as in the passage where

---

[1] The speaker is Proteus.

Ὀδυσσέως ἐκ τῆς νυκτεγερσίας ἀνακομισθέντων· καὶ γὰρ οἵαν ὠφέλειαν ἔχει τὰ λουτρὰ διὰ τούτων μάλιστα δηλοῖ·

θυμῆρες κεράσασα κατὰ κρατός τε καὶ ὤμων (κ 362).
φανερὸν οὖν ὅτι ἐντεῦθεν ἔχοντα τὴν ἀρχὴν τὰ νεῦρα εἰκότως ἀπ' αὐτῶν καὶ τὴν ἴασιν τοῦ κόπου λαμβάνει· αὕτη δέ ἐστιν ἡ διὰ τοῦ θερμανθῆναι καὶ ὑγρανθῆναι· ξηραίνουσι γὰρ οἱ κόποι.

210. λοιπόν ἐστι σκοπεῖν ὅπως καὶ τὰ τῆς χειρουργίας κατηνόησε. τὸν μὲν δὴ Μενέλαον ὁ Μαχάων ἰᾶται, πρῶτον ἐκκομισάμενος τὸ βέλος, ἔπειτα σκεψάμενος τὸ ἕλκος καὶ ἐκπιέσας τὸ αἷμα καὶ ξηρὰ φάρμακα ἐπιπάσας· καὶ τοῦτο πρόδηλον, ὅτι τεχνικῶς αὐτὸ πράσσεται. τὸν δὲ Εὐρύπυλον κατὰ τοῦ μήρου τετρωμένον Πάτροκλος πρῶτα μὲν τῷ εὐπορηθέντι μαχαιρίῳ διαχειρίζει, ἔπειτα ἀπονίψας ὕδατι λιαρῷ, ὡς ἀνωδυνώτερον γένοιτο, ῥίζαν ἐπιβάλλει· πολλαὶ γὰρ πανταχῇ πρὸς ἴασιν ἑλκῶν πεφύκασιν. ἔγνω δὲ καὶ τοῦτο, ὡς τὰ πικρὰ φάρμακα πρὸς τὸ ξηραίνειν ἐστὶν ἐπιτήδεια· ξηραίνεσθαι δὲ χρῄζει τὰ ἕλκη. καὶ οὐκ εὐθέως ἰασάμενος ὁ Πάτροκλος ἀπῆλθεν, ἀλλ'

ἧστό τε καὶ τὸν ἔτερπε λόγοις (Ο 393)·
ἔδει γὰρ τῷ ὀδυνωμένῳ παραμυθίας. τὸν δὲ Μαχάονα τρωθέντα οὐ μεγάλην οὐδὲ καίριον πληγὴν ἐπὶ τοῦ ὤμου εἰκότως ἀφυλακτοτέρᾳ διαίτῃ ποιεῖ χρώμενον· ἴσως καὶ τὴν τέχνην αὐτοῦ δείκνυσι· ὁ γὰρ τὰ ἄλλα ὡς ἔτυχε διαιτώμενος ἑαυτὸν ἰᾶσθαι ἐδύνατο.

211. κἀκεῖνο δὲ ἔστι κατανοῆσαι παρ' αὐτῷ, ὅτι οὐκ ἀγνοεῖ τῶν ἰατρικῶν φαρμάκων τὰ μὲν ἐπίπλαστα καὶ ἐπίπαστα, ὡς ὅταν εἴπῃ

ἐπ' ἄρ' ἤπια φάρμακα...
πάσσε (Δ 218-19),
τὰ δὲ ποτά, ὅπου ἡ Ἑλένη τῷ κρατῆρι μίσγει φάρμακον

Diomedes and Odysseus return from their nocturnal exploits. In the following verse it is also clear what value baths have:

> She poured soul-pleasing water over my head and shoulders
> [Od. 10.362].

Since the nervous system begins in this part of the body, it is appropriate that the treatment of fatigue should start here. This is accomplished by warming and wetting because fatigue dehydrates.

210. It remains to see in what way he was aware of surgery. Machaon treats Menelaus by first removing the arrow, then examining the wound, pressing out the blood, and applying dry drugs, and it is immediately clear that he does this with knowledge of his craft. Patroclus, taking care of Eurypylus who was wounded in the thigh, first works on him with the knife that was available, then washes him with warm water to make the wound less painful, and finally applies a root. Many sorts of roots found everywhere are good for the treatment of wounds. Homer also knew that drugs that are bitter are suitable for drying, for wounds need to be dried out. Moreover, Patroclus did not go away immediately after treating him, but

> sat and cheered him with words
> [Il. 15.393],

for he was in pain and needed consolation.

Homer appropriately shows Machaon, when wounded very slightly and not at all critically in the shoulder, using a rather less rigorous regime. He may also be demonstrating Machaon's skill, for he who told the others how to take care of themselves was able to cure himself as well.

211. One can tell that Homer was not ignorant of the fact that some healing drugs are applied externally and sprinkled on, for he says,

> He sprinkled on gentle drugs
> [Il. 4.218-19],

and that some are drunk, as where Helen puts drugs in the wine bowl,

νηπενθές ... ἄχολόν τε, κακῶν ἐπίληθες ἁπάντων (δ 221).

τὸν αὐτὸν δὲ τρόπον καὶ τῶν δηλητηρίων φαρμάκων τὰ μὲν ἐπίχριστα οἶδεν, ὡς ἐν τούτοις·

φάρμακον ἀνδροφόνον διζήμενος, ὄφρα οἱ εἴη

ἰοὺς χρίεσθαι χαλκήρεας (α 261-2),

τὰ δὲ ποτὰ ἐν ἐκείνοις·

ἐν δὲ βάλῃ κρητῆρι καὶ ἡμέας πάντας ὀλέσσῃ (β 330).

ταῦτα μὲν καὶ περὶ τῶν παρ' Ὁμήρῳ ἰατρικῶν.

212. ὠφελοῦνται δὲ οἱ ἄνθρωποι, ὥσπερ ἀπὸ τῆς ἰατρικῆς, οὕτως ἔστιν ὅτε καὶ ἀπὸ τῆς μαντικῆς. ταύτης μέντοι τὸ μὲν τεχνικόν φασιν εἶναι οἱ Στωικοί, οἷον ἱεροσκοπίαν καὶ οἰωνοὺς καὶ τὸ περὶ φήμας καὶ κληδόνας καὶ σύμβολα, ἅπερ συλλήβδην ὅτταν καλοῦμεν, τὸ δὲ ἄτεχνον καὶ ἀδίδακτον, τουτέστιν ἐνύπνια καὶ ἐνθουσιασμούς. οὐδὲ ταῦτα οὖν Ὅμηρος ἠγνόησεν, ἀλλ' οἶδε μὲν μάντεις καὶ ἱερεῖς καὶ ὀνειροπόλους, ἔτι δὲ καὶ οἰωνιστὰς καί τινα ἐν Ἰθάκῃ σοφὸν

ὄρνιθάς τε γνῶναι καὶ ἐναίσιμα μυθήσασθαι (β 159)·

καὶ Ὀδυσσεύς φησιν εὐχόμενος

φήμην τίς μοι φάσθω ἐγειρομένων ἀνθρώπων

ἔνδοθεν, ἔκτοσθεν δὲ Διὸς τέρας ἄλλο φανήτω (υ 100-1).

> to calm pain, drive away anger, and make all evils forgotten
> [Od. 4.221].

In the same way, he knows that some poisons are spread on, as in these lines:

> wanting a deadly drug to spread on his bronze
> arrowheads   [Od. 1.261-62],

and that some are drunk, as in this [where the suitors worry about Telemachus, lest he]

> put poison in the wine bowl and kill us all
> [Od. 2.330].

This much about medicine is found in Homer.

212. People sometimes receive benefits from seercraft, just as from medicine. The Stoics divide this field into technical seercraft, including the examination of sacrificial victims, bird omens, oracles, casting lots, and the examination of various other signs, which, taken together, we call *otta*.[1]—and nontechnical or untaught seercraft, that is, dreams and ecstatic visions. Homer was not ignorant of this either, for he knows of "seers" and "priests" and "dream-interpreters" and "bird-interpreters" and [says that] a wise man in Ithaca

> knew birds and spoke ominous words
> [Od. 2.159].

Odysseus says in his prayer,

> Let some sign come to me from one of those awake
> indoors, and let some other sign from Zeus appear outside
> [Od. 20.100-01].

---

[1] This is the ms. reading, but the word is otherwise unknown in the sense required, and no convincing emendations have been brought forward. It is probably to be taken as related to the fairly common verb ὀττεύομαι, used of divination, usually from a sound or voice (ὄσσα, though in this context the spelling with double sigma does not occur). This word would then be the equivalent of the infrequent word ὀττεία, used to designate this sort of divination. The distinction between "artificial" and "natural" divination is discussed by Cicero in *On Divination* 1.72 and 1.109.

καὶ πταρμὸς δὲ παρ' αὐτῷ σύμβολον ἀγαθὸν γίνεται. τοῖς δὲ μνηστῆρσιν ἐφίσταται ἔνθεος μάντις, ἔκ τινος ἐπιπνοίας σημαίνων τὰ μέλλοντα. ἐπεὶ δὲ καὶ ὁ Ἕλενος αὐτήκοός φησι θείας φωνῆς γεγονέναι

ὣς γὰρ ἐγὼν ὄπ' ἄκουσα θεῶν αἰειγενετάων (Η 53),

παρέχει πιστεύειν ὅτι καὶ Σωκράτης ἀπὸ τῆς τοῦ δαιμονίου φωνῆς ἐμαντεύετο.

213. τίς ἔτι καταλείπεται λογικὴ τέχνη ἢ ἐπιστήμη; ἀλλὰ μὴν καὶ ἡ τραγῳδία τὴν ἀρχὴν ἔλαβεν ἐξ Ὁμήρου, εἰς ὄγκον πραγμάτων καὶ λόγων ἐπαρθεῖσα. ἔστι γὰρ παρ' αὐτῷ πᾶν εἶδος τραγῳδίας, ἔργα μεγάλα καὶ παράδοξα καὶ θεῶν ἐπιφάνειαι καὶ λόγοι φρονήματος μεστοὶ καὶ ἠθῶν παντοίων μιμητικοί. συνελόντι δὲ εἰπεῖν ὅτι οὐδὲν ἄλλο ἀλλ' ἢ δράματα αὐτοῦ ἐστι τὰ ποιήματα, σεμνὰ μὲν καὶ ἐπηρμένα τῇ λέξει καὶ τῇ διανοίᾳ καὶ τοῖς πράγμασιν, οὐκ ἔχοντα δὲ ἀνοσίων ἔργων ἐπιδείξεις, γάμους ἀθεμίτους ἢ παίδων ἢ γονέων σφαγὰς ἢ ὅσα ἄλλα ἡ νεωτέρα τραγῳδία τερατεύεται· ἀλλὰ καὶ ὅταν τοιούτου τινὸς ἐπιμνησθῇ ἐπικαλύπτειν μᾶλλον ἢ ὀνειδίζειν πειρᾶται τὸ ἁμάρτημα, ὡς ἐπὶ τῆς Κλυταιμνήστρας πεποίηκε. φησὶ γὰρ ὅτι

φρεσὶ κέχρητ' ἀγαθῇσιν (γ 266)

τὸ πρότερον, ἕως παρόντα εἶχε τὸν ἀοιδόν—τούτεστι διδάσκαλόν τινα—ὑπὸ τοῦ Ἀγαμέμνονος ἐπισταθέντα, ὅπως αὐτῇ τὰ ἄριστα παραινῇ. τοῦτον δὲ ἐκποδὼν ποιήσας ὁ Αἴγισθος παρέπεισεν αὐτὴν ἐξαμαρτάνειν. καὶ ὅτι ὁ Ὀρέστης δικαίως ἐτιμωρήσατο τῷ πατρὶ τὸν Αἴγισθον ἀποκτείνας, τὴν δὲ τῆς μητρὸς ἀναίρεσιν ἀπεσίγησε. καὶ ἄλλα πολλὰ τοιαῦτα ἰδεῖν ἔστι παρὰ τῷ ποιητῇ, τραγῳδίαν σεμνὴν καὶ οὐκ ἀπάνθρωπον γράφοντι.

A sneeze is likewise a good portent in Homer. An ecstatic seer appears in front of the suitors, revealing the future by some sort of inspiration, and when Helenus declares that he has heard a divine voice [this is another example of nontechnical seercraft]:

> for thus I heard the voice of the ever-living gods
> [Il. 7.53].

This encourages one to believe that Socrates as well prophesied by listening to the voice of his attendant spirit.[1]

213. What field of language or thought, what science is left? Well, there is tragedy, with its massiveness both of content and of language, which also had its source in Homer.[2] Every element of tragedy is found in him: great and extraordinary actions, apparitions of the gods, words full of wisdom, and imitations of characters of all sorts. In short, his poems are nothing other than dramas, solemn and sublime in diction, thought and content, and without the presentation of such unholy monstrosities as forbidden marriages and murders of children or parents which more recent tragedy has. Rather, when he mentions something of this sort he tries to hide the crime rather than denounce it openly, as in what he says about Clytemnestra. He says that she

> had a good heart   [Od. 3.266]

at first, while she had her bard with her—that is, a sort of mentor—who was assigned his task by Agamemnon, to recommend the best course to her. But Aegisthus put him out of the way and coaxed her into sinful paths. Likewise Homer says that Orestes justly avenged his father when he killed Aegisthus, but he passes over in silence the murder of his mother. Many other such passages may be found where the poet is writing solemn and by no means inhumane tragedy.

---

[1] Socrates and his δαιμόνιον were a popular subject of discussion in the high Empire, represented in the surviving literature by a dialogue of Plutarch and an essay of Apuleius (both generally cited under the same Latin title: *De deo Socratis*, "On the God of Socrates").

[2] Aristotle, of course (*Poetics* 1448a) saw Homer as the ancestor of tragedy in that he presented men as "better than they are," but our author seems rather to be concerned with stories known from tragedy that are told in the epics.

214. οὐδὲν δὲ ἔλασσον καὶ ἡ κωμῳδία ἐνθένδε ποθὲν ἔλαβε τὴν ἀφορμήν· εὗρε γὰρ ὅτι καὶ παρὰ τῷ τὰ σεμνότατα καὶ ὑψηλότατα διηγουμένῳ ἐπεισόδιά τινα ἔστι γέλωτα κινοῦντα, ὥσπερ ἐν τῇ Ἰλιάδι ὁ Ἥφαιστος χωλεύων εἰσάγεται οἰνοχοῶν τοῖς θεοῖς,

ἄσβεστος δ' ἄρ' ἐνῶρτο γέλως μακάρεσσι θεοῖσιν (Α 599).

ὁ δὲ Θερσίτης, τῷ δὲ σώματι αἴσχιστος καὶ τὴν ψυχὴν κάκιστος, ἐκ τοῦ θορυβεῖν καὶ κακολογεῖν καὶ αὐχεῖν, ἐφ' οἷς οὐδεὶς τῶν ἐν δυνάμει καθεστηκότων, καὶ ἐπὶ τούτοις κολάζεσθαι γελᾶν ἐπ' αὐτῷ παρασκευάζων

οἱ δὲ καὶ ἀχνύμεμοί περ ἐπ' αὐτῷ ἡδὺ γέλασσαν (Β 270).

ἐν δὲ τῇ Ὀδυσσείᾳ ὁ παρὰ τοῖς ἡδυπαθοῦσι Φαίαξι μελῳδὸς ᾄδει τὴν Ἄρεος καὶ Ἀφροδίτης μοιχείαν καὶ ὅπως ἐμπεσόντες εἰς τὰ τοῦ Ἡφαίστου δεσμὰ κατάφωροί τε ἐγένοντο καὶ γέλωτα παρέσχον τοῖς ἄλλοις θεοῖς, οἳ καὶ ἔσκωψαν χαριέντως πρὸς ἀλλήλους. καὶ παρὰ τοῖς ἀσώτοις μνηστῆρσιν εἰσάγεται ὁ πτωχὸς Ἶρος, τῷ γενναιωτάτῳ Ὀδυσσεῖ ἐρίζων εἰς πάλην καὶ ἐν τῷ ἔργῳ φαινόμενος καταγέλαστος. καθόλου γὰρ οἰκεῖόν ἐστι τῇ τοῦ ἀνθρώπου φύσει μὴ μόνον ἐπιτείνεσθαι ἀλλὰ καὶ ἀνίεσθαι, ἵνα καὶ διαρκῇ πρὸς τοὺς ἐν τῷ ζῆν πόνους. τοιαύτη μὲν καὶ ἡ θυμηδία παρὰ τῷ ποιητῇ εὑρίσκεται. εἰ δὲ οἱ μετ' αὐτὸν εἰσαγαγόντες τὴν κωμῳδίαν λόγοις αἰσχροῖς καὶ ἀποκεκαλυμμένοις εἰς παρασκευὴν γέλωτος ἐχρήσαντο, οὐκ ἂν εἴποιεν ἄμεινόν τι εὑρηκέναι. καὶ γὰρ τῶν ἐρωτικῶν διαθέσεων καὶ λόγων Ὅμηρος μὲν ἐγκρατῶς ἐπεμνήσθη· ὥσπερ ὁ Ζεύς φησιν

οὐ γάρ πώ ποτέ μ'... ἔρως φρένας ἀμφεκάλυψε (Γ 442)

καὶ τὰ ἑξῆς. καὶ ἐπὶ τῆς Ἑλένης

214. No less did comedy have its source here,[1] for it found, in the author who described the most solemn and elevated things, episodes that provoke laughter, as when in the *Iliad* the limping Hephaestus is brought in as cupbearer of the gods, and

> deathless laughter sprung up among the blessed gods
> [Il. 1.599].

Likewise there is Thersites, the ugliest in body and the basest of soul [of all the Greeks], for his outbursts and badmouthing and arrogance—characteristics foreign to all of those in authority—who provides laughter at his own expense when he is punished for these things:

> angered though they were, they all laughed well at him
> [Il. 2.270].

In the *Odyssey* the bard of the pleasure-loving Phaeacians sings of the adultery of Ares and Aphrodite, how they fell into Hephaestus' net and so were caught in the act and provided a good laugh for the other gods, who stood around and made witty remarks to one another. Likewise, among the depraved suitors the beggar Irus is brought in to challenge noble Odysseus to wrestle and, when this happens, appears ridiculous.

It is a fact of human nature that we cannot live in a constant state of alertness and tension but need also to be relaxed at times in order to be equal to the toils of life. The amusing parts of Homer will be found to be aimed toward this goal, and if those who have come after him and written comedy have introduced disgraceful and obscene language to excite laughter, they could not say they have made any improvement. Homer describes even erotic situations and language with moderation. Note how Zeus says,

> Never has love . . . enveloped my mind
> [Il. 3.442],

and so forth. Likewise he has the old men say about Helen,

---

[1] This rather inadequate account of comedy in Homer is concerned primarily with passages in which Homer describes laughter.

ού νέμεσις Τρώάς τε και εύκνήμιδας Αχαιούς
τοιῇδ' ἀμφὶ γυναικὶ πολὺν χρόνον ἄλγεα πάσχειν (Γ 156-7)·

καὶ ὅσα ἄλλα τοιαῦτα. οἱ δὲ ἄλλοι ποιηταὶ ἀκρατῶς καὶ ἀμέτρως ἁλισκομένους τῷ πάθει τοὺς ἀνθρώπους ἐποίησαν. καὶ ταῦτα μὲν ἐπὶ τοσοῦτον.

215. ἔστι δέ τι χαρίεν εἶδος λόγων καὶ τὸ τῶν ἐπιγραμμάτων ὅπερ εὑρέθη ἐπὶ τῶν ἀγαλμάτων καὶ αὖ πάλιν ἐπὶ τῶν μνημάτων, σημαῖνον συντόμως τὸν τούτων τινὶ τετιμημένον. ἀλλὰ καὶ τοῦτο Ὁμήρου, ὅπου φησὶν

ἀνδρὸς μὲν τόδε σῆμα πάλαι κατατεθνειῶτος,
ὅν ποτ' ἀριστεύοντα κατέκτανε φαίδιμος Ἕκτωρ (Η 89-90).

καὶ πάλιν

Ἕκτορος ἥδε γυνή, ὃς ἀριστεύεσκε μάχεσθαι
Τρώων ἱπποδάμων, ὅτε Ἴλιον ἀμφεμάχοντο (Ζ 460-1).

216. εἰ δὲ καὶ ζωγραφίας διδάσκαλον Ὅμηρον φαίη τις, οὐκ ἂν ἁμαρτάνοι. καὶ γὰρ εἶπέ τις τῶν σοφῶν ὅτι ἐστὶν ἡ ποιητικὴ ζωγραφία λαλοῦσα, ἡ δὲ ζωγραφία ποιητικὴ σιωπῶσα. τίς οὖν πρῶτος ἢ τίς μᾶλλον Ὁμήρου τῇ φαντασίᾳ τῶν νοημάτων ἔδειξεν ἢ τῇ εὐφωνίᾳ τῶν ἐπῶν ἐκόσμησε θεούς, ἀνθρώπους, τόπους, πράξεις ποικίλας; ἀνέπλασε δὲ τῇ ὕλῃ τῶν λόγων καὶ ζῷα παντοῖα καὶ μάλιστα τὰ ἀλκιμώτατα, λέοντας, σύας, παρδάλεις· ὧν τὰς μορφὰς καὶ διαθέσεις ὑπογράψας καὶ ἀνθρωπείοις πράγμασι παραβαλὼν ἔδειξεν ἑκατέρας τὰς οἰκειότητας. ἐτόλμησε δὲ καὶ θεοῖς μορφὰς ἀνθρώπων εἰκάσαι· ὁ δὲ τὴν ἀσπίδα τῷ Ἀχιλλεῖ κατασκευάσας Ἥφαιστος καὶ ἐντορεύσας τῷ χρυσῷ γῆν, οὐρανόν, θάλασσαν, ἔτι δε μέγεθος Ἡλίου καὶ κάλλος Σελήνης καὶ πλῆθος ἄστρων στεφανούντων τὸ πᾶν καὶ πόλεις ἐν

> There can be no blame that Trojans and well-greaved Achaeans
> should suffer long for such a woman
> [Il. 3.156-57],

and there are many other such passages. The other poets have depicted men as prey to their passion in an unrestrained and immoderate manner. This will suffice on this subject.

215. Another pleasing literary form is the epigram,[1] such as is found on statues and on gravestones, succinctly describing the individual honored by such a monuments. This too belongs to Homer, who says in one place,

> This is the grave of a man long dead
> whom glorious Hector killed, when he stood out among the warriors   [Il. 7.89-90],

and elsewhere,

> This is the wife of Hector, the greatest of fighters
> among the horse-taming Trojans, when they fought around Troy
> [Il. 6.460-61].

216. If one were to say that Homer was a teacher of painting as well, this would be no exaggeration, for as one of the sages said, "Poetry is painting which speaks and painting is silent poetry."[2] Who before, or who better than Homer displayed for the mind's eye gods, men, places, and various deeds, or ornamented them with the euphony of verse? He sculpted in the medium of language all kinds of beasts and in particular the most powerful: lions, boars, leopards—and by describing their forms and dispositions and drawing in human matters for comparison, he demonstrated the special properties of each. He dared also to give the gods human shapes. Hephaestus, making the shield of Achilles and sculpting in gold the earth, the heavens, the sea, even the mass of the sun and the beauty of the moon, the swarm of stars that

---

[1] Though the epigram was an important genre form the Hellenistic period, its juxtaposition here with tragedy and comedy points to its high status in the Imperial period, from the mid-first-century *Garland of Philip* onward.

[2] Simonides (Plutarch, *The Glory of Athens* 346F); cited as traditional by Plutarch, with no author specified, at *How the Young Should Read Poetry* 18A.

διαφόροις τρόποις καὶ τύχαις καθεστώσας καὶ ζῷα κινούμενα καὶ φθεγγόμενα, τίνος οὐ φαίνεται τέχνης τοιαύτης δημιουργοῦ τεχνικώτερος;

217. ἴδωμεν δὲ καὶ ἐπὶ ἄλλου ἑνὸς ἐκ πολλῶν παραδείγματος ὅτι ὁρωμένοις μᾶλλον ἢ ἀκουομένοις ἔοικε τὰ ποιήματα, ὥσπερ οὖν καὶ ταῦτα, ἐν οἷς τὴν οὐλὴν τοῦ Ὀδυσσέως φράσας ἐπιφέρει τὰ τῆς Εὐρυκλείας

τὴν γρηῢς χείρεσσι καταπρηνέσσι λαβοῦσα

γνῶ ῥ' ἐπιμασσαμένη, πόδα δὲ προέηκε φέρεσθαι.

(ἐν δὲ λέβητι πέσε κνήμη, κανάχησε δὲ χαλκός,)

ἂψ δ' ἑτέρωσ' ἐκλίθη· τὸ δ' ἐπὶ χθονὸς ἐξέχυθ' ὕδωρ,

τὴν δ' ἅμα χάρμα καὶ ἄλγος ἕλε φρένα· τὼ δὲ οἱ ὄσσε

δακρυόφιν πλῆσθεν, θαλερὴ δέ οἱ ἔσχετο φωνή.

ἁψαμένη δὲ γενείου Ὀδυσσῆα προσέειπεν·

ἦ μάλ' Ὀδυσσεύς ἐσσι, φίλον τέκος· οὐδέ σ' ἐγώ γε

πρὶν ἔγνων, πρὶν πάντα ἄνακτ' ἐμὸν ἀμφαφάασθαι.

ἦ καὶ Πηνελόπειαν ἐσέδρακεν ὀφαλμοῖσι,

πεφραδέειν ἐθέλουσα (τ 467-77).

καὶ τὰ ἑξῆς. ἐνταῦθα γάρ, ὡς ἐν πίνακι γραπτῷ δεδειγμένων τῶν ὑπὸ τὸν ὀφθαλμὸν πεσεῖν δυναμένων, ἐμφαίνεται πλείω τὰ μηδὲ τῇ ὄψει ἔτι καταληπτὰ ἀλλὰ τῇ νοήσει μόνῃ, ἥ τε διὰ τὴν ἔκπληξιν ἄφεσις τοῦ ποδὸς καὶ ὁ ψόφος τοῦ χαλκοῦ καὶ τὸ ἐκχεόμενον ὕδωρ καὶ ἡ τῆς γραὸς λύπη τε ἅμα καὶ χαρὰ καὶ τὰ ῥηθέντα πρὸς τὸν Ὀδυσσέα καὶ ἃ πρὸς τὴν Πηνελόπην ἀποβλέψασα εἰπεῖν ἐμέλλησε. πολλὰ δὲ καὶ ἄλλα γραφικῶς παρὰ τῷ ποιητῇ δείκνυται, ἅπερ ἐν αὐτῇ τῇ ἀναγνώσει θεάσασθαι ἔνεστιν.

218. ἐνταῦθα καιρὸς καταπαύειν τὸν λόγον ὄν, ὥσπερεὶ στέφανον ἐκ λειμῶνος πολυανθοῦς καὶ ποικίλου πλέξαντες, ταῖς Μούσαις ἀνατίθεμεν. καὶ οὐκ ἂν φροντίσαιμεν, εἴ τις ἐπιτιμήσειεν, ὅτι, πονηρῶν πραγμάτων ὑπόθεσιν

crowns the universe, cities of various sorts and fortunes, and moving, speaking creatures—what practitioner of arts of this sort can you find to excel him?

217. Let us examine another of the many examples that show that his creations are such that we seem to see them rather than hear them.[1] Talking of Odysseus' scar, he speaks of Eurycleia:

> As she was rubbing it with her palms the old woman
> saw the scar and dropped the foot, so that
> it fell in the bowl and the bronze clanged, then
> the bowl tipped to one side and water splashed out on the ground.
> Joy and anguish gripped her heart—her eyes
> were filled with tears and her voice was choked to silence.
> Still she touched Odysseus' chin and started to address him:
> "You are truly Odysseus, dear child! I didn't know you
> before—before I had touched my king with my own hands."
> She spoke and looked toward Penelope, wanting to tell her
> [Od. 19.467-68, 470-77],

and so forth. Here, while everything that can be displayed to the eye is presented as if in a painting, there is still more—things that the eye cannot grasp, but only the mind—the surprise that makes her drop the foot, the noise of the bronze bowl, the water splashing out and the old woman's simultaneous joy and anguish, and the things said to Odysseus as well as those that she is on the verge of saying, as she looks toward Penelope. Many other things are described in the same graphic manner by the poet, as one can see simply from reading him.

218. It is time to bring this essay to a close. I dedicate it, like a wreath gathered and plaited from a meadow rich in every sort of flower, to the Muses. I would not be concerned if someone should accuse me of attributing to Homer physical, political, and ethical discourse and all sorts of wisdom, when in fact the subjects of his poems are wicked deeds.

---

[1] It is striking that this passage was singled out as well by Erich Auerbach (*Mimesis*, ch. 1) as emblematic of Homeric style, and for qualities not unrelated to those stressed here. See "Introduction," above, 27.

ἐχουσῶν τῶν τοῦ Ὁμήρου ποιήσεων, προσάπτομεν αὐτῷ λόγους φυσικοὺς, πολιτικοὺς καὶ ἠθικοὺς καὶ ἐπιστήμας ποικίλας. ἀνάγκη μὲν γὰρ ἦν τῷ ποιητῇ πράξεις παραδόξους καὶ πάθη καὶ ἤθη διάφορα ὑποθέσθαι· ἐπεὶ τὰ μὲν ἀγαθὰ καθ' ἑαυτὰ ἁπλᾶ ἐστι καὶ μονοειδῆ καὶ ἀκατασκεύαστα, τὰ δὲ τοῖς κακοῖς ἀναμεμιγμένα πολλοὺς ἔχει τρόπους καὶ παντοίας διαθέσεις, ἐξ ὧν ἡ ὕλη τῶν πραγμάτων συνίσταται· ἐν ᾗ παρατιθεμένων τῶν χειρόνων ἡ τῶν ἀμείνων γνῶσις καὶ αἵρεσις ῥᾴων καθίσταται. καὶ τὸ ὅλον ἡ τοιαύτη ὑπόθεσις παρέσχεν ἀφορμὰς τῷ ποιητῇ παντοδαποὺς κινῆσαι λόγους, τοὺς μὲν ἀπ' αὐτοῦ, τοὺς δὲ ἀπὸ τῶν εἰσαγομένων προσώπων· ὥστε τὴν ἀπὸ τούτων ὠφέλειαν τοῖς ἐντυγχάνουσι παρασχεῖν. πῶς δὲ οὐκ ἂν πᾶσαν ἀρετὴν ἀναθείημεν Ὁμήρῳ ὅπου καὶ ὅσα αὐτὸς μὴ ἐπετήδευσε ταῦτα οἱ ἐπιγενόμενοι ἐν τοῖς ποιήμασιν αὐτοῦ κατενόησαν; καὶ χρῶνται μέν τινες πρὸς μαντείαν τοῖς ἔπεσιν αὐτοῦ καθάπερ τοῖς χρησμοῖς τοῦ θεοῦ· ἄλλοι δὲ ἑτέρας ὑποθέσεις προθέμενοι ἁρμόζουσιν ἐπ' αὐτὰς τὰ ἔπη μετατιθέντες καὶ συνείροντες.

The poet was forced to base his poem on extraordinary actions and to introduce all sorts of emotions and characters—things that are good in themselves are simple and uniform and unornamented, but mixtures of good and evil generate multiple possibilities and a multitude of situations, these form the material of the tale. Since this material has things of the worse sort mixed into it, the recognition and choice of the better becomes easier. In general, such a plot provided the poet with reasons for composing speeches of all sorts, some on his own behalf and some by the characters he introduces, so that the audience receives the benefit of them.

How then could we possibly not attribute every virtue to Homer, when those who have come after him have even found in his poetry all the things he did not himself think to include? Some use his poetry for divination, just like the oracles of god, while others put forth entirely different subjects and ideas and fit the verses to them, transposing them and stringing them together in new ways.[1]

---

[1] The last reference seems to be to the pastiches or *centones* of Homer current at least from the second century CE. Cf. "Introduction," above, 27-29.

APPARATUS

NOTE: Included here are the readings we have chosen that lack manuscript support and represent conjectures or doubts on the part of earlier scholars or (in a few cases) our own. A full apparatus with variant readings will be found in Kindstrand's edition of *De Homero*.

54B: The Essay on the Life and Poetry of Homer

5   <ποιητὴν> γὰρ ὄντα δεῖ Wyttenbach; παρόντα δέ codd.

8   [μέν] seclusimus

19   <λέξις> suppl. Kindstrand
        κατὰ τὴν ἀμφοῖν ἀνάλογον ὁμοιότητα Dübner; μετά codd.

20   <οὕτω> suppl. Chalcondyles (ed. princeps)

22   <τὸ> Bernardakis
        <οἷον> Kindstrand

35   <τό> Bernardakis

53   <τό> Kindstrand

68   <τό> Dübner

74   <ὁ δὲ θεωρητικός> Wyttenbach
        αἰτία secl. et suppl. Kindstrand (cf. chs. 75-82)

86   <καθιπταμένοις> Kindstrand

92   τούτου γὰρ αἴτιον Wyttenbach; τοῦτο codd.
        <ἡ> Kindstrand
        ποιητική Wyttenbach; ποιητικῆς codd.
        <τό> Wyttenbach

94   <εἰ> J. Mehler

103   [πάλιν ἐν οἷς] secl. Aldine[2]

105	<εὐ>διάλειπτον Stephanus; ἀδιάλειπτον codd.
107	<τοῦ δέ> Aldine²
110	<ἐπί ... κυλίνδων> Wyttenbach
113	<τῇ> Wyttenbach <ᾧ> Dübner
118	<εἰν> Xylander et Stephanus
123	<τι> Kindstrand
127	<ἀυτμῇ δηλοῖ> Wyttenbach; ἀποδιδοῖ codd.
130	<ἐν δὲ σθένος ὦρσεν ἑκάστῳ> suppl. Stephanus
132	[τρόπον] secl. E. Mehler
133	<οἷσί τε> suppl. Stephanus
140	τοῦ ...τό Pohlenz (in Deicke [1937]); τό ... τοῦ codd.
153	ο<ὖν>τυγχάνων Valckenaer
165	<διδούς> Wyttenbach
169	προ<ς τὸ> Bernardakis
172	<καί> scripsimus, cf. Kindstrand
192	<παραδίδωσιν> vel sim. Bernardakis
195	[τό] seclusimus
206	<παρα>τίθησι suppl. Wyttenbach
217	<ἐν ... χαλκός> suppl. J. Mehler

INDEX

*Note: The index covers both the introductory material and the translation, the former by page number (e.g. 99), and the latter by chapter number, in boldface (e.g. **99**), in **A**, or **B**.*

Achilles, 24, 26; **A: 7-8**; **B: 4, 24, 25, 31, 68, 69, 78, 108, 115, 117, 120, 122, 125, 129, 134, 136, 142, 144, 145, 151, 163, 164, 165, 168, 169, 170, 175, 185, 190, 194, 198, 199, 202, 216**
Aegina, **A: 3**
Aegisthus, **B: 183, 213**
Aeolic dialect (*see also* dialect, Homeric), **B: 10**
Aeolians, **A: 3**
Aeschylus, **B: 157**
Agamemnon, **A: 7**; **B: 20, 24, 48, 57, 78, 129, 163, 164, 165, 166, 168, 169, 177-78, 183, 185, 194, 197, 199, 213**
Aiaia, **B: 126, 136**
Ajax, **B: 63, 108, 129, 132, 145, 149, 169, 194, 199**
Alcinous, **B: 147, 150, 182**
Aldine Press (*see also* Manutius, A.), 2
allegory, 4, 8, 15-18, 27, 28; **B: 70, 96, 102**; mystical, 8-9
alloiosis, **B: 41-64** (*for the varieties, see "Contents"*)
Amphiareus, **B: 143**
anacephalaeosis, **B: 174**
anadiplosis, **B: 32**
anastrophe, **B: 30**
Andromache, **B: 188, 190**
Antilochus, **B: 125, 199**
Antimachus, **B: 2, 183**
Antipater of Sidon, **A: 4**
antiphrasis, **B: 25**
antithesis, **B: 173**
antonomasia, **B: 24**
Apelles, **A: 2**
Aphrodite (*see also* "Ares and Aphrodite"), 20; **A: 6**; **B: 44, 84, 101-02, 214**
Apollo, **A: 4, 7**; **B: 17, 22, 24, 78, 102, 139, 143, 202**
apostrophe, **B: 57**
Aratus, 20, 21, 27; **B: 106, 160**
Archilochus, **B: 155**

Ares (*see also* "Ares and Aphrodite"), 20; **B: 34, 53, 101-02, 111, 214**
"Ares and Aphrodite", 20; **B: 101-02, 214**
Argos, **B: 2**
Aristarchus, **B: 2-4, 175**
Aristippus, 11; **B: 150**
Aristotle (*see also* Peripatetics), 12, 13, 19, 20, 21, 22, 25; **A: 3**; **B: 2, 105, 120, 128, 132, 133, 145**; *Metaphysics*, 19, 25; *Poetics*, **A: 3**
arithmetic calculation, **B: 146**
arithmology (Pythagorean), **B: 145**
armies of Greeks and Trojans, size, **B: 146**
Artemis, **B: 84, 102, 202, 204**
Ascra, **A: 2**
astronomy (*see also* Dog Star), 20; **B: 104-06**
asyndeton, **B: 40**
asyntakton, *see* alloiosis
Athena, **A: 6**; **B: 12, 24, 102, 114, 117, 121, 129, 139, 143**
Athens, **B: 2**
Attic dialect (*see also* dialect, Homeric), **B: 12-13, 28, 42**
Auerbach, E., 27
Aulis, **A: 7**; **B: 77**

Barnes, J., 6
Benseler, G. E., 7
Bernardakis, G. N., 30
Boeotia, **A: 2, 7**
Boeotians, **B: 146, 182**
Boivin de Villeneuve, J., 5, 6
Briseis, **A: 7**; **B: 169**
Budé, G., 4
Buffière, F., 8
burial customs, **B: 189-91**

Calliope, **A: 4**
Calypso, **B: 76, 136, 150**
Camerarius, I., 4
catachresis, **B: 18**
cattle of the sun, 24; **B: 120, 125**
centones, 29
Chalcondyles, D., 4

Chios, **A: 4**; **B: 2**
Chiron, **B: 202**
Christ, 24
Chryse, **A: 7**
Chryseis, *see* Cressida
Chryses, **A: 7**; **B: 78, 164**
Circe, 24, 27; **B: 124, 126, 136**
Clarke, S., 6
Clytemnestra, **B: 213**
Colophon, **A: 4**; **B: 2, 93**
comedy, 27; **B: 214**
Constantine, 10
constellations, **B: 106**
Cornutus, 5
cosmology, 16, 19-20; **B: 93-111, 119**; love and strife, **B: 99-102**
Crates of Mallos, **B: 3**
Cressida, **A: 7**
Critheis, **A: 2-3**; **B: 2**
Crete, **A: 4**
Cronius, 8, 29
Cyclopes, **B: 76, 135, 206**
Cyme, **A: 2**; **B: 2**

Demeter, **B: 23**
Democritus, **B: 150**
Demodocus, 27;
Demosthenes, **B: 72, 157**
demonology, 9, 24
dialectic, 19
dialect, Homeric, **B: 8-14**: archaisms in, **B: 14**; Aeolic element in, **B: 10**; Attic element in, **B: 12-13, 28, 42**; Doric element in, **B: 9, 10, 13**; Ionic element in, **B: 11**
diatyposis ("vivid description"), **B: 67**
Dio Chrysostom, *On Homer* 2, 4
Diomedes, **B: 53, 58, 168, 180, 199, 209**
Dionysius of Halicarnassus, 4, 6, 7
Dionysius Thrax, **B: 2**
Dios, **A: 2**
discourse, historical, 18-19
discourse, political, 18, 19, 26-29
discourse, theoretical, 19-27
divination, 27-28; **B: 212, 218**
Dog Star, **B: 202**
Dolon, **B: 135**
Doric dialect (*see also* dialect, Homeric), **B: 9, 10, 13**
doxography, 12, 21

ethics, **B: 132-44**
elements, 19; **B: 93-98**
ellipsis, **B: 39**

emotions, **B: 129-32**
Empedocles, 19, 20; **B: 99-101**
emphasis, **B: 26**
enallage, **B: 30**
epanaphora, **B: 33, 36**
epanodos, **B: 34**
Ephorus of Cyme, **A: 2**; **B: 2**
Epicurus, 11; **B: 150**
Epicureans, 12, 13
epigram (as genre), 27; **B: 215**
epigrams about Homer, **A: 4**
epiphonesis, **B: 65**
epithets, **B: 17, 24**
Ernesti, J. A., 6
Essay on the Life and Poetry of Homer, The, passim; authorship, 2-4, 6-9, 12; content, 10-29, 45-53; date, 7-9, 29; editions, 1-4, 33-35; history, 1-10; interpretive techniques, 10, 12-13, 26; manuscripts, 2-3, 30; "Shorter Life", 4, 6, 14; translations, 2, 37-38
ethics, 19, 25-26
etymology, 23
Eumaeus, 15
Euripides, **B: 153, 156**
Eurycleia, **B: 217**
Eurypylus, **B: 210**
Eustathius, 5

fate, 22; **A: 4**; **B: 115, 118, 120-21, 134, 189, 196**
figures (of Homeric diction), **B: 27-71** (*see under specific figures*)
Francinus, A., 4

Gale, T., 4, 6
Gnostics, 24, 29
gods (*see also* providence; Homer: anthropomorphic gods in) passim, esp. 21-22; **B: 5, 112-18, 203**; "Battle of the Gods", 20; **B: 102**
government, types of, **B: 182-83**
grammaticus, 9, 27
Greeks, passim

Hades, 19, 23, 27; **B: 97, 105, 111, 122, 126, 186**
Hadrian, 28
harmony, **B: 99, 102, 145, 147**; personified, **B: 102**
Hector, **A: 7**; **B: 57, 72, 79, 83, 115, 125, 129, 135, 169, 171, 188, 190, 197, 198, 215**
hedonism, 11-12

Index

Helen, **A: 7**; **B: 4, 183, 211, 214**
Helenus, **B: 212**
Hephaestus, 27; **A: 7**; **B: 23, 75, 79, 101, 102, 176, 214, 216**
Hepp, N., 5
Hera, 16; **A: 6**; **B: 12, 96-97, 100, 102, 108, 187**; as *aer*, **B: 96**; suspended by Zeus, **B: 97**
Heracleidae, **B: 3**
Heracles, **B: 29, 123**
Heraclitus (*Homeric Allegories*), 2, 5, 10, 29
Hermes, 24; **B: 102, 117, 126, 138**
Hermogenes of Tarsus, 7-8
Herodotus, 13, 22
[Herodotus] *Life of Homer*, 2, 4, 5
Hesiod, 13; **A: 2**
hexameter (heroic) verse, **B: 6-7**
Hillgruber, M., 30
historical discourse (for the elements, see "Contents"), **B: 74-90**
Homer, passim, esp. 10, 13; ancillary texts: editions, 2-6; anthropomorphic gods in, 15, 21-22; **B: 112-14, 216**; as educator, 14; as philosopher, 10, 11, 13, 19-26; **B: 92-160**; as rhetorician, 10, 13, 27; **B: 15-73, 161-74**; biography of, **A: 1-5**; **B: 1-3**; date of: **A: 5, B: 3**; dialects of, **B: 8-14**; diction of, 15, **B: 7-73**; divination by, 28; encomia of, 4-5; interpretive literature on, 2-3; meter of, **B: 6-7**; myth and mythic language in, **B: 6, 92, 114**; originator of all forms of human discourse, **B: 74-199**; psychology of, **B: 122-31**; similes of, **B: 84-90**; theology of, **B: 112-21**; types of style (*plasmata*) in, **B: 72-73**; works: *Battle of Frogs and Mice*, **A: 5**; *Iliad*, passim, esp. **B: 4, 162, 163**; *Margites*, **A: 5**; *Odyssey*, passim, esp. **B: 4, 162, 163**
homoeoteleuton, **B: 35, 36**
homoioptoton, **B: 35**
hyperbaton, **B: 30**
hyperbole, **B: 53, 71, 90**
Hyperion, **B: 17, 104**

Idomeneus, **B: 87, 149, 157, 193, 198, 199**
indifference (ἀπάθεια), 11; **B: 134, 135**

Ionia, **A: 3**; **B: 3**
Ionic dialect (*see also* dialect, Homeric), **A: 2**; **B: 11**
Ios, **A: 3-4**; **B: 2**
irony, 15; **B: 68, 69**
Irus, **B: 150, 214**

Kindstrand, J. F., 30
Kranae, **A: 7**

law, **B: 175, 181, 183**
le Fèvre, T., 5
Leto, **B: 78, 102**
Lesbonax, 31
Ludwich, A., 1
Lycaon, **B: 135**
Lydia, **A: 3**

Machaon, **B: 206, 210**
Maion, **A: 2-3**; **B: 2**
Manutius, A., 4
Marcus Aurelius, 7-8
Melanthius, 15; **B: 70, 150**
Meleager, **B: 169**
Meles, **A: 2-4**; **B: 2**
Melesigenes, **A: 2-3**
Menelaus, **A: 7**; **B: 13, 135, 171, 172, 183, 185, 210**
medicine, 27; **B: 200-11, 212**
Meriones, **B: 193, 198, 199**
metalepsis, **B: 21**
metaphor, **B: 19-20**
metensomatosis, 24; **B: 125-26**
meteorological phenomena, **B: 107-11**
metonymy, **B: 23**
Micyllus, I., 4
military tactics, **B: 192-98**
Minos, **A: 4**; **B: 175**
Muses (*see also* Calliope), 21; **A: 3**; **B: 49, 56, 159, 163, 218**
music, 26-27; **B: 145, 147-48**
myth, **B: 6, 92, 101, 114**
"Myth of Er", 24

narrative, elements of, 18-19
nekyia, 24
Neleus, **A: 3**; **B: 47**
Neoplatonists, 8, 9, 10, 17, 24
Nestor, **A: 7**; **B: 129, 141, 145, 165, 167-68, 172, 199, 206**
Nicander, **B: 2**
Numenius, 8, 9, 17, 29

obligations, **B: 184-91**

Odysseus, 11, 24, 26; A: 4, 7; B: 4, 22, 28, 30, 40, 52, 68, 117, 120, 121, 124, 125-26, 135, 136, 141, 143, 145, 149, 150, 162, 163, 166, 167, 169, 172, 174, 178, 181, 185, 188, 199, 206, 207, 209, 212, 214, 217
Olympus, 19; B: 35, 57, 94-95, 98, 103, 114
onomatopoeia, B: 16
Orestes, B: 185, 213
organization (οἰκονομία), B: 162

painting, B: 216-17
Palatine Anthology, A: 4
palillogy, B: 32
parembole ("insertion"), B: 31
Paris, A: 6-7; B: 48, 171, 183
parison, B: 37
paronomasia, B: 38
pastiches, *see* centones
Patroclus, 26; A: 7; B: 83, 89, 108, 122, 134, 142, 145, 151, 185, 190, 210
Peleus, B: 24, 44, 57, 66, 144, 169
Penelope, B: 84, 149, 182, 185, 188, 190, 207, 217
Peripatetics, 11-12; praise of moderate emotion by, B: 135; classification of good things by, B: 137
periphrasis, B: 29
Phaeacians (*see also* Alcinous), 11; B: 174, 182, 207, 214
Phemius, 27; A: 2; B: 181
Philoctetes, B: 146
Phoenix, B: 142, 144, 169-70
physics, 19, B: 92-131, 218
Pindar, B: 2
Planudes, M., 1-3, 9, 20
Plato, 10, 12, 17, 22, 23, 25, 29; B: 12, 120, 122, 128, 175; *Cratylus*, 23, 24; *Protagoras*, 17; *Republic*, (*see also* "Myth of Er"), 10, 24; *Second Alcibiades*, 17
Platonists (*see also* Neoplatonists), 12, 17, 22, 23, 26, 29
Plutarch, *passim* ("Introduction"), esp. 2, 7, 9, 10, 16; editions, 2-4, 7; *Moral Essays*, 2; "Education of Children, The", 2; *Homeric Studies*, 3-4; pseudepigrapha, 2-3; Lamprias Catalogue of, 3
pleonasm, B: 28, 39
poetry, enigmatic language in, 17; B: 92

poles, B: 106, 110
political discourse, B: 161-99
Poliziano, A., 4
Porphyry, 4, 7, 9, 24, 29; *Homeric Questions*, 4, 10; "On the Cave of the Nymphs in the *Odyssey*", 4, 8
Poseidon, 19, B: 97, 101, 102, 107-08, 114, 136, 145
Presocratics, 19, 21
Priam, A: 7; B: 77, 117, 138, 183
proanaphonesis ("prediction"), B: 65
Proclus, 9, 10, 28
prologues, B: 163
prosopopoeia, B: 66
Protesilaus, A: 7
providence, divine, 15, 22; B: 115-21
Pykimede, A: 2
Pythagoras, 9, 12, 13, 23-27; B: 122, 125, 145, 149, 151, 154
Pythagorean *Carmina aurea*, B: 153
Pythagoreans, 8, 19, 23-26, 28, 29; arithmology of, 26, B: 145, 147

rhetoric, 10, 13, 27
riddles, 17-18

Salamis (in Cyprus), A: 4; B: 2
sarcasm, 15; B: 69
Sarpedon, B: 108, 209
Sartre, J.-P., 14
scholiasts, 20
Schrader, H., 10
scripture, 28
seercraft, 27; B: 212
Sidon (Phoenicia), A: 4, 7
Simonides, B: 2
similes, 19, B: 84-90
Sirens, 21, 26-27; B: 147
Smyrna, A: 2, 3-4; B: 2
Socrates, 10, 29; B: 212; rejection of Homer by, 10
Solomon, 6
Sophocles, B: 158
sortes Vergilianae, 28
souls, 10, 20-25; A: 4; B: 4-5, 44, 106, 111, 122-31, 133, 135, 136, 137, 145, 147, 163, 207, 209, 214; immortality of, 9, 12, 22-25; B: 122-26; imprisoned in bodies, B: 124; reincarnation of: *see* metensomatosis
Sparta, A: 7; B: 68
states, B: 176-83
Stephanus, C., 2
Stobaeus, 2, 24

Stoics, 11-12, 16, 22, 23, 25-26; **B**: **119**, **127**, **130**, **134**, **136**, **143**, **212** materialism of, 12; **B**: **127**; praise of indifference by, **B**: **134**; "ruling principle" of, **B**: **130**
synecdoche, **B**: 22

Telemachus, **B**: **68**, **162**, **181**, **185**, **202**, **211**
Thales, 13,19; **B**: **93**
Theagenes of Rhegium, 16
Thebes, **A**: **4**
Theocritus, 27; **B**: **159**
Theophrastus, 22; **B**: **120**
theoretical discourse (physics, ethics, dialectic), **B**: **92-160**
Thersites, **B**: **75**, **149**, **214**
Thessaly, **A**: **4**
Thetis, **A**: **7**
Tiresias, **B**: **44**, **123**, **145**
tragedy, 27; **B**: **213**
Trojan War, passim, esp. **A**: **5-8**; **B**: **3**
Trojans, 16; **A**: **7-8**; **B**: **12**, **48**, **51**, **53**, **57**, **75**, **77**, **102**, **119**, **135**, **145**, **146**, **149**, **183**, **190**, **214**, **215**

tropes (of Homeric diction), **B**: **15-26** (*see under specific tropes*)
Troy, passim
Tyndareus, **B**: **202**

Virgil, 28
virtues and vices, **B**: **5**, **6**, **124**, **133-44**, **218**
Volkmann, R., 7, 8

winds, **B**: **10**, **35**, **59**, **71**, **72**, **90**, **108-11**, **127**, **208**, **209**
Wyttenbach, D., 2, 7

Xenophanes, 19; **B**: **93**
Xylander, W., 2

Zeus, 16, 19; **A**: **7**; **B**: **17**, **48**, **56**, **67**, **75**, **77**, **78**, **79**, **94**, **96-97**, **105**, **108**, **111**, **114**, **115**, **118**, **119**, **120**, **132**, **133**, **138**, **143**, **153**, **155**, **156**, **166**, **175**, **179**, **182**, **187**, **201**, **212**, **214**; "Deception of Zeus", 19; Zeus' chain, **B**: **94**; as *aither*, **B**: **96**

GREEK INDEX

Note: The Greek index covers only the Greek words that occur in the introductory material and those cited as technical terms in the English translation, the former by page number (e.g. 99), and the latter by chapter number, in boldface (e.g. 99), in A, or B. A complete word index, along with an index of proper names, can be found in Kindstrand, 127-68. An asterisk (*) indicates words otherwise unattested.

ἀγαθά, **B 136**
ἀειδής, 23; **B 122**
ἀήρ, 16,19; **B 96**, **108, 122**
ἀγαθά, 12; **B 136**
αἴνιγμα, 18
αἰνίττομαι, 17-18
αἶνος, 17-18
αἴσθησις, 22
ἀλληγορέω, 16
ἀλληγορία, 15-17
*ἀντιπνεύσασα, **B 127**
ἀόρατον, **B 122**
ἀπάθεια, 11; **B 134**, **135**
ἀπαθές, **B 189**
ἀρετή, 11, 12; **B 136**
ἀρχή, 18
ἀσώματος, 21

Γαιήοχος, **B 107**
γνώμη, 19

δέμας, 23; **B 124**
δεσμός, 23
δύη, **B 145**

ἐάων, **B 137**
εἴδωλον, **B 150**
εἱμαρμένη, 22
εἰρωνεία, 15
ἐλεεῖν, **B 132**
ἔμφρων, 24
ἐνηείη, **B 145**
ἐνηής, **B 145**
Ἐνοσίχθων, **B 107**

ἐπιστάμενος [πάντα], 22
εὐδαιμονία, 11, 26; **B 136-37, 150**
εὐνομία, **B 175**

ζόφον ἠερόεντα, **B 97**

ἡγεμονικόν, **B 130**
ἠθικὸν μέρος φιλοσοφίας, 25

θεωρητικὸς λόγος, 18
θυμός, **B 129**
θυμικὴ ὀργή, **B 129**

ἱστορικὸς λόγος, 18

λόγος, 18, 24

μένος, **B 131**
μετριοπάθεια, 11; **B 135**
μῦθος, 18

νέμειν, **B 175**
νέμεσθαι, **B 175**
νέμεσις, **B 132**
νόησις, **B 114**
νοητός, **B 114**
νόμος, **B 175**
νοῦς, 22, **B 114**

οἰκονομία, **B 162**
ὅλον λαμπρόν, **B 95**
*ὄττα, **B 212**

πάθος, **B 81**

πάντα, **B 103**
πνεῦμα, 23; **B 127**
πνευματικόν, **B 128**
παράδοξος, 14
πολιτικὸς λόγος, 7, 26, 27
πρόνοια, 22

σαρκασμός, 15
σῆμα, 23
σῶμα, 23; **B 124, 128**

τεχνίτης λόγων, 27
τύραννος, **B 183**

ὑπόνοια, 16, 17

φρήν, **B 129**
φρόνησις, **B 129**
φύσις, 21

ψύξασα, **B 127**
ψυχή, **B 127**